*PLANNING
AND
IMPLEMENTING*

*Health
Education
in Schools*

PLANNING AND IMPLEMENTING

Health Education in Schools

MARION POLLOCK
with Chapter 6 by Evalyn Gendel
with Chapters 9 and 10 by Peter Cortese

Mayfield Publishing Company
Palo Alto, California

Copyright © 1987 by Mayfield Publishing Company

All rights reserved. No portion of this book may be reproduced in any form or by any means without written permission of the publisher.

Library of Congress Catalog Card Number: 86-062998
International Standard Book Number: 0-87484-563-7

Manufactured in the United States of America
10 9 8 7 6 5 4 3 2 1

Mayfield Publishing Company
285 Hamilton Avenue
Palo Alto, California 94301

Sponsoring editor: James Bull
Manuscript editor: Sylvia Stein
Cover designer: Richard Kharibian
Production management: Miller/Scheier Associates, Palo Alto
Compositor: Carlisle Graphics
Printer and binder: Maple-Vail

Contents

Foreword   vii
Preface   ix
Acknowledgments   xii
Chapter   1   *A rationale for health education in schools*   1
Chapter   2   *Curriculum development: Problems and procedures*   45
Chapter   3   *Formulating health teaching goals and objectives*   83
Chapter   4   *Creating curriculum guides and lesson plans*   113
Chapter   5   *Health teaching methods and techniques*   143
Chapter   6   *Avoiding controversy and criticism in health teaching*   189
Chapter   7   *Evaluating school health education*   229
Chapter   8   *Constructing and using evaluation tools and measures*   263
Chapter   9   *Administration and management of school health programs*   295
Chapter   10   *Community relationships with school health programs*   327
Appendix   A   *Selected federal health information clearinghouses and information centers*   351
Appendix   B   *Criteria for evaluating the school health services program*   361
Appendix   C   *Administration of the school health program*   375
Appendix   D   *Criteria for comprehensive school health education*   383
Appendix   E   *Sample test specifications*   389
Appendix   F   *Responsibilities of the generic health educator*   397
Index   399

Foreword

This is the kind of book that health educators have been seeking and not finding—a *complete* and *even* treatment of planning and conducting health education in the school setting. There is solid theoretical and practical material on the complete range of topics for the study of school-based health education programs: the rationale, the factors and forces that influence the nature and scope, considerations in developing or selecting curriculum and teaching methods, and specifics on how to go about evaluating the outcomes.

The text will be most appreciated by experienced faculty members who find in it substance that is often lacking elsewhere. There are exceptionally complete and lucid presentations of philosophy, law, curriculum development, community controversy and evaluation—topic areas that are often slighted or omitted.

It is tailor-made for the professional preparation of health educators at the undergraduate level but sophisticated enough for graduate or in-service courses. The questions, exercises, and references at the end of each chapter make the teacher's job easier. And the availability of appendices with current statements about comprehensive school health programs, health services, and responsibilities of the generic health educator save much searching for important supplementary material.

The book is also an appropriate resource for use by school-community committees and coalitions.

Marion Pollock and her collaborators, Evalyn Gendel and Peter Cortese, all eminent health educators and teachers as well, have produced a highly professional book. In the hands of an expert teacher who can add examples, stimulate discussion, and inspire confidence, it can go far in improving the quality of that basic of basics: health education in schools.

> Marian V. Hamburg, Ed.D.
> Professor of Health Education
> New York University
> July 18, 1986

Preface

This textbook has been written primarily for students enrolled in colleges and universities offering at least an undergraduate major in school or community health education. The theory and practical examples of its application provided throughout will also be useful to graduate students of health education, those teaching health as a secondary assignment, principals and others responsible for school administration, and health care professionals employed by schools. For example, school administrators, members of boards of education, school physicians, school nurses and nurse practitioners, and public health personnel whose responsibilities include the provision or supervision of certain health services or care in schools.

Although the book focuses on the practice of school health education in secondary schools, this is because health instruction as a separate class is seldom if ever scheduled in elementary schools. Any health teaching done below the sixth grade is provided by elementary teachers along with all of the other basic studies. However, the skills and procedures employed in the development of a curriculum for health education, whatever the level of schooling, are exactly the same. Usually such curriculum plans, as developed by a school district or state office of education, build upon sets of long range goals whose achievement is expected as the result of the subsumed objectives proposed for each grade, K through 12. In that sense, secondary school health curricula are an extension of that planned for elementary grades and dependent in many ways upon the quality and comprehensiveness of the health education provided in those earlier years.

Planning and implementing are in some ways discrete and in other ways inseparable sets of activities. Planning health education curricula must be based upon assessment of individual and community needs. Its principal procedures involve date gathering, synthesizing, and decision making. Implementing is concerned with designing, managing, and evaluating the success of the activities or interventions provided as appropriate and valid means of achieving the purposes of such plans. There is, therefore, inescapably a circularity between them. However carefully plans are made, it is the implementation stage of a program that tests their worth and feasibility. Evaluation of the results of a curriculum or program means some amount of replanning and that in turn means redesigned objectives and activities, more evaluation and so on.

School health educators have long been required to learn how to plan lessons and develop curriculum materials at least for their own use. Similar coursework has seldom been required of community health educators. Very few have been persuaded that there was value in taking such a course because "community health educators are not going to be teachers." It is the thesis of this book that the skills particular to curriculum development and pedagogy are not, however, the exclusive responsibility of school health educators. Health education means education for health. A health educator needs to know how to plan and carry out educational programs capable of promoting health. As Mabel Rugen has remarked sagely, "I found out early in my career that school health people and community health people do much the same things. They just use different words when they talk about it."

Every health educator needs to know how to plan and implement health education because differences in settings or in the subject matter of interest don't change the processes involved. There are other reasons. First, children don't spend all of their time in schools. They do encounter health education in the other settings. That education ought to be based upon knowledge of what is being provided or not provided in the schools, and it needs to be planned with care so that it complements, reinforces or if necessary supplements school programs. Second, health educators of all kinds often serve as resource persons for schools: as consultants, demonstrators of health related techniques such as cardiopulmonary resuscitation (CPR), guest speakers on specific topics, or providers of field-trip experiences designed to acquaint students with community health facilities. Third, community-based health educators are more and more participating in local- and state-level curriculum decision making and in developing curriculum guides for classroom teacher use. That means that they have to know how to prepare meaningful and measurable instructional objectives appropriate to the needs and abilities of specified students. They also have to know how to design learning and evaluation activities that match those objectives. Just as importantly, they have to be aware of the constraints under which health teachers work if they are to avoid causing controversy or criticism of their teaching or the school.

Further justification is explicit in the description of a proposed undergraduate health education curriculum that would develop a "generic health educator." The generic health educator is hypothesized as the individual whose professional preparation has not been biased in favor of any of the settings and who theoretically could perform acceptably in any of them, albeit in a subordinate role without further study and experience. Four of the seven areas of responsibility specified as essential in the professional preparation of the generic health educator include the following:

1. Assessing individual and community needs for health education
2. Planning effective health education programs
3. Implementing health education programs
4. Evaluating the effectiveness of health education programs

These happen also to be the focus of much of this text, not because the text has been written to conform to the logic of the framework, but because the framework adheres to the state of the art.

School health education is not synonymous with the school health program. A comprehensive school health program involves far more than provision of health instruction. It involves every teacher and all of the school personnel. It also encompasses many health services and environmental arrangements designed to promote and protect the health of both students and staff while on campus or en route between home and school. It should be noted that, as indicated by the title, this text is concerned almost entirely with curriculum and instruction. Each of its chapters has been written so as to lead logically from the first, which presents a rationale for the provision of health instruction in schools, through the last two chapters, which discuss the role of administrators and the community in determining the quality and nature of the curriculum.

The intention has not been to tell you *what* students should be taught about health and health behavior. Rather it has been to explain how to plan and carry out meaningful and effective health instruction, whatever the setting in which it is provided. Secondarily, it has been our intention to provide health instructors intending to work in other settings an understanding of the special goals, constraints, and techniques with which school health educators must be concerned. Surely communication among health educators will be facilitated and the quality of their collaborations enhanced when all of them, not just school health educators, have had an opportunity to work with curriculum planning.

The book has not been written for some safely ambiguous reader or student, but for you. You will often be asked to pause and think about what has been said or explained and to make a decision about it before you go ahead. The intention of the book is to instruct, and the questions and the exercises at the end of each chapter are there for you to test your comprehension of what you have read. Most of them can be done, but need not be done by yourself. Some of the exercises may be more interesting if you collaborate with a few classmates. If you understand what you have read, all of the questions and exercises should be easy for you. Don't look for the answers in so many words in the text. What is wanted is evidence of your ability to apply what you have just learned in a new situation so that your answer is not an echo but an application of your own. Any items that give you trouble are indicators that related sections of the chapter may need to be reviewed. Having done that, if you still have difficulty we would appreciate your telling us about it.

ACKNOWLEDGMENTS

Many people have helped, either directly or indirectly, to move this book along the road between proposal and completion. I am deeply grateful to every one. First and foremost among them, in terms of primacy and impact, was the late Delbert Oberteuffer. In a very real sense, it is his book, too. Obie participated actively during the first stages of its development, reacting to the preliminary outline and suggesting specific sections of his prior works that he very much wanted to see updated and included. What he wanted to do at this point in his career was to edit and to advise. And that is what he did, as long as he could. His support and encouragement as the project was begun were as prized as they have been sorely missed.

I am also grateful to Evalyn Gendel and E. J. Bonner who shared in the discussions carried out during the early planning period and later collaborated in the preparation of the chapter on Controversial Subjects in Health Education. Thanks are due Peter Cortese and Beverly Bradley as well for their help during the planning and developmental stages of the project. Peter Cortese also prepared and wrote key chapters on administration and school-community relationships.

Other contributors include those who reviewed parts of the manuscripts at various stages of its development and whose comments and suggestions guided the many revisions made along the way. These were William Creswell, University of Illinois; Larry Olsen, Pennsylvania State University; Phyllis Ensor, Towson State University; Peter Cortese, California State University, Long Beach; Marshall Kreuter, Center for Health Promotion and Education, (CDC); Ann E. Nolte, Illinois State University; Robert D. Russell, University of Southern Illinois at Carbondale; Carl Nickerson, Comprehensive Health Education Foundation, Seattle; and William Cissell, East Tennessee State University.

More were colleagues, primarily Don A. Beegle, whose tireless library research made the writing go much faster, and former students at California State University at Long Beach, especially Rick Loya, Kathy Middleton Owen, and Beverly Bradley. I am indebted also to staff members of various local and national health agencies and organizations in particular Susan Seffrin, American Dental Association, Brenda Martin of Planned Parenthood of Los Angeles, Perry Brown, Los Angeles County Department of Health Services, Joy Cauffman, Department of Family and Preventive Medicine, University of Southern California, and others who cooperated in validating statements made in the text. Thanks also are due the secondary school students in South Pasadena and Pasadena, California, and in Muncie, Indiana, who demonstrated their role-playing abilities in the pictures featured throughout the book, as well as to the adults who so generously donated their time and skills in the process of obtaining those pictures. These were Warren Schaller, Joan Sturkie, Armi Lizardi, Jeff Cox, and Michelle Barrett. Nancy Schmitt, of the Huntington Memorial Hospital in Pasadena made available the picture of the volunteer Candy Striper.

I am deeply indebted to Marian and Morris Hamburg for giving so much of their time and expertise to the analysis of the materials on school administration, and to Marian Hamburg for reading the entire manuscript and writing the book's foreword.

Special thanks are due Lansing Hays whose encouragement and advice were invaluable as the project was begun, and to Jim Bull who later took over his work and cheerfully tolerated my preliminary grumbling about losing Lans as editor, and so ably guided the manuscript's development through its necessary revisions to the point of publication. Additionally, the expert copyediting of Sylvia Stein and the friendly competence of Bernie Scheier in supervising the production of the book have made my part of that process not just painless, but educational and enjoyable.

Finally, I am grateful to all of the health educators and educational theorists whose writings have together shaped the organization and content of this book. I wish that it were possible to acknowledge every one of them, as well as of the faculty and students who together have taught me all that I know about health education. But if that is not feasible, let me admit with all humility and sincerity that, in a way, this is their book, as well.

Marion B. Pollock

*PLANNING
AND
IMPLEMENTING*

*Health
Education
in Schools*

1
A rationale for health education in schools

Health education is health education whatever the setting in which it is practiced. Today those settings are usually categorized as school, community, clinical, and business or industrial. Undergraduate programs designed to meet the need for professional health educators tend to focus either on school health or community health. Those who major in community health can serve as health educators in any of the last three settings. Those who major in school health are unique in that they are qualified to hold positions in any one of them. Although both programs prepare students to be health educators, only the school health major requires certain courses and field experiences focused specifically on teaching skills.

Preparation for health teaching in schools is much like that in community, clinical, and work site settings in most ways, yet different in some ways. For example, school health education is more concerned than the others with learning theory, pedagogy, and immediate evaluation of results. School health educators are more accountable to the community for the nature and acceptability of their activities. Health education is more closely scrutinized for its content and methods than any other subject commonly taught in schools. Unlike the target groups in other health education settings, students constitute a captive audience. Parents and taxpayers have the right to question how and what children are being taught. The concern is that teaching activities do not intrude on family privacy or provide information not appropriate for any particular age group.

Children may not attend school unless their health has been certified by a physician. Effective health education designed for a healthy young audience in schools must be more comprehensive in scope and involve the learner more directly in the learning experiences than in the other settings. The target group includes the total population of youngsters of school age, not just groups defined by a common health problem or need. As of this writing, only school health education specialists are expected in most states to be credentialed if they wish to be full-time teachers.

This book focuses on health education as it is taught in schools and has been written for school health education majors. Yet there are many good reasons why every health educator should be equally as familiar with its content. First, almost all the concepts and skills required of school health educators are also needed by health educators in any setting. Second, schools are part of the community, and school health programs can be depended upon to complement and promote adult health education programs in community settings. The reverse is also true. Only if community and other health educators understand the purposes and methods engaged in by their colleagues in the schools will the kind of collaboration and cooperation needed to promote the health of the nation be possible. Adolescents will soon be the adults whose decisions and actions can significantly enhance or compromise the health of their families, neighbors—even the health of their entire community. Third, health educators in all settings are increasingly serving as consultants to schools and boards of education when curriculum guides are being developed or revised. Knowledge of community health problems is not sufficient background for curriculum development. Construction of teaching-learning guides requires a grasp of curriculum theory and special skills in curriculum development. Fourth, teaching materials specific to certain health problems (e.g., cardiovascular disease, drug and alcohol abuse, sexually transmitted diseases, and tobacco dependence) created and provided by health educators and agencies outside the school need to be educationally sound and appropriate for use with the specified age group.

In sum, sooner or later every health educator finds it necessary to participate in planning for health instruction. There is much more to curriculum writing than outlining the subject matter that describes a health problem. Health instruction is not merely providing health-or disease-related information. Beyond the subject matter, there must be meaningful and feasible objectives, worthwhile learning opportunities, effective organization and administration, and evaluation of results. Without good planning, there cannot be successful implementation of any program of health education, whatever its setting.

THE ORIGINS OF HEALTH EDUCATION

Health education had its beginnings in schools in Massachusetts under the leadership of Dr. William A. Alcott, an influential writer and educator, Horace Mann, the first secretary of the first state board of education in the United States, and other prominent educators early in the nineteenth century. Alcott, called the "father of school health education" in the United States, wrote a prize-winning book on the healthful construction of schoolhouses in 1829, was the first to suggest that schools should have an attending physician, and was the first to write a health book suitable for children. Horace Mann, probably the most influential educator of his day, strongly recommended that physiology and hygiene be included in the curriculum of the common (elementary) schools in all six of his annual reports between 1837 and 1843. He said: "The study of Human Physiology, however—by which I mean both the Laws of life, and Hygiene or the rules and observances by which health can be preserved and promoted—has claims so superior to every other, and, at the same time, so little regarded or understood by the community, that I shall ask the indulgence of the Board, while I attempt to vindicate its title to the first rank in our schools, after the elementary branches." He gave direct responsibility for this to the schools, adding, "I see no way in which this knowledge can ever be universally, or even very extensively diffused over the land, except it be through the medium of our Common Schools" (Means, 1962, p. 34).

Subsequently, in 1850, Massachusetts became the first state to require physiology and hygiene by law as a compulsory subject in all the public schools of the commonwealth. That same year Lemuel Shattuck's famous Report of the Sanitary Commission of Massachusetts gave school health education further strong support. Although the Shattuck report dealt with public health concerns, he had been a teacher and served as a member of the school committee charged with reorganizing the public schools in Concord, Massachusetts. It was not surprising that he saw the implications for school health in the recommendations made by the Sanitary Commission. He said:

> Every child should be taught early in life, that, to preserve his own life and the lives and health of others, is one of the most important and constantly abiding *duties*. By obeying certain laws, or performing

certain acts, his life and health may be preserved; by disobedience, or performing certain other acts, they will both be destroyed. By knowing and avoiding the causes of disease, disease itself will be avoided, and he may enjoy health and live; by ignorance of these causes and exposure to them, he may contract disease, ruin his health and die. Every thing connected with wealth, happiness and long life depend upon *health;* and even the great duties of morals and religion are performed more acceptably in a healthy than in a sickly condition. (Means, 1962, p. 44)

Between 1880 and 1890, the Women's Christian Temperance Union led by Mary Hanchett Hunt was successful in motivating thirty-eight states and territories to pass laws mandating certain aspects of health teaching described as "the evil effects of alcohol, tobacco, and narcotics."

By 1921, Charles Chapin, superintendent of health in Providence, Rhode Island, freely admitted that schools and departments of education were more systematic in their approach and accomplished more with their health teaching than did the public health departments of the day. At that time, public health education was limited to propaganda, pamphlets, and publicity. (The present-day Public Health Education section of the American Public Health Association was titled the Section on Health Education and Publicity when founded in 1921.) Eventually, public health workers began to move away from propagandizing to adopt the schools' more successful organized teaching in their work with adults. So it was that education for health began in the schools and has been expanded first to community and by now to clinical and industrial settings.

Professional preparation of health education specialists began during the 1920s. The first undergraduate degree in school health education was granted by the Georgia State College for Women in 1923. In that same year, the first specialist preparation program in a U.S. school of public health was given by the Harvard-Technology School of Public Health (a short-lived alliance between Harvard and the Massachusetts Institute of Technology). The degree was a CPH (Certificate of Public Health), later changed by Harvard to the now familiar MPH, entitling the recipient to work either in school health or public health education fields (Means, 1975, p. 178).

Separation of health education into two fields of concentration—school health education and adult health education—is first mentioned as having been established at the University of Michigan in 1935. The latter field was soon renamed public health education (Rugen, 1972, p. 9). By 1950, a national survey revealed that students could major in health education in a total of thirty-eight institutions of higher education. Today more than three hundred colleges and universities offer professional preparation programs in school or public health education at undergraduate or graduate levels or at both.

WHAT DO WE MEAN BY "HEALTH"?

Does that seem like a foolish question? Surely everybody knows what health is, or at least what it *isn't*. Nevertheless, nobody yet has been able to devise a definition that is clear-cut and comprehensive enough to gain universal acceptance. Statements describing health range from the comfortably direct "Health is what enables a person to be what he wants to be and to do what he wants to do" (Hochbaum, 1978, p. 33) to more elaborate statements such as "Health is a dynamic, ecological resultant involving the interaction of many complex predisposing, precipitating, and perpetuating factors and conditions" (Hoyman, 1965, p. 114).

Health has also been referred to as "high-level wellness," "biological well workingness," "a comprehensive, generalized concept, not a fact," a "positive direction or position on a theoretical continuum between wellness and death," and perhaps most often as "not being sick." Analysis of those definitions most frequently cited in the literature reveals a number of common elements. Let's look at a few that might be considered representative of current beliefs.

First, if there *is* a universally accepted definition, it has to be that of the World Health Organization (WHO), which has been approved by every one of its member nations as they joined over the years since its founding in 1947: "Health is a state of complete physical, mental, and social well being and not merely the absence of disease and infirmity." When that was written, it was far from earlier notions of health as a state of being, determined by the lack of discernible disease or infirmity. Moreover, it was the first to specify dimensions of health other than the purely physical. The definition has often been criticized as describing health in terms that are impossible to achieve. Nevertheless, it was a landmark statement and remains the official statement for most of the world. Other definitions, devised more recently, include:

> "Health is the condition of the organism which measures the degree to which its aggregate powers are able to function" (Oberteuffer, 1960, p. 47).

> "Health can be regarded as an expression of fitness to the environment, as a state of adaptation" (Dubos, 1965, p. 350).

"Health is a quality of life involving dynamic interaction and interdependence among the individual's physical well being, his mental and emotional reactions and the social complex in which he exists" (School Health Education Study, 1967, p. 10).

"Health is a state of well-being sufficient to perform at adequate levels of physical, mental, and social activity, taking age into account" (Lalonde, 1974, p. 6).

"Health is the quality of physical, psychological, and sociological functioning that enables the individual to deal adequately with self and others in a variety of situations . . . a dynamic and relative state of functions (Bedworth and Bedworth, 1978, p. 347).

"Health is a relational concept . . . not an entity that can be directly promoted but a relationship between capacities and demands" (Baranowski, 1981, p. 254).

"Health is the capacity to cope with or adapt to disruptions among the organic, social, and personal components of the individual's health system." (Bates and Winder, 1984, p. 36).

Some of the terms that recur in these statements seem to view health as a *quality* (e.g., dynamic, multidimensional, interdependent, relational). Others perceive health as an indicator of successful coping abilities (e.g., adaptation, interaction, functioning, performance). In essence, these definitions are more alike than they are different. All of them reflect a notion of health as an active rather than a passive concept, as optimal functioning, as wellness, and as indicating a strongly positive position on a continuum of well-being.

Inasmuch as "health" as described is the goal of health education, the selection of subject matter for health teaching logically focuses on health promotion rather than on information about the disease of the month or year and its prevention. Study of anatomy and physiology or the etiology of certain diseases is not the stuff of health education unless that information is demonstrably essential to the promotion of health, never as an end in itself.

WHAT IS HEALTH BEHAVIOR?

Probably every purposeful human reaction or goal-directed action is to some extent health related or health directed. If that is true, then everything we do is health behavior. McAlister (1981) defines health behavior more specifically as "any action that influences the probability of immediate and long-term physical and physiological consequences affecting physical well-being and longevity."

The terms "health practices" and "health habits" are sometimes used interchangeably with "health behavior." There are differences among them, however, that need to be recognized and adhered to in use. Health practices are ways of coping with or satisfying immediate health needs (e.g., as in food selection; care of teeth and gums; personal grooming; maintaining balance among sleep, rest, and recreation; use or abuse of harmful substances). Health practices are not always consistent, but whether their effect is health enhancing or health compromising, each action is taken deliberately. A decision has been made, one way or the other. For example, a person may choose a candy bar for a snack, although fresh fruit is also available and was the choice the day before, or visit a dentist for a scheduled checkup rather than spend the day at the beach.

Health habits are learned and consistent ways of coping with health-related urges or needs. A health practice can become a health habit and often does. The transition occurs when the individual carries out the practice without giving it any thought at all. Habits differ from health practices in precisely that way. Habits are actions taken at an unconscious level. For example, often smokers are so accustomed to a cigarette as an accompaniment to coffee drinking that no decision is necessary or made; they simply reach for a cigarette as a part of the coffee-drinking pattern. Habits may be positive or negative in their effect, but they are always automatic rather than deliberate actions.

Implicit in the term "health behavior" is the assumption that what we are talking about is *healthful* behavior. Its meaning varies, depending on the context in which it is used. Used in a global sense, it refers to an individual's life-style (defined as the pattern of behavior representative of the aggregate of the decisions that affect one's total health). The term also defines the objective of a health education program, usually community based, which is to change a specified unhealthful behavior. In the case of school health education, it is not always change in health behaviors that is sought so much as reinforcement or development of health *practices* believed to promote lifelong wellness. (An unhealthful life-style is the product of long years of practice. It is not until we are adults that changes in life-threatening health behaviors, begun when we were children, become so critical a need.)

Curriculum goals for school health education generally describe health behaviors that are the expected outcome of health instruction. Some of those behaviors (e.g., parenting and family planning) will not be elicited or even possible until the students have become adults and have full responsibility for their decisions and actions. Health behaviors expressed as goals encompass all the subordinate and supporting actions that together contribute to their achievement. Moreover, they are not limited to personal health care practices and habits, but include responsible actions that support and promote family and community health as well.

WHAT IS HEALTH EDUCATION?

Anyone who intends to become a health educator, particularly a school health educator, will often be asked that question. The best answer may be "It depends." In any field of specialization, the meaning of certain key terms depends upon the perspective of the speaker. A necessary assumption is that those who are doing the listening are thinking along the same lines. For example, health educators use the term "health education" to refer to the parent discipline or body of knowledge, to the profession or primary occupation of those employed as health educators in a given setting, to the outcome of the activities planned to achieve it, and to the processes or methods by which it is accomplished. It is also often used in quite another context in connection with programs designed to train certain health *care* specialists. For the purposes of this discussion, each of the principal meanings of health education will be explored as it relates specifically to education for health in schools.

Health education as discipline

The focus in this instance is on the body of knowledge with which health education is concerned. Health education has been described as an eclectic discipline with its roots firmly established in medicine, public health, social-behavioral sciences, and education (Kreuter, Christenson, and Davis, 1983, p. 30).

School health education omits any mention of input from medicine and public health in defining its subject matter as "a relatively new discipline . . . derived from the biological, behavioral, sociological, and health sciences" (Joint Committee NEA-AMA, 1973). Although health education has been provided in schools far longer than in any other of its settings, as the emphasis shifted from physiology and anatomy to hygiene and finally to the comprehensive curriculum and behavioral concepts of today, it has achieved the status of a separate discipline. The fact that its body of knowledge has been derived from many other sciences does not mean that the subject matter consists merely of bits and pieces snipped from those other disciplines. School health education borrows concepts, principles, and facts pertaining to healthful living, but interprets them differently in ways that apply to human needs, human values, and human potential. For example, the study of nutrition in health education is not presented as watered-down facts of the sort that nutrition majors must know. Instead, health education seeks to provide the learner with the kind of information and skills needed by every individual who must make daily choices of foods that can maintain or promote her or his own nutritional status. Nor is health instruction limited to what the learner needs to know in order to choose a healthful diet. Mental, social, emotional, and even economic influences on food choices are explored. The effects of diet choices on energy, appearance, and every other desirable quality and goal are identified. Students are helped to see how the effect of nutritional choices overlaps with other areas of the health curriculum.

The subject areas included in today's health education discipline, analyzed and interpreted in these many ways, together comprise the irreducible amount of information a person needs in order to choose wisely among the many alternative health actions open to him or her.

Health education as profession or occupation

Health educators, whatever the setting in which they plan and carry out their programs, when asked to indicate their field of work or profession, usually describe it as "health education." This does not mean that the professional preparation of every health educator has been the same or even that all those carrying out health education activities have had professional preparation for the job. There are a number of reasons for that. First is the fact that the term "health education" has long been misunderstood by employers and even by health educators in other settings. Responsibility for health education has often been allocated to people in allied health or communication fields on the basis of unstated assumptions regarding both the tasks and the skills needed in order to accomplish them. This means that those who do the hiring often don't themselves know what a health educator needs to be able to do in any particular setting. In clinical settings, health care personnel have not always been receptive to the notion that health education could be entrusted to people whose background is educational rather than medical in emphasis. In the case of school health education, the mistaken belief persists that anyone can teach health. The equally erroneous belief that anyone can write a health curriculum guide also persists, and those "anyones" keep churning out attempts to prove it by the bushel. Even where health instruction is mandated by state law, the same misconception explains why school administrators tend to assign "anyone" to teach the health course. In areas where legislative support is either lacking or not enforced, a certain apathy or even resistance to school health education exists, based on the conviction that as a frill course nobody needs it. Further, there has been no consensus in the profession regarding acceptable standards for preparation and practice in health education. Certain professional groups have proposed guidelines for undergraduate and graduate studies in health education, but these have reflected their own special interests and goals rather than those of health educators in all settings.

Fragmentation of the profession based on practice settings and the absence of a common basis for quality assurance in the preparation of health educators seemed to be the underlying causes of these problems. Leaders in the field became convinced that development of a set of standards acceptable to the total profession might be the solution to both problems. Accordingly, representatives of eight national organizations with a major commitment to health education organized a workshop in February 1978 that brought together health educators representing all the principal practice settings. The purpose was to (1) analyze existing commonalities and differences in the professional preparation of health educators for different settings and (2) determine the potential for developing a baccalaureate curriculum whose graduates, as entry-level health educators, were prepared to perform the role of a generic health educator. The generic role was viewed as representing the common core of responsibilities, functions, and competencies of health educators, independent of setting. Competencies essential to practice unique to schools or other settings would be achieved by means of electives or as determined by individual professional preparation programs.

As the outcome of this meeting, a National Task Force on the Preparation and Practice of Health Educators (NTFPPHE) was established. The charge to the task force was to pursue the development of a comprehensive credentialing system for the health education profession that would be applicable to all of its practice settings. Subsequently, funds were obtained, and a project dedicated to the achievement of this charge was begun.

Since then, and as of this writing (1986), three phases of the project have been completed: (1) specification of the role competencies required of the entry-level health educator, (2) refinement and validation of the initial set of competency statements, and (3) development of a curriculum framework designed to help faculties in colleges and universities review existing undergraduate professional preparation programs in health education and develop a curriculum consistent with the delineated generic role. A copy of the first draft of the curriculum framework was sent to each established department of health education in the universities and colleges of the nation. In addition, regional workshops were held across the country. The purposes of both actions were to (1) acquaint health education faculty members with the preliminary curriculum framework and its rationale and (2) obtain the necessary feedback from the field for its further development and refinement.

The curriculum framework has been rewritten to incorporate these responses and recommendations (see appendix E). The next phase will be the development of instruments capable of assessing a health educator's level of competence. Until these have been tested and validated, implementation of a comprehensive credentialing system must remain a goal. However, when that system has been established, the quality and effectiveness of the curricula provided for the education of competent health educators should be dependably consistent. Health education will have moved from the somewhat ambiguous title of a job or occupation to the recognized status of an accepted profession. Once that is a reality, health educators may no longer have to explain what health education is all about.

Health education as outcome

"Health education" is also the term used to describe the result of a program. Health education is the purpose of health teaching and of the curriculum planned to guide that instruction. Health education used in the sense of outcome describes achievement of the cognitive, affective, and behavioral goals set for an instructional program. The potential outcome of an effective K–12 curriculum in health education would be health-educated adults, capable of making health-related decisions sensibly and responsibly. Moreover, such health-educated adults should be better prepared for harmonious family membership and parenting. They should be better equipped to participate in or support programs designed to promote the health of all people.

Health education as process

The word "process" is defined as a "series of actions, changes, or functions that bring about an end or result." Many define health education as the process involved in bridging the gap between supplying people with information about health and teaching them how to use it in solving or preventing health problems. Representative statements include the following:

> "the process of assisting individuals, acting separately and collectively, to make informed decisions about matters affecting their personal health and that of others" (Henderson, 1982)
>
> "a process affecting intellectual, psychological, and social dimensions that increase our capability to make informed health decisions affecting self, family, and community well being" (Bedworth and Bedworth, 1978, p. 347)
>
> "Health education is a planned opportunity to learn about health which occurs in a setting at a given point in time and involves an interaction between teacher(s) and learner(s)" (Bates and Winder, 1984).

Behavioral change is not a primary or immediate purpose of health teaching, first, because it cannot be assumed that young people need to have all of their health behaviors changed. A comprehensive school health curriculum covers the entire scope of health knowledge, not just those areas in relation to which specific behavioral changes might seem critical for some students. Second, schools and teachers can be accountable only for changing students' command of health concepts and problem-solving abilities, not their actual health behaviors (Kreuter, 1984).

Carlyon (1981) supports this point of view: "As I understand it, health instruction curriculum shares the overall goal of the entire school curriculum, which is to help students become knowledgeable, critical, independent learners. Health curriculum more than the rest of the curriculum, focuses upon knowledge, critical abilities, and learning skills related to normal growth and development and maintenance of well being. It is assumed that people so equipped are more likely to live healthful lives than those who are not." That is what health education means to school health educators—not changing health behavior, but teaching youngsters how to choose the kinds of health behaviors that can enhance the quality of every aspect of their lives, not just for today, but for all the tomorrows they will have.

WHAT ARE THE GOALS OF SCHOOL HEALTH INSTRUCTION?

The goals of school health instruction might be outlined in this way:

1. to promote ability to choose health-related actions (habits, practices, patterns of behavior) favorable to the promotion of high-level wellness and the enhancement of the quality of life
2. to promote development of a well-integrated personality, allowing enjoyment of life based upon a realistic acceptance of individual limitations and strengths
3. to replace misconceptions and superstitions with accurate information about matters concerning personal and public health
4. to facilitate the development of the confident ability to cope with health problems based upon acquisition of problem-solving skills and knowledge of sources of sound health information
5. to develop the ability in students to discern cause and effect, to take appropriate preventive or remedial steps when needed, and thus to improve the quality of living to the extent possible
6. to contribute to the health of the community through the development of health-educated citizens who have learned the advantages and accept

the necessity of supporting health-related measures designed to improve the common good

WHY HEALTH EDUCATION IN SCHOOLS?

Health education in schools is not limited to classroom instruction, but includes the provision of health services and a healthful environment. The latter two program elements complement and reinforce many of the concepts and skills promoted in the classroom and vice versa.

Justification for the provision of health education in schools is solidly based upon accepted school obligations, legislation, student needs and interests, the goals of general education, parental and community support, national support, and the recommendations of health and educational authorities. Discussion of each of these factors follows.

An obligation of the schools

The schools' responsibility for the health and safety of students is based upon the following beliefs. Having received children certified as being well upon entry, a school must:

1. *Help maintain those students' health in order to ensure their continued fitness to learn.* Schooling can be helpful or harmful, enhance growth and development or hinder it, afford the student an integrating experience or one that is frustrating and disintegrating. The school health program is committed to the promotion of the health of the students and to their growth and development in every dimension.
2. *Provide an environment that protects and promotes the health of both students and staff.* A school's environment includes the people who interact with students (teachers, nurses, administrators, and all the supporting staff); the nature and quality of the curriculum; the fairness and appropriateness of evaluation and grading procedures; the effectiveness of the sanitation and safety provisions in protecting students as they live and work in classrooms, laboratories, or athletic fields; and the emotional climate of the school, the neighborhood, and the community in which students and faculty reside. Youngsters learn best when every element of the school environment is healthy itself and healthful in its effect upon their well-being.
3. *Maintain health services as a means of appraising, protecting, and promoting the health of students.* Appraisal establishes a chain of action that finds the youngsters who are in need of medical, dental, psychological, or social services and cooperates with the family in coping with or

solving the problem. For several million students, these basic screening and appraisal activities conducted by the schools may be the only chance they have for the early discovery of and compensation for or correction of remediable handicaps. Moreover, it may be the first real experience many students have with health care professionals or the only real test for any minor but potentially handicapping lack of visual or audio acuity. The school's business is to provide education, not practice medicine, but medical advice is often needed in order to develop the best educational program for certain students.

4. *Provide health instruction that stresses development of a life-style reflecting responsible health behavior and application of critical thinking skills in making health-related choices and decisions.* Such instruction is not effected by an assembly lecture program, rainy day activities offered in lieu of physical education, or physiology and anatomy or "health crisis of the year" units haphazardly tacked onto such other courses as biology, home economics, or social studies.

Supportive legislation

Authorization for any element of school health education must be established in law. Public money may not be spent by local schools without express enabling legislation. Mandated or permissive legislation requires or permits specified school activities and services to be provided students in schools. Existing legislation in forty-three states requires or strongly recommends health education or specific aspects of health instruction. Completion of semesters or units of health education is a requirement for graduation in more than half of the states. Legislatures in seven states (California, Colorado, Florida, Illinois, New York, North Carolina, and Vermont) have reexamined health instruction as a part of the curriculum and reaffirmed its importance in the education system (ECS, 1982). As health care costs continue to escalate, the number of similarly committed states is likely to increase dramatically in the next few years. Effective health instruction during childhood and adolescent years could do more to prevent premature death or disability than even the finest patient or community health education in later years focused on changing long-established unhealthful behaviors.

Student health needs

No one knows how great a difference the provision of comprehensive health education at every grade (as is afforded the other basics such as reading and mathematics) would effect in diminishing the health problems of both children and adults in our society. No one has ever tried it. Yet the fact is that most health behavior is learned (and from role models in the adult world) during childhood. As many as 40 percent of children aged 11 through 14 are estimated to have one or more risk factors for heart disease (overweight, high blood pressure, elevated serum cholesterol, cigarette smoking, and diabetes) (McGinnis, 1981, p. 12). Among adults, the major causes of death (heart disease, cancer, and stroke) are largely due to behaviors and exposures begun when they were young.

A life-style does not suddenly evidence itself once adult status has been attained. It is shaped day by day, beginning in childhood as one makes health-related choices and acts upon them. Nor does the appearance of major health problems resulting from poor health habits, misinformation, or irresponsible behavior wait for the advent of physical maturation or legal majority. Many of the major health problems experienced by young Americans could have been avoided. Most of them are the result of unhealthful actions taken deliberately and often. Consider the following statistics reflecting teenage problem behaviors:

- About one in every two hundred adolescents—nine out of ten of whom are girls from all socioeconomic levels—is literally starving herself. Anorexia nervosa, bulimia, and bulimarexia are learned behaviors stemming from a preoccupation with food (Food and Nutrition News, Nov. 1984).
- The self-reported use of cocaine among young adults in the U.S. tripled between 1974 and 1979 (*Data Track II*).
- Deaths from suicide in the U.S. increased from 22,364 in 1969 to 27,206 in 1979, a rise of about 22 percent. As of 1982, suicide was in tenth place as the cause of death, and the rate was actually probably higher because many self-inflicted deaths are not recorded as such. Death rates from suicide at ages 15 through 19 rose by more than 60 percent among males and by more than 30 percent among females (*Metropolitan Life Foundation Statistical Bulletin,* 1982, p. 3).
- Teenage women are smoking at earlier ages and at higher rates than ever before (Howe, 1984, p. 3).
- Each year in this country, thirty thousand teenagers under age 15 become pregnant (Hatcher, 1986, p. 18). The U.S. is the only developed country where teenage pregnancy has been *increasing* in recent years, with the rate for 15-to 19-year-olds standing at ninety-six per thousand, compared to fourteen per thousand in the Netherlands, thirty-five in Sweden, forty-three in France, and forty-five in England and Wales. The teenage abortion rate *alone* in the U.S. is as high or higher than

the combined abortion and birth rates of any of those countries (Guttmacher Institute, 1985).

- At least one of every sixteen high school seniors is actively smoking marijuana on a daily basis, and one in sixteen drinks alcohol daily. About two-thirds of all young people try an illicit drug before they finish high school, and about one-third try an illicit drug other than marijuana. Nearly all (93 percent) of the 1982 seniors surveyed reported that they had tried alcohol, and the great majority (70 percent) had used it in the previous month ("Alcohol and other drug abuse," 1984).
- There is increased prevalence of the use of smokeless tobacco, particularly among teenage males—a practice seriously compromising oral health and inducing heart rate and blood pressure increases (Glover et. al., 1984, p. 25). Eight percent of high school students in Massachusetts reported regular use of smokeless tobacco in 1984. The Oklahoma Health Systems Agency found that snuff or chewing tobacco was used by 7 percent of third-graders and 22 percent of eleventh graders (*Nation's Health,* 1985, p. 20).
- Teenagers between the ages of 15 and 19 have one of the highest STD rates of the total population (Brown, 1986). Teenagers are more at risk for chlamydial infection than adults because they are more likely to have intercourse with multiple partners and less likely to use condoms (Hatcher, 1986). As reported in 1983, there were 97,015 cases of gonorrhea among males and 138,071 cases among females in the age group 15 to 19 (*STD Statistical Letter,* 1983, p. 5).
- Today motor vehicle crashes are the leading cause of death among persons aged 5 to 34. Youths aged 15 to 24 are almost three times more likely to die from a motor vehicle crash than from any other cause. Seat belt use rates among teenagers are consistently the lowest of all groups observed (3 to 5 percent) (Lawson, Sleet, and Amoni, 1984, pp. 27–29).

Statistics about health problems are only indicators of needs, however. The next question must be, "What do today's youngsters need to know and know how to do if problems like these are to be avoided or at least minimized in incidence?"

They need to be able to distinguish between fact and misinformation, misconception, or superstition concerning health and health behavior. They need to know how to protect and care for their own bodies. They need to know how to discover reliable information required for the solution of a new health problem. They need to master problem-solving and decision-making skills. They need to learn how to be wise consumers, not just of health products, but also of health information and health services. They need to find out who they are and learn to be comfortable with that person. They need to know how to live agreeably with others and how to handle stress so that it becomes a positive rather than a negative force in their lives. They need to build a system of values that views health as a means of attaining one's goals, not as an end in itself. They need to learn how to be what Postman and Weingartner (1969, p. 2) have termed "crap detectors." That term is based on the authors' conviction that the schools must serve as the principal medium for developing in youth the attitudes and skills of social, political, and cultural criticism. Gardner (1965) also speaks of teaching habits of mind useful in new situations, such as the capacity to think critically. The goal is the kind of person who lifelong will continue to question, to learn, and to grow.

If health education in schools can help students learn these kinds of concepts and skills, the incidence of many of the behavioral problems cited above ought to be significantly diminished. Needs like those are not often perceived as such by school-age youngsters. Yet they share a great many needs that they do recognize and often voice. Needs that are perceived are usually referred to as interests or concerns.

Student health interests

The most recent survey of student health concerns and interests was conducted in the state of Washington (Trucano, 1984). Over five thousand students participated in the study, which was patterned on the earlier Connecticut study, *Teach Us What We Want to Know* (Byler et al., 1969). It was not the intention of the Washington study to make comparisons, but instead to make a report on the present. Nevertheless it is interesting to see how many more commonalities than differences there were as identified by these two studies conducted more than a decade apart. Commonalities included concerns and interests in learning about topics related to growth and development, food and nutrition, physical fitness, first aid and accident prevention, mental health, diseases, sexuality, peer relationships, family relationships, pregnancy, development and care of babies, smoking, alcohol and drug abuse, weight control, and fear. The concerns revealed by the Washington survey that were different in that they were new reflect current problems in the larger society. For example, the young people of today had far more specific fears and worries than their predecessors. They were worried about not being loved and wanted, about divorce, death, stress, and suicide. They were concerned with handicapping conditions and birth defects, child and sexual abuse, and improving their self-concept. All these commonalities and differences were mentioned at almost every grade level and with varying amounts of interest, depending on the relevance of the concern to the age group involved.

Significantly, nearly 85 percent of the responding students said "yes" to the question, "Do you think it is important to study about health?" A twelfth grader added, "If I could have the opportunity of learning/studying all of these things you have mentioned in your survey, it would not only be fantastic . . . but a great blessing and a miracle" (Trucano, 1984, p. 9).

Knowledge of students' needs and interests is important for two primary reasons: first, because it tells the teacher what subject matter is most relevant to a given group of students and, second, because motivation is high when instruction is based upon real concerns. It is a vital, but not the only, source of information to be considered when designing a curriculum plan.

Health education is general education

General education refers to the common core of subjects believed essential to the education of every American child. Everybody agrees in principle that one of its primary goals is the promotion of health, as stated in the following:

> The school must be guided, in pursuing its central purpose or any other purposes, by certain conditions which are known to be basic to significant mental development. The school has responsibility to establish and maintain these conditions.
>
> One of them is physical health. The sick or poorly nourished pupil, the pupil suffering from poor hearing or vision, is hampered in learning. An adequate physical basis for intellectual life must be assured.
>
> Mental health is also of profound importance. With it, the pupil can have that desire and respect for learning which promote the satisfactory development of his capacity for effective mental performance. Without it, the likelihood of such development is drastically reduced, if not rendered impossible. . . . As the child is helped to view himself and the society in a healthy way, to develop self-discipline, and to feel secure in his relationships, he becomes better able to respond positively to the school. (Educational Policies Commission, 1961, p. 15)

Are today's schools committed to the provision of curricula that meet all these standards and satisfy student needs and interests? Studies show this to be so only partially and in some places. There are well-established courses such as biology, life science, physical education, social studies, and home economics that touch on some of it, but none of them comes to grips with health needs directly or comprehensively. Pieces of health information tucked into these other studies may afford students some categorical facts, but it will not be health education. Students need health instruction, and if its provision is dependent on the assumption that piecemeal is good enough, then they are being cheated and so is society. Sliepcevich (1963, p. 155) argues, "Is it not just as important that a student have as part of his general education health education, as it is to have science, mathematics, foreign languages, or the fine arts? . . . The majority of students will not become scientists or mathematicians, and for them an understanding and appreciation of these other scientific fields will be adequate. But *every* person will need to make intelligent decisions about his own health, that of his family and community. Good health is more than a personal problem. The individual has a responsibility to society to maintain a high level of health."

The Paideia Proposal (Adler, 1982) (paideia signifying the general learning that should be the possession of all human beings) avers that general education is better than any other kind of schooling because it prepares children to be good citizens and to lead good human lives. In short, the goals of general education are those also of health education, and achievement of the concepts and skills of the one contributes to those of the other. There can be no general education without the inclusion of health education. It is the most basic of all the basic studies. The parallels between the goals of general education and of health education were defined in a national report on health issues in these words: "Many people think . . . that to be truly healthy requires a clear sense of self, a full ration of confidence and self-esteem, and opportunity to realize physical, emotional, and intellectual potentials. At this level, general education and health education have similar goals. There may come a time when health education and general education becomes [sic] fully integrated—it may be hard to tell where one leaves off and the other begins," (*Promoting Health: Issues and Strategies,* 1979, p. 15).

Parent and community support

Although not every community member is a parent, every parent is a member of the community. However, parents are typically surveyed in their role as parents of specified school-age children, whereas community surveys are usually administered to categories of adults based upon their profession or business or their membership in a special-interest group, such as the PTA. In any case, the great majority of parents and community members consistently supports the provision of health education in schools in both words and deeds.

Many local studies of parents' attitudes have focused on sex education because this is a controversial aspect of school health education and because many states and local districts require that parents be polled before instruction is begun. The result is always the same. The majority of parents and the public endorses school family life and sex education (Yarber, 1979). For example, a study in Galveston, Texas, indicated that parents were in agreement with the sex education objectives provided their eighth graders, thought the course was a valuable experience for their child, and said that the course made it easier for them to discuss sexual matters with their children (Parcel and Coreil, 1985). Ryder (1983) found that a large percentage of parents and students surveyed in Orange County, California, supported the provision of sex education programs encompassing a broad range of topics, some of which might be considered controversial. A 1981–1982 statewide study in California reports that parents of ninth and tenth graders were strongly supportive of family life education and that less than 1 percent of the parents withdrew their children from instruction in the program that year (Koblinsky and Weeks, 1984).

A community-wide poll conducted in Texas asked a group of parents, students, former students, educators, and members of the business and professional community to rate sixty-two competencies listed under nine categories of skills needed by high school graduates. Decision-making skills were ranked first, with life-coping and physical, social, and personal health ranking third and fourth, *ahead* of communication and computational skills (Killian, 1983).

Among the findings of the sixteenth annual Gallup poll (Gallup, 1984) of the public's attitudes toward the public schools were these concerning health education. First, a majority of those polled would require high school students to take a course in health education. Further, among the top nine topics the public believed should be provided and required of *all* students, drug abuse was first, alcohol abuse was second, and parent/parenting was eighth.

Nor is community support of school health education limited to verbally expressed approval of such instruction. Almost every kind of community professional and industrial organization offers some amount or kind of health-related materials and services to the schools. For example, official health agencies such as local, county, and state health departments will often provide speaker services, offer audio-visual aids and films, and supply pamphlets concerning specific reportable health problems. Voluntary health agencies such as the American Cancer Society, the American Heart Association, and the American Lung Association have helpful teaching aids (posters, pamphlets, audio-visual materials, charts, and teaching-learning guides) available for the asking. Some also have speakers bureaus. Professional societies such as medical or dental groups or individual practitioners often will assist the schools in solving short-term medical problems or host field trips to medical or dental facilities for small groups of students. Private industry such as insurance companies, manufacturers, and various councils and institutes (e.g., those that represent the dairy industry or cereal, meat, and livestock producers) are active in developing and distributing teaching aids and student materials concerning nutrition. Service clubs such as the Lions, Elks, and Shriners are so called because community service is their primary goal. Almost every one of them focuses its services upon a specific health problem. Many of those problems affect the school-age child. For example, the Lions focus on vision problems, the Elks are concerned with cerebral palsy, and the Shriners support hospitals that provide care and treatment for crippled or seriously burned children.

The National Congress of Parents-Teachers (NCPT) is both community based and school based, but its members are dedicated to the promotion of comprehensive school health education and the health of schoolchildren. Finally, there are the youth groups (e.g., Boy Scouts, Girl Scouts, Campfire Girls, Four H Clubs). Although the membership of these clubs is school based, the leadership is community based. The programs of youth groups focus on the promotion of healthful living and serving the community and the school. Schools often call on youth groups to assist as leaders in projects that benefit the safety and sanitation of the school and its grounds or to serve as tutors of younger or educationally disadvantaged students.

The quantity and quality of the community assistance available to schools and teachers in planning for classroom teaching is almost limitless, especially in urban areas. But even in rural areas, county health departments can be contacted for assistance both in the form of speakers and teaching aids. State and national health agencies will often respond to mailed inquiries with single copies of the educational materials or lists of materials that may be borrowed or obtained at small cost. One precaution should always be observed: Preview any materials obtained from sources outside the school to be sure that no objectionable commercial copy is included, that the vocabulary and subject matter of the presentation are appropriate for use with the students for whom it is intended, and that the subject matter and emphasis of the message are consistent with school policy.

National support for health education

Health education of the people as a means of preventing disease and promoting health is not a new idea. What is new today is the recognition that maybe health educators have been right all along. It looks as if health education may be the best means of motivating young people and adults to think first and act later when it comes to life-style choices. Admitting that other forces (social, economic, personal attitudes, environment, and politics) will always also be influences does not mean that ability to discover and apply the best information obtainable in making health-affecting decisions cannot also play an important role. Green (1981, p. 10) says that one of his biases regarding the value of health education is that it "does work in varying degrees and in the long run is potentially more cost effective, humane, and therefore more socially acceptable in the prevention of or solution of anticipated health problems."

Support for health education as a primary strategy in effecting health promotion objectives has led to and at the same time grown from the beliefs and related activities of federal, professional, and private sector foundations and organizations. It is also reflected in the statements of authorities in education, medicine, public health, and health-concerned industries and agencies. For the purposes of this text, the following will focus on support for health education in schools, although much of it will also apply to health education in the other settings.

Recommendations of health and educational authorities

The Report of the President's Committee on Health Education Much of what is happening today at the national level supportive of health promotion had its beginnings in the *Report of the President's Committee on Health Education* (1973). Among its recommendations were the following:

> That health problems based on behavior—or which can be worsened or bettered primarily through behavior—be identified and made the basic content of health education programs. And that guidelines be developed for each that can be followed by a person alone or with the help of a health adviser.
>
> That extended and intensified health education programs be developed for appropriate groups in every community to focus on health problems which apparently can be prevented, detected early or controlled through individual action.
>
> That cost analysis studies be made to determine the long-term effectiveness of health education programs in reducing personal health care costs for persons with specific types of health problems. . . .
>
> As our primary finding, we believe very strongly that the nation needs a National Center for Health Education to stimulate, coordinate, and evaluate health education programs. At the present time there is no organization or agency in or outside of government even approaching it. Nor does anything appear on the horizon to indicate that the need for a Center might be filled in some other way.
>
> The over-all objective of the National Center would be to improve the health of the American people through health education. It would approach that goal by continuing and vastly expanding the work of the Committee in determining exactly what is being done now in health education; how well it is being done; how more can be done; and how what is done can be made to deliver results. (*Report of the President's Committee on Health Education,* 1973, pp. 23, 28–29)

The National Center for Health Education was established in 1975 in accordance with the committee's recommendation and is discussed later in this chapter.

Healthy People—the Surgeon General's report Later, the Surgeon General's report, *Healthy People* (1979), proposed a national agenda of four goals for the reduction of disease, disability, and premature death among all age groups by 1990. The central theme of this report was that "the health of the people can be significantly improved through actions they can take themselves, and through actions decision makers in both public and private sectors can take to promote a safer and healthier environment for every American, at home, at work, and at play." The era of health promotion and disease prevention had begun. The five health promotion goals were these:

1. to continue to improve infant health and, by 1990, to reduce infant mortality by at least 35 percent, to fewer than nine deaths per thousand births
2. to improve child health, foster optimal childhood development, and, by 1990, reduce deaths among children ages 1 to 14 years by at least 20 percent, to fewer than 324 per 100,000
3. to improve the health and health habits of adolescents and young adults and, by 1990, to reduce deaths among people aged 15 to 24 by at least 20 percent, to fewer than ninety-three per hundred thousand
4. to improve the health of adults and, by 1990, to reduce deaths among people aged 25 to 64 by at least 25 percent, to fewer than four hundred per hundred thousand
5. to improve the health and quality of life for older adults and, by 1990, to reduce the average annual number of days of restricted activity due to acute and chronic conditions by 20 percent, to fewer than thirty days per year for people aged 65 and older

Schools were identified as having major responsibility in achieving these goals in these words: "No group is more able than school teachers to provide information and instruction that can help young people make decisions that promote good health. Comprehensive school health education activities can: enhance a child's skills and personal decision-making; promote understanding of the concepts of health and the causes of disease; and foster knowledge about the ways in which one's health is affected by personal decisions related to smoking, alcohol and drug use, diet, exercise, and sexual activity" (*Healthy People,* 1979, p. 143).

Objectives for the nation As a direct outcome of the Surgeon General's report, a companion volume, *Objectives for the Nation*, was published in 1980. More than five hundred individuals and organizations from both private and government sectors were involved in the lengthy process of developing it. Objectives were established for each of the fifteen priority areas identified in the report, categorized as either *health promotion* (smoking reduction, reduction of alcohol and drug misuse, nutrition, physical fitness and exercise, and stress management), *health protection* (occupational environment, safety, infectious agent control, control of toxic wastes, and fluoridation of water), and *preventive health services* (immunizations, maternal and infant care, family planning, STD control, and high blood pressure control) (Green, 1981, p. 18).

For each of the fifteen priority areas, a number of objectives were specified. They were confined to what might feasibly be attained by 1990 and focused on interventions and supports intended for well people, to reduce their risks of becoming ill or injured at some future time. The objectives were presented within a framework of supportive information, the principal assumptions underlying the framing of the objectives, and a list of prevention/promotion measures with the potential of achieving the objectives. In every case, health education in all settings is indicated as one of such measures. Health education in schools is specifically referred to more than the other settings.

For example, relative to pregnancy and infant health, this is a recommended measure: "developing, implementing, and evaluating the quality and quantity of health education in schools and communities, with emphasis on life style risk factors (poor nutrition, and use of alcohol, cigarettes, and drugs)" (*Promoting Health/Preventing Disease*, 1980, p. 16). Another recommended measure is for the area of infectious agent control: "school health and public and professional education, to improve individual awareness of and responsibility for disease prevention practices such as handwashing and obtaining immunizations for one's self and one's children" (*Promoting Health/Preventing Disease*, 1980, p. 58). The current status and supportive function of school health programs is also mentioned in some of the assumptions, for example, relative to nutrition, "Comprehensive school health education, including nutrition education, will become a more integral part of the K–12 curriculum" and for the problem of family planning, "Education can result in behavioral change," (*Promoting Health/Preventing Disease*, 1980, p. 76).

Subsequent to the publication and dissemination of the objectives, a two-day conference, *Prospects for a Healthier America: Achieving the Nation's Health Promotion Objectives (1984)*, was held in Washington, D.C., for the purpose of expanding the support and cooperation of national organizations from a variety of public and private sectors. The invited participants were organized into five working groups as follows:

1. *health care settings* (such as hospitals, health maintenance organizations, community health centers)
2. *health professions* (physicians, psychologists, dentists, nutritionists, and nurses)
3. *business and industry*
4. *voluntary associations* (for example, National Safety Council, American Lung Association, National Boards of the YMCA and YWCA)
5. *schools* (for example, the American School Health Association, Association for the Advancement of Health Education, National Association of Elementary School Principals, and the National Center for Health Education)

More than fifty organizations were represented by the group.

The ten-member school working group quickly agreed that schools could best contribute to the achievement of the 1990 health promotion objectives by offering quality comprehensive school health programs. Current program obstacles were identified, and sixteen recommendations to federal agencies, and as many others to professional education associations, were made. An example of the recommendations aimed at federal agencies was "#9 Categorical school health interventions (e.g., drug abuse, smoking, or cardiovascular diseases) developed through federal agencies should be designed to be integrated with the broader comprehensive school health curriculum and school health services" (*Prospects for a Healthier America,* 1984, p. 16).

A sample recommendation from the list intended for professional education associations was "#11 Educational associations should collaborate with health education associations and relevant health associations to generate appropriate legislative and administrative requirements for school health education programs and for appropriate teacher preparation in health education" (*Prospects for a Healthier America,* 1984, p. 18).

It should not be concluded that the curriculum for health education in schools today should be limited to study of those fifteen preventable health problems. Health education in schools looks at human behavior in all of its dimensions, not just at information specific to the nation's health promotion objectives, which is not to say that those objectives could not be successfully integrated within its curriculum.

Iverson and Kolbe (1983) estimate that, of the recommended 227 national prevention objectives proposed relative to the Surgeon General's 1979 promotion goals, 67, or about a third of them, could be attained directly or indirectly by the nation's schools. It was judged that achievement of 34 of them would be impossible in the absence of school health education and that the schools could potentially enhance achievement of 33 more. Whether there are only those 67 objectives to which school health education could contribute is not certain. The basis for their selection is explained as "the authors reviewed each of the national prevention objectives and judged whether or not each of the 226 [*sic*] national prevention objectives could be achieved without the existence of school health programs, (Iverson and Kolbe, 1983, p. 298). Green (1981) has said, "Clearly, health education is the primary mode of effecting the health promotion objectives, but health education is a necessary element in all of the other priorities for action as well." Education for health can be effective in changing adult behavior and life-styles. School health education can contribute to the prevention of those harmful life-styles and behaviors.

There is a problem with the operationality of the objectives as stated. In education, an objective is a statement describing what the learners are to be able to do following instruction that they could not have done before. (Chapter 5 will discuss the formulation of educational objectives.) Actually, these "objectives" are more precisely subgoals. They tell you how much change in the incidence of the health problem is the goal, but they don't tell you very much about what students have to be able to do with the specified information if that action is to be facilitated by the educational experience provided. Translation of those subgoals into feasible, functional statements organized sequentially, K–12, within the framework of a comprehensive curriculum, remains to be accomplished. When that has been done, and teaching and learning plans have been carried out accordingly, those sixty-seven objectives will have had the best treatment possible. And if it is successful, not just some specified percentage of the students should have achieved the objectives, but all of them who have had that instruction. In any case, provision of comprehensive school health education can make a valuable and valued contribution to the goals established in the Surgeon General's report.

NATIONAL OFFICES RESPONSIBLE FOR SUPPORT OF HEALTH EDUCATION

Bureau of Health Education

One of the recommendations the president's committee report listed was "that a focal point be established within the Department of HEW to work with all federal agencies to help make the federal government's involvement in health education more effective and more efficient," (*Report of the President's Committee,* 1973, p. 24). There was no such office or agency at the time, although there were many public and private efforts aimed at the health education of Americans. In answer to that recommendation, in 1974, the Bureau of Health Education (BHE) was established as a component of the Center for Disease Control of the Public Health Service, Department of Health, Education and Welfare. Its mission was "to provide leadership and direction to a comprehensive national health education program for the prevention of disease, disability, premature death, and undesirable and unnecessary health problems" (BHE, 1975, p. 1). In addition to the office of the director, the bureau included the National Clearing House for Smoking and Health (which administered a national program to reduce death and disability due to smoking), the Community Program Development Division (which initiated, monitored, and evaluated community health projects), and the Professional Services and Consultation Division (which provided technical assistance and consultation to public and private agencies and groups concerned with health education. Bureau staff provided direct project support at national, regional, state, and local levels, as well as project management of all bureau contracts and grant programs.

Early in 1981, the Center for Disease Control was reorganized as the Centers for Disease Control. As a consequence, the Bureau of Health Education was combined with the Family Planning Evaluation Division and the nutrition program to form the new Center for Health Promotion and Education (CHPE), and what was the Bureau of Health Education is now the Division of Health Education within that center. The charge of the Division of Health Education remains much the same as for the bureau, although changes occur as national health needs necessarily change both program support and priority setting.

National Center for Health Education

During its first year of existence, the BHE's principal initiative with the private sector was a contract with the National Health Council to conduct a feasibility study of a proposed private sector–based National Center for Health Education, as recommended by the President's Committee on Health Education in 1973. The center was to be uniquely both private and governmental in that it was to be mandated by the Congress and financed by both the federal government and private sources.

When complete, the council's report included these recommendations:

> The Center should be a free-standing, non-profit private organization. . . . It should be a non-bureaucratic, national health education

problem-solving mechanism, which would depend to a major degree on other organizations for input, resources, funding and implementation of policies and projects. . . .

The Center should concentrate its resources on the performance of leadership functions no other agency can deliver, and avoid duplication of other public and private resources.

Seven major leadership functions were identified as appropriate to the Center: Consensus building . . . Policy determination . . . National strategy design . . . Health Education advocacy . . . Data base development and information exchange . . . Technical assistance . . . and Evaluation, testing, and demonstration. (U.S. Department of Health and Human Services, 1975, p. 2)

The present National Center for Health Education was incorporated in New York and first established in San Francisco, California, in October of 1975. From the first, advocacy of health education has been the Center's most important function. Other primary functions include convening and strategy design, technical assistance, research and evaluation, and information exchange. It has worked closely with the Bureau and Division of Health Education (CDC) in the further development, promotion, and dissemination of the School Health Education Project's curriculum materials, was awarded the Bureau of Health Manpower contract for the Role Delineation Project, and conducted the Kellogg Foundation–funded School and College Initiative Project. The Center provides office space and certain facilities to the National Task Force for the Professional Preparation and Practice of Health Education. It also publishes a magazine *Health Link News* and other printed materials. The "Healthy Me" curriculum program is sponsored by the center, as are other health education projects funded by the private sector and administered by Center staff.

Office of Comprehensive School Health

The Health Education Act of 1978 (Public Law 95–561) provided strong legislative support for school health education as follows: "The Congress finds and declares that: there is an increased concern for physical health and well being; and understanding of the principles of good health can play a vital role in preventing illness and diseases; and a Federal program is needed to assist state and local educational agencies in developing health education programs." As a result, an office of comprehensive school health (OCSH) was established in the Department of Education in 1979 with the intention of implementing the purposes of that act. The charge was to encourage and support state and local programs that teach children and youth how to maintain their health and avoid preventable illness and disease.

The office was an effective advocate for school health, and its director was successful in establishing viable links among federal, local, and professional groups concerned with school health objectives. Although the office was never funded as authorized and was abolished by the Reagan administration, the concept and value of comprehensive school health education was given wider attention and interpretation than had been the case until then.

Office of Disease Prevention and Health Promotion

This office, established in 1976 in the Office of the Assistant Secretary for Health, has had several titles during the interim. At its inception, it was titled Office of Health Information and Health Promotion (OHIHP or OHIP). In 1980, its title and responsibilities were expanded to Office of Health Information, Health Promotion, and Physical Fitness and Sports Medicine (OHP). Now the acronym is ODPHP, but it remains in the Office of the Assistant Secretary of Health (OASH) and in the now-titled Department of Health and Human Services (DHHS). The ODPHP coordinates policy and program development in prevention. Its many responsibilities include coordinating the development of implementation plans for the federal contribution to the 1990 objectives for the nation.

Based upon the framework provided by the Surgeon General's report, DHHS activities are coordinated around five key settings: the community, the schools, the work site, the medical treatment setting, and the home. Within ODPHP, a school program component is staffed and budgeted separately, its staff working closely with the Health Education Division of CHPE, NCHE, and private groups as appropriate. Collaboration first with the Bureau of Health Education, now the Health Education Division of the Center for Health Promotion and Education, has been close. Beginning in January 1980, the production and distribution of the center's *Focal Points* has been a joint effort. This means that information about the activities, grants, and contracts awarded by both groups can be found in the same publication.

Since the abolition of OCSH in the Department of Education, the ODPHP school program has built upon current awareness of the potential of health education in schools for preventing disease and promoting health that had been generated by that office during its brief tenure.

National Institutes of Health

The mission of the National Institutes of Health is the discovery of knowledge for the prevention and control of disease and the extension of life. Almost all the research is conducted outside the institute but administered by institute personnel. The bulk of the institutes' appropriation of more than $2 billion a year goes to this extramural program of grants to scientists and research institutions throughout the nation. Another program promotes health personnel development through the provision of traineeships and fellowships in public health and other scientific fields.

One action specifically supporting research in school health was the National Conference on School Health Education Research (1983) sponsored by the National Heart, Lung, and Blood Institute and the Office of Disease Prevention and Health Promotion. Even though the conference focused on the institute's special health areas, most of the state-of-the-art review, issues, problems, and recommendations for future research were generic to all areas of school health education. Sixty specialists invited from biomedical, behavioral, and social science fields and health education researchers participated in the conference. This mix of interests and expertise was intended to increase the likelihood that ideas from these other fields might be applied to school health education research.

Conference proceedings were published in 1984 as supplemental issues of the *Journal of School Health* (American School Health Association) and *Health Education* (Association for the Advancement of Health Education—AAHE). Hence, the conference and proceedings represent a collaboration among federal agencies, professional health organizations, voluntary health agencies, and researchers from many disciplines in support of school health education and the health of the nation's youth (Stone, 1984, p. 216).

The great number and range of activities and projects conducted or funded by these federal or national agencies cannot be described adequately here. For further information, refer to National Clearing Houses as appropriate and to other health-concerned data bases. The Center for Health Promotion and Education operates a data base on health education including citations and abstracts of current journal articles, monographs, conference proceedings, reports, and unpublished documents acquired and selected by the center. It also contains descriptions of programs in health education selected by the Center. Only documents published or programs of relevance since 1977 are included. Single copies of documents and supporting documentation for each program can be obtained by consulting with local public, medical, and university libraries. Each citation provides sufficient information to enable users of the data base to locate copies or contact programs.

OTHER NATIONAL ORGANIZATIONS SUPPORTIVE OF SCHOOL HEALTH EDUCATION

Generally speaking, national organizations supportive of school health education are supportive of all health education. Organizations of this sort can be categorized as either official or nonofficial. Those discussed so far have been of the first category. Nonofficial organizations include (1) voluntary health agencies (American Heart Association, American Lung Association, March of Dimes), (2) professional associations (Association for the Advancement of Health Education, American School Health Association, American Public Health Association), (3) commercial organizations and alliances (Metropolitan Life Insurance Company, Kimberly-Clark Corporation, National Dairy Council, Meat and Lifestock Institute), (4) integrating agencies (United Way, Welfare Planning Councils), (5) private philanthropical foundations (Rockefeller Foundation, W. K. Kellogg Foundation), and (6) coalitions of health-concerned organizations (Coalition of National Health Education Organizations, National School Health Education Coalition). Specific information about most of these will be found in chapter 10. The Coalition of National Health Education Organizations and programs in progress that demonstrate the impact of private foundation support will be discussed here.

Coalition of National Health Education Organizations

The CNHEO is composed of professional health-concerned organizations that have identifiable memberships of health educators and have an ongoing health education program. Seven national organizations and eight health education groups are represented. These eight organizations or sections with a combined membership of more than twenty-five thousand include the following:

- American College Health Association (Health Education section)
- American Public Health Association (Public Health Education section)
- American Public Health Association (School Health Education and Services section)
- American School Health Association
- Association for the Advancement of Health Education (American Alliance for Health, Physical Education, Recreation, and Dance).
- Conference of State and Territorial Directors of Public Health Education.
- Society for Public Health Education
- Society of State Directors for Health, Physical Education, and Recreation.

Member organizations accept responsibility to appoint a delegate and alternate delegate to the coalition, to consider coalition recommendations, and to take action when appropriate. Each organization contributes $50 a year to help defray coalition expenses. Delegates are responsible for representing their parent organization at all coalition meetings and for providing two-way communication between the coalition and its member organizations. They are also responsible for obtaining coalition action relative to parent organization issues and obtaining parent organization action or approval on coalition recommendations or actions.

The coalition has five primary goals:

- facilitate national-level communication, collaboration, and coordination among the member organizations
- provide a forum for the identification and discussion of health education issues
- formulate recommendations and take appropriate action on issues affecting the member interests
- serve as a communication and advisory resource for agencies, organizations, and persons in the public and private sectors on health education issues
- serve as a focus for the exploration and resolution of issues pertinent to professional health educators

Funds to support coalition meeting expenses are sought from sources outside the member organizations. Meetings are often sponsored by health-related agencies in return for technical assistance, and consultation is provided to the host group. On many issues, the coalition serves as the voice of the health education profession, generating greater visibility for the profession and its member organizations. Consequently, coalition statements can have greater impact on legislation, public policy, and issues than those emanating from any one organization alone. The coalition's response to the report by the National Commission on Excellence in Education, *A Nation at Risk,* sent to all chief state school officers and published in the *Journal of School Health* (August 1984) is an example of this kind of statement and action. The intention was to make a significant rebuttal on behalf of the entire health education profession to the report's derogation of health education in schools. These are some of the points that were stressed:

> The Coalition would like to point out that health is basic to "the basics." Learning cannot occur in children who are physically or emotionally distressed. Children's health should be a national priority if for no other reason than the view proposed by the Commission on Excellence in Education. Today's children are the future workers of our nation . . . workers need good health.
> Not only is the current health status of children critical to their achievement in school, but their future health status is very much dependent on the health promoting or health debilitating habits which may become a part of their lifestyle. In 1976, medical scientists concluded that perhaps as much as 50% of the mortality occurring that year was due to unhealthy behaviors or lifestyles. There is an urgent need to assist children to understand that their lifestyle can affect their physical and emotional health. Prevention of disease in the adult is very much dependent on the early adoption of a healthy lifestyle. (Coalition of National Health Education Organizations, 1984, pp. 256–257)

The coalition has supported legislation and appropriations concerned with health education, health promotion, and disease prevention (e.g., urging restoration and funding of the Office of Comprehensive School Health, funding for OHIP and extension of Title XVII, and passage of the Older Americans Personal Health Education and Training Act). For more information, see Cauffman, 1982.

Private foundations

Much of the financial support of curriculum and research projects in school health has come from federal sources, primarily from the Division of Health Education (CHPE), formerly the Bureau of Health Education; the Office of Disease Prevention and Health Promotion, and the National Institutes of Health (e.g., for heart, lung and blood; on drug abuse; on alcohol abuse and alcoholism). State and national voluntary health agencies have a long history of contributions to school health education as well.

Significant as the support of these governmental and national groups has been and continues to be, there are some unavoidable disadvantages to accepting their support. First, such funds are usually targeted at categorical health problems. Second, particularly with regard to government funding, the purpose and nature of the program is specified in advance by the funding agency owing to the nature of the announced RFP (request for a proposal). If a contract or grant is awarded, the work must be done under the direct supervision of officers from the funding agency.

Philanthropic foundations interested in promoting school health education are generally open to new ideas and friendly to creativity and experimentation. Awardees are allowed more flexibility and freedom in carrying out a proposed program once it has been agreed to. Furthermore, foundations are more likely to be dedicated to comprehensive school health education, rather than focused on a single health problem or area of concern.

Among the foundations that have allocated large sums of money in support of health education in schools are the R. K. Kellogg Foundation, the Metropolitan Life Foundation, the Robert Wood Johnson Foundation, the Rockefeller Foundation, the Bronfman Foundation, the Exxon Foundation, the Zellerbach Family Fund, and the Kaiser Family Fund. There are many more that have contributed to school health education over the years. In general, they have contributed to the development and testing of experimental curriculum materials at all levels of school and college health education and to providing scholarships and fellowships for the encouragement of individual research interests. Some examples of current foundation-sponsored projects are:

- the National Preventive Dentistry Demonstration Program, a six-year research project to culminate in a report supported by data on the cost-effectiveness of each of various combinations of preventive procedures, funded by the Robert Wood Johnson Foundation
- *Quest,* a widely adopted curriculum and program to help students and their parents learn basic life skills in problem solving, communicating, enhancing self-esteem, and resolving conflicts, funded by W. K. Kellogg Foundation
- the SHES study, a national survey of health education in the schools, K–12, followed by the creation and field testing of experimental curriculum materials based upon a conceptual approach to health teaching and learning, a two-year project funded by the Bronfman Foundation
- a curriculum titled "Growing Up Healthy" designed for use with primary grade students, developed and piloted in the San Francisco Unified School District and funded by the Zellerbach Family Fund
- the Health Activities Project (HAP), an entirely experiential and equipment-based program for fourth- to eighth-grade students, involving them with their own health and safety in a discovery approach, funded by the Robert Wood Johnson Foundation
- a nation-wide program titled "Healthy Me" in support of comprehensive school health education to which $4 million has been allocated by the Metropolitan Life Foundation to be awarded in $5000 grants to innovative programs and effective coalitions for school health every year for four years (the first awards were announced early in 1986).
- the National Center for Health Education's "Education for Health by the Year 2000," with the support of the Exxon Foundation
- the University of Texas Medical Branch School Health Program, a five-year, $2 million comprehensive demonstration project in school health, funded by the Robert Wood Johnson Foundation
- the School and College Initiative (SCI), seeking to expand and improve school health education at all levels and to increase and promote the distribution and communication of existing comprehensive school health education curriculum models and resources, under the aegis of the National Center for Health Education and funded by the W. K. Kellogg Foundation

Private foundations have played an important part in promoting quality health education in schools. Indeed, private sector funding and support at all levels of spending and involvement is likely to be the critical element in shaping the decisions affecting health teaching in schools, even ultimately whether those health objectives for the nation are actually achieved at proposed and hoped-for levels.

Other voices, related views

Statements like those published by federal agencies and offices and issued by the national health institutes, associations, and coalitions are impressive and effective in supporting health education. Yet individual voices have a special kind of impact as well. When respected leaders in any field, in or out of health fields, speak about health education, people listen. The list of individual educators, educational philosophers, health educators, physicians, school administrators, and other community leaders whose convictions and efforts have promoted health education in schools is long. A selected few are presented as representative of all those whose voiced convictions have helped build the discipline and facilitate its application over the years.

- "If our values are straight and we value human health above all else, then health education becomes one of the master areas in all of American education, along with language. It deals, or should deal with all those phenomena indigenous to being human, that develop or retard, create or kill. Nothing is more important. Time must be found for it," (Oberteuffer, 1977).
- "With more than 48 millions of children and youth in the United States attending our schools, this is surely the greatest opportunity we have to make a difference in the positive health habits of our citizenry. I realize that school health education is no panacea because there are no easy solutions to the many complex health problems confronting our society. However, the schools, through a well-planned health promotion and health education program, will provide students with relevant learning activities that can assist them in making wise health decisions immediately and later on as adults," (Earl, 1984,).
- "Clearly, no knowledge is more crucial than knowledge about health. Without it, no other life goal can be successfully achieved. Therefore, we recommend that all students study health, learning about the human body, how it changes over the life cycle, what nourishes it and diminishes it, and how a healthy body contributes to emotional well-being" (Boyer, 1983).
- "We ought to be developing a much better system for general education about human health, with more curricular time for acknowledgement and even some celebration of the absolute marvel of good health that is the real lot of most of us, most of the time (Thomas, 1972, p. 83).

- ". . . one of the best systems available in our society for health promotion and the prevention of health problems, but probably the most neglected and underused are the schools. The potential for the promotion of positive health lifestyles in the schools is very great because: Prevention is primarily an educational program and belongs in the schools; We have access to almost every individual during early and impressionable years of their lives. . . . We have an extensive transportation system already in place; We have highly intelligent and professional staff who know and relate well to their constituents; Schools are in the business of education and skilled in the transmission of ideas and concepts; and schools are accustomed to dealing with role model issues" (Wilson, 1978).

- ". . . physicians, social workers, hospital administrators, health educators, dentists, nutritionists, health economists, even congressmen, and many more, differ in terms of their particular professional objectives, foci of intervention, strategies, methods, and functional targets. But they all strive to affect peoples' health-related behaviors in one way or another within their own professional confines. What sets the health educator apart is his *primary* set of objectives, which is to create in children and adults the cognitive/affective states and processes which are necessary for, or at least favorable to, the kinds of behaviors which are deemed health-promoting. With *these* objectives being characteristic of and primary to health education, their achievement—or nonachievement—presents also the criteria of educational effectiveness, criteria by which, and only by which, health educators should be judged" (Hochbaum, 1981, p. 5).

- "The single most important contribution school health programs can make to promote health is to emphasize the importance of lifestyles, and the environment, and to teach children to use the health system. Our recent attempts to contain health costs may be successful in the short run. The hope for the future, however, rests with the next generation of health consumers, the children of today. Effective health education early in life can help to prevent the major diseases of adulthood. We must learn even more about the development of living patterns at a young age that will lead to healthier adult lives" (Califano, 1977).

- "School leaders throughout our country want and need to provide the leadership for a good comprehensive school health education program. To research, plan, implement and evaluate such a program is indeed challenging as well as time-consuming. . . . The effort expended by each school district to ensure that a comprehensive school health pro-

gram is implemented would depend on the district's locality, size, and the individual makeup of its staff and community. However, the demand for such a program and the need are common to all" (Bartow, 1984).
- ". . . an educational system that hopes to prepare youth adequately for the future must be concerned with student feelings, attitudes, beliefs, understandings, values—the things that make us human—as well as with student behavior" (Combs, 1981).
- "With the nation's health bill soaring, the information dispensed in health classes—on alcohol and drug abuse, nutrition and diet, first aid, common communicable diseases and preventive health care, sex education, and mental health—could well save more needless misery, suffering and expense than any other course in the curriculum" (Honig, 1985).

In sum, all the foregoing constitutes the rationale for health education in schools as generally accepted by the profession and by authorities in and out of the field. The remainder of this book will address the problems and procedures involved in developing and implementing the sort of curriculum that is consistent with the goals that have been described. Essential steps in curriculum development, selection of appropriate teaching strategies, ways of avoiding controversy or criticism, the design and application of effective evaluation procedures, as well as chapters on administration and management of school health programs and ways to facilitate and integrate community interrelationships will be presented.

SUMMARY

1. Health education is health education whether practiced in school, community, clinical, or work settings.
2. Every health educator needs to know how to plan and carry out effective health instruction.
3. Health, as a concept denoting optimal functioning and high-level wellness, is the focus of health instruction in schools.
4. The primary goal of the program is promotion or maintenance of behaviors consistent with a healthful life-style.
5. Health education is a term with more than one meaning.
   a. as referring to the discipline, the subject matter or body of knowledge studied

b. as referring to the profession, describing one's occupation or field of employment
   (1) The professional preparation of those describing themselves as health educators may or may not be in health education.
   (2) A credentialing system would serve to standardize professional preparation in health education.
c. as referring to an outcome, the actual, measurable result of a program of health education
d. as referring to a process, the strategies or interventions employed as means of effecting desired changes in knowledge, attitudes, and actions related to health behavior

6. The goals of health instruction are not limited to the transmission of sound health information, but are concerned also with the development of the cognitive skills and abilities, attitudes, and values essential to its meaningful application in meeting health needs.

7. Health education belongs in the schools for many reasons, including the following:
   a. The school is responsible for the protection and promotion of the health of students and school personnel.
   b. Supportive legislation mandates and authorizes specified health services and specifies some amount of instruction in almost every state.
   c. Students need and want to learn how to promote and protect their own health as well as that of family and friends.
   d. Health education is considered one of the basic disciplines, hence an essential element, of the school curriculum.
   e. Studies consistently show that parents and community groups approve and support the provision of health education for all children and youth.

8. Federal support for health education, and particularly school health education, has markedly increased in the past decade.
   a. Federally sponsored programs and reports, such as that of the President's Committee on Health Education (1973); the Surgeon General's report, *Healthy People* (1979); "Objectives for the Nation" (1980); and "Prospects for a Healthier America" (1984), have motivated new interest and action.
   b. Establishment of national offices responsible for promoting health education in schools has added weight and prestige to proposals for the development or improvement of programs of education for health. These include the Bureau of Health Education (1974), the Division of Health Education (CHEP-CDC) (1981), the Na-

tional Center for Health Education (1975), the Office for Disease Prevention and Health Promotion (1976), and the Office of Comprehensive School Health (1979).
   c. Funding of research and grants related to health instruction in schools has been provided by the National Institutes of Health.
9. Other national organizations that fund research, demonstration projects, or in other ways promote school health programs include voluntary health agencies, industrial alliances, private foundations, and coalitions of private or professional health education groups.
10. Publication of statements made by authorities in education, health education, public health, medical, and other fields who recommend the provision of health education in schools provides a growing source of community or individual voices complementing official or organizational recommendations.

QUESTIONS AND EXERCISES

Questions

1. Describe ways in which the work of health educators in other settings can promote and be promoted by health education in schools.
2. Why is it sometimes difficult and even impossible for school health educators to demonstrate success in changing specified health behaviors?
3. How could one's belief about the meaning of health influence the nature of a health education program?
4. How many of the listed goals of school health instruction focus directly on provision of information? What implications for emphasis in planning the curriculum do you see in that fact?
5. Differentiate among health behaviors, health practices, and health habits. Give examples of each to illustrate your explanations.
6. In your view, is the primary meaning of health education descriptive of the discipline, the profession, its outcome, or the process by which it is conducted? Defend your belief.
7. Seven reasons why health education should be provided by schools have been discussed. How would you rank them in terms of their potential influence on school administrators? Next rank the seven reasons as they seem most to least important to you as a school

health educator. Is there a difference in the two sets of rankings? What do you conclude?

Exercises

1. Look for and clip from local newspapers or news magazines any stories reporting health-related trends or issues concerning America's children and youth. Suggest ways that each of those you discover could serve as the focus of meaningful health education activities.
2. Review the content areas recommended for inclusion in comprehensive school health education curricula (appendix C,). If you were asked to integrate study of the fifteen priority areas specified in "Objectives for the Nation," which of the ten content areas would you choose as the logical host for each? Which would not be taught if the curriculum were based upon the fifteen priority areas?
3. Consult the education and health and safety codes for your state. What are some key health services and safety provisions that schools must provide by law? What is the nature and quantity of health instruction that is mandated?
4. Assume that the health chairman of the PTA of your school has asked you to give a thirty-minute talk at the next scheduled meeting of the group on the topic "What is health education and why should it be included in every school's curriculum?" Prepare an outline of the key points you would make, along with the information you would want to give them in support of each point.

REFERENCES

Adler, M., *The Paideia Proposal*. New York: Macmillan, 1982.

"Alcohol and other drug abuse among adolescents." *Metropolitan Life Foundation Statistical Bulletin* 65:1, Jan.-March 1984.

Baranowski, T., "Toward the definition of concepts of health and disease, wellness, and illness." *Health Values* 5:6, Nov.-Dec. 1981, pp. 246–255.

Bartow, G. "Foreword." In "Comprehensive school health education," *Journal of School Health*, Sept. 1984, p. 312.

Bates, J., and Winder, A., *Introduction to Health Education*. Palo Alto, CA: Mayfield, 1984.

Bedworth, D. A., and Bedworth, A. E., *Health Education—A Process for Human Effectiveness*. New York: Harper & Row, 1978.

Block, P., "Working with anorexic and bulimic adolescents." *Food and Nutrition News* 56:5, p. 33.

Boyer, E. L., *High School: A Report on Secondary Education in America*. New York: Harper & Row, 1983.

Boyer, E., *Los Angeles Times,* Part I, page 23, February 23, 1985.

Brown, Perry, Epidemiological analyst, STD program, Los Angeles County, CA, Health Department. Personal communication. March 1986.

Bureau of Health Education, *FACTS,* Aug. 1975, whole issue.

Byler, R., et. al., *Teach Us What We Want to Know.* New York: Mental Health Materials Center, 1969.

Califano, J., Speech given to the National School Health Conference. Minneapolis, 1977.

Carlyon, W. H., "The seven deadly sins of health education." *Eta Sigma Gamman* 13:1, Spring-Summer, 1981, pp. 3–8.

Cauffman, Joy G., "A history of the Coalition of National Health Education Organizations: its first ten years and future directions" Muncie, IN: Eta Sigma Gamma Monograph I:2, Dec. 1982.

Coalition of National Health Education Organizations, "Limitations on excellence in education." *Journal of School Health* 54:7, Aug. 1984, pp. 256–257.

Combs, A. W., "What the future demands of education." *Phi Delta Kappan* 62:5, Jan. 1981, p. 372.

Data Track II. American Council of Life Insurance, 1983.

Dubos, R., *Man Adapting.* New Haven, CT: Yale University Press, 1965.

Earl, A. S., "Why health education must be in our nation's educational policy." *Statistical Bulletin, Metropolitan Insurance Company* 65: 4, Dec. 1984, p. 4.

Education Commission of the States, *State Policy Support for School Health Education.* Denver: Education Commission of the States, 1982.

Educational Policies Commission, *The Central Purpose of American Education.* Washington, D.C.: NEA, 1961.

Gallup, G., "The 16th annual gallup poll of the public's attitudes toward the public schools." *Phi Delta Kappan,* Sept. 1984, pp. 23–32.

Gardner, J. *Self Renewal.* New York: Harper & Row, 1965.

Glover, E., Edwards, S., Christen, A., and Finnicum, P., "Smokeless tobacco research: An interdisciplinary approach." *Health Values* 8:3, May-June 1984, pp. 21–25.

Green, L., "Emerging federal perspectives on health promotion." *Health Promotion Monographs,* Teachers College, Columbia University, Center for Health Promotion, 1981.

Green, L., Krueter, M., Deeds, S., and Partridge, K., *Health Education Planning: A Diagnostic Approach.* Palo Alto, CA: Mayfield, 1982.

Guttmacher Institute, *NEWS.* New York, March 1985.

Hatcher, R. A., "Commentary." *Contraceptive Technology Update,* Feb. 1986, p. 18.

Healthy People: The Surgeon General's Report on Health Promotion and Disease Prevention. Washington, D.C.: DHEW (PHS), 1979.

Henderson, A., "The refined and verified role for entry-level health educators." Muncie, IN: Eta Sigma Gamma Monograph, 1982.

Hochbaum, G., "Some select aspects of school health education." *Health Education* 9: 2, March-Apr. 1978, pp. 31–33.

Hochbaum, G., "Behavior change as the goal of health education." *Eta Sigma Gamman* 13:2, Fall-Winter 1981, pp. 3–6.

Hochbaum, G., "Health education as a profession: Reality or illusion." *Eta Sigma Gamman* 15:1, Spring-Summer 1983, pp. 3–6.

Honig, Bill, *Last Chance for Our Children*. Reading, MA,: Addison-Wesley, 1985.

Howe, H., "An historical view of women smoking and advertising." *Health Education* 15:3, May-June 1984, p. 3.

Hoyman, H., "An ecologic view of health and health education." *Journal of School Health* 35:3, March 1965, pp. 110–121.

Iverson, D., and Kolbe, L., "Evolution of the national disease prevention and health promotion strategy: Establishing a role for the schools." *Journal of School Health* 53:5, May 1983, pp. 294–302.

Joint Committee on Health Problems in Schools of the NEA and the AMA, *Why Health Education in Your School*. Chicago: AMA, 1973.

Killigan, M. G., "Community poll defines key skills and assesses schools' performance." *Phi Deta Kappan* 65:3, 1983, pp. 218–219.

Koblinsky, S., and Weeks, J. "Family life education in California ninth and tenth grades." *Journal of School Health* 54:5, May 1984, pp. 181–184.

Kreuter, M. W., "Health promotion, the public health role in the community of free exchange." *Health Promotion Monograph No. 4*. New York: Center for Health Promotion, Teachers College, Columbia University, 1984.

Kreuter, M. W., and Christensen, G. M., "School health education. Does it cause an effect?" *Promoting Health Through the Schools, Health Education Quarterly* 8:1, Spring 1981, p. 30.

Kreuter, M. W., Christensen, G. M., and Davis, Roy, "School health education research. Future issues and challenges." *Health Education* 15:4, 1983, p. 30.

Lalonde, M., *A New Perspective on the Health of Canadians*. Ottawa: Information Canada, 1974.

Lawson, D., Sleet, D., and Amoni, M., "Priorities for motor vehicle occupants protection for children and youth." *Health Education* 15:5, May 1984, pp. 27–29.

McAlister, A. L., "Social and environmental influences on health behavior." *Promoting Health Through the Schools, Health Education Quarterly* 8:1, 1981, pp. 25–31.

McGinnis, M., "Health problems of children and youth: A challenge for schools." *Promoting Health Through the Schools, Health Education Quarterly* 8:1, 1981, pp. 11–14.

Means, R. K., *A History of Health Education in the United States*. Philadelphia: Lea and Febiger, 1962.

Means, R. K., *Historical Perspectives on School Health*. Thorofare, NJ: C. B. Slack, 1975.

Metropolitan life Foundation, *Statistical Bulletin* 63:4, Oct.-Dec. 1982.

Metropolitan Life Foundation, *Statistical Bulletin*, Jan.-March 1984, p. 1.

Nation's Health. Washington, DC: American Public Health Association, 1985.

Oberteuffer, D., *School Health Education*. New York: Harper & Row, 1960.

Oberteuffer, D., "Health education: An appraisal II." In *Concepts and Convictions.* Washington, DC: AAHPER, 1977.

Parcel, G., and Coreil, J., "Parental evaluations of a sex education course for young adolescents." *Journal of School Health* 55:1, Jan. 1985, pp. 9–12.

Postman, N., and Weingartner, C., *Teaching as a Subversive Activity.* New York: Delacorte Press, 1969.

Promoting Health: Issues and Strategies (regional forums in community health promotion). Washington, DC: OHIP/DHEW, 1979.

Promoting Health/Preventing Disease: Objectives for the Nation. Washington, DC: Office of Disease Prevention and Health Promotion, 1980.

Prospects for a Healthier America: Achieving the Nation's Health Promotion Objectives. Washington, D.C.: U.S. Department of Health and Human Services (PHS), Office of Disease Prevention and Health Promotion, 1984.

Report of the President's Committee on Health Education. New York: President's Committee on Health Education, 1973.

"Results of the school health education evaluation study." *Journal of School Health* 55:8, October 1985, entire issue.

Ross, H., and Mico, P., *Theory and Practice in Health Education.* Palo, Alto, CA: Mayfield, 1980.

Rugen, M., *History of the Public Health Education Section.* Washington, DC: American Public Health Association, 1972.

Ryder, K., "Parent and student curriculum expectations of school sex education programs." Unpublished master's thesis, California State University, Long Beach, 1983.

School Health Education Study, *Health Education: A Conceptual Approach.* St. Paul, MN: 3M Education Press, 1967.

Sliepcevich, E., "Should public health be interested in school and college health programs." *Journal of School Health* 33:4, 1963, p. 155.

STD Statistical Letter, no. 132, USHHS-CDC, p. 5.

Stone, E., "A national perspective of school-based research. *Journal of School Health* 54:5, 1984, pp. 215–216.

Thomas, Lewis, *The Lives of a Cell.* New York: Viking Press, 1974, p. 83.

Trucano, L., *Students Speak.* Seattle: Comprehensive Health Education Foundation, 1984.

U.S. Department of Health and Human Services, PHS, *Health Education Focal Points,* Sept. 1975–1986.

Wilson, V., Keynote address to Wisconsin Wellness Commission. 1978.

Yarber, W., "Instructional emphasis in family life and sex education: Viewpoints of students, parents, teachers, and principals at four grade levels." *Journal of School Health* 49:5, May 1979, pp. 263–265.

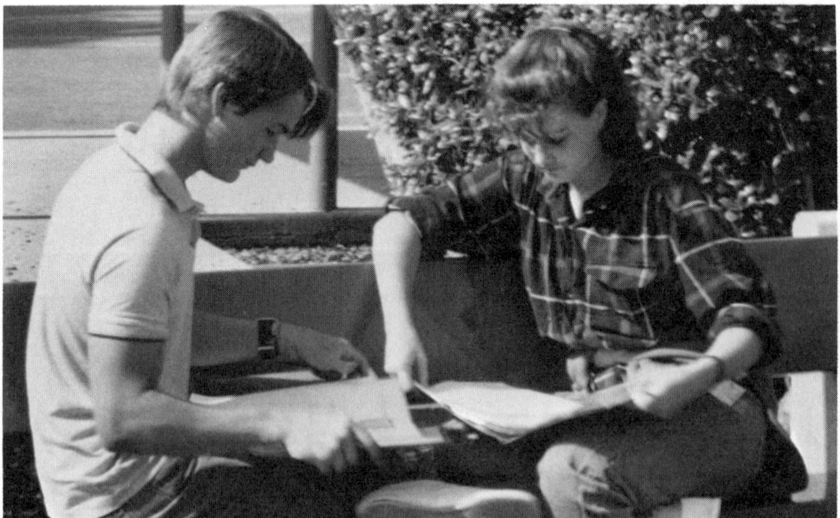

2
Curriculum development: problems and procedures

Anyone who is a health educator, whether in a school, community, workplace, or clinical setting, needs to know how to develop a curriculum. The procedures are much the same in every case. The data sources are essentially the same as well. Any differences stem from the nature of the learner, or audience, and the setting in which the educational interventions are to occur.

Although we are discussing curriculum development for health education in a school setting, not only school health educators are concerned with the health instruction of children and youth. All health educators are involved in on one way or another. First, because students live most of their lives outside school walls, they sooner or later experience health education in other settings. Second, health educators of all kinds frequently serve as resource people in schools. For example, they are often asked to be guest speakers, to provide or demonstrate instructional materials and aids, or to facilitate field trips. Third, community-based health educators commonly play an important role in curriculum planning for school health education. Not only do they participate actively in curriculum planning, but they provide valuable information about community needs as a part of that process.

When *you* hear the word "curriculum," what does it mean to you? Inasmuch as you are a college or university student, you may view curriculum as simply the courses you have to take in order to get that degree you want. Definitions vary, depending on whether a student, a teacher, or a curriculum developer is speaking. They also depend on the intended application of the plan. A curriculum planned for the health education of all students in a given state will be far more broadly described than one intended for the use of a teacher or teachers in a specific school or for a specific course of study. In its broadest sense, "curriculum" usually refers to the whole body of courses offered by an educational institution or by any one department thereof. The term is also used to describe a series of related courses leading to a specified degree, as for a health education major. In its narrowest sense, it refers to a plan for the organization and teaching of a single course, usually during one semester. It is in this last sense that we use the word in this text.

Curriculum has been defined most simply as both "the stuff-to-be taught" and "the stuff-to-be-used" in working toward the objectives that go beyond that stuff (Wilhelms, 1962, p. 14). If it is simply stuff to be taught, then the only question that needs to be answered is "What knowledge is of most worth?" The answer to that question is important, but it doesn't tell us enough. There is far more to curriculum development than deciding what the subject matter ought to be. The more fundamental questions that must also be answered are "What goals—what changes—what personal developments—are of most worth?" "What sorts of curriculum materials are likeliest to carry them forward?"

A curriculum designed for health education must be inferred from life as it is. Education that can facilitate optimal development of decision-making skills and positive health values has to be directly drawn from the real world. If it is to seem relevant to the learners, curriculum planning has to be based on relevant data. The following are some of the problems to be addressed:

- Who are the learners for whom it is intended?
- What do they need and want to know?
- What are the skills that they will need, and what are the health behaviors and attitudes expected by the society in which the learners will live and function as citizens?
- What are the important ideas or generalizations representative of health education?
- How can this subject matter be employed as a means of organizing new facts as they are discovered and accumulated?

Answers to those questions serve as the basis for the decision making fundamental to a curriculum.

SOURCES OF A SCHOOL HEALTH CURRICULUM

Tyler is universally recognized as the originator of the rationale upon which most curriculum development is based today. His *Basic Principles of Curriculum and Instruction* (1949) continues to be a standard reference some thirty printings later. Recently, a select group of professors of curriculum rated it number one among the top thirteen publications that have had a major influence on the curriculum during the past seventy-five years (Shane, 1981). Tyler believes that no single source adequately serves as the basis for defining educational objectives. Instead, investigation must be made of the following:

1. the learners themselves
2. contemporary life outside the school (the community)
3. recommendations made by subject matter specialists (the body of knowledge)

Investigation of these three sources is a necessary first step in the Tylerian approach to curriculum development.

The learners

A primary source of data from which the goals of health education may be inferred is the person who is to be doing the learning. What are the needs, interests, concerns, state of maturation, present abilities, knowledge, and experience of a given age group of students in a school, community, or state? Although it is not possible to explore these problems thoroughly in a book of this nature, a brief overview of the sort of information to be sought as well as a description of some ways to obtain it should serve as an introduction to this source.

Student needs and interests One view of a need is as the degree to which the present condition of an individual differs from some acceptable standard. An educational objective based on this notion of needs would specify the skill and related subject matter to be learned in order to bridge that gap. For example, it is important to find out what students already know and do about health and health behavior. A number of standardized health knowledge and health behavior inventories are available and can be used as pretests to reveal student present knowledge, beliefs, attitudes, and practices (Solleder, 1979). Not just what students know or do *not* know, but also something about misconceptions can be ascertained in this way. That kind of information provides a baseline for planning future instruction and evaluation. You have to know where you are now if you want to plan a sensible step ahead and later find out if you got where you wanted to be. Data from which to infer needs of this kind are obtained in a number of ways, including analysis of student health records or computer-assisted health risk appraisal surveys; direct observation of student practices affecting health as shown by their food choices, use of tobacco or other drugs, and personal health habits; and personal interviews with parents, teachers, or other adults who have a close relationship with a youngster.

Another kind of need arises from the innate urge to maintain a balance or equilibrium between internal drives and external conditions. Internal drives may be physiological, emotional, or integrative. External conditions define the realities of the world around us. As long as reality does not limit our ability to satisfy those drives, balance is restored easily.

Physiological drives are those such as for food, water, warmth, and sleep. All of them are unending needs that are unnoticed by most of us most of the time because ways of satisfying them are so well learned. For example, if you feel thirsty, you get yourself a drink, often without thinking. But a person becomes increasingly aware of the need for water if thirst is not soon slaked. How long does it take, every day, before you find yourself longing for sleep? In fact, how long can you stay awake even if you try?

Yet powerful as physical needs are in motivating human behavior, their satisfaction does not guarantee good health. Unless physiological drives are provided for in an environment warm with affection and acceptance, there will be serious problems. No less important to human health are the psychological and integrative drives. Psychological drives are those such as the need for affection, status, and belongingness. The family is of primary importance in satisfying the lifelong hunger for satisfaction of those needs. Many of the things we choose to do, or not do, are directly the result of these kinds of innate needs.

Integrative needs are those such as for feelings of identity, self-fulfillment, and self-respect. Seeking association with the people whom we admire, selecting a mate, and pursuing the kind of employment or career that seems worthwhile are reflections of these kinds of drives. How effective would you be in your daily life without any satisfaction of psychological and integrative needs? Think about it for a moment. Can you remember a time when your need in one of those areas was so acute that your health was affected? What are the implications in the universality and power of those drives for planning a curriculum for health?

"Interests" is a term often used interchangeably with needs in reporting studies of the learner. If a person is interested in something, it is because the object, behavior, or information seems important or desirable in some way. It is a sort of felt need. Felt needs are most easily identified because they are more apparent to the learner. It is temptingly easy to develop a curriculum based entirely on what students say they want to know, but to do so would be doing them a disservice. The problem is that needs are not always interests, and vice versa. There are things students need to know of which they are unaware. The expression of interests in a topic is unlikely in the absence of any knowledge of it. There are too many equally compelling variables influencing curriculum development decisions. For example, legislative mandates and community expectations must be considered. One person's interests don't stay the same over time, and they are never exactly the same for all learners. In sum, interests are important elements that describe the learner, but they are just one of many.

Research relative to needs and interests Identification of student health needs and interests has been the purpose of many investigations. Oberteuffer's (1930) study of the needs and interests of Ohio schoolchildren is an early example. Since then, many master's theses and doctor's dissertations, usually limited to available samples of the children in a few schools, have been completed. Three major studies merit special mention: the Denver study (Denver Public Schools, 1952), the Connecticut study (Byler, 1969), and the Trucano study in Washington state (Trucano, 1984).

The Denver study surveyed interests of thirty-six hundred K–12 students relative to eighteen health content areas. The survey instrument consisted of two hundred fifty topics such as "To find out how food affects your weight," "To find out why boys' voices change," and "To find out how to develop confidence in yourself." The respondents were to indicate which ones interested them. The resulting data were charted according to level of interest and by sex. No attempt was made to assess interest in any topics other than those listed.

A number of conclusions drawn from the data gathered from this study are no less valid today. For example, it was demonstrated that girls had an intense interest in personality development all through their junior and senior high years. Boys' primary interest during that same period was physical fitness, except during the ninth grade, when it focused temporarily on personality development. The study confirmed the notion that students' interests shift in ways parallel to patterns of physical and social growth.

The Denver study report continues to be a useful source of information about the health interests of children at every grade level. A great deal can be learned about differences between teachers' and parents' perceptions and what students really want to know. And it is clear that what they wanted to study, or did not want to study then, is not greatly different from the interests that surveys reveal today.

The more recent Connecticut study surveyed the health interests, concerns, and problems of five thousand Connecticut schoolchildren from kindergarten through the twelfth grade. Results were categorized by topics and in relation to age groups. To the question "Should a health course be taught in the secondary schools?" the response was almost unanimously yes. The following list summarizes what these youngsters thought should be taught and in which school grades (Byler, Lewis, and Totman, 1969):

- sex education   (7–12)
- drugs, drinking, smoking   (7–12)
- physical development   (7–12)
- food, nutrition, diet   (7–12)
- personal hygiene   (7, 9, 10–12)
- diseases   (7,8, 10–12)
- first aid and safety   (7, 8, 10–12)
- understanding self and others or related topics   (8–12)
- community health or related topics   (7, 8, 10–12)
- grooming   (9–12)
- what health is: maintenance   (7,9, 11)
- family life and health   (8, 10–12)
- birth control, birth defects   (10–12)

During secondary school years, the major interests and concerns were much the same at every level, 7–12. Chief among these were the topics of sex education, mental health and understanding the self, problems of the entire society such as disease, abuse of drugs, alcohol, and tobacco, weight control, peer relationships, and relationships with parents. The study reports specific questions about these and other health concerns by grade. There are differences as the student matures. For example, younger students' interests tend to focus on themselves as growing and developing individuals and on learning how to be accepted by peers. After the tenth grade, concern with peer relationships lessens, and interest in learning about the responsibilities of parenthood increases.

Overall, it was discovered that the major health interests at any age were the same for all students whether they lived in the inner city or in rural, suburban, or high socioeconomic areas. However, the researchers caution against any dependence on these reported findings as universals for two reasons: first, because health information keeps changing so fast and, second, because no group of youngsters is ever exactly the same as any other. They conclude: "Identifying the concerns and interests of the students is the first step that all good teachers take in preparing for meaningful learning experiences. The teacher's plan, then, is timed and focused around the local and individual needs" (Byler, Lewis, and Totman, 1969, p. 172).

Students Speak (Trucano, 1984) reports the health interests and concerns of over five thousand Washington State public school students, K–12. Although patterned on the 1969 Connecticut study, the Trucano study was not meant to make comparisons, but to discover interests of students in the eighties. New instruments and procedures were developed to meet specific needs of Washington State nutrition and health educators.

Common areas of high interest reported by these students included handicapping conditions/birth defects, genetics, childhood and sexual abuse, fears and worries (about suicide, divorce, stress, death), one's self-concept, understanding human behavior, drugs, nutrition, aging, first aid/accident prevention, and sexuality (families, babies, pregnancy).

Eighty-seven percent of the respondents felt that it was important to study about health. Of the total number of students responding to the question "How much studying about health do you feel you have had in school?" 31 percent said "a lot" and 65 percent said "some."

Although concerns related to family relationships, drugs, mental health, and nutrition continue to be areas of high interest over the years, many of the subtopics are new to those categories, reflecting changes in life expectancy, health values, the changing nature of the family, and life-styles. Awareness of these shifts and of the fact that they will continue to occur is essential if curriculums are to meet the needs of today's students and tomorrow's adults.

Growth and developmental considerations The interrelationship between young people's needs and interests and their developmental age is well established. As children mature physically, the other aspects of growing and developing change as well. Teenagers' interests are different from those of young children because the older youngsters are growing so fast and in so many ways. Body proportions, size, and certain functions often change too rapidly for their social, mental, and emotional correlates to keep pace.

For example, girls seem to change overnight from children to young women, often towering over their male classmates in height. They experience the growth spurt some years before boys of the same age. As a result, they begin girl-boy relationships sooner, and often with boys older than themselves. When boys experience the growth spurt, they find themselves temporarily lacking body coordination. It's disconcerting to reach out for something and find that your hands now overshoot the target. Legs once proportional to the rest of the body suddenly lengthen and temporarily cause awkwardness. For a while, a boy's voice cannot decide whether it will be tenor or baritone.

Adolescents sometimes find themselves expected to behave as if they were adults before they are free of the rules governing the child. New social roles have to be learned. Responsible behavior must be evidenced as the price that must be paid for new privileges. Rapidly growing bodies require increased intake of foods; teenagers seem to be hungry all the time. Interest in food and nutrition rises, but for different reasons in different people and also depending on the sex of the learner.

Every aspect of growth and development has significance for curriculum development. Whatever the age group, the learner's characteristics must be identified and considered.

However much individuals differ in timing, the sequence of physical growth and development is universal. Every society expects those of a certain age to do the things they are capable of doing (Hurlock, 1973). In our society, the expectations are often referred to as "developmental tasks"—the tasks young people are expected to complete successfully during these years. It is believed that otherwise social disapproval and unhappiness result, and continuing growth and development are hindered. Havighurst (1952) proposed ten such tasks as expected of young people between the ages of 12 and 18. Most of these are concerned with social growth and development. Examples of the five emphasizing the social dimension include "achieving new and more mature relationships with agemates of both sexes" and "preparing for marriage and a family life." One of them, "achieving emotional independence of parents and other adults," focuses on the emotional aspect. Another addresses the physical tasks: "accepting one's physique and using the body effectively." The others focus on mental tasks such as "developing intellectual skills and concepts necessary for civic competence." Clearly, these are expectancies based upon the growth and development characteristics of the secondary school student. Although they are proposed as goals of education in general, most of them could have been written specifically for health education.

Considering growth and development characteristics as descriptors of the learner allows us to view expected changes as the genesis of needs and interests and links them to achievement of social expectancies. Both kinds of information about the learner must be studied.

The community

What is the meaning of "community" as a source of data for curriculum development? The concept of community has broadened in the past several years. It has been defined for health teaching as follows: "A community may be thought of in various ways—from the limited context of one's family, neighborhood or school, to the broader scope of the world and universe" (School Health Education Study, 1970). Basically, a community is a group of people bound together by common needs, problems, and interests. In that sense, this country is a community, every state is a community, and every neighborhood and school is a community.

Today's America is increasingly an informational rather than an industrial society. The trend toward urbanization is being reversed; decentralization is becoming the pattern not only for people but in business (Naisbitt, 1982).

Rapid change is no longer an occasional happening, but a way of life. Those who will join the work force in the twenty-first century will need to be flexibly ready to accept change as it comes in every aspect of living. What will students need to know in order to achieve some measure of the good life in such a society? What are the health concepts, skills, and abilities needed today, as well as tomorrow, if they are to participate effectively in the many kinds of communities in which they will spend their lives? Some answers to those questions can be inferred from study of the social, economic, and political aspects of our world. National, state, and local health issues and problems must be examined for their significance in shaping curriculum decisions. No matter how much data we gather to identify student needs, it must be remembered that no one lives in a vacuum, but in the real world.

National needs At the federal level, the surgeon general's report on health promotion and disease prevention, *Healthy People* (U.S. Department of Health, Education and Welfare, 1979), identified four major factors that affect the nation's health: unhealthy life-styles, inadequacies in the existing health care system, environmental hazards, and human biological factors. Priority areas for prevention of disease or promotion of health were specified. These included high blood pressure control; family planning, pregnancy, and infant health; immunization; sexually transmitted disease; toxic agent control; occupational safety and health; accident prevention and injury control; fluoridation and dental health; surveillance and control of infectious diseases; smoking and health; misuse of alcohol and drugs; nutrition; physical fitness and exercise; and control of stress and violent behavior.

Among the report's many recommendations, this one specifically links national health needs to health education in schools: "The schools may be the richest source for potential behavior change. Comprehensive school health education should include promoting health knowledge, the causes of disease, and the influence on health by personal decisions related to smoking, alcohol and drug use, exercise, and sexual activity" (U.S. Department of Health, Education and Welfare, 1979, p. 5).

As a follow-up to that report, *Objectives for the Nation* (U.S. Department of Health and Human Services, 1980) outlined for each of the above priority areas its health implications, specific objectives for attainment by 1990, and related information. All these data are relevant to a curriculum for tomorrow's health classes. However, because the focus is narrowly confined to health *problems* rather than wellness as an asset to be promoted and protected, the national objectives describe only a partial view of U.S. health needs.

National health curriculum research Only one study has ever been attempted at the national level. This was the School Health Education Study

(1961–63), which surveyed instructional practices and the health knowledge, attitudes, and practices of sixth-, ninth-, and twelfth-grade students across the nation. The following problems revealed by that investigation led to a "call for action" and recommendations for change:

- failure of the home to encourage practice of health habits learned in school
- ineffectiveness of instruction methods
- parental and community resistance to certain health topics
- insufficient time in the school day for health instruction
- lack of coordination of the health education program throughout the school grades
- inadequate professional preparation of staff
- disinterest on the part of some teachers assigned to health teaching
- failure of parents to follow up on needed and recommended health services for children
- indifference toward and hence lack of support for health education on the part of some teachers, parents, administrators, health officers, and other members of the community
- neglect of the health education course when combined with physical education
- inadequate facilities and instructional materials
- student indifference to health education
- lack of specialized supervisory and consultative services

Those needs seem as critical today as when they were delineated. For example, during the 1980s, a national study of the schools found that health education took a secondary place to physical education when the two were combined (Goodlad, 1984), just as had been reported in the SHES findings more than twenty years earlier.

Analysis of the data obtained through administration of standardized tests to students in sixth, ninth, and twelfth grades revealed lack of knowledge related to specific health content areas and acceptance of many misconceptions. The average sixth grader could answer just over half the questions asked. Dental health, mental health, and safety education were the weakest areas for them. Ninth-grade students demonstrated least competence in the area of consumer health, followed by habit-forming substances, fatigue, rest and sleep, defense against disease, mental health, dental health, and safety and first aid. High school students' greatest needs were for knowledge about nutrition, community health, chronic disease, and consumer health. The complete report is rich in information reflecting the needs of both the learner and the community (School Health Education Study, 1964).

Local community health needs and concerns Green and his colleagues (1980) suggest that local community needs assessment is too often overlooked in school health education planning. National health objectives need to be considered among community needs, but they describe a perspective that is too specific to be useful as the principal source for all communities. Moreover, it is at the local level that things get done. Naisbitt (1982) says that today it is the smaller local political units—cities, counties, and communities—that are claiming local authority over and responsibility for social issues that hit hard at the local level. There are always special local needs that are more sensitive and crucial for a given school, neighborhood, or community than those identified at national levels. However, a need that is crucial in one state may be minimal in others. For example, drug abuse is more likely to be a problem in border or coastal areas than in the Midwest. Local differences in needs must be recognized when developing teaching plans for a school.

Current health issues and needs are never difficult to identify. In 1986, there are health problems stemming from the changing nature of the family, urbanization, the need to absorb large numbers of Asians into our social and economic world, growing numbers of homeless people, epidemics of hitherto unknown communicable diseases (AIDS) and chronic diseases (Alzheimers), and a host of other critical social, mental, and physical health problems and issues reported in the literature and in the media every day. It's easy to find items reporting health problems; bad news always gets the most attention. But there will be news of a positive nature, too, such as new immunizations, medical and dental health advances, descriptions of better safety procedures, and so on. A curriculum that is responsive to what is happening where you are is not only more motivating for the students, but wins far more support from community leaders.

Community influences on curriculum planning Although community needs are considered when devising a curriculum for health education, it is also a product of the community. For example, suppose local morbidity and mortality statistics reveal a sudden increase in the incidence of sexually transmitted diseases among school-age people. Parents may actively support better education about disease prevention; yet some may be so opposed to any education about a problem of this nature that the school is prevented from providing it. The following are some of those influential factors.

Various ethnic or socioeconomic factors may be unique as data sources motivating curriculum emphases not so imperative in other communities. No one has yet devised a curriculum plan that is right for every community in the nation. Ethnic factors such as race, religion, language, and cultural preferences and biases interact in ways that distinguish the needs of one community from another. Socioeconomic factors such as social class, education, age, occupation, and income not only influence health need priorities but also determine whether or how they are satisfied. For example, poor nutrition may be a problem in an upper-class area, but for different reasons and it may be of a different nature than the same problem in the barrios. Nutrition choices are often dictated by necessity or by cultural forces rather than by wilful neglect or ignorance of what is necessary to provide balanced nutrition. In many ways, the curriculum reflects the community.

Legislative and political factors have a powerful impact upon curriculum planning. State legislators decide whether health education must be taught by qualified health educators. Lawmakers, not educators, decide whether health education will be required and if so how comprehensive it is to be. Local and state boards of education are also usually elected bodies. No public school can carry out a program counter to board policy, however urgent a community health need may be judged to be by school personnel.

Conventional wisdom, that common core of beliefs about what's good for health and prevents or cures certain illnesses, is the most subtle curriculum influence. Many of the folk practices and superstitions that are a part of this problem have persisted for a long time. Hundreds of them have been identified and probably direct at least some of the health behavior of even highly educated people. These are the kinds of things that "everybody knows" and that are not so much taught as caught: "Feed a cold and starve a fever." "An apple a day keeps the doctor away." "Fish is brain food." "Brown eggs are more nutritious than white eggs." "Drunkards can be sobered up by giving them lots of hot black coffee." "Venereal disease can be inherited." "Aches and pains during adolescence are normal 'growing pains.' " Are there any in that list that are new to you? Unless there is a systematic plan to replace misconceptions with scientific information, there is no way to counter their influence on health behavior.

The values or philosophy of the community regarding the worth of or need for health teaching is another external influence on decisions about health instruction. It's unlikely that health educators would propose an educational goal that was inconsistent with their own value systems. However, an educator's values may conflict with those of certain members of the community. This kind of conflict is exemplified by the commotion sometimes stirred up by the inclusion of health topics such as human sexuality or family planning. Somehow such community issues must be resolved, but with the learner's needs as the primary concern.

Crisis-generated community pressure is more often the source of curriculum changes in health education than in most subjects commonly taught in public schools. Unfortunately, this results in a categorical, disease-oriented, reactive curriculum, whereas health instruction should be comprehensive, wellness oriented, and proactive in emphasis. Effective health teaching considers the whole person and not just the diseases and disorders to which humans are prey. Youngsters want and need to know far more about their health and health behavior than how to cope with specific potential diseases that might threaten them in the years to come. A more exact title for that kind of curriculum is "disease education." Still, health teaching for the coming decade will probably continue to reflect the continuing national and local concern with drug abuse and the equally crucial problems of unwanted teenage pregnancy, environmental pollution, unmanaged stress, and violence. These will get the most attention at least until or unless different health problems are subsequently perceived as having greater urgency and are given priority in their place.

The body of knowledge

The third source of a curriculum is its special body of knowledge. Both *content,* or subject matter, and *process* are involved. "Content" refers to the concepts, principles, and generalizations that make up the information to be learned. "Process" refers to all the cognitive operations associated with the creation, acquisition, and application of that knowledge. A curriculum focused on content alone ends with the passive assimilation of information. One that stresses process uses knowledge as a means of learning, but never as its total goal. The difference between the two approaches is that one ends in students knowing something and the other in their knowing what to do with it.

Knowledge as content Because what is identified as being important to teach and learn is inseparable from the values of a society, the question that specialists in every field must address is "What knowledge is of most worth in your discipline? What knowledge *does* an educated person need in order to function effectively as a human being and as a worthwhile member of our society? The answers keep changing as the stuff of health education changes and as needs and interests change.

Health education has been described as "an applied science that draws upon the physical, biological, medical, and behavioral sciences for its body of knowledge. It is a discipline that synthesizes concepts and theories from these several areas and interprets them in the context of human needs, human values, and human potential. It is deeply concerned with promotion of personal effectiveness and the quality of life" (American Association of School Administrators, 1973).

It ought to be easy to say what the content of health education includes, but it isn't. First, you have to choose a scheme for listing its components. There being several possible designs, whichever one you choose will affect its description. A curriculum using the systems of the body as its organizing elements cannot be the same as one using content areas. Second, there is no one set of curriculum elements accepted by everyone. There is more agreement than differences among the several lists of health topics in use, but there *are* differences. Third, new topics keep emerging as old ones are temporarily abandoned. This has been termed the "revolving door syndrome" with the same problems considered crucial a decade or more ago emerging once again (*Education for Health,* 1974). To illustrate this point, notice that the popularity of death and dying as a health topic is beginning to wane already (Rosenbaum, 1982). At the same time, interest is beginning to focus on aging, which reflects the shift in the numbers of people who are reaching retirement years in good health. It is expected that by the year 2000, one in five people will be over age 65. Can you predict what effect that might have on health education curricula?

Most recently, the Education Commission of the States (1981) recommended the following as *minimum* elements of a comprehensive school health curriculum:

1. personal health
2. mental and emotional health
3. prevention and control of disease
4. nutrition
5. substance use and abuse
6. accident prevention and safety
7. community health
8. consumer health
9. environmental health
10. family life education

Most states have their own health curriculum guides that recommend or prescribe a set of organizing elements similar to this. A recent survey of the states revealed that these guides were either current or under revision (Education Commission of the States, 1982), which means that health content in those states has been defined for the schools, at least in general.

Knowledge as process Application of problem-solving skills, often referred to as the scientific method, exemplifies the processes by which health knowledge is advanced, just as in any other discipline. What do we mean by "problem" in this context? A problem should not be thought of as defined by the existence of a disease or other unhealthy situation that needs to be combated. As we will be using the term, it simply means that some need exists that the individual's past experience and present knowledge do not equip him or her to satisfy or meet. If you are hungry and you have quick means of remedying that problem, you are not really aware that it was a problem. But suppose some giant hand picked you up and set you down in the desert far from civilization. How would you satisfy hunger in that situation?

Practice of problem-solving and decision-making skills stimulates creative as well as critical thinking. Students learn how to locate reliable information about a defined need or concern, how to analyze, compare, and thoughtfully choose among the alternate solutions that emerge as the outcome of these processes. They learn how to test the effectiveness of the most promising of those solutions and what to do if it proves inadequate. Practice in solving hypothetical problems today facilitates successful coping with new needs or problems in the future. Information that is valid today can be totally invalid tomorrow, but well-learned cognitive skills transfer to new situations.

Process rather than content should be the primary concern of health education. Human beings are feeling, thinking, acting organisms who need to grow and develop as long as they live. Knowledge is the vehicle, not the destination, in a process-centered approach to teaching and learning. A teacher must be a facilitator of learning, not simply a communicator of information, however vital it may be. Subject matter should be chosen because it meets the learners' needs, never as an end in itself. Bruner (1963) says: "One thing seems clear, if all students are helped to the full utilization of their intellectual powers, we will have a better chance of surviving as a democracy in an age of enormous technological and social complexity."

The goal of health education in every setting is to help people learn about and adhere to the kind of life-style that prevents illness and promotes wellness. School health educators just may have the best chance of achieving that goal because the target audience is young and its health habits are being shaped rather than being firmly established and already negative in their effect.

ALTERNATE CURRICULUM MODELS

Once analysis of the three sources of a curriculum has been completed, what happens next? What are the procedures involved in moving from what has been learned to the health education of children and youth? It depends upon the model selected for planning and implementing a program that meets those needs and facilitates acquisition of that knowledge. In addition to the Tyler rationale, the health belief model, and the PRECEDE framework have been applied in every health education setting, including schools. What are the commonalities and differences among these curriculum models?

The Tyler rationale

The Tyler rationale is in essence a goal attainment model. Once study of the sources has been completed, a set of goals and objectives is formulated based upon a synthesis of the obtained data. These statements are next screened in order to be sure that each is consistent with (1) educational philosophy and (2) accepted theories of learning. Those surviving this process become the framework on which the instructional program is built and evaluation is based. Learning experiences are devised to permit practice of the behaviors specified in the objectives. Suggested evaluation activities are designed to assess the learner's ability to exhibit success in the achievement of those objectives. Discussion of this aspect of curriculum will be found in chapters 7 and 8.

The health belief model

The HBM was formulated during the mid-fifties to explain preventive health behavior or its absence (Rosenstock, 1974). It also is a goal-oriented model, the goal being health. Research carried out by Hochbaum and others demonstrated that preventive health behavior is a function of two principal interacting variables: *perceived susceptibility* and *perceived benefits* (Rosenstock, 1974, p. 361). The first of these proved to be the best single predictor of health behavior. In other words, the person who believes that there is real danger of contracting a serious disease is most likely to take appropriate preventive action. The person who does not know how serious it is or does not believe that it constitutes much of a threat is least likely to do so. The second variable means that the greater the perceived benefits of a given health action, the less likely that the cost or barriers to that action will outweigh them (Cummings, Jette, and Rosenstock, 1978).

Originally, the HBM focused entirely on the desire to avoid a specific disease threat. That approach has been revised to include general health motivation. A third major variable of the model is the cue for action that stimulates preventive behaviors. Such a cue can be internal, coming from the individual, or external, coming from significant others or society in general.

The HBM has been proposed as a possible framework for the development of school health curriculums as follows: "Primary prevention is economically and socially less expensive than sickness care. Furthermore, the acquisition of appropriate health beliefs and practices should, in principle, be simpler in childhood than in adulthood. We must bring to bear our educational expertise—based on good social-psychological theory—

during the early socialization years, to produce more preventively-oriented children" (Rosenstock and Kirscht, 1974).

Whether the model can adequately serve as a framework for a school health education curriculum is arguable. It has, however, been employed successfully in developing health education interventions related to specific health problems (for example, in situations where the intention is to intervene in specific health behavior problems such as smoking, obesity, and drug experimentation).

Preventive action is at least partly dependent upon an individual's knowledge and attitudes about its necessity and potential effectiveness. Health teaching in schools can provide opportunities for students to learn what can be done to prevent illness or reduce the threat of disease. Prevention is important, but it is only one of the goals of health education. The HBM may be more useful in developing specific school health curriculum units than a total program.

The PRECEDE framework

The PRECEDE framework has its roots in community health programming, although its proponents suggest that it is applicable to health education in every setting. This model views health education as intervention, "the purpose of which is to short-circuit illness or to enhance the quality of life through change or development of health-related behavior" (Green et al., 1980). Planning the PRECEDE way requires the user to start at the other end of a program. One identifies a desired outcome first and then works backward to discover what has to precede it. There are seven phases of analysis:

1. assessing the quality of life of a population (What are the social problems?)
2. identifying the health problems underlying those social problems
3. diagnosing contributing health behaviors and nonbehavioral factors
4. diagnosing the predisposing, enabling, and reinforcing factors affecting health behavior
5. determining which of these shall be the focus of the intervention
6. developing and implementing the program
7. evaluating the results

Actually PRECEDE is more like the Tyler Rationale than it is different. In fact, the principal differences seem to be that it works backward and its focus is problem oriented rather than comprehensive health teaching. Both approaches analyze the nature and the needs of the learner (patient, worker, student, client, or consumer), the needs of the community (the society or target audience), and the body of knowledge (the subject matter of concern and the skills needed to apply that knowledge). Both base program (curriculum) development on clearly stated general objectives (goals) and specific (measurable) objectives.

Perhaps any differences depend more upon the nature of the learner (whether it is a student, patient, worker, client, or consumer) and on the setting in which the health program is provided (school, clinic, workplace, or community).

There *are* differences between health teaching in schools as a part of general education, and as planned and practiced in the other settings. Sliepcevich (1978) says:

> Health education audiences in other community-based structures become candidates for education, specifically because of a health concern or problem. These health educators function in a medical or problem-oriented model which is a reflection of the way in which the other professionals in that setting have been trained. . . . And, usually, the problem is very specific and categorical—a result of the funding sources of the program.
>
> This is not to say that health educators outside of educational institutions are not capable of planning and carrying out educational programs focused on wellness and total health. It is simply a reality that the orientation of the social structure and setting determines the boundaries of the health educator's role and functions.

Yet if the school health curriculum is to be designed in ways that complement health education in other settings, as it ought to be (and vice versa), then teachers need to be knowledgeable about those programs and the models upon which they are based.

Ideological models

Although the foregoing three curriculum planning models have applications whatever the setting in which health educators practice, they are discussed here as particular to health teaching in schools. It would be an oversimplification to think that other systems of belief do not also influence program decisions. Carlyon (1981) suggests that there are ideological models, basic assumptions about the purpose of health education and the way it ought to be structured, that shape school programs and public health education programs differently. The educational programs of schools are based on developmental models such as those of Freud, Piaget, and Erikson. The medical/public health model, he says, always assumes that intervention is a necessary function of health education. The developmental model assumes that children are essentially well and will grow and develop normally, given enough physical, social, intellectual, and emotional nourishment. He puts it in neat contrast as follows:

School-Developmental Model

The purpose of the schools is to encourage normal growth, development and enquiry so as to produce knowledgeable, self-directed, independent learners.

Schools view education as the provision of information and learning experiences that encourage and guide the child's natural and irrepressible drive to learn.

The goals of education are long term, cumulative and enabling.

Medical/Public Health Model

The purpose of medicine and public health is to solve or prevent disease problems.

Public health views education as an intervention to change specific deviant (unhealthful) behaviors.

The goals of medicine and public health are short term, specific, and problem solving.

Of course, health teachers are as much concerned with health behavior as with health information. Although it is difficult to predict the long-term effects of health teaching in schools, the goals specified in the action domain (desired actual behaviors outside of school and sometimes in the future) give direction to curriculum planning.

DEFINING THE SCOPE OF THE HEALTH CURRICULUM

The term "scope" in this instance refers to the accepted range of subject matter or information special to health education. In order to develop a curriculum plan, its subject matter has to be logically arranged in some way. The segments or components of a curriculum are usually referred to as its "organizing elements." Although the body of knowledge doesn't change very much, the form in which it is presented may differ, depending on the sort of organizing element employed. Organizing elements commonly used for this purpose include the following: the major body systems, major or critical health problems, traditional content areas, health topics, concepts or generalizations, and competencies. Whichever scheme is employed, basic differences in perception of the body of knowledge are implicit in that choice. These differences determine not only the stuff that will be taught, but how it will be taught and even by whom.

The body system design

The most traditional of all the designs, the body system design focuses on anatomical-physiological study of the body and its care. Curricula based on the body systems are typified by the Primary Grades Health Curriculum Project (PGHCP) and the School Health Curriculum Project (SHCP) as it was originally developed in the 1970s. The curriculum for each grade focused on body systems, parts, or the senses (for example, PGHCP—grade

K: "Happiness is Being Healthy" [study of the teeth], grade 1: "Super Me" [senses of taste, touch, and smell], grade 2: "Sights and Sounds" [seeing and hearing], grade 3: "The Body, Its Framework and Movement" [skeletal and muscular systems]; SHCP—grade 4: "Nutrition, Digestion, and Health" [digestive system], grade 5: "About our Lungs and Health" [respiratory system], grade 6: "Our Health and our Heart" [circulatory system], grade 7: "Living Well with our Nervous System" [nervous system]). These eight curriculum elements constitute the "Growing Healthy" health education program so widely in use across the country today. Although the K–7 grade level themes remain the same, the total program is now greatly expanded and comprehensive in scope (National Center for Health Education, 1984).

A similar program developed by the University of California at Berkeley in association with the Albany, California, School District has been adopted by other school districts in California and in Australia. The goal of that curriculum is expressed in this statement: "My body is mine, my emotions are mine, my environment is mine. All these are my responsibility to understand and care for" (University of California, 1980). The plan calls for about an hour's time a week and considers specific body systems for each grade, K–8. Kindergarteners learn how general body parts work; first graders study the digestive system; second graders study hearing and general anatomy; third graders study vision; fourth graders concentrate on the respiratory system; fifth graders focus on the circulatory system and sexual maturation; sixth graders study the gastrointestinal system and nutrition; seventh graders concentrate on the central nervous and the reproductive systems; and eighth graders learn the interrelationships of all body systems.

Young children have been shown to have great interest in learning about their bodies (Byler, Lewis, and Totman, 1969). Use of the body system design can be justified for the elementary schools on that basis. However, the outcome is apt to be more in the nature of physiology than health education. It is unlikely that comprehensive health education will result because so much of the content of health education will not fit a format defined by the systems or functions of the body.

The health problems design

Some health educators believe that effective use of the limited time and resources available for health instruction is possible only if the curriculum focuses on the crucial health problems faced by a given age group. An example of this approach is the study made by the Curriculum Commission of the Health Education Division of the American Association for Health, Physical Education, and Recreation in 1967. The first move was to identify the most crucial health problems as projected for the 1960s and 1970s. By inference, any not specified did not satisfy the criterion of cruciality. Here are the problems that did:

- accidents
- hazardous environmental conditions
- inadequate teenage diets
- obesity
- mental and emotional problems
- sexual experimentation
- early marriage
- early parenthood
- illegitimacy
- abortions
- changing roles of men and women
- smoking
- quackery
- need for comprehensive medical care
- lack of fluoridation
- periodontal diseases
- venereal diseases
- chronic and degenerative diseases and disorders
- aging
- exploding population problems
- need for disaster preparedness
- better understanding of international health problems

This list was not proposed as representative of the scope of health education, but the exclusion of drug misuse and abuse as a crucial problem for the 1970s is surprising.

More recently, the fifteen priority areas identified in the surgeon general's report, *Healthy People* (U.S. Department of Health, Education and Welfare, 1979), are health problems. The recommendations for school health education later inferred from those priority areas reflect the health problems design approach.

The advantage of using health problems to structure health teaching and curriculum is that emphasis is given to the prevention or control of those threats to health that today's youngsters are most likely to encounter. As such, they are not only current problems but also theoretically more meaningful to the student. However, health instruction in such a plan is limited to the selected problems, which may or may not be so crucial by the time the instruction is given. Moreover, what seems crucial to adults who plan the teaching may seem far less threatening to healthy youngsters. Nor are all the selected problems equally likely to seem crucial to all students.

A problem-centered curriculum is based upon the assumption that students need to know nothing more about health-related decisions than how to cope with the specified problems. Whether this ability is transferable to other problems is far from certain. Learning to solve specific problems by rote memorization doesn't equip the learner to make the everyday choices that affect health in small but important ways. It tends to ignore the social, economic, and other pressures that motivate unhealthful behaviors. To talk about *health* as if knowledge about symptoms, causes, and prevention or risk reduction of disease were the primary or only requisite factor in health promotion is the very antithesis of comprehensive health education.

The health content area design

The use of content areas as the framework for a health curriculum is probably the most familiar form in which the scope of health education is organized. A content area is described by a short title covering a broad range of related subject matter. Nutrition is a content area. There are many advantages to the content area design. First, when fully developed and carried out, it provides comprehensive coverage of the body of knowledge. Second, the format is so well accepted that a wealth of resource materials (references, textbooks, pamphlets, articles, films, filmstrips, tapes) keyed to those areas is easily located and frequently updated. Third, for those reasons, school health educators anywhere in the country are more likely to interpret and teach the subject matter similarly. Fourth, the titles are consistent with the subject matter and help define the boundaries of the information considered in each.

Content areas are often the sort of organizing elements recommended in official documents such as those developed by state boards of education or by federal departments or agencies concerned with health education. Two representative lists proposed by state agencies illustrate how nearly universal content area titles are. Oddly enough, although there are often slight variations in the exact areas specified, there are almost always ten of them.

California State Framework
(health education, K–12)
1. personal health
2. family health
3. nutrition
4. mental-emotional health
5. use and misuse of substances
6. diseases and disorders
7. consumer health
8. accident prevention and emergency health services

Pennsylvania State Curriculum Plan
(health education, K–12)
1. community health
2. consumer health
3. disease prevention and control
4. family health
5. safety and first aid
6. fitness
7. growth and development
8. nutrition
9. personal health

California State Framework *Pennsylvania State Curriculum Plan*
(health education, K–12) (health education, K–12)
9. community health 10. tobacco, alcohol, and other drugs
10. environmental health (*Pennsylvania Health Curriculum*
(California State Board of Educa- *Progressive Chart,* 1982)
tion, 1978)

Of course, the very compactness and neatness of those titles can lead to compartmentalization of instruction. Unless care is taken in planning nice transitions among and between the areas, it gets to be a series of short courses. And because the cue for subject matter selection comes from those titles, subject matter tends to become the focus; hence, the emphasis may be on knowing rather than doing. In addition, when there is not enough time to cover all ten content areas fully, those left until last are given short shrift or are simply omitted. If that happens, the intended comprehensiveness is lost or at least diminished.

The health topic design
A topic differs from a content area in that is is usually a subarea or theme. A subarea might be "personality development," "accident prevention," or "boy-girl relationships." A health theme is often stated as "choosing health products wisely," "coping with excessive stress," or "contributing effectively to community health."

The advantage of using a health topic design is that it allows teachers greater flexibility in planning health instruction to meet the needs and interests of their own students. Because the subject matter is delimited by the topic of interest, it can be investigated more thoroughly and given more time in the schedule. Topics tend to focus on life-styles or day-to-day health decisions or choices, so they relate well to the needs and concerns of the learner and the community. A shortcoming is that topics may not encompass much of the scope of health education, even as added together. This design has to be promoted vigorously by the school administrator and coordinated by someone qualified and given authority to do so. It probably is best utilized as supplementary to a plan that covers the total scope.

The conceptual approach
Beginning in the 1960s, curriculum specialists began to study the rapidly expanding body of knowledge in disciplines such as biology, physics, chemistry, and mathematics for the purpose of identifying their most powerful ideas and processes. Use of the concepts that resulted from these analyses as a framework for curriculums seemed to promise better organization and increased effectiveness in teaching in those fields. Two major curriculum

projects in health education with similar goals were begun at that time: the School Health Education Study and the Project of the Commission on Curriculum Development of the Health Education Division of AAHPER. The formulation of concepts for use in curriculum development was central to both projects.

What is a conceptual approach to the scope of health education? Briefly, it is one that employs concepts, generalizations, or conceptual statements as organizing elements. The key term that needs to be defined in speaking about conceptual planning is the word "concept." Actually, authorities don't agree on the exact form of a concept. The problem is that concepts can be stated at more than one level of abstraction. For the purposes of this discussion, the word or generalization used to structure the content of a discipline must be abstract enough to facilitate categorization of related but less important ideas, facts, or perceptions.

What are some useful guidelines in formulating conceptual statements, as opposed to questions, goals, facts, or topics? First, they are abstractions representing classes of perceptions resulting from direct or indirect but related experiences. One's concept of heat is usually an outcome of direct experience of many kinds, such as the pain resulting from touching something that is too hot. A concept of things not directly encountered, such as dinosaurs or viruses, is gained through indirect experiences, such as those provided by books or pictures.

Second, a concept is a sort of mental summary of an individual's perceptions not only of many positive instances of a class of things, but also of a number of related negative examples. For example, one's concept of "soft" is as much the product of experience with hardness as with softness. Can you really have a true concept of softness without any experience with hardness? Formulation of a concept, termed "internalization," is evidenced by the ability to generalize from a class of things to newly experienced instances of class identification and to exclude things that, however similar in many ways, are not members of that class (discrimination). For example, the concept of food may differ in small ways among cultures, but in general, all people know what constitutes food and what does not. The vast number of perceptions and concepts stored in human memory banks and instantly scanned on demand challenges the data-processing abilities of the finest computers.

Third, a word or generalization broad enough to serve as a conceptual statement, especially when human health behavior is involved, often possesses strongly affective qualities. The concept of food is a case in point. We all would agree that meat fits into a concept of food, but not all kinds of meat. In our society, we don't eat the meat of dogs or grasshoppers or ants as a rule. Yet such things are edible and are eaten by humans in other societies, even in ours if starvation is a problem, which is to say that if you get hungry enough, the concept of food is sufficiently flexible to admit a great many things ordinarily excluded.

Conceptual statements are often used to define content, but primarily as an expansion of a health topic or content area. Their function in this case is to present factual information related to the actual organizing element. The California health instruction framework uses content areas as its organizing elements and conceptual statements to outline the content. Examples of the generalizations used to structure the content of environmental health are environmental quality (an interrelationship exists between human health and environmental quality) and environmental protection (maintaining a safe and healthful environment is a shared responsibility of the individual, family, and society).

Another example of concepts used within other curriculum designs is the statements developed by the Commission of the Health Education Division of AAHPER (American Assocation for Health, Physical Education and Recreation, 1967). Sets of concepts serve as the focus of instruction for each of the twenty-two health problems defined by that project. However, it was not the concepts, but problems, that were used as the organizing elements of that plan.

> For the problem of smoking, here are some of the "concepts" listed as descriptive of the content.

1. The evidence linking cigarette smoking and lung cancer is very substantial.
2. Certain diseases other than lung cancer are found more commonly among cigarette smokers than nonsmokers: coronary artery disease, pulmonary emphysema, chronic bronchitis, and stomach ulcers.
3. The habitual use of tobacco is related to psychological and social drives and is strengthened by the drug effects of nicotine on the body and specifically on the central nervous system.

Would you say that those are concepts, or facts?

Probably the best known example of the use of concepts as the organizing elements of a curriculum for health education was prepared by the writing team of the School Health Education Study (1967, p. 20). These ten conceptual statements represent the body of knowledge and serve as a framework for curriculum development.

1. Growth and development influences and is influenced by the structure and functioning of the individual.
2. Growing and developing follows a predictable sequence, yet is unique for each individual.
3. Protection and promotion of health is an individual, community, and international responsibility.

4. The potential for hazards and accidents exists whatever the environment.
5. There are reciprocal relationships involving man, disease, and the environment.
6. The family serves to perpetuate man and to fulfill certain health needs.
7. Personal health practices are affected by a complexity of forces, often conflicting.
8. Utilization of health information, products, and services is guided by values and perceptions.
9. Use of substances that modify mood and behavior arises from a variety of motivations.
10. Food selection and eating patterns are determined by physical, economic, and cultural patterns.

The advantage of a conceptual framework for curriculum development is that it provides an efficient system for organizing the body of knowledge and at the same time a more stable link to current health content than do the other designs. Problems keep changing as new ones emerge or solutions are found for old ones. Certain content areas gain or lose importance as time passes. New content areas reflecting changes in community needs are added, as in the case of "aging." Usually when that happens, something else is dropped. Whenever organizing elements are changed, everything else has to be changed. If revision is not complete, there will be some loss of comprehensiveness and currency. Because concepts are abstractions, they are much less vulnerable to these kinds of changes. If there is new information or new concerns emerge relative to a concept, they can be accommodated without changing the concept itself.

As one example, "Use of substances that modify mood and behavior arises from a variety of motivations" is a complete idea that probably has been true as long as there have been humans and drug-producing plants. When you reduce the statement to something like "substance abuse," you not only lose the concept, but you lose its meaning as well. In the first place, there are many substances in this world. Which of them is intended by the word as used to describe a content area depends upon the reader's perception. The complete statement tells us that it is specifically those substances that modify mood and behavior, but that isn't enough, either. Lots of substances modify mood and behavior, including warm milk and candy. The rest of the statement adds to its meaning. In total, it says that whatever the substance used to modify one's mood and behavior, its use is always the result of many motivating forces. In fact, the focus is not on the substances at all, but on those motivations. They are the common denominator in drug abuse. Information about the kinds of substances used for that purpose is interesting, but it doesn't explain behavior. Guided by a content area titled "substance abuse," a teacher will be preparing lessons that are very different, both in subject matter and in process, than when teaching toward that concept.

Concepts used as organizing elements provide guidelines to logical progression from kindergarten through the twelfth grade. Each year's plan is engineered to contribute in measurable ways to the formulation and internalization of the concepts. Because they always describe the same body of knowledge, the only thing that changes at succeeding levels is how the learner treats that content. As the student grows in ability and understanding, the depth and breadth of the subject matter and the complexity of the cognitive skills increase.

The disadvantage of the conceptual approach is that it needs to be carefully planned by a teacher who understands it and is well qualified to teach health. Green and his colleagues (1980) comment, "Paradoxically, the philosophical and conceptual strength of the SHES curriculum may have been its major weakness. Many health educators apparently found it difficult to understand and apply in the classroom situation." Unquestionably, it takes more skill and more planning than other approaches. The problem is not that conceptualization is too complicated a process. Actually, conceptualization is a natural and lifelong process. All children come to school with a great many concepts already firmly in place in their minds. Anybody who has ever tried to feed a baby something that doesn't fit what that baby has learned about the concept of food finds that out in a hurry. The problem is that the teacher has to arrange the kinds of perceptions (lessons) that will lead students to formulate the *desired* concept. Some teachers may not have the background in health science that is needed in order to plan these kinds of lessons. In-service training may be required, and the school administrator may not be able to allocate the necessary funds. Still, although the conceptual design for health education was introduced in the late 1960s, it remains viable today, for it was in many ways far ahead of its time.

Kreuter and Christenson (1981) support this view, saying, "the SHES approach to health education remains the most conceptually and philosophically sound guide to the development of school health education."

The competency-based model

During the 1970s, competency-based education (CBE) achieved wide acclaim as the way both to improve instruction and to meet public demands for better accountability by the schools. At every level of administration, state, district, and school, there was a rush to define the competencies that seemed essential. By the end of that decade, thirty-eight states and numberless schools and districts had mandated minimum competency testing for both elementary and secondary school graduates. Minimum competency testing, of course, assumes that the student has experienced a curriculum based upon the same competencies.

On the face of it, competency-based designs are those employing competencies as their organizing elements. We have found none that do. The competencies in CBE curriculum plans are instead subordinate to more conventional designs, usually content areas. The problem with competencies is much like that discussed regarding concepts. Both words are abstractions, or constructs, not specifics that can be pinned down neatly and measured. Both are often developed at more than one level of complexity. There is no single, agreed-upon definition of either.

Spady (1977) defines competencies as "indicators of successful performance in life role activities, e.g., producer, consumer, citizen, family member, etc." Other definitions include "learner outcomes or experiences which evolve from the knowledge, attitudes, and skills that are important to function as an adult in society" and "whatever is required to do something adequately." For the purposes of the present discussion, in general, a competency-based design is goal-directed, and the competencies are the goals. They are not the organizing elements. They are more exactly the criteria by which successful performance is to be measured. For example, a competency-based curriculum developed by the National Task Force on the Preparation and Practice of Health Educators, Inc., employs seven areas of responsibility as its organizing elements. A set of terminal competencies and supporting enabling competencies was devised for each . These competencies will serve as the basis for criterion-referenced tests to assess student performance. More detailed discussion of the role and form of competency statements will be provided in chapter 3.

PLANNING CURRICULUM SEQUENCE

Decisions determining the scope of a curriculum necessarily precede those concerning sequence. However, the problem of ordering the selected organizing elements comprising the scope must be addressed next. Scope represents a set of decisions that set the boundaries on *what* is to be taught. Sequence focuses on planning *when* each of the organizing elements will be taught.

Sequence has two principal dimensions: *vertical* and *horizontal*. Vertical sequence is concerned with planning for progressive study year by year, K–12. Not just what subject matter will be taught at a particular grade is involved, but also at what depth and complexity it will be treated. Horizontal sequence deals with ordering the selected curriculum elements during a given grade or course of study. However many subject areas are to be studied, one of them must be studied first, another immediately thereafter, and so on. There has to be a logic for each placement of this nature. Some of these kinds of decisions are appropriate at the administrative level. Others are usually and better left to the classroom teacher.

Administrative decisions

Decisions governing grade placement or *vertical sequence,* are typically made at the administrative level, although teachers may be involved in the deliberations. There is no standard practice relative to grade placement; every school or district seems to decide on its own. What is recommended and often found in secondary schools is a semester course during the seventh grade and another during the tenth grade. Theoretically, some health teaching is given each year during elementary school years.

Grade placement of health instruction is scheduled according to either a cyclical or a spiral plan. In a *cycle* plan, rather than attempt to cover the total scope, only certain of the organizing elements are offered in any one year. Selection of those to be taught in every grade is based upon what is known about the growth and developmental characteristics, needs, and interests of the students in that grade. A chart employing the scope as one axis and the successive grades or levels of instruction as the other is often devised. A series of checks indicates every subject area to be considered in any given grade. In the cyclical plan, each area is revisited several times throughout the total school experience.

The *spiral* plan is much the same in rationale for placement, except that the plan covers the total scope. What changes during each course or level of education is the depth and complexity of what is to be studied. The term "spiral" comes from the fact that teaching at first focuses on concrete facts and elicits simple cognitive skills in working with them. As students mature, they continue working with the same scope, but the curriculum encompasses broader and broader concepts and requires the application of skills and abilities that build in complexity on what has been mastered earlier—hence, the analogy of a spiral that starts with a small loop and widens as it proceeds.

Some curricula, as in the case of the School Health Education Study (1972), combine the cycle and the spiral plans. The SHES curriculum is spiral in nature over four levels of instruction (K–3, 4–6, 7–9, and 10–12), as illustrated in the scope and sequence chart. Only vertical sequence is provided, in that ordering of the concepts is left to local school adaptation. The intention was that readers would prepare their own cycle plan within the level with which they were concerned. All the scope could be covered within a level, but the exact sequence and scope would be different each year. Actual planning was intended to be a local procedure, with the broader scope and sequence serving only as a starting point.

Continuity

Tyler (1949) believes that any effective plan for vertical sequence must include one more factor, which he calls "continuity." Continuity refers to the reiteration of major curriculum elements, such as concepts, values, and skills. He refers to these elements as the "organizing threads" of the curriculum. In the case of health education, these might be health concepts, health values, and skills (in this case, problem solving and decision making). Whatever the grade and whatever the subject matter, these three elements should be stressed and developed throughout. It's rather like weaving, with the organizing threads as the warp and the organizing elements as the woof.

Classroom level decisions

Teacher decisions affecting sequence focus most directly on *when* as it concerns planning for teaching and learning. The problems primarily relate to horizontal sequence and planned linkages between elements of study.

Ordering the scope   When horizontal sequence is concerned with ordering subject areas defined in the scope, those decisions may be made by a small, representative group of health teachers on behalf of all such instructors in a school district. Determining when study of any particular organizing element will be scheduled is far more complex a problem than simply placing one first, then picking another, and so on until all of them have been given a place. Decisions must not be either whimsical or haphazard; they should be based on careful study of the students in the community for which the curriculum is intended. Although there is no one most desirable or best sequence, all teachers must adhere to the one selected. Given the same scope and sequence, the goals, objectives, choice of subject matter, time allotments, teaching strategies, and evaluation activities prepared by qualified health teachers ought to be very similar. Yet each teacher is free to develop enabling objectives, lessons, and evaluation activities as they meet the needs of specific students.

Planning linkages between areas of study   Another aspect of horizontal sequence for which individual teachers are responsible has to do with presenting each of the subject areas in ways that make the relationship of the next to the one preceding not just logical but dynamic. The student must be able to see very clearly what each has to contribute to the concept of health and health behavior. If this aspect of horizontal sequence is neglected, there is danger that the scope will be perceived as a set of minicourses. No one can arrange for these linkages so effectively as the classroom teacher. No one else can take a curriculum plan and turn its words into actions that give it life.

Once the scope and sequence of a curriculum have been established, the next move must be to infer meaningful goals and objectives to serve as guidelines for developing instructional strategies. Chapter 3 discusses ways of stating objectives appropriate for this sort of description and planning.

SUMMARY

1. Curriculum development considers not just *what* should be taught and learned, but how it should be organized and when certain subject areas should be provided or emphasized.
2. The purpose of comprehensive school health education is to help students learn how to make decisions and choices that contribute to a healthful life-style and promote community well-being.
3. A health education curriculum should be based on study of three basic sources.
    a. the learner:
        (1) needs and interests
        (2) growth and development considerations (physical, social, intellectual, and emotional stages of maturation and developmental tasks)
    b. the community:
        (1) national and local community needs and concerns
        (2) community influences on curriculum (ethnical and socioeconomic factors, legislative and political factors, popular beliefs about health and health behavior, community values and philosophies of health, and local health and health-related crises)
    c. the body of knowledge:
        (1) as content (the range of concepts, principles, or generalizations that define the scope of the discipline of health education)
        (2) as process (the scientific method—cognitive processes by which knowledge is generated and applied in health education)
4. Three curriculum planning models are applicable in school and other health education settings.

a. the Tyler rationale (a goal-attainment model based on learning theory)
b. the health belief model (explaining preventive health behavior, based on health behavior theory)
c. the PRECEDE framework (focusing on factors preceding desired outcomes—medical and and community health education theory)
d. the school-developmental model (emphasizing goals that are long term and enabling, focused on developing self-directed, independent learners)

5. Ideological models shaping health education programs differ in important ways between schools and public health settings.
6. Definition of the scope of a health education curriculum depends upon the nature of the organizing elements employed for that purpose. Organizing elements commonly used include the following:
   a. the body systems design (e.g., respiratory, circulatory, digestive)
   b. the health problems design (e.g., hypertension, obesity, accidents)
   c. the health content area design (e.g, personal health, consumer health, community health, etc.)
   d. the health topic design (e.g., stress reduction, accident prevention, boy-girl relationships)
   e. the conceptual approach (conceptual statements or generalizations broad enough to encompass major curriculum components)
   f. competency-based curriculums are those whose organizing elements are specified as health-related skills and abilities.
7. Sequence planning decisions are made at administrative and at classroom levels.
   a. Administrative decision usually determine grade placement (problems of vertical sequence)
      (1) A cycle plan schedules specific elements of instruction and designated intervals and is most typical of elementary schools.
      (2) A spiral plan covers the total scope of the curriculum in successive courses but at increasing levels of complexity and depth as the student progresses through the grades.
      (3) A plan for continuity establishes organizing threads for the curriculum (such as concepts, values and skills) to be emphasized at every level of instruction.
   b. Classroom level decisions affect problems of horizontal sequence, determining when and what will be taught to specific students.
      (1) Teachers generally decide how the subject areas will be ordered during a course.

(2) Interrelationships or linkages between one subject area and the others depend upon the skill and planning of the classroom teacher.

QUESTIONS AND EXERCISES

Questions
1. What would be the advantages and disadvantages of basing a curriculum on data gathered relative to any single source? If you were to depend on any one, which would you perceive as the most important? State your reasons for your belief.
2. What, in your view, is the difference between teaching and intervention in health education?
3. For any one physical change due to normal growth and development, describe the social, emotional, and intellectual maturation that would be expected at about the same time.
4. If you were asked to carry out the essential research basic to the development of a strong school health education program, what would be the best means of gathering data descriptive of each of the basic sources?
5. Considering the alternatives in curriculum models, which do you support as the best framework for a meaningful school health curriculum? Which kind of organizing element would you urge be adopted and why?
6. How might current variations in family composition require modifications in a health education curriculum?

Exercises
1. Describe a hypothetical group of learners of a given age, detailing their interests, needs, and prior health education experiences if any. Add information about major social, economic, cultural, physical, or other health-related aspects of the community in which they live. Next, using a curriculum design of your choice or one in current use in local schools, prepare a proposal that lists all the organizing elements that would define the body of knowledge and order them from first to last as you would recommend they be provided. Then write brief explanations of the links that you would establish between each ele-

ment. Be sure to emphasize how each would be clearly related to the overall concept of health and health behavior.
2. Construct a chart to illustrate a cycle plan for a curriculum in health education during the elementary school years. Use the scope you recommended in the above exercise as its horizontal axis and grades K–8 as the vertical axis. Justify your placement of content emphasis at each year by citing data obtained through study of the three sources.

REFERENCES

American Association for Health, Physical Education and Recreation, *Health Concepts: Guides for Health Instruction*. Washington, DC: 1967.

American Association of School Administrators, "Health Education." In *Curriculum Handbook for School Administrators*. Arlington, VA: American Association of School Administrators, 1973.

Bruner, J., *The Process of Education*. Cambridge, MA: Harvard University Press, 1963.

Byler, R., Lewis, G., and Totman, R., *Teach Us What We Want To Know*. New York: Mental Health Materials Center, 1969.

California State Board of Education, *Health Instruction Framework for California Public Schools*. Sacramento: Department of Education, 1978.

Carlyon, W. H., "Myths, mindsets, and the medical model, misunderstanding school health education." *Health Values* 5:5, Sept–Oct 1981, pp. 207–210.

Cummings, K. M., Jette, A., and Rosenstock, I., "Construct validation of the health belief model." *Health Education Monographs* 6:4, 1978, pp. 394–405.

Denver Public Schools, *The Health Interests of Children*, rev. ed. Denver: School District #1, 1952.

Education Commission of the States, *Recommendations for School Health Education*. Denver: Education Commission of the States, 1981.

Education Commission of the States, *State Policy Support for School Health Education*. Denver: Education Commission of the States, 1982.

Education for Health in the School Community Setting. Position paper, School Health Section, APHA, 1974.

Goodlad, J. I., *Planning and organizing for teaching*, Washington, DC: NEA, 1964.

Goodlad, J. I., *A Place Called School*. New York: McGraw-Hill, 1984.

Green L. W., Kreuter, M. W., Deeds, S. J., and Partridge, K. B., *Health Education Planning: A Diagnostic Approach*. Palo Alto, CA: Mayfield, 1980.

Havighurst, R. J., *Developmental Tasks and Education*. New York: Longmans, Green, 1952.

Hurlock, E. B., *Adolescent Development*. New York: McGraw-Hill, 1973.

Kolbe, L. J., and Iverson, D. C., "Implementing comprehensive health education: Educational interventions and social change." *Health Education Quarterly* 8:1, 1981, pp. 57–80.

Kreuter, M., and Christenson, G., "School health education: Does it cause an effect?" *Health Education Quarterly* 8:1, Spring 1981, pp. 43–56.

Naisbitt, J., *Megatrends*. New York: Warner Books, 1982.

National Center for Health Education, *Growing Healthy*. New York: National Center for Health Education, 1984.

Oberteuffer, D., "Health education research for Ohio schools." *Ohio Schools* 8: 1, 1930, pp. 26–27.

Pennsylvania Health Curriculum Chart. Pennsylvania Department of Education, with the Pennsylvania Association of Health, Physical Education, Recreation, and Dance, 1982.

Pollock, M. B., and Johns, E. B., "Health education." In *Curriculum Handbook for School Executives*. Washington, DC: AASA, 1973.

Rosenbaum, R., "Turn on, tune in, drop dead." *Harpers*, July 1982, pp. 32–42.

Rosenstock, I. M., "Historical origins of the health belief model." In *The Health Belief Model and Personal Health Behavior. Health Education Monographs* 2: 4, 1974, pp. 328–335.

Rosenstock, I. M., and Kirscht, J. P., "Practice implications." In *The Health Belief Model and Personal Health Behavior. Health Education Monographs* 2: 4, 1974, pp. 470–473.

School Health Curriculum Project, *PGHCP/SHCP Curricular Progression Chart*. San Bruno, CA: School Health Education Project, National Center for Health Education, 1980.

School Health Education Study, *Summary Report*. Washington, DC: School Health Education Study, 1964.

School Health Education Study, *Health Education: A Conceptual Approach to Curriculum Design*. St. Paul, MN: 3M, 1967.

School Health Education Study, *Concept Three, Teaching-Learning Guides*. St Paul, MN: 3M, 1970.

School Health Education Study, *Scope and Sequence Chart*. St. Paul, MN: 3M, 1972.

Shane, H. G., "Significant writings that have influenced the curriculum." *Phi Delta Kappan* 62:5, Jan. 1981, pp. 311–314.

Sliepcevich, E. M., *Summary Report of the School Health Education Study*. Washington, DC: School Health Education Study, 1964.

Sliepcevich, E. M., *Proceedings* of the workshop "Preparation and practice of community patient and school health educators." Bethesda, MD: DHEW, Bureau of Health Manpower, 1978.

Solleder, Marian, *Evaluation Instruments in Health Education*. Washington, DC: AAHPERD, 1979.

Spady, W. G., "Competency-based education: A bandwagon in search of a definition." *Educational Researcher*, Jan. 1977, p. 10.

Toffler, A., *Learning for Tomorrow*. New York: Vantage Books, 1974.

Trucano, L., *Students Speak*. Seattle, WA: Comprehensive Health Education Foundation, 1984.

Tyler, R., *Basic Principles of Curriculum and Instruction*. Chicago: University of Chicago Press, 1949.

University of California, *U C Clipsheet* 55:31, March 25, 1980.

U.S. Department of Health and Human Services, *Objectives for the Nation*. Washington, DC: U.S. Government Printing Office, 1980.

U.S. Department of Health, Education and Welfare, *Healthy People: The Surgeon General's Report on Health Promotion and Disease Prevention*. Washington, DC: U.S. Government Printing Office, 1979.

Wilhelms, F. T., "Curriculum sources." In *What are the Sources of the Curriculum*. Washington, D.C.: Association for Supervision and Curriculum Development, 1962, pp. 14–25.

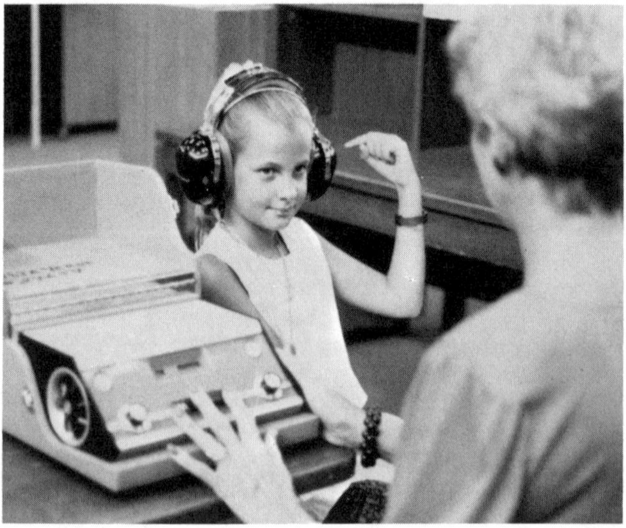

3
Formulating health teaching goals and objectives

If one of your goals is to become a health teacher, then you probably accept the necessity of having to get there one step at a time. Let's call those steps your objectives. And, if you are planning to teach, learning how to set worthwhile goals and define measurable objectives for your students has to be one of them. But what if you aren't sure as you read this chapter whether you want to be a teacher, a patient educator, a community health planner, or something else entirely? Why spend time studying and learning something you may never use? Is the need to determine and communicate one's goals and objectives limited to teaching? Before you answer, let's look at some other opinions regarding the function and worth of clearly stated, measurable objectives.

- "The identification and description of objectives—the first step in planning—is absolutely essential to the success of any plan. One cannot specify how he will accomplish a vague and indeterminate purpose" (O'Donnell, 1972).
- "Objectives must be *operational*. They must be capable of being converted into specific targets and specific assignments. They must be

capable of becoming the basis, as well as the motivation for work and achievement" (Drucker, 1974).

- "Instructional goals that are clearly communicated are more likely to be attained than goals that are not clearly communicated" (Melching et al., 1966).
- "Where behavioral change is desirable, possible, and appropriate, utmost care should be given to stating objectives precisely" (Green et al., 1980).
- "Objectives are the touchstone against which achievement is measured. Hence, objectives must be measurable . . . and their sum must equal achievement of the goal" (Ross and Mico, 1980).
- "If objectives are to be actionable, they must be clear and verifiable to those who pursue them" (Koontz and O'Donnell, 1972).
- "Because instruction represents an intervention designed to benefit those instructed, it seems only sensible to describe those intended benefits with as much clarity as possible (Popham, 1975).

All these people are saying much the same thing: If you want to get someplace else, first decide exactly where you want to go. What makes that agreement significant in this instance is the fact that none of these statements has been quoted from the literature of school health education. They are taken from that of business and management, community health planning, community health education, military training programming, curriculum development, and educational evaluation. Nor are these the only sources that might have been cited here. In short, clearly stated objectives aren't just for teaching about health. They are basic to good planning whatever the field of endeavor. Knowing how to set worthwhile goals and define related, measurable objectives is a skill as valued as it is valuable.

GOALS AND OBJECTIVES DEFINED

Often the words "goals" and "objectives" are used interchangeably. For example, instead of goals, words like "aims," "expected outcomes," "purposes," and even "objectives" may be used. Instructional objectives are given even more varied titles. Depending on the source, they may be termed "behavioral," "measurable," "precise," or "learning" objectives, to mention just a few variations. As a means of avoiding terminology problems of this kind, this text uses "goal" to mean a desired, long-range, accumulative, curriculum-level outcome. An *objective* is a statement specifying what students are expected to know, be able to do, prefer, or believe as the result of specific instruction.

FORMULATING GOALS

In effect, health education goals are descriptors of what is perceived as desirable outcomes of the total curriculum. Accordingly, they serve as the source and focus of all the instructional objectives. In principle, they are curriculum constants, never changing as students progress through the public school experience. They are usually categorized as concerned with cognitive, affective, or psychomotor domains of learning. In health education, an alternative domain (action) is often substituted for the psychomotor to permit formulation of goals descriptive of positive life-style behaviors.

Traditionally, few have expected much more of the required goal statements than that they exist, sound nice, and can be exhibited on demand. A case in point is the classic *Cardinal Principles of Secondary Education* (National Education Association, 1918). Among its seven famous principal objectives of education, "health" stands proudly first. It would be nice if all educators since then had given health education that prominence. However, most often its achievement through education has depended more upon assumption than planning. This dilemma may be partly due to the abstract nature of the word "health." In the absence of further advice, nobody has known exactly what ought to be done about it. That one word does not really convey the notion that health education needs to be given a place in the curriculum. And if it does not, how might a goal statement be stated so that it does so more clearly?

Characteristics of goal statements

To begin with, a goal is best written as a complete sentence. That sentence should be composed both of a behavior (cognitive, affective, or action oriented) and the subject matter with which the learner is expected to be able to employ that behavior. Particularly in the cognitive and affective domains, the behavior tends to be ambiguous rather than measurable (knows, understands, and believes or appreciates). The subject matter encompasses very broad areas or very abstractly described topics, intentions, or conditions. Goals focus on desired *ends* of instruction. They are not concerned with means or process.

However many goals may be proposed to serve as guidelines to a K–12 curriculum, the behaviors reflect all three domains, and the statements are categorized accordingly. Cognitive goals focus on behaviors or intellectual skills such as comprehending, knowing, applying, analyzing, and evaluating. Affective goals propose changed or reinforced attitudes and values promoting a healthful life-style. Action goals describe desired life-style patterns and coping behaviors that will be exhibited in real-life situations usually far removed in time from the instruction planned to help shape them. No classroom evaluation is intended or required as a test of the achievement of the goals in any of the domains.

In the following examples of goal statements, look for the two essential components (the behavior and the content).

- *Cognitive*. understands the interrelationships among physical, social, and mental/emotional aspects of health
- *Affective*. accepts the need to maintain personal health care habits that protect and promote wellness
- *Action*. adheres to a life-style that tends to promote well-being and manage stress constructively

Ways that goal statements aid in curriculum development

What are the advantages to be gained by investment of time and effort in the formulation of goals? There are more than a few.

1. Statements of this level of abstraction and instructional remoteness from the learner can be more profound, reflecting social values more eloquently and directly than can objectives.
2. Because they describe long-range purposes applicable at all levels of planning, they provide stability and consistency to the overall curriculum.
3. Their format permits description of major course objectives in succinct and economical terms.
4. They provide the rationale for and promote the cumulative effectiveness of successive levels of health teaching.
5. They provide a framework for the development of the supportive, operational objectives that must be defined at both institutional and instructional levels of specificity.
6. They facilitate communication between school and community by providing a shorthand view of the purposes of health education as an aspect of general education.

Competencies as goals

In recent years, competency statements have often been employed as broad descriptors of desired student outcomes. Competency-based curriculum planning gained quick and wide acceptance during the 1970s. Soon competencies had been prepared for every level of instruction, from kindergarten through graduate school. The form and level of generality demonstrated by statements labeled "competencies" vary widely, however. This is probably because there is no commonly accepted definition of the term. Some words like "motherhood" and "apple pie" are so familiar and so well regarded that definitions are seldom deemed necessary. "Competence" seems to be one of those words. Its meaning is taken as self-evident. Attempted definitions are characterized by a kind of circularity so that competence is "whatever is required to do something adequately," and "adequate performance" of something is defined as "competence."

Actually, there is no such thing as "competence." It's an abstraction, a construct, like "health." We assume its existence based upon observation of certain indicators accepted as evidence of adequate performance. When enough indicators of competence are exhibited, the sum of them is accepted as evidence of the whole. Try to form a mental image of "competence" or to draw a picture of it. It can be done only for specific examples of competence, not for competence in general.

Still, with or without an accepted definition, somebody's notion of competence is implicit in whatever is proposed as descriptive of such an outcome. Published lists of them abound. Some are broad and ambiguous, such as "appreciates the value of daily health practices in relation to grooming and personal appearance." Some are fuzzy but focus on facts, such as "recognizes that a calorie is a measure of the energy value of food." Some describe desired abilities, such as "the ability to communicate well in teaching-learning settings." Most competency statements are in no way distinguishable from behavioral objectives, however.

Competency statements versus goal statements

Which of the above examples represents the best way to state a competency? What are the guidelines used in determining that any statement in fact describes a competency? As it happens, validation of statements proposed as competencies has largely depended upon consensus of opinion. Often a wide range of outside expert opinion has been elicited to substantiate the work of those who have originated a list, especially when the originator has been a lone investigator, as in the case of a thesis or dissertation author. But when competencies have been developed by groups of professionals, such as teachers, the group in effect has served as its own panel of experts. The assumption has been that the statements they produce are competencies because they have been identified by persons acknowledged to be competent in that field themselves.

Use of a panel of experts in this way is an accepted procedure in this kind of endeavor. Yet strictly speaking, consensus is all that can be claimed by way of validation; it is not proof of anything. After all, for some time, it was the consensus of opinion that malaria was caused by bad air. Whether a list of statements is actually a set of competencies because a panel of experts says it is remains simply a matter of opinion.

Still, consensus means a lot in this context, and the consensus among educators appears to be that a behavioral objective describes a competency. Or to put it the other way around, a competency can be stated in the form of a measurable objective. Programs described as competency based almost always use such objectives to describe proposed competencies. Usually at least two levels of competence are defined. In that case, the higher level, broader competencies resemble statements labeled "goals" in other programs.

The principal difference between levels of competency statements, as is the case with goals and objectives, is that the behavior in the case of the higher level is ambiguous (knows, comprehends, believes); that of the objectives is measurable (defines, identifies, analyzes). To illustrate this point, here are examples of a competency statement and a long-range goal, along with their supporting objectives. The first is adapted from a set devised by the faculty in a high school district in California (1980). The second is cited from the SHES curriculum (School Health Education Study, 1967):

I. Competency: Students will understand the effects of nutrition on their immediate and long term personal well being.
   Objectives: Names the essential nutrients and their functions.
   Identifies beneficial effects of common foods.
   Explains long term effects of poor nutrition.

II. Long Range Goal: The student comprehends that the choice of foods determines the nutritive balance vital to effective functioning of the body.
   Objectives: Describes food nutrients and their functions as they relate to health.
   Interprets relationships between nutritional status and disease.
   Compares ways that nutritional status enhances or deters physical, mental, and social attainments.

Nothing of form has changed very much between the two higher level statements, the competency and the goal. Only the labels are different. Perhaps the competency movement did not so much introduce a new means of describing desirable educational outcomes as it promoted the use of clearly stated objectives in a new way. Educators once resistant to the notion of "behavioral" objectives are now comfortable with the same sort of objectives based upon a competence, not entirely because of the change in terminology either. For one thing, objectives written with competency as the desired outcome are far more likely to focus on meaningful subject matter.

In addition, the focus is more apt to be on process, or learning to *do,* than on subject matter alone, or learning *that.* This means that developing a set of objectives for use in competency-based teaching has to be done with special thought and care. If competence is to be the outcome of a set of objectives, then the form, generality, and quality of those statements must be impeccable.

Viewed as competencies, a set of related objectives should be consistent in the nature of their behaviors. Whether a set focuses on what the competent student is to know *about,* know *how to do,* or what a competent adult or practitioner *does,* the objectives ought to be grouped accordingly. Moreover, such groupings of objectives should, in sum, be comprehensively facilitative of achievement of the higher level competence from which they have been inferred.

FORMULATING OBJECTIVES

Although, like goal statements, objectives specify a behavior and some amount of health information, they focus more directly on *means* of instruction. "A well stated instructional objective describes in unequivocal terms the desired postinstruction status of the learner" (Popham, 1975, p. 48). Whether the objective is general or specific, some amount of measurable growth or change in the learner is explicitly proposed.

The function of objectives in curriculum development

Each objective specifies some aspect of the content relevant to the goal, along with a cognitive, affective, or other behavior appropriate to the ability and experience of the students for whom it is intended. Its function is to serve both as an organizing center for the subsequent development of teaching-learning plans and as a criterion for later evaluation activities.

Objectives are always subordinate to a goal and designed to contribute to its ultimate achievement. Taken together, objectives in effect define the purposes of the goal from which they have been inferred. The answer to the question "Has the learner achieved a given long-range goal?" should be implicit in postinstruction evaluation based upon the objectives designed and implemented to that end.

No instructional objectives are proposed relative to goals in the action domain. Those goals represent desired choices among alternative health-related behaviors. As such, they depend upon command of the concepts and skills described by the cognitive and affective objectives of the health curriculum. The assumption is that success in achieving the first two sets of objectives equips the learner to choose wisely and enhances the possibility that he or she will do so. In any case, few if any objectives can be devised that reliably gauge the probability of future behaviors.

The specificity of an objective varies, depending on its role in curriculum design and the immediacy of its impact on the learner. General objectives are used to structure curriculum guides or units of study. Specific objectives give guidance to classroom projects or individual lesson plans. Whether general or specific, effectiveness in communicating its intent should always be a test of the quality of an objective.

Action words acceptable for instructional objectives

Opinions differ regarding the kinds and numbers of verbs acceptable for use in defining an objective. However, most authorities agree that certain action words communicate intentions more reliably than others. The number of verbs deemed acceptable for this purpose ranges from as few as nine (American Association for Advancement of Science, 1969) to nearly three hundred (Guilbert, 1976). The longer the list, the greater the variety of terms admitted.

Cognitive behaviors are generally not observable as they are being practiced, but their product can be observed and measured. Cognitive terms tend to be perceived similarly by most of us. Even though individual teachers might interpret them in slightly different ways, most would agree in general what would be happening when a person was naming, identifying, or analyzing.

Affective behaviors reflect some amount of self-direction and positive attitudes toward the content specified in an objective. They are concerned with changing attitudes, values, and interests. Affective behavior categories range from the nearly cognitive level of "awareness" through "responding," "valuing," "organization" to the highest, "characterization by a value" (Krathwohl, Bloom, and Masia, 1964).

Activity descriptors specify a *means* of exhibiting a cognitive or affective behavior. For example, can anyone discuss something without explaining, describing, comparing, or using some other cognitive skill? "Discuss" is simply a means of allowing the student to verbalize what the intellect delivers on demand if the needed data are stored in its memory banks. Here is an example of that kind of objective: "Observes experienced health educators in classroom situations." We know what is to happen, but we don't know why it is to happen. The real objective is not stated but ought to specify the intended outcome of such an experience. It might be "identifies special teaching techniques employed by experienced health educators." Activity-specific objectives are always ends in themselves and therefore have limited potential for transfer.

Because differences between behaviors are seldom clear-cut, overlaps in meaning are unavoidable. Nevertheless, an attempt has been made to categorize verbs commonly used in defining instructional objectives as follows:

Cognitive	Affective	Activity Descriptors
name	realize	discuss
define	examine	write
list	master	observe
identify	determine	report
explain	accept	draw
describe	believe	state
interpret	be aware	tell why
predict	deduce	indicate
analyze	reject	demonstrate
categorize	support	formulate
classify	advocate	cite
differentiate	volunteer	design
synthesize	argue	investigate
compare	offer	read
evaluate	persist	develop a plan

Can you see a pattern differentiating one category of verbs from the others?

Each of these three categories of objectives has its uses. Whichever one you choose in any particular situation, what is most important is (1) that you know when you select it exactly what the behavior requires the student to be doing and (2) that the behavior you select fits the purpose you have in mind. This is particularly so in the case of cognitive behaviors for several reasons. First, cognitive objectives are most often evaluated, and the evaluation must match a behavior that is known in advance of instruction. Second, cognitive outcomes are inescapably an aspect of every affective outcome. Third, cognitive objectives typically are used, in the form of general objectives, to structure curriculums.

Defining cognitive terms

Before formulating a set of instructional objectives for teaching or for constructing a curriculum guide, it is wise to establish the meanings of the terms that are to be used throughout. An agreed-upon glossary of terms facilitates communication, provides consistency, and helps implement objectives as effectively in use by a single teacher as among many teachers.

The following definitions have been developed for the cognitive domain. The format is based upon the framework designed by Bloom et al. (1956), but any plan that facilitates quick reference to meanings will do. The important thing is that each definition specifies what the learner is doing when practicing that behavior. The rationale of the Bloom taxonomy or hierarchy of educational objectives assumes that at each level of cognition, all the skills listed in the previous category have been mastered. Only the lowest or simplest level of cognition, "knowing," does not depend upon that assumption.

To categorize a given skill with absolute precision is difficult if not impossible, but it has been attempted for the behavioral skills that follow. The placement of one or more of them might differ, depending on the view of those making those decisions. These definitions do not necessarily provide the best or only possible description of the behavior, but if teaching plans are based upon terms with agreed-upon meanings, the quality of both the teaching and the learning should be enhanced.

A Glossary of Cognitive Terms

I. *Knowledge:* remembering of an idea or phenomenon in a form very close to that in which it was first encountered
  1.1 To name: to use the word or title by which an object, person, or idea is usually designated
  1.2 To define: to give the precise meaning of a word or sense of a word
  1.3 To list: to itemize, to record a number of things or persons of a like nature

II. *Comprehension:* those behaviors that represent an understanding of the literal message contained in a communication
  2.1 To identify: to discover the nature or special characteristics of a thing or to determine the class to which a thing belongs
  2.2 To explain: to offer reasons for or a cause of—to clarify the nature or meaning of something
  2.3 To describe: to give a detailed account of in words, to picture verbally or graphically
  2.4 To distinguish: to recognize as being different or distinctive from otherwise similar things

III. *Application:* those behaviors exhibited by the learner in bringing to bear abstractions such as theories, principles, ideas, rules, and methods needed for the solution of a problem
  3.1 To interpret: to clarify its meaning by restating an idea or theory in another way
  3.2 To illustrate: to clarify an idea or theory by using examples or comparisons
  3.3 To predict: to foretell or make known in advance what will happen at a later time

3.4 To translate: to put in simpler terms or to convey from one form to another
IV. *Analysis:* those behaviors employed in breaking down a theory or plan into its separate parts and determining the relationship of those parts and how they are organized, also the techniques used to convey the meaning or to establish the conclusions of a communication
   4.1 To analyze: to separate into parts so as to determine the nature of the whole
   4.2 To classify: to sort things or ideas according to a set of shared characteristics
   4.3 To categorize: to determine the placement of an idea or object in a specified division of a classification system
   4.4 To differentiate: to note or demonstrate characteristics establishing the uniqueness of a thing or an idea
V. *Synthesis:* those behaviors involved in putting new elements and parts together so as to form a new pattern or structure not clearly there before
   5.1 To synthesize: to combine data or information so as to form a new or more complex product
   5.2 To conclude: to reach a decision or form an opinion about something following careful study of a problem or issue
   5.3 To propose: to put forward a plan or an idea for consideration, discussion, or acceptance
VI. *Evaluation:* those behaviors involved in the making of judgments about the worth of ideas, works, solutions (The criteria may be quantitative, qualitative, or both.)
   6.1 To evaluate: to examine and judge the worth or value of something
   6.2 To compare: to examine in order to note similarities among or between things
   6.3 To contrast: to show how one thing is strikingly different from another or others
   6.4 To appraise: to estimate the quality, amount, size, or other features of an object or a product

Current variations in stating cognitive objectives

How should an instructional objective be stated? Curriculum experts do not entirely agree on the answer to that question. Some assert that an objective is not complete unless the exact conditions under which the resulting learning is to be demonstrated are spelled out. Certain words are accepted as appropriate descriptors of desired behavioral change by some but not by others. Some believe that an ambiguous behavior can be used so long as the statement goes on to explain what is meant by the word in that situation; others prefer that the word used be measurable in and of itself. Some insist that precise criteria for the evaluation of learner performance be included in the statement; others are satisfied with a statement whose behavior can be measured in several ways so long as it is measurable in *some* valid manner.

Differences in point of view often stem from the nature of the discipline itself. For example, mathematics objectives can and probably need to be more specific than those for health education. But human beings just don't line up in neat columns; nor can they be required to behave according to one rule or one prescribed choice defined as "right." Youngsters need to learn how to solve human problems that may never occur or will not occur for many years. A curriculum that can meet those kinds of needs is much more complicated to plan and evaluate than one that deals with more concrete and specific objectives. It isn't easy to teach *anything,* but health education presents the teacher with some unique problems and challenges.

It is generally agreed that an objective must specify a behavior that can be practiced and demonstrated in the classroom and that each must define some amount of subject matter. Beyond that, most health educators pattern objectives according to one of three accepted models: the programmed instruction model, the Bloom taxonomy model, and what we shall term an operational model.

The programmed instruction model The popularity of narrowly prescribed objectives began with Robert Mager's delightful small book, *Preparing Objectives for Programmed Instruction.* Programmed instruction was an innovation in teaching that received brief but considerable attention during the early 1960s. Interest in this sort of self-paced, mechanized instruction soon waned, but enthusiasm for precisely stated objectives did not. There were a number of reasons for this, but principally it was because sudden public demands for greater teaching accountability made better specification of teaching objectives imperative. Teachers at that time had not been taught how to write measurable objectives, and suddenly they needed to learn how, and fast. Before a year had passed, Mager's book became so widely popular as the means of in-service education for teachers that a new printing with a new title was made available to meet the demand. The title, *Preparing Instructional Objectives,* was new; the content was the same. The result was mass adoption of the programmed instruction model for educational objectives. Whether the same precision is appropriate for all teaching is arguable, but the book's contribution to the behavioral objectives movement was unique and powerful.

An objective written for health education based on the programmed instruction model might be something like this: "Given a list of twenty commonly used foodstuffs, the student will be able to classify each according to its principal nutrient, with 80 percent accuracy." Yet it should be remembered that objectives serve more than one function in curriculum development. Some are used to structure a total program; others are the focus of a single lesson. The closer their impact on the learner, the more precise they need to be, and vice versa. Those objectives written at the institutional level or even at course or unit levels do not need to be so narrowly defined, nor do they need to describe evaluation criteria. The minute analysis of purpose for the development of precisely defined objectives typical of the Mager model is at once its strength and its weakness. Attempts to write objectives so narrow in their scope and prescriptive of achievement end in long lists of statements. The outcome is more often overwhelming profusion than constructive precision. Further, it is easier to describe valid performance indicators for the cognitive than for the affective domain. That means that worthwhile, but less measurable, affective objectives are rarely proposed.

At any level, the effect of such specificity is sometimes to deny teachers the right to vary lesson plans and evaluation activities to suit their own talents or to meet the needs of their own students. However, used as originally intended, to structure individual steps or lessons as in programmed instruction, objectives of this nature are undeniably effective.

The Bloom taxonomy model At the other extreme of specificity in writing objectives, especially at the lowest level of cognition, "knowledge" (and research has shown that most educational objectives are defined at that level), is the previously described taxonomy model (Bloom et al., 1956). Bloom and his colleagues defined knowledge as the remembering of ideas, material, or phenomena in a form very like that in which they were originally encountered. Those who have employed the Bloom taxonomy as the basis for developing objectives have tended to focus on cognitive behaviors such as "knows" or "is aware of." Categorization of the total statement depends largely on the subject matter involved (for example, "to know the criteria by which the major nutrient of a given foodstuff can be identified").

The primary goal of education, and particularly health education, is to develop the ability to think critically, not just to regurgitate information much as it was presented in prior learning experiences. When designing instructional objectives, care must be taken to give balanced emphasis to the other, more complex behaviors represented in the total hierarchy of cognitive skills and abilities (those calling for comprehension, application, analysis, synthesis, and evaluation). When this is done, the taxonomy can be a useful tool in developing worthwhile instructional objectives for health education.

The operational model A third model for the development of measurable objectives lies somewhere between these two, accepting as useful any objective clearly describing what the student is to be able to do following instruction. The verb must be acceptably measurable in the classroom and feasible of application by the students for whom the objective is designed. The subject matter dimension may be abstract or concrete and factual, depending on the purpose. The higher the level of instruction (K–12), the more abstract the subject matter. Similarly, general objectives (those designed to structure overall curriculum plans) describe content in broader terms than those prepared for individual lessons. An operational objective appropriate for health instruction at the secondary level might be "classifies foodstuffs of various kinds according to their principal nutrient."

This last model may have the most utility for health education because both teaching and instruction can be based upon the behavior in any way the teacher chooses so long as what happens matches the objective as stated. Objectives that are too prescriptive tend to stifle creativity and hinder individualization of instruction. The effectiveness of objectives whose behaviors are ambiguous is limited, no matter how precisely the subject matter may be defined. Without a measurable behavior, a teacher lacks guidelines either to the appropriate cognitive skill to be practiced or the best method of practicing it.

Characteristics of functional health education objectives

Whichever model for objective development is selected, functional statements are consistent with the following characteristics. First, an objective statement includes two basic components; a measurable skill or behavior and some amount of clearly specified health information or subject matter, for example:

1: *The effects of drug abuse* (simply a topic)
   1–2 *To analyze critically* (This is simply a behavior; there must be some subject matter to which it can be applied.)
   1–3 *The student describes the effects of drug abuse on the individual and the community.* (Both components are present.)

Second, an objective is stated in terms of the learner's activity, rather than descriptive of a teacher's plan, for example:

2: *To teach reasons why so many people continue to smoke despite published warnings* (Learning is the desired outcome, and it can happen only in the student. This objective could be implemented in an empty room.)
   2–2 *The student analyzes forces motivating cigarette smoking.* (The statement clearly describes what the student is expected to do, yet the teacher has considerable latitude in planning for appropriate practice.)

Third, an instructional objective defines but one behavior or skill and only one complete idea or topic as subject matter, for example:

3: *Names methods of disease control and explains how each is most effectively applied* (Obviously this is two objectives pasted together. Not only are they easier to work with as two separate objectives, but the outcome is more apt to be what was wanted.)
   3–2 *Names and lists methods of disease control* (Here we have two behaviors, the first of which is redundant in any case inasmuch as listing involves naming.)
   3–3 *Describes methods of disease control and how each control is applied* (This is one behavior but two separate topics. Better would have been *Describes methods of disease control* and *Explains how given methods of disease control are applied*. Notice that once separated, the content may be better explored with separate behaviors rather than with the same in each case.)

Fourth, an objective is operational, which is to say that the learner can practice working with it and demonstrate its achievement, to some degree at least, in the classroom, for example:

4: *Refrains from using substances that are dangerous to health* (No one would quarrel with the value of this kind of outcome, but you'd have to follow the learner about for life in order to prove that it had been accomplished.)
   4–2 *Differentiates between uses of mood modifying substances that are helpful and those that are harmful to health* (Although ability to do so does not guarantee that such a skill will be applied, the student *can* demonstrate its achievement in classroom evaluation activities.)

Fifth, an instructional objective for health education should describe a learning outcome that looks beyond accomplishing the immediate task. What is to be learned should have promise of lifelong utility and meaning. At the minimum, such objectives should provide preliminary information and practice with skills needed in order to handle later objectives that do have such potential for competent decision making. It is a rare decision we make that does not in some way affect health, our own and that of others. Health education should seek to equip the learner for a lifetime of reasoned health behavior choices. Whether it does or not depends upon the nature and quality of the instructional objectives that structure teaching, for example:

5: *Names the principal bones of the human skeleton* (How does ability to name bones help the student live better or choose wisely? Will knowledge of the names of bones help anyone walk better, stand more erectly, or run better?)

5–2 *Explains how adequate amounts of fluoride in drinking water affect the development of teeth and bones* (Abilities and information obtained by means of working with this objective have applications beyond obvious classroom objectives. American voters have often been asked to decide whether public water supplies shall be fluoridated. Parents need to know the effect of topical application of fluoride or use of fluoride-enriched toothpaste when making decisions about dental care for their children. The health-educated adult is better qualified to make decisions of this sort than the individual whose perceptions of the function of fluorides are based upon hearsay or propaganda.)

Finally, an instructional objective must be feasible. As Bloom has observed, the precision and operationality of an objective neither assures its educational worth nor guarantees that students can attain it (Bloom, Hastings, and Madaus, 1971, p. 32). Feasibility is a problem influencing the design of objectives in several ways. First it has to do with the realities of school administration, time allocations, money, personnel, and equipment. Objectives cannot be proposed that involve projects that would take too much time, cost too much, require materials or equipment that are unavailable, or are similarly unrealistic in any way.

A feasible objective can be achieved by the students for whom it is intended. You can't ask elementary grade students to "analyze the effects of urbanization on the quality of human life," for it expects them to deal with concepts and exhibit a cognitive skill that few of them are likely to possess. Selection and design of an objective must be based upon knowledge about the past experience and learnings of the students for whom it is intended.

A related factor influencing the feasibility of an objective is the readiness of a group of students to receive and work with it. Readiness of this sort is a function of maturation in association with experience. It can also be an outcome of a need or interest. Other factors influence readiness—for example, age, sex, health status, strength, the quality of family relationships, attitudes, economics, and beliefs. Variables such as these must be considered when writing objectives if they are to be feasible and motivating for students at any level of instruction.

Readiness to learn about a health matter is not the same as readiness to act in accord with what is learned. Although it cannot be argued that learning how to solve a health problem guarantees desirable future behaviors, neither can it be denied that possession of that skill is a lifelong asset, ready to be called upon when needed.

Objectives in the affective domain

The affective domain of educational objectives includes those that focus on feelings, interests, attitudes, appreciations, and values. Cognitive objectives are concerned with what the student is to learn to *do;* affective objectives propose what it is hoped the student will *feel* like doing or not doing. That the two domains of objectives are being discussed separately does not mean that it is ever possible to separate one from the other, however. Rarely, if ever, is there an objective defined that is solely cognitive or totally affective in nature. Those who developed the affective domain of the taxonomy of educational objectives emphasize this fact repeatedly, for example: ". . . at all levels of the affective domain, affective objectives have a cognitive component, and one can find affective components for cognitive objectives" (Krathwohl, Bloom, and Masia, 1964, p. 63). Although course objectives may appear to be concerned only with cognitive outcomes, there is inescapably an affective outcome in every case.

Krathwohl and his colleagues used the term "internalization" to describe real changes in attitudes, appreciations, or values. This process of continuous inner growth is viewed as ranging from a point of mere awareness of a phenomenon to a level of complete commitment making it part of an individual's personal philosophy or value system.

There are five categories of the hierarchy of affective objectives:

1. awareness
2. responding
3. valuing
4. organization
5. characterization by a value or a value concept

A number of exemplary objectives are suggested by Krathwohl, Bloom, and Masia (1964) for each of these categories of that domain, from which a single statement is here cited as an illustration.

I: recognition that there may be more than one acceptable point of view
II: willingness to comply with health regulations
III: desires to obtain optimum health
IV: forms judgments as to the responsibility of society for conserving human and material resources
V: acceptance of objectivity and systematic planning as basic methods in arriving at satisfying choices

Although the above statements were presented as "objectives" in the affective domain, the term was used interchangeably with "goal." Today, most educators would view these kinds of statements as goals rather than as instructional objectives.

Characteristics of affective objectives The form of an affective objective differs from that of its more disciplined cousin in several ways. First, the behavior is often less precise and therefore difficult to use as a guide. Second, it describes outcomes likely to be long term rather than immediate, which makes measurement even more a problem. Third, the subject matter is often concerned with personal beliefs, attitudes, and personality characteristics that may be too sensitive in nature to be taught or evaluated directly. In this regard, Tyler (1973) reminds us that educators must be guided by certain principles. He says that there are two main principles that should be carefully considered in reviewing proposed objectives in the affective domain. One is the political principle that the function of the school in a democratic society is to help the student gain the means for increasing independence in judgments and action, but not to indoctrinate particular political or sectarian views. The other is the ethical principle that each individual has the right to privacy that must not be invaded by the school.

An affective objective may be laudable but not necessarily essential to success in the course. For example, "appreciation of community health services" has been proposed as a desirable attitude objective. It's not really likely that a student who knows what community health services are available and how they may best be used will fail the course for lack of enough appreciation of that information.

The following statements have been taken from materials specifically developed for affective education (Thayer and Beeler, 1975). Notice that although there is always a behavioral term, it is the subject matter that is identified with the affective domain.

- Be able to identify strong personal emotional states.
- Will gain awareness of how rapidly levels of affectivity change.
- Becomes aware of the possible incongruence between an individual's overt behavior and covert emotions.
- To clarify and bring into conscious awareness the participant's own feelings, beliefs, and values.

Assessing achievement of affective outcomes Achievement of an affective objective is as difficult to implement as it is to measure. For this reason, many teachers do not attempt to write such a statement or to consider affective objectives either feasible or necessary. Yet the goals of health education are vitally concerned with changes in attitudes and values. Knowledge is not enough. The health-educated person has to value health and believe that certain behaviors and choices can be effective in maintaining it. Learning opportunities *can* be devised to help students examine their values and make a reasoned analysis of alternative behaviors and consequences.

Popham (1975) recommends that unmeasurable, affective objectives should be kept if they meet the following guidelines. If they are so praiseworthy on the face of it that they warrant the risk that it may be impossible to prove their achievement and (1) there is no known means of measuring such objectives, (2) most authorities agree that they are truly significant, and (3) the proportion of nonmeasurable to measurable objectives is small.

We believe that the development of affective objectives should be given as much care as are competencies or other cognitive objectives and that learning opportunities should be devised to carry out any deemed essential to health teaching. We also believe that implicit in every meaningful health lesson is an unstated affective component. Krathwohl, Bloom, and Masia (1964, p. 55) support this view in these words: "The careful observer of the classroom can see that the wise teacher as well as the psychological theorist uses cognitive behavior and the achievement of cognitive goals to attain affective goals. In many instances she does so more intuitively than consciously. In fact, a large part of what we call 'good teaching' is the teacher's ability to attain affective objectives through challenging the students' fixed beliefs and getting them to discuss issues."

Roles of objectives in curriculum planning

The role of the most specific or enabling objectives is to serve as the focus of a single lesson or a few at most. The role of the more broadly conceived, general objectives is to provide a framework of statements to serve as organizing centers for a course, a unit of study, or an entire curriculum plan, K–12. Each general objective becomes the focus of all the precisely stated instructional objectives devised by individual teachers as they plan the lessons needed to facilitate its achievement.

Criteria differentiating general from specific objectives

Whether general or precise, instructional level objectives do not differ in form. The behaviors, with the exception of those that are simply activity descriptors ("states," "discusses"), are the same. Both kinds of statements must satisfy the requirements for a functional objective.

What distinguishes a general from a specific, lesson-oriented objective in that case? According to Popham (1975), there are no sure guidelines. He says, "Most objectives are carved out at a level of specificity intuitively derived by the objective specifier." This means that with practice you come to have a feel for it. However, three criteria, "duration," "cruciality," and "transferability," are suggested. *Duration* refers to the amount of time that would be needed to accomplish an objective. A general objective describes complex outcomes that would take the learner a week or more to achieve, whereas a specific objective focuses narrowly on a single outcome. *Cruciality* requires that a general objective be broadly representative of essential or significant health education concepts and behaviors. The subject matter defined in specific objectives is limited to that necessary for the related lesson. *Transferability* has to do with the fact that a general objective leads to the development of a capacity for action that is transferable to other times, situations, or problems. In other words, a general objective does not describe a purpose or an outcome so specific that its achievement is simply an end in itself. Specific objectives are not expected to promote transference so much as to facilitate some part of the learning implicit in the broader objective.

These are some ways to judge the *power* of general objectives to serve as organizing centers structuring plans for a large teaching unit or course of study. The problem is somewhat different when general objectives are used to frame a sequence of instruction K–12. How are objectives stated that satisfy the guidelines for generality but also are feasible and appropriate to the needs and abilities of students at successive levels of progression through the grades?

Defining objectives sequentially—K–12

Competence in cognitive skills and abilities increases with education and experience. Secondary school students presumably have mastered a great many skills and can deal with abstractions more easily than can younger children. There will always be some overlap of capacities among students of the same age, but in general, those at the same level of education will be more alike than they are different. Objectives that reflect expected changes in abilities and experience at successive levels of schooling are developed by appropriately adjusting the two components of an objective.

Cognitive behaviors range from simple recall, as in "naming" or "listing," to those as complex as "synthesizing" or "evaluating." Similarly, the subject matter component may be narrowly specific or very general. Four combinations of the two components of every objective are possible. For example, the lower the level of schooling, the simpler the behavior and the more concrete the content dimension of the objective. As the student progresses, subsequent objectives might specify continued practice of simple behaviors, but now in dealing with more broadly described content. More complex behaviors are attempted gradually, first in dealing with simple topics, then with generalizations. At the fourth, or high school level, the behaviors can be as complex as desired and the subject matter as comprehensive as past learning activities permit.

Knowledge of the hierarchy of educational objectives helps us develop objectives appropriate to differing levels of experience. In other words, students have to know the facts before they can demonstrate comprehension, they have to comprehend the facts before they can apply them, and so on. Objectives proposed for students at varying levels of instruction should be based on recognized growth and development characteristics of the learners and on their past experience with that subject matter.

Complete scope and sequence charts such as those discussed in chapter 2 illustrate this kind of progression by levels. We will not attempt to create such a plan for the sole purpose of demonstrating how general objectives are differently stated according to level. Instead, a single statement at each level may serve to illustrate the gradual increase in expectations from levels I through IV.

- level I: defines the meanings of health and illness (a simple behavior and a concrete topic)
- level II: defines qualities characterizing a healthy community (a simple behavior but subject matter that is abstract)
- level III: analyzes ways that peer pressure affects individual diet choices (more complex behavior but subject matter that is more factual than abstract in nature)
- level IV: analyzes the interrelationships between heredity and environment in the development of a healthy individual (a complex cognitive behavior and subject matter that is relatively abstract)

There are a great many possible variations of these combinations. Be sure that the objectives selected for any one level are all of the same pattern. That means don't mix those using a simple behavior in connection with a narrowly described topic with others exhibiting more sophisticated patterns. Inconsistency in form as a result of mixing combinations at the same level destroys the logic that established their generality for a given group. Some objectives in such a situation will be less powerful than others, hence inappropriate, nonchallenging, and possibly also noncontributing to stated goals. Whatever the objective, it must be attainable by the students for whom it has been proposed. They must be capable of exhibiting the skill, and they must know enough about the subject matter to find it not only comprehensible but motivating.

Inferring specific objectives from the general objectives

Although general objectives are usually determined at school, district, and state levels, specific objectives are best left for the classroom teacher to work out. Only the teacher is able to define instructional objectives appropriate for a given class. Every group of students is in some ways different from any other, whether as to past experience, skill development, current interests, or chief concerns. Small variations in the enabling objectives (preparatory subobjectives) or in the number that are needed make no difference in the long run. Achievement of the competence implicit in mastery of the general objective is what matters, however the teacher arranges for this to happen.

Let us assume that the general objective has been established as follows: *"The student differentiates between inherited and acquired traits and characteristics."* Then here are some possible enabling objectives that a teacher might perceive as necessary means to that end:

1. names ways people are different from others of the same age
2. lists commonly possessed personality traits and characteristics
3. explains the role of genes in transmitting physical characteristics
4. identifies environmental factors influencing growth and development
5. illustrates ways the environment can promote or deter physical, social, and mental dimensions of development
6. describes ways social and mental/emotional characteristics are learned

More objectives than these might be necessary for some groups and fewer for others. Different objectives than these might be more effective with some students. Teachers should be free to do whatever works best with the students in their own classes.

How clearly stated objectives facilitate health teaching

There is no one set of general curriculum level objectives whose mastery is by agreement essential to health education. There are too many differences among students and needs for that to be the case. The subject matter itself changes so rapidly that it taxes the specialist to keep up on it in even one area of interest. However, if the objectives that you devise are clearly stated, meaningful, and feasible, they will facilitate teaching and planning both in general and in particular. Several advantages are derived from care taken to formulate crisply stated objectives.

First, they make it easier for the teacher to make the curricular decisions that are necessary to achieve the stated goals. It is a lot easier to plan the most efficient means of getting somewhere if you know at the start where it is you are supposed to go. Not only do clearly stated objectives provide better direction, but they make it easier to spot those that are trivial or irrelevant so they can be deleted or rewritten.

Second, clearly stated objectives act as guidelines to every other aspect of planning for their implementation. An instructional objective provides clues to four essential aspects of teaching. The verb, or behavior, tells you exactly what the students are to be doing during the lesson (e.g., "naming," "explaining," "analyzing"). At the same time, it indicates what kinds of teaching techniques can be used to provide appropriate practice of that behavior. For example, if the cognitive skill is "synthesizes," panel discussion or debate might be used. Lecture or demonstration will not give the students practice in synthesizing. In effect, the behavior specified in the objective tells you both what is and what is not appropriate as a teaching strategy.

The content component of the objective defines the subject matter to be studied and learned. If an objective is "describes the effects of drug abuse on the individual and his or her family," then the focus is on those effects. These may and should include effects of many kinds—physical, social, mental, and emotional—but any other information about drug abuse is irrelevant to that objective. This doesn't mean that you can't teach about other aspects of drug abuse. It does mean that inasmuch as you are limited to the content specified in the objective, if more content is wanted, you must either broaden the original objective or develop others that deal with any desired additional topics. The rule is, as the objective defines that subject matter, so the learning opportunity must be faithful to its intention.

Finally, a clearly stated objective serves as the criterion of its achievement. Whatever the objective, its evaluation must require the students to demonstrate competence in doing just what it says. No other test of its achievement is valid. There are other uses of this connection between objectives and evaluation. Students can be pretested if desired to discover what they already know about the proposed task. Then teachers have an established basis for determining their success in changing the behaviors as planned and for revising objectives once they have been implemented in the classroom. Pretesting also provides a means of checking the feasibility of objectives. Depending on the outcome, an objective might be confirmed as worthwhile and workable, rewritten if need be, or discarded.

Decisions about objectives are clearly the most important that have to be made in planning for teaching; every other decision depends upon them. They must be designed and used thoughtfully, giving careful attention to every clue they provide. The learning opportunities and evaluation activities that result ought to mirror the intentions of the objective so unmistakably that an observer could correctly infer the original statement based upon what the students were asked to do.

SUMMARY

1. The first step in planning is the definition and description of goals and objectives, whether it be for business management, public health administration and planning, education, or any other achievement-oriented endeavor.

a. An educational goal is a desired, long-range, accumulatively achieved outcome of instruction.
b. An educational objective is a proposed change in knowledge, abilities, or beliefs resulting from a lesson or lessons.
2. Goals are the source and focus of all instructional objectives.
   a. Curriculum goals are concerned with desired ends of instruction.
   b. Health education goals are usually categorized according to cognitive, affective, psychomotor (sometimes action) domains of learning.
   c. Goals reflect social values, provide stability and consistency to curriculum plans, define major course purposes in economic terms, promote the logical development of sequential course activities, provide a framework for the instructional objectives, and facilitate school-community communication.
3. Competency statements in their broadest form typically do not differ in form or function from statements proposed as goals.
4. Objectives are concerned with the *means* of instruction and are stated at the classroom level of implementation.
   a. Objectives are subordinate to a goal and designed to contribute to its achievement.
   b. Clearly stated objectives propose some amount of measurable growth or change in the learner.
   c. The role of an objective is to serve as the focus of teaching and evaluation plans.
5. The verb or behavior specified in an instructional objective should usually be an observable or measurable skill.
   a. Some words communicate intended cognitive behaviors more dependably than others.
   b. Words such as "discuss," "write," and "state" reflect ways of demonstrating cognitive skills.
   c. Words that describe affective behaviors can be measurable within certain limits.
6. There are three generally accepted variations in stating cognitive objectives.
   a. the programmed instruction model
   b. the taxonomy model
   c. the operational model
7. Essential criteria defining a functional objective include the following: It should
   a. be two-dimensional
   b. describe what the student will be doing or learning

c. describe one objective only
d. be operational
e. be meaningful, having worth in its own right
f. be feasible
8. Objectives may be stated at different levels of generality, depending on their role and function in curriculum development.
   a. A general objective should describe outcomes not attainable in less than a week's work, should be broadly representative of essential health behaviors and concepts, and should involve practice of transferable capacities.
   b. General objectives range from simple to complex, depending on the age group for whom they are designed, but must be consistent in form for a given level.
   c. Whether you are developing general or specific objectives, the same criteria defining clearly stated objectives apply.
9. Affective objectives are concerned with hoped-for changes in feelings, interests, attitudes, appreciations, and values.
   a. Cognitive and affective objectives are never separable—some of both kinds of outcomes being implicit in the achievement of each.
   b. Affective behaviors tend to be less measurable than the cognitive.
   c. Desired outcomes of an affective objective are perforce long range, and for this reason, their achievement is difficult to assess.
10. The roles of general objectives differ from those of specific objectives.
    a. General objectives provide a framework of statements that serve as organizing centers for a course or a curriculum plan.
    b. Specific, or enabling, objectives serve as the focus of one or only a few related lessons.
11. General objectives satisfy criteria of greater duration, cruciality, and transference as compared to specific objectives.
12. General objectives can be modified to meet varying levels of student ability by manipulating the complexity of the behavior in connection with the breadth of the subject matter described.
13. Specific objectives should be inferred from the general statement and based upon what is known about the past experience and present abilities of the students for whom they are being proposed.
14. Clearly stated objectives facilitate health teaching in several ways:
    a. providing overall directions for planning sequence and scope
    b. specifying the content and appropriate teaching strategies
    c. serving as the criteria for assessment of teaching-learning outcomes

QUESTIONS AND EXERCISES

Questions

1. What is the difference between the psychomotor and the action domain of health education goals? Why is it not possible to develop instructional objectives for an action domain of goals?
2. What is the relationship between accountability requirements and the need for clearly stated, operational objectives?
3. Compare statements labeled "competencies" as proposed in a given curriculum plan with goals and objectives specified in other curriculums. How are they similar? How are they different?
4. Why is it not possible to write objectives that are totally cognitive or affective in their purpose and outcomes?
5. What are the principal differences in style between an affective objective and a cognitive objective?
6. Differentiate between the role of a general objective and that of a specific objective in curriculum planning.
7. Comment on the following statement: Affective objectives should be discarded when their achievement cannot be measured. Do you agree or disagree? List the reasons why you believe or do not believe that the statement is correct.

Exercises

1. Obtain a current health education curriculum guide structuring a K–12 curriculum. Identify its stated goals and objectives or other system for indicating progressive study of the subject matter. Prepare a written analysis of these curriculum components in terms of their clarity, operationality, ability to communicate purpose, consistency by level (level I being grades K–3, level II being grades 4–6, level III being grades 7–9, and level IV being grades 10–12), and the relevance of any objectives to the stated goals. In the case of objectives, assess their adherence to the criteria for stating functional objectives.
2. Develop an exemplary health education long-range goal for the cognitive, affective, and action domains of outcomes. Next prepare an illustrative, course level objective for both the affective and the cognitive goal. Finally, suggest as many enabling or instruction level objectives as you can that would logically facilitate achievement of each general objective. How many of those that you devise would be objectives that every student would need to accomplish? Which ones might be omitted, depending on the students and even perhaps the

nature of the community or the school? What reasons could justify omitting any particular objective?

3. Compile a list of ten instructional objectives derived from any health education curriculum materials you choose. Evaluate each of them for its acceptability in terms of the role proposed for its application. Rewrite and correct any statement that does not meet all the criteria for operationality or for generality level. Is one problem or weakness encountered more often than others? How many different kinds of problems do you find among the ten objectives?

REFERENCES

American Association for Advancement of Science, *Science, a Process Approach.* Washington, DC: American Association for Advancement of Science, 1969.

Bloom, B. S., Englehart, M. D., Furst, E. J., Hall, W. H., and Krathwohl, D. R., *Taxonomy of Educational Objectives. Handbook I: The Cognitive Domain.* New York: McKay, 1956.

Bloom, B. S., Hastings, J. T., and Madaus, G. F., *Handbook on Formative and Summative Evaluation of Student Learning.* New York: McGraw-Hill, 1971.

Drucker, P. E., *Management. Tasks, Responsibilities, Practices.* New York: Harper & Row, 1974.

Green, L. W., Kreuter, M. W., Deeds, S. G., and Partridge, K. B., *Health Education Planning: A Diagnostic Approach.* Palo Alto, CA.: Mayfield, 1980.

Guilbert, J. J., *Educational Handbook.* Geneva: WHO, 1976.

Koontz, H., and O'Donnell, C., *Principles of Management.* New York: McGraw-Hill, 1972.

Krathwohl, D. R., Bloom, B. S., and Masia, B. B., *Taxonomy of Educational Objectives, Handbook II: Affective Domain.* New York: McKay, 1964.

Mager, R. F., *Preparing Objectives for Programmed Instruction.* Palo Alto, CA: Fearon, 1961.

Mager, R. F., *Preparing Instructional Objectives.* Palo Alto, CA: Fearon, 1962.

Melching, W. H., Ammerman, H. L., Whitemore, P. G., and Cox, J. A., *Deriving, Specifying, and Using Instructional Objectives.* Alexandria, VA: Human Resources Research Office (under contract with the Department of the Army), 1966.

National Education Association, Commission on the Reorganization of Secondary Education, *Cardinal Principles of Secondary Education.* Washington, DC: U.S. Bureau of Education Bulletin no. 35, 1918.

O'Donnell, C., "Planning objectives." In *Management. A Book of Readings,* edited by H. Koontz and C. O'Donnell. New York: McGraw-Hill, 1972.

Popham, W. J., *Educational Evaluation.* Englewood Cliffs, NJ: Prentice-Hall, 1975.

Ross, H. S., and Mico, P. R., *Theory and Practice in Health Education.* Palo Alto, CA: Mayfield, 1980.

School Health Education Study, *Health Education, a Conceptual Approach to Curriculum Design*. St. Paul, MN: 3 M, 1967.

Thayer, L., and Beeler, D. D., eds., *Activities and Exercises for Affective Education*. Ypsilanti, MI: Special Interest Group, American Educational Research Association, 1975.

Tyler, R. W., "Assessing educational achievement in the affective domain." *NCME Measurement in Education* 4:3, Spring 1973, pp. 1–8.

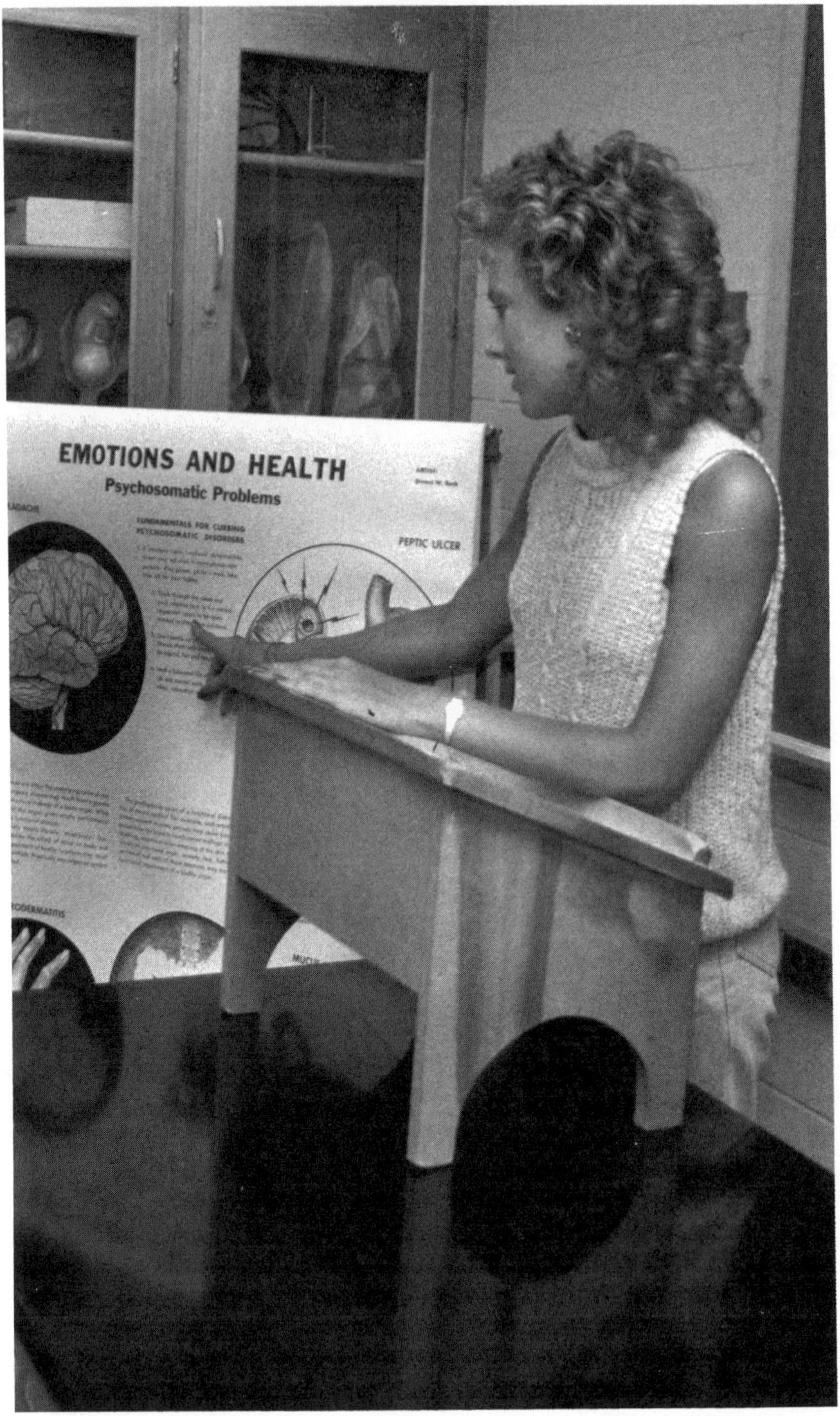
EMOTIONS AND HEALTH
Psychosomatic Problems
FUNDAMENTALS FOR CURBING PSYCHOSOMATIC DISORDERS
PEPTIC ULCER

4
Creating curriculum guides and lesson plans

A fundamental assumption of this book is that *every* health educator needs to know how to plan and carry out educational programs appropriate to the needs of specific target populations. For school health educators, the population of concern includes every youngster in school in every one of the states.

School health educators are first of all teachers, which means that, like any other teacher in the public schools, they must earn a teaching credential. A qualified health teacher is a specialist in the subject matter of health education and must be skilled in all the essential functions of curriculum development (assessing, planning, implementing, and evaluating). Typically, the implementation of a curriculum plan is a school or district responsibility because the outcome of such deliberations affects the total program.

CURRICULUM PLANS

Beauchamp (1975) defines curriculum implementation as the general process of moving from a curriculum plan to instruction. Ideally, the decisions that shape a discipline-specific curriculum design such as for health education are based upon input from many people, including school administrators, supervisors, curriculum and subject matter specialists, community health educators, classroom teachers, and sometimes students. The product of these deliberations is almost always a written document referred to as a *curriculum guide*.

Health education guides are not exclusively the products of schools and teachers. If all the health-related guides, whether categorical (focused on a single health problem such as cardiovascular disease) or comprehensive (addressing the total scope of health instruction), were piled one upon the other, the resulting stack of paper might rival the Eiffel Tower in height. In addition to those prepared by educators, health-related curriculum guides are also being developed and promoted by federal and state educational agencies, local and national voluntary health associations, health-related industries, and professional health education associations. Many guides are put together by corporations whose primary business is curriculum development, often financed by federal grants or contracts.

If there are differences in the philosophy or design of guides that are the products of such widely diverse community-based sources, most of them are the result of unstated assumptions held by their developers. Two are the belief that anybody can put together a workable guide once the subject matter has been identified or, conversely, that subject matter can easily be plugged in, given that a guide has been designed by curriculum specialists.

As an example, in the 1980s, it was proposed that health education should focus on persuading people to change their health behaviors. Hence, "risk reduction" strategies intended to effect these changes in connection with specified health problems were vigorously promoted and supported by federal grants. The assumption here was that all young people need to change the same behaviors. The fact that this was a disease-oriented curriculum plan aside, major health problems affecting the nation do not represent the scope of comprehensive school health education. Curriculum guides built upon such assumptions are necessarily very different in subject matter emphasis and methodology from those whose scope is comprehensive and *health* oriented.

There are probably few guides so poor that a skilled teacher couldn't use them at all. However, neither is there a guide so foolproof that it can make a star performer out of an inept teacher! A curriculum guide developed through the cooperative efforts of those as expert in curriculum development as in the discipline of school health education, that focuses on health promotion, and that is carried out by qualified school health educators probably has the best potential for facilitating the preparations of lesson plans that can be as stimulating as they are effective.

Purposes of curriculum guides

Health education curriculum guides are constructed at differing levels of generality, depending on their purpose. Those developed for statewide or national use usually include at a minimum a recommended list of organizing elements (content areas, health problems, topics, concepts, body systems, etc.), a general plan for sequence, and a set of goals and illustrative objectives. This sort of framework or guide is intended to provide a unifying basis for the construction of more detailed guides by school districts. Content outlines are frequently provided in the form of generalizations or concepts, but suggestions for teaching activities and evaluation are rare. Probably one of the best and most comprehensive state guides is that produced by the State of Connecticut, Board of Education (1982). This document is not limited to scope and sequence but also discusses such topics as the total school health program and curriculum development processes and problems and provides sample evaluation materials as well as an exemplary unit on nutrition.

State and national guides tend to be more alike than they are different. The scope cannot vary beyond the boundaries of the body of knowledge commonly accepted as representative of health education. The choice of organizing element does provide a slightly different approach, but in general, the content is the same. "Content areas" are most often chosen to describe the subject matter units that make up state or local guides, although they may be sequenced differently. In addition, the goals and objectives are often remarkably similar, which can be partially explained by the fact that they are tied to much the same scope. A further unifying force has evolved since the publication of the School Health Education Study's basic document, *Health Education,* and widely distributed scope and sequence chart (School Health Education Study, 1967). The impact of the curriculum design formulated by the SHES writing team continues to be far-reaching and considerable. This assertion is supported by the fact that the book *Health Education: A Conceptual Approach to Curriculum* was that most frequently cited in health education journals between 1970 and 1979 (Price, Newell, and Miller, 1982). Sometimes the indebtedness of a current curriculum to the SHES design is specifically acknowledged, but even when it is not, the derivation is often obvious. For example, here is an objective written by the SHES group, followed by three taken from more recent selected state curriculum guides.

- "Defines heredity and is aware of inherited and acquired characteristics"(School Health Education Study, 1967)
- "Differentiates between traits that are inherited and acquired" (1978)
- "Compares acquired and inherited personal characteristics" (1981)

- "Defines heredity and distinguishes between inherited and acquired characteristics" (1982)

Developing curriculum guides for classroom implementation

Every health educator needs to know something about curriculum design for several very good reasons. First, because he or she is very apt to be asked to assist, either as a consultant or participant, in the development of health curriculum materials at some level of education. Second, anyone responsible for recommending adoption of a guide to be used in teaching children what they need to know about health needs to be able to identify the best among those available.

How do you choose the best and most useful among them? First, you examine the document to see if all the essential characteristics are included and nicely developed. Second, you analyze the logic of its organization and development. For example, does the subject matter expand, and is it faithful to the content dimension of the objectives? Are the suggested learning opportunities clearly designed to provide practice in the behavior specified in the objectives? Is there a sequence explicit in the plan that builds to the achievement of its goals? Third, you read the directions and suggested activities to see if the explanations are clear without being rigidly prescriptive. Finally, you assess the potential contribution of its goals and objectives to the achievement of those defined by the school or district with which you are working. Knowing how to discover the answers to those questions is as useful in developing an effective guide as it is in evaluating one prepared by others.

CURRICULUM UNITS

The development of a curriculum guide that attempts to cover the total scope of health education is not just time-consuming but ends in a product of considerable bulk if it is to be useful. There probably is no easy solution to the time-cost problem short of assembling a guide from bits and pieces borrowed from other guides (the patchwork quilt curriculum design). The second problem is usually solved by treating each of the organizing elements that makes up the scope as a separate unit or guide in itself. In any case, the processes involved are the same for the parts as for the total plan. A major advantage of the unit approach is that each area is more apt to receive equal time and attention when it is developed independently. The major potential disadvantage is the danger that the curriculum can become a set of minicourses designed by different people. Care must be taken that the long-range goals of the total program be kept in mind by all of those given responsibility for preparing any unit. Each guide has to provide planned linkages between the concepts it explores and those that precede and follow it.

Elements of a functional curriculum unit

Suppose you were asked to work with a group of educators to develop a series of teaching-learning guides keyed to each of the organizing elements comprising the scope of the instructional curriculum. How much specific direction is essential, and how much freedom in making plans could you leave to the creativity and expertise of the teacher? Or to put it another way, what needs to be included and what can safely be left out? The suggestions that follow might be helpful as you begin your work. Guides that are intended for use by teachers in planning their lessons typically include at least the following elements:

1. overview or explanation of the rationale underlying the instructional plan to be presented, and instructions for its use
2. stated long-range goals and unit-specific objectives appropriate to the needs and interests of the students for whom the guide is designed
3. general description of the subject matter essential to the achievement of those objectives
4. series of learning opportunities derived from the objectives and providing an array of suggested activities that might contribute to their achievement
5. feasible schemes for evaluating the success of the learning opportunities and appraising the effectiveness and validity of the guide itself
6. list of suggested resources and materials available to the teacher as aids in teaching

Unit overview Ideally, the overview includes data supporting the need for that unit of study at the specified grade or level of instruction. These data ought to reflect pertinent, up-to-date research findings; incorporate significant statements made by school health education authorities, recommendations made by health education professional groups, and state and national curriculum guides; include morbidity and mortality statistics as relevant; and list related needs and interests determined through local studies of students and the community in which they live. In addition, the overview should explain how to use the guide and give a brief description of the approaches that will be suggested as means of attaining the objectives.

Comprehensive overviews such as this are too long for reproduction here. At the other extreme, many guides either have none at all or one limited to the briefest announcement of the subject matter to be studied.

118 Planning and Implementing Health Education in Schools

For example, here is a one-sentence statement labeled "Overview":"The purpose of this Nutrition Education Curriculum is to teach the principles of good nutrition in school in order to help students develop the proper eating habits and nutrition awareness essential for a healthy life." The statement is straightforward and concise, but it is completely teacher-oriented and prescriptive rather than focused on descriptions of those for whom the unit is really designed. We don't know anything about the learners for whom the unit is intended, except for some unstated assumptions: first, that they don't now know the principles of good nutrition and, second, that if one knows the principles of good nutrition, proper eating habits will result.

What is your opinion of the following, more complete statement? What would you add to it, if anything?

> At all levels and ages, prevention is the primary objective of education in substance use and abuse. Programs should include effective educational strategies that stress the concept of individual responsibility for the daily decisions that affect health.
>
> Cigarette smoking is a crucial school health issue. In recent years, children have begun to smoke at even earlier ages, and there have been dramatic increases in smoking among teenage girls. Smoking has been identified as the cause of most cases of lung cancer and as a major factor increasing the risk of heart attack. Cigarette smoking, therefore, is the single most preventable cause of death. Every effort should be made to deter the onset of smoking among children and adolescents.
>
> There is no question that drug misuse is a national problem, although reliable information on the extent of use is difficult to obtain. Alcohol and drug misuse exact a substantial toll of preventable deaths, illnesses, and disabilities. The misuse of these substances not only increases the risk of accidents, suicides, and homicides, but also contributes to family problems as well as poor school and job performance. Substance misuse can lead to long-term chronic disease. Since 1962, drug experimentation and frequency of use have increased greatly. Successful education may be one way to combat this trend. (State of Connecticut, Board of Education, 1982)

As a test of an overview, ask yourself after you have read it if you are persuaded that the unit is justified as part of a health education curriculum and whether you would have any questions regarding its use before you could work with it comfortably. The test of a functional overview is its ability to satisfy the reader's need to know (1) how the unit is justified as a part of a health instructional program designed to meet the needs of a given age group of students and (2) how the guide is to be used to facilitate lesson planning that might help the students satisfy those needs.

Goals and objectives If you believe that health education is concerned with more than simply transmitting information, then you must define your goals accordingly. Most certainly there must be cognitive goals, but affective goals and action goals need to be identified and sought just as vigorously. These kinds of long-range purposes of health instruction might be described as what it is hoped that the learner will know, believe, and do about health and health behavior as a consequence of instruction.

Goals are established at the institutional level of instruction and represent the desired outcomes of the total health education curriculum, K–12. Because they are long range in purpose, they remain constant for each unit and grade and provide a common referent for classroom planning. It is not intended that they be considered the specific focus of every lesson or that their achievement can be evaluated in a classroom situation. Both the behavior and the subject matter described in goal statements are therefore stated in very broad terms. Examples of each domain or category of goal follow:

- Cognitive: The student knows that there are inescapable interrelationships among the physical, mental, and social aspects of growing and developing and that a change in one affects the others.
- Affective: The student respects himself and his fellows [sic] as individuals, alike in some ways, yet possessing unique capabilities and able to make a special contribution to the well-being of the community.
- Action: The student chooses alternatives in behavior that tend to promote rather than hinder his [sic] own growth and development. (School Health Education Study, 1969, p. 10)

The role of an instructional objective in the development of a curriculum guide or unit should be to serve as an organizing center for the development of either a learning opportunity or a lesson plan. Such an objective has to be stated so clearly that any teacher reading it could devise a means of implementing it. Even though the plans that a dozen individual teachers worked out for any particular objective were very different in methodology, the outcome in every class ought to be just about the same. Why should that be true?

General objectives can be stated just as clearly and measurably as the more specific, enabling objectives. And they afford the curriculum unit developer both a unifying and an economical means of structuring study of the topic of interest. (See chapter 3 for detailed discussion of the purpose and form of the general versus the enabling objective.) Classroom teachers are expected to translate the purposes of the broader curriculum objectives into a set of enabling objectives appropriate to the needs of their own students. In order to do this, a teacher first has to determine what his or her own students need to know and be able to do before they can be expected to show that they have mastered the broader, curriculum level objective.

The teaching-learning plans, or *learning opportunities,* proposed as ways to implement general objectives are just as broadly designed. The number of lessons required for their achievement varies according to the plan and the level of readiness among a given group of students. For example, a learning opportunity might suggest a term project, the completion of which would involve working with it for weeks.

Achievement of general objectives requires more or less time, depending on the entering knowledge and skills of the students concerned. Enabling objectives are usually designed as means to accomplish the broader purpose and are short term and achievable within one or two class meetings.

Examples of unit level objectives along with some possible enabling objectives a teacher might employ as a means of preparing his or her class for the larger purpose follow:

1. *General Objective:* evaluates the relationships among physical, social, and intellectual aspects of growth and development
   Enabling Objectives:
   a. defines the meanings of "growth" and "development"
   b. classifies behaviors as indicators of physical, social, or mental growth and development
   c. analyzes ways physical growth influences social and mental growth and development
   d. explains how a balance among the three major aspects of growth enhances developmental well-being
II. *General Objective:* describes factors influencing diet choices and food preferences
   Enabling Objectives
   a. identifies family, cultural, and other sources of personal food preferences
   b. describes social situations that influence the amount and kinds of foods eaten
   c. compares diets and food selection patterns at different ages and in relation to differing activities
   d. analyzes physical, social, and emotional aspects of appetite and hunger as motivators of eating patterns

No one can prescribe a set of curriculum level objectives that every child in this country needs to master. There are too many differences in community and student needs and interests to make that either feasible or logical. But that does not mean that it is sensible to try to construct a curriculum guide without the structure that thoughtfully designed goals and objectives can provide. If you find a guide that seems to have managed without them, you will also find a guide that lacks coherence or direction; or you will find that whatever direction the guide takes is the result of objectives that are implicit in the plans, even if unrecognized by the authors. The problem then is that, without guidelines, the outcome is far less likely to be comprehensive or even health education.

Content outline In constructing the content dimension of a guide, you need to describe the key ideas or subject matter that is to be explored relative to each of the general objectives that structure the unit. It need not and should not be comprehensive, for just as in the case of the enabling objectives, it is the teacher who decides what specific content is needed for each lesson. The guide should include just enough to be sure that the teacher is given a clear description of the breadth and limitations of the essential content, but never so much as to be wearisome. The content provided for the teacher should expand upon, but not go beyond, that defined by the objective. It can be presented as a set of concepts or big ideas, as a series of powerful generalizations, or in typical outline form.

The *California State Health Instruction Framework* (1978) develops the content for each of the ten content areas in the form of concepts. For the area of community health, these are the concepts proposed for study from preschool through young adult years.

1. Community health resources. Community health resources are necessary to protect and promote individual, family, and community health.
2. Shared responsibility. The health of the community is a shared responsibility of the individual, the family, and the community.
3. Health planning. Cooperative health planning enhances the health of the people and reduces unnecessary expenditures of human and material resources.
4. Health careers. A wide range of opportunities exists for careers in health.

Curriculum guides directly designed for teacher use give greater attention to the content related to each of the general objectives. For example, here are ten generalizations that have been used to spell out the content that matches a general objective. The objective is *analyzing forces motivating personal health decisions*.

1. Stress, strain, tension, anxiety, and pressure are forces that control, persuade, or influence a person making a decision about his own health.

2. One or more forces influence one's decisions about body care, general appearance, nutrition, rest, relaxation, and exercise.
3. An individual's goals reflect his needs and wants and are considered when making good personal health decisions.
4. Personal health decisions are governed by daily patterns (e.g., smoking, eating habits), self-motivation, and an ability to control emotions.
5. *Family forces* (e.g., lifestyle and tradition, parental authority, marital strain, sibling rivalry) shape an individual's first impressions and attitudes, equip him with decision making skills, and guide his physical, emotional, and social development.
6. *Peer pressure* (e.g., fad behavior, impressing friends, gang activities) encourage positive or negative attitudes and behaviors according to group standards.
7. *School and authoritative forces* add dimension and foresight into formulating practical and useful decisions regarding personal health.
8. *Mass media forces* (e.g., advertisement appeals, violent television programs, newspaper editorials) provide a variety of perceptual experiences but often influence the individual subconsciously.
9. *Disease, illness, and accident forces* cause specific immediate responses which stimulate the formation of different actions and behavior.
10. *Technological advances* (e.g., new medical equipment, nuclear power plants, birth control devices) influence personal health decisions. (Developed by Diana Monroe and Marilyn Carter, Health Science 440, California State University, Long Beach, 1975.)

The School Health Education Study guides outline the content material. In relation to the objective "Identifies principles of community organization used in the solution of health problems," the following fragment illustrates the format that was followed:

3. The specific design for achieving community organization varies according to the level of community involved (e.g., family, neighborhood, local, state, nation, world). However, certain principles used in the solution of health problems are common to any community.
   a. A need for change must be perceived by the people who will be most affected.
   b. Change must begin with the people as they are and the community as it is. Acknowledged problems, as well as existing problems of which the public is not aware, must be considered.
   c. Programs for change must recognize existing community beliefs and customs and integrate the desired action as much as possible within that structure.
   d. Planning and carrying out programs must be allotted adequate time.

(1) Active involvement of interested, representative, and capable individuals and groups is essential for effective action.
(2) Too fast or overvigorous approaches can result in resistance to change.
e. Consultants or specialists should be involved to aid in solving problems beyond the abilities of the community team. (School Health Education Study, 1970, p. 32)

Learning opportunities A learning opportunity is to a lesson plan as a general objective is to an enabling objective. The learning opportunity is typically broadly described, requiring several lesson plans at least. Two benefits justify the use of learning opportunities as a means of structuring the study of unit objectives. First, a learning opportunity takes less space to describe and can be explained with less detail than lesson plans. Second, as a consequence, the teacher can consider an array of good ideas, no one of which is required and all of which can be modified as desired. The learning opportunity simply suggests some ways that the general objective could be implemented. Whether it is used as is, changed to meet class needs, or rejected is the instructor's decision.

Creating and clearly explaining teaching plans in a few words isn't easy. There are other challenges, too. It is not enough that the suggested activity be related to the content in general; it must be unarguably relevant to the objective it is supposed to be implementing. Remember that the fundamental assumption of a learning opportunity must be that *the student does not now know the subject matter defined by the objective and therefore cannot work with it, whatever the specified cognitive skill*. If the proposed activity could not be attempted unless the student already knew the information and could use the skill competently in dealing with it, then what you have is an evaluation activity, not a learning opportunity.

Most curriculum guides developed for teacher use list objectives and often also some suggested learning opportunities. Guides intended for use by elementary teachers tend to be more detailed and prescriptive than those for high school instruction. This may reflect the belief that health education at the secondary level will be taught by specialists who need less direction than the generalist elementary teacher. This is true in some school districts, but not in all of them by any means. And the policy governing teaching assignments keeps changing, sometimes faster than the guides, which is to say that not every teacher assigned to teach a health course is a school health educator.

Depending on the experience and philosophy of those charged with developing a curriculum guide, what is presented under the heading "learning opportunity" can vary widely. Typically, procedures or ideas labeled "learning opportunity" in such guides are either too short or too detailed, and their relevance to the objective depends more on hope than on design. For example, a guide from a school district in Southern California offers the following ideas in connection with the associated objectives:

1. Identifies the cause of dental caries and disease of the gums. (Demonstrate production of acid by microorganisms of the mouth using acid indicator and have student demonstrate and discuss proper dental prophylaxis.)
2. Lists skin defects and problems. (The student writes on how they overcome skin blemishes and problems anonymously [sic]. The teacher may read some of these to the class and discuss them with the class. Note: The teacher can add comments on the hormonal changes taking place in adolescence and how this is only a temporary phase everyone goes through.)
3. Identifies the basic cause of heart disease. (Have a physician come to class [or tape a physician's talk and play the tape to the class] to talk about cardio-vascular diseases. Select a group of students to visit a large medical center to especially see coronary and intensive care units. Have students learn to take pulse, use a stethoscope and appreciate and understand its use by physicians. Have students learn to use a sphygmomanometer.)

How many of these suggestions allow the student practice appropriate to the objective in terms of the subject matter or the skill?

Notice how often suggestions for learning opportunities begin with "have," an overworked word in curriculum guides second only to "discuss." What does it mean to you as a suggestion for teaching? Does it mean "ask them to. . . . " or "Arrange for them to. . . ."? Does it always mean the same thing, or does it mean different things, depending on the rest of the statement, as in "Have (invite?) a physician come to class"? If you use "have" as the word that introduces a teaching plan, be sure you tell the reader what you mean when you say that. What will the learners be doing when the teachers are "having" them do whatever the activity suggests?

Consider another series of instructional objectives and related learning opportunities suggested for high school health teaching.

1. Understand that dietary inadequacies in early periods of life contribute to permanent physical and mental defects. (Develop a testimonial for news letter, TV, radio stations, public display, school cafeterias on importance of good nutrition for life.)
2. Recognize that health problems may occur which require that certain foods be avoided or added to the diet. (Invite a physician, a dietitian, or another appropriate professional to discuss nutrition-related health problems of adolescents.)

3. Examine personal eating behavior and analyze nutritional adequacy of his/her own diet. (Examine case studies illustrating how life style, characteristics, emotional problems, money or time management, health problems, popular fads, role models, etc. may contribute a barrier to good nutrition. Offer suggestions to overcome these barriers.)

The COIK fallacy

Would those learning opportunities be helpful as described? If you were asked to design a set of lessons with only those objectives and the above suggestions, what else would you need to know? Where does one find case studies like those referred to in the last plan? What "other suggestions" did the author have in mind? Is it clear how the listed factors "contribute" a barrier to good nutrition? If the reader has to ask questions like these, the chances are that the guide will end up in a drawer. Edgar Dale (1972) terms the kind of directions that leave the reader as puzzled as this the COIK fallacy. The letters stand for "Clear Only If Known." Ask yourself what is the very least a teacher needs to know in order to make suggested activities work in the classroom. Remember that he or she will have to make do with what the learning opportunity says. The writer of the plan will not be there to clarify what is not adequately explained.

There is no sure recipe for preparing the perfectly described learning opportunity. There are some things to do that should make them better than those above, however. First, describe the suggested activity as fully as you think is necessary when it must stand alone. Then take out every nonessential word. If your first version was complete and clearly described, what is left ought to be just about right.

The plans that follow depend upon the assumption that earlier learning experiences have prepared students to work with the concepts and apply the behavior specified in the objective. The purpose here is simply to illustrate how much the addition of more detail helps to communicate a plan to those expected to carry it out. Type 1 is the kind of one-line description often seen in guides that doesn't add much to the information provided by the objective. Type 2 provides more specifics yet without being overly prescriptive.

Objective: *Explains the interrelationships among physical, mental-emotional, social, and spiritual dimensions of health.*

Learning Opportunity Type 1: Discuss ways each dimension of health affects and is affected by the quality of the others.

Learning Opportunity Type 2: Using a circular sketch on chalkboard or transparency, illustrate and explain how the effect of one dimension is linked to that of the others (for example, how a physical handicap or temporary health problem like acne, a cold, or an injury have social and emotional effects; how peer group relationships, family harmony, or other social situations can affect mental, physical, or spiritual well-being; how unrelieved stress, social rejection, or personality disorders can cause both short-term and chronic illnesses of many kinds; and how meditation can be used to diminish tension and enhance social and emotional health).

Ask the students to think of ways that positive health behaviors could benefit another dimension of health. Encourage them to describe situations they have experienced or know about that were primarily emotional, social, or physical problems but had an impact on the other dimensions of well-being. Suggest that they speculate about ways that a given action could have a positive or negative effect on other aspects of health. Ask questions like the following: "How might a physical handicap be compensated for by a person's growth in social poise or intellectual ability?" "In what ways do balanced patterns of sleep, rest, and activity contribute to total health?" "What would be the social and physical benefits of using stress-reducing techniques effectively?"

As a means of culminating the activity, ask the students to write and hand in the next day a paragraph or two explaining ways health-related actions can detract from or enhance all dimensions of well-being.

Evaluation activity The fundamental assumption of an evaluation activity is that the *learner knows the subject matter defined by the objective and has learned to deal with it competently, employing the specified cognitive skill*. Hence, students must be given a task that requires them to show that they can do what they were supposed to have learned to do.

One way to evaluate the success of the above learning opportunity in teaching students how to explain those interrelationships would be to arrange for small group dramatizations. Randomly assign single dimensions of health to two or three students. Ask each group to identify a health problem that might affect that dimension of well-being and then to plan a short skit explaining ways positive actions in other dimensions might prevent or control that problem. As each group presents its skit, encourage the others to comment on the accuracy and quality of the suggested actions.

Whatever the suggested activity, it should be as clearly described as was the learning opportunity. The focus should be on application, not recitation, and on problem-solving and health-promoting actions rather than on facts about causes of diseases or their treatment. Some criteria for appraising the product of the activity ought to be included. Otherwise it is not evaluation but only a plan requiring the learners to carry out an assignment. Fuller discussion of evaluation and measurement techniques will be provided in chapters 7 and 8.

Resources and materials The final section of a curriculum guide often details recommended textbooks, references, and articles in professional or popular periodicals; audiovisual aids; prepared transparencies; pamphlets; films; audiotapes; charts; posters; and other effective and easily obtained teaching materials. In a curriculum unit intended for teachers, what is included may be limited to that specifically related to the learning opportunities that have been suggested. Guides intended for statewide or national use tend to be more extensive in anticipation of the differing needs and interests that will exist across the country and because the wider the range of comparable resources described, the greater the chance that some will be available to any one community. However extensive the list, the materials should be cataloged separately as either teacher or student oriented and by kind (books, articles, pamphlets, films, etc.). Bibliographical data should be complete and enough information provided so that a teacher would be able to obtain any material not readily available at school.

Keeping this section current is always a problem. A teacher needs to add new titles to those listed in the latest school guide as soon as they can be approved for school health instruction or for a specific group of students.

LESSON PLANS

The objectives and learning opportunities that structure a curriculum guide tend to focus on instructional ends, whereas lessons are concerned with instructional *means* to those ends. A guide is just a lot of words printed on a lot of paper unless someone has the ability to translate those words into action. It takes the classroom teacher's special skills and insight to bring it to life.

Essential as teacher input is to the development of a curriculum framework or unit, the actual number of teachers who take part is small. Even in a school district large enough to justify construction of its own guide, only a few of the teachers who will use it are ever involved. At the state level, the number of teachers who participate in curriculum decision making is even smaller proportionate to the total number active in a given subject area.

Lesson planning is the teacher's primary and most significant role in curriculum implementation. Every day, for every class, there must be a teaching-learning plan. That plan can be devised only by the teacher who is to carry it out with a given group of students. No one else knows the capabilities and needs of those students so well. Other teachers may suggest broadly described learning opportunities, but only the classroom teacher can make the specific day-to-day plans necessary for achieving that larger purpose. An effective plan reflects answers to the following questions:

1. What does the learner need to know in order to achieve the curricular objective?
2. What should the learner be able to do as the outcome of the activity?
3. What will this lesson contribute to the achievement of the curricular objective?

Process versus content-oriented plans

In planning a lesson, choose teaching techniques for their potential for involving the learner intellectually, emotionally, sometimes even physically. Teaching should be *process* as well as *content* oriented. First, let us define these two terms. "Content," as perceived by curriculum specialists, has been defined as the totality of information that comprises the learning material for a particular course or a given grade. "Process" is a generalized term referring to all the intellectual operations associated with generating, organizing, and using information.

Where the emphasis in teaching is placed upon process, the acquisition of information is a goal, but the *way* it is acquired and used thereafter is part of it. Knowing something isn't very useful without knowing what it is good for. In process-focused teaching, content is not limited to subject matter but includes process itself as a system for learning and thinking. The subject matter is not changed in any way, only the way the learner works with it. The kind of cognitive skill called for in the learning activity tends to be more complex, and in most cases, learning is a lot more fun. Even more important, learning how to think and make reasoned choices among alternative solutions transfers to any problem, any time, anywhere.

The process model for learning situations consists of three major interacting operations: *intake, manipulation,* and *application*. Intake has to do with the purposeful provision of the new information indicated in the instructional objective. This process is necessarily linked to the senses, so the techniques that facilitate intake are those that involve listening, reading, observing, handling, tasting, or smelling. Manipulation processes are those that require the learners to work with new information in ways that allow them to understand it better and to organize it for future use. Behaviors such as comparing, categorizing, interpreting, and conceptualizing are data-manipulating cognitive skills. Application involves the deliberate use of the material in solving problems and testing such solutions in terms of their consequences. It is the purpose of a lesson plan to sketch the means by which these three operations will be carried out relative to a given enabling objective.

A process-oriented lesson plan avoids the temptation to focus solely upon the simplest or lowest level of cognitive skills. At the same time, it promotes desired affective outcomes because the students use the information in dealing with problems that are not just real, but significant in their own lives. The end product of process-oriented teaching is increased ability to solve human, health-related problems and not merely the acquisition of soon-forgotten facts about health and disease.

The Bloom taxonomy of educational objectives (Bloom et al., 1956) identified six categories of cognitive skills (knowing, comprehending, applying, analyzing, synthesizing, and evaluating). The lowest level of cognition, knowing, differs from the others (for knowledge about a given subject is fundamental to them all) in that *remembering* is the only process expected of the learner. Remembering bits of information is not the goal of health instruction. Thinking, decision making, and problem solving require higher level, more complex skills such as applying, categorizing, interpreting, synthesizing, evaluating, analyzing, and reorganizing. These kinds of cognitive processes cannot be learned or sharpened by means of lessons limited to memorization reinforced by recitation.

Lesson planning

Lesson planning goes far beyond the selection of techniques or even their effective application. Hunter (1971) says that there are three tasks basic to lesson planning: (1) determination of what is to be learned, (2) determination of what the learner will be doing in order to accomplish the desired learning, and (3) determination of what the teacher will need to do in order to facilitate that accomplishment. The lesson plan that reflects the outcomes of those decisions successfully communicates not just *what* is to be taught or *how* it will be taught, but also *why* it has been taught.

In planning a lesson, the problem is first to define an enabling objective that is feasible (in the sense that it can be achieved within the time frame of a single class session). Then, to work out a plan for the teaching-learning activity that implements its purposes. A number of subproblems related to the instructional objective must be solved in order to do this:

1. What are the key ideas or generalizations that can be inferred from the content dimension of the objective?
2. What is the best way to communicate this new information to the students so that it can be used in the learning situation?
3. How can the lesson be introduced to the students in a realistic and motivating way?
4. Which technique or techniques can best facilitate practicing the specified skill as the learner works with the related information?

5. How can the lesson be concluded in such a way that the students are given an opportunity to demonstrate the quality of their achievement of the objective?

Which of these subproblems is related most directly to intake, which to manipulation, and which to application? Would the solutions to the subproblems be at all different if memorization of specified information were the goal and recitation and lecture were the primary activities? In your own experience, is listening to a lecture the most stimulating and effective means of acquiring new information? Have you ever been dismissed from class merely because the clock indicated that the time was up, not because the lesson had been brought to a purposeful close?

Typically, lesson plans are designed by each teacher for his or her own classes and sketched out for at least a week or to encompass plans for a given unit of study. That series of plans structures instruction and is available to a substitute teacher in the event that the regular teacher must be absent.

Such a block of lesson plans outlines *what* is supposed to be taught (the subject matter) and specifies *when* it is to be taught or scheduled. *Why* or *how* the lesson is to be carried out is usually not spelled out. Experienced teachers have a great number of tested instructional approaches to any given objective filed in their mental data banks. Rather than tie themselves in advance to any specific technique, they are free to select the one that promises to work best on that day, given a set of circumstances that cannot always be known in advance. Yet, if asked to do so, a master teacher has no difficulty explaining why a strategy is being employed and is appropriate in that instance.

Nobody ever began to student teach with a full kit of teaching tools ready to go. The ability to plan a lesson that is as absorbing as it is effective has to be learned. And, like any other skill, it gets better with practice. Student-teachers are required to work out each component of every lesson plan in explicit detail for this reason. Adherence to a format similar to that provided on page 132 is often required.

Constructing a working lesson plan

A lesson plan is in essence a small piece and an essential step toward implementation of a curriculum level learning opportunity. The principal difference between the two is that the lesson plan is delimited by the more narrowly defined enabling objective and describes its plan in greater detail. A completely developed lesson plan would include all or most of the following components:

1. a measurable enabling objective derived from a specified curriculum level objective

2. clues to the subject matter that will be the focus of instruction
3. a plan for introducing the lesson and linking what is to happen to what has been learned in the preceding lesson or lessons (the initiation)
4. a scheme for communicating or facilitating the students' discovery of the information with which they will be working during the lesson
5. a description of the proposed teaching-learning activities
6. a planned application of what has been practiced as a capping and summarizing experience (the culminating activity)
7. a list of things that could easily go wrong, along with well-thought-out coping or preventive measures

Components unique to lesson plans

Of the above seven components, those that are special to a lesson plan are the initiation, the culminating activity, and the anticipated problems. The others are common to learning opportunities and have been discussed earlier.

Initiation Every lesson has some sort of an initiation activity, whether excellent or mediocre. Two things have to be accomplished if an initiation is to be effective. First, the stage has to be set for what is to follow, and in a way that sparks student interest. Next, as evenly as can be arranged, everyone must be ready to pick up where yesterday's lesson ended. The simplest way to do that is to make some announcements: "Today we are going to see a film that presents and explains the new U.S. dietary guidelines. Yesterday, as you remember, we talked about the four food groups and the functions of the basic nutrients." That may also be the dullest way to get a lesson under way.

One way to initiate a lesson that can interest youngsters is to involve them in the action from the start. Let *them* tell you what they learned yesterday. You might find out that yesterday's lesson just didn't work. If it didn't, it's not too late to do something about it. Pose some thought-provoking questions about the food choices they make every day. Ask them what standards, if any, are being applied in deciding what they eat. Before you show the film, give them some points to watch for that will be important in the discussion that will follow.

Culminating activity A good lesson is even better if it ends in a meaningful way. A lesson plan needs a concluding activity that is an integral part of the total scheme for learning. For example, students can be asked to restate what has been learned in their own words. Ask them to write a short paragraph that finishes the sentence "The most important things I learned today were." Give them an assignment that will require the appli-

Model Lesson Plan Format

Instructor _____ Date _____ Unit _____

GENERAL OBJECTIVE _____

Enabling Objective for this lesson: _____

Initiation:

Subject matter outline	Time estimates	Resources to be used	Teaching-learning strategy

Culminating Activity:

Anticipated problems	Possible solutions

cation of what has been learned in a new situation. Ask them to brainstorm ways in which this information and skill can be applied in making choices today and in the future. The strategy employed in a lesson gives its own direction for the culminating activity that fits.

Actually, in some ways, this aspect of the lesson may be the most crucial to the success of the entire plan. The benefits are many. When the information is used in some practical way, learning is reinforced. Instead of leaving the room with relief that the lesson is over, the students find satisfaction is being able to do something useful with what they have learned. They are better able to understand the relationship between health education and the quality of their own lives today and in the future. The instructor finds out whether the teaching-learning activity has been successful in helping the students achieve the objective. If it has, the next steps can be planned with confidence in student readiness. If it has not, the next lesson can be planned in ways to correct that failure.

Anticipated problems Often new teachers and even not so new teachers forget to take account of Murphy's famous law, which predicts that whatever can go wrong *will* go wrong. For every lesson, there are a few things that are crucial to the success of the plan. Therefore, it is sensible to identify these in advance and decide what you will do if things don't work out as intended. Some kinds of problems can be prevented; others cannot and are always a possibility. You need to have alternative strategies in mind for these, just in case. For example, your lesson is built around the presentation of an extremely interesting thirty-minute film. The projector breaks down, the sound won't work, the film doesn't arrive on time, or the take-up reel isn't large enough. How do you handle any one of those dilemmas?

You have asked your students to interview at least five adult smokers in order to find out why they began to smoke and why they now continue smoking despite the warning printed on every package that smoking cigarettes is dangerous to health. You planned that they would break into small groups to pool the information that they had gathered. The conclusions reached in the groups would be shared with the total class as the basis for generalizations about cigarettes and the difficulties involved in quitting smoking. Everything is nicely planned, but the strategy is a failure because few of the students gathered the information as they were asked to do. If the problem had been anticipated, what might have been done to avoid it?

You have arranged for a speaker from a voluntary health agency to talk to your classes in regard to the epidemic of AIDS. The students are very eager to hear this presentation and have spent the last two class meetings putting together a list of questions they would like the speaker to address.

When you get to school the morning of the appointed day, you learn that the speaker has had to cancel out. What could be done in that case?

Experienced teachers learn to keep a sure-fire alternate plan ready for quick substitution if need be. No one can avoid every problem, even if care is taken to plan for those that seem most likely. However, by thinking ahead, you can prevent some of them, and if you're lucky, most of those you anticipate won't happen. But never risk disaster for lack of a little forethought.

A sample lesson plan

It is difficult to develop a single example of a lesson plan in isolation from those that would logically have preceded it. Nevertheless, the following represents an attempt to illustrate how each of the components might be detailed as part of a total plan. It is necessarily based upon two assumptions: first, that previous lessons have explored peer pressure and family preferences as forces influencing consumer health decisions and choices and, second, that these students have agreed to find and bring to class two full-page magazine advertisements promoting some personal health care product. One ad is to be concerned with a product that they have used in the past or are using now, the other with a similar product that they have never used.

General Objective:
describes forces influencing consumer health decisions and choices
Enabling Objective:
evaluates the impact of advertising on selection and use of personal health care products
Content Generalizations:

1. Most advertisements provide useful information about a product, but their primary purpose is to promote its sale.
2. We tend to be most easily influenced by advertising claims for products with which we have had no experience.
3. The wise consumer needs to be able to distinguish between the claims made for a product and the product itself.

Initiation:
Volunteer students will be asked to make short statements summarizing what they have learned about peer pressure and family preferences as forces influencing the choices a person makes among health products. Today's objective will be introduced by means of an exhibit of current advertisements clipped from one issue of a popular teenage-oriented magazine. All

of them will be a full page so that they can be taped together to graphically illustrate the amount of space given to these kinds of ads in such a publication. Students will be asked to speculate about the investment that so much advertising represents and to note how many of the products are already known to them.

Information Input:

A set of prepared transparencies will be used to illustrate typical potential benefits or desirable results promised in advertisements for personal health care products such as shampoos, toothpastes, and skin creams. Students will be helped to analyze each promise or claim critically and to pose significant questions that should be asked (for example: "Is such a benefit sure to follow use of the product?" "Would the outcome be appropriate to the needs of anyone who might buy and use the product?" "Are any of the claims irrelevant to the purposes of such a product?"). Those questions that the group agrees are most significant will be listed on the chalkboard for quick reference during the learning activity.

Activity:

The class will next be divided into small groups of four to five students. Each group is to evaluate the ads brought to class by its members. The procedures will be those as practiced during the intake phase of the lesson. This time they are to look first at the ads that have to do with a product with which they have had actual experience. Next, they are to evaluate the ads that describe products that are new to them. Then each group is to develop a list of claims that they identified in their two sets of ads that seem to be exaggerated, misleading, or irrelevant. In addition, each group will list those statements that can be accepted as probably true and informative. These lists are to be shared with the total class. A class total of the number of items in each of the two lists will be obtained. It is hypothesized that the dubious claims will far outnumber the factually correct statements.

Concluding Activity:

Once these data have been reported and recorded, the students will be encouraged to draw some conclusions based upon what they have discovered. Questions to give this task some direction include: "Did the fact that an advertisement was describing a product that you use have any effect on your view of the truth of its claims?" "If so, did it make you more or less critical of the advertisement?" "Did you find that you are more or less easily influenced by claims about products you have never tried?" "Can you explain why that should be so?" "Based on the analysis of the ads we have worked with today, what would you say is the proportion of factual statements to those intended to beguile the reader into buying a personal health care product?" As a capping activity, each student will be asked to write a paragraph summarizing what the smart consumer ought to know about the influence of advertising on one's choices and use of personal health care products. These are to be done at home and handed in at the beginning of the next class.

Anticipated Problems	Possible Solutions
The overhead projector won't light.	Be sure to have spare light bulb and know how to replace it.
No overhead projector available.	Keep the original drawings of your transparencies available.
The school is temporarily without power.	Use original drawings.
Some students forget to bring ads for evaluation.	Have extra sets of ads ready for distribution to those students.

Admittedly, lesson plans developed in so much detail represent much more thought and work than one-liners such as "Have students discuss the value of information provided by health-related advertisements." Nevertheless, all things considered, it's worth it. Try it. You'll know where you are going and exactly how you're going to get there. Moreover, so will your students. If you are a new teacher, that's a great way to start out. Substitute teachers who find a plan like that waiting for them will love you.

Some dos and don'ts of lesson planning

Not very long ago, the key advice to would-be teachers went something like this: "Tell them what you're going to tell them. Tell them. Then tell them what you told them." Health teaching can't be done that way. If it is to be more than communicating information, it has to be done in ways that interest, stimulate, and motivate students. Whatever the objective, a lesson plan ought to lead the student to *think about* and *apply* what has been learned. There are many things you can do to facilitate that kind of outcome. There are also things you ought not to do. After you've been teaching for a year or so, you'll probably discover some dos and don'ts of your own. Meantime, start with these:

- Plan your lessons so that the focus is on learning how to solve health problems in general, rather than on learning the answers to specific problems as we know them today.
- Make student learning, not demonstration of your teaching skills, the purpose of every lesson.
- Develop plans that are flexible enough to be adaptable to the abilities and experience of every student in your class and to day-to-day emergencies or events needing discussion.
- Make sure that your students understand the purpose of each lesson, as well as its relevance to those that preceded it and are to follow.

- Develop activities that engage as many of the senses as possible. Seeing and hearing have more impact together than seeing or hearing alone. Students learn less by watching an experiment and hearing it explained than by having the hands-on experience of conducting the experiment themselves.
- Choose activities that are clearly and logically related to the instructional objective.
- Plan lessons that motivate thinking and deciding rather than memorizing and reciting.
- Design lessons that can be carried out within the time limitations of a class meeting.
- Don't develop lesson plans that depend upon the assumption that pooled student opinions can be substituted for the provision of reliable information relevant to a meaningful objective. If the students have already learned what they need to know elsewhere, you will be wasting their time with that lesson. If they don't already know it, you will also be wasting their time.
- Don't start your lesson planning by choosing a technique that you like and are skilled at applying. The best technique for a lesson is the one that allows students to practice the skill specified in the objective.
- Don't use novel or faddish activities simply as ends in themselves. Fun and games are entertaining, but unless you have a worthwhile outcome firmly in mind, that is all they will be.
- Above all, don't be afraid to admit you don't know everything there is to know about the subject matter to be covered in the lesson. You won't lose your students' respect. Take advantage of their interest and teach them how to discover the answers for themselves. They will have practiced a skill with lifelong utility, and you will have learned something you didn't know before. Everybody will be satisfied.

SUMMARY

1. Curriculum development is a skill needed by health educators in every setting.
2. Curriculum implementation is the process that ties instruction to planning.
3. Curriculum guides are written documents developed as means of implementing the larger plans.
    a. Health education curriculum guides are either comprehensive or categorical in scope.

b. Such guides are created by educational institutions and by a host of commercial and health-concerned organizations in the private sector.
4. Guides developed for national or statewide use tend to describe the curriculum in broad terms and for several reasons are more alike than different from each other.
5. Health educators must be able to participate effectively in guide development and to evaluate the potential usefulness of packaged curriculum material offered to them.
6. Typically, each major curriculum organizing element is developed in the form of a subguide or curriculum unit of instruction.
7. A functional curriculum unit is characterized by its provision of six major components.
   a. An overview that justifies instruction of the material and sketches the instructional intentions in broad terms is provided.
   b. Goals and Objectives: Long-range goals ordinarily describe expected K–12 outcomes in cognitive, affective, and behavioral or psychomotor domains of learning. Objectives are general rather than specific and represent broad achievements proposed for a given level of instruction.
   c. An indication of relevant content is provided in some form, whether limited to a few key ideas or topics or more broadly defined generalizations or a subject matter outline.
   d. Learning opportunities are suggested for teaching-learning activities for which at least several enabling lessons would be necessary.
   e. Evaluation activities that would allow students to demonstrate achievement of the general objective in a real-life problem-solving situation are described.
   f. A listing of recommended textbooks, references, films, and other related and obtainable teaching materials is provided.
8. Lesson plans focus on instructional means to the ends proposed in curriculum guides. Whereas guides are devised by a wide range of specialists, including teachers, lesson planning is primarily the special responsibility of teachers alone.
9. Lesson plans for health teaching must focus on process (how the content is handled by students), not simply on learning some amount of subject matter.
10. The process model for learning consists of three interacting operations: intake, manipulation, and application.

a. Process-oriented teaching-learning plans necessarily involve the higher level cognitive skills.
   b. Use of higher level cognitive skills leads to lessons that deal with more meaningful and transferable outcomes.
11. Lesson planning requires the solution of several subproblems critical to achievement of its objectives.
12. The principal difference between a learning opportunity and a lesson is that the latter represents but a part of the former and is planned in greater detail.
13. An initiating activity, a culminating activity, and proposed solutions to possible problems that might be encountered in carrying out the plan are special to lesson plans.
14. A lesson plan must interest, stimulate, and motivate students to think about what has been learned and to use it in their daily lives.
15. Attention to some "dos" and "don'ts" of planning lessons can help the new teacher design more effective lessons.

QUESTIONS AND EXERCISES

Questions

1. Why should health educators in every setting know how to plan and implement curricula for health teaching?
2. What are the advantages of developing separate curriculum units as opposed to a guide that encompasses the total scope of health instruction? Are there any disadvantages? All things considered, which design do you recommend? What are your reasons?
3. Explain the essential relationships among long-range goals, general objectives, and enabling objectives as concerned with curriculum guide construction.
4. Compare the assumptions upon which the development of learning opportunities and evaluation activities is based.
5. What is the difference between lessons that are content oriented and those that are process oriented? How does that difference alter what is taught and learned in each approach?
6. Research has shown that new material placed first in a lesson is easiest to learn and that placed last is the next easiest. What does that suggest relative to the importance as well as the content and structure of an initiation and a culminating activity?

140 Planning and Implementing Health Education in Schools

7. Suggest some ways that a teacher could discover how much time would be needed in order to carry out a given lesson plan.
8. What questions would you need to ask if you had to teach a health class with this idea as your only guide: "Have the students compile a list of several factors from the environment that contribute to various forms of disease"? What are the unstated assumptions implicit in that suggestion?

Exercises

1. Obtain a copy of a curriculum guide for analysis of its purpose and format. Is it comprehensive or categorical in scope? Are all the essential characteristics of a guide adequately developed? What are its strengths? Are there any weaknesses or omissions? Would you recommend its adoption and use in health education classes? Defend your recommendations with specific reasons why or why not.
2. Select a learning opportunity as proposed in the guide you have just analyzed. Does it fit the general objective? Does it clearly describe a plan that allows the students to practice the specified behavior? If not, how would you rewrite the plan to make it more appropriate and communicate its intention more clearly?
3. Scan the list of learning opportunities compiled in connection with one objective and identify any that you believe are actually evaluation activities. Justify your point of view.
4. Using the format on page 132, develop and fill in all the components of a working lesson plan. When you have written a rough draft of your plan, go through the copy and delete every word not essential to its clarity and ability to communicate. Test the result by asking a friend to read and react to your shorter version. Revise it as necessary to improve its ability to communicate your plan.
5. For any curriculum organizing element of your choice, propose an enabling objective. Then consider whether you would furnish the data with which the students would work or whether you believe it would be more meaningful if they were helped to discover them for themselves. Then describe a procedure by means of which they would either be given the necessary information or helped to discover it.

REFERENCES

Beauchamp, G., *Curriculum Theory,* 3rd ed. Wilmette, IL: Kagg Press, 1975.
Bloom, B., Englehart, M., Furst, E., Hill, W., and Krathwohl, D., *Taxonomy of Educational Objectives: Cognitive Domain.* New York: McKay, 1956.

California State Health Instruction Framework, Sacramento, CA. State Department of Education, 1978.

Dale, E., *Building a Learning Environment.* Bloomington, IN: Phi Delta Kappa Foundation, 1972.

Hunter, M., "The science of the art of teaching." In *Controversy in Education,* Philadelphia; Saunders, 1971.

Monroe, D., and Carter, M., "Content generalizations derived from an instructional objective." Long Beach, CA. California State University, 1975. (unpublished paper)

Price, J. H., Newell, S., and Miller, P., "Most cited authors and publications in health education journals for 1970–79." *Journal of School Health* 52:10, 1982, pp. 586–591.

School Health Education Study, *Health Education: A Conceptual Approach to Curriculum.* St. Paul, MN: 3 M, 1967.

School Health Education Study, *Concept One: Teaching-Learning Guide, Level IV.* 1969.

School Health Education Study, *Concept Three: Teaching-Learning Guide, Level IV.* 1970.

State of Connecticut, Board of Education, *A Guide to Curriculum Development in Health and Safety.* 1982.

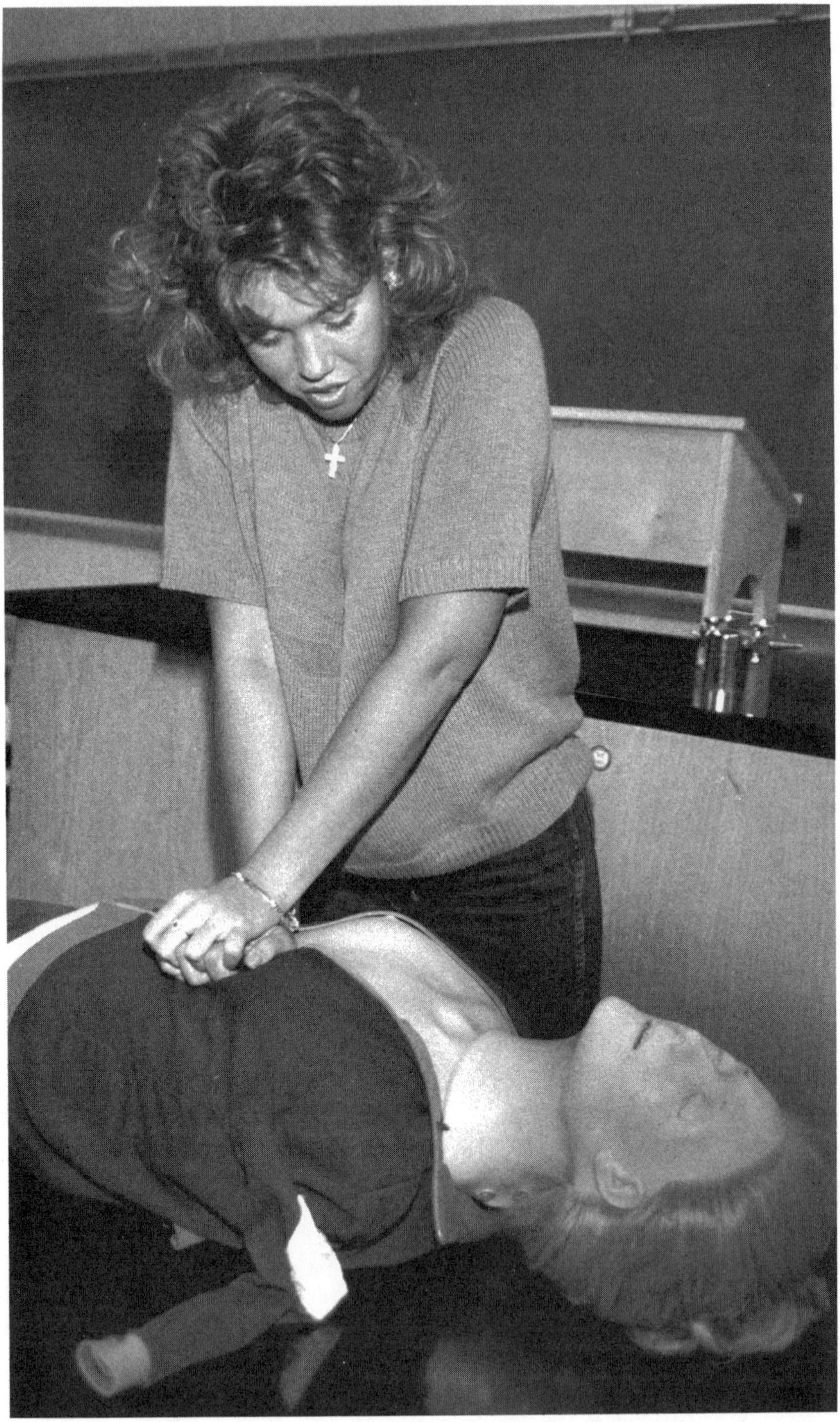

5
Health teaching methods and techniques

If you are the typical college or university upperclass student, you are an expert at judging how well teaching activities work. At least you ought to be; you've been exposed to teaching for sixteen or more years by now. Of course, in all that time, you've been sitting in the audience watching a long parade of individual teachers. Think about the instructors you've observed over the years. Which of them stand out in your memory as the best? What was it about their teaching that makes you remember them so favorably? Was it *what* they taught you or *how* they taught it? Undoubtedly, it was something of both, for it has to be. But the most successful teachers, those who make learning an adventure as well as an outcome, focus much more on process than on content.

What do we mean by "process"? Briefly, the term refers to all the cognitive skills used in dealing with knowledge. Processes involve inquiring, discovering, conceptualizing, applying, theorizing, and more. Where the emphasis is primarily on subject matter, teaching tends to depend upon telling, and learning is typically a passive experience. Where the stress is on process, the approach is active. Student participation is the learning mode. Content becomes the means rather than the primary goal of instruction.

Combs (1981) suggests that two factors in combination have rendered the role of teacher as information provider obsolete. One is the knowledge explosion, which has made it impossible for anyone to know even a fraction of what is available to be known. The other is technological advances such as computers, satellite-assisted television, radio, and other media that have made rapid communication and dissemination of information possible. He says: "Only the process aspects of curriculum meet the criterion 'essential' to prepare youth adequately for the world they will inherit. . . . An educational system unable to predict the knowledge or behaviors demanded by the future will have to concentrate instead on producing persons able to solve problems that cannot presently be foreseen. Tomorrow's citizens must be effective problem solvers, persons able to make good choices, to create solutions on the spot. That is precisely what intelligence is all about. Unable to forecast the future in specific terms, schooling must be directed toward the production of intelligent persons" (Combs, 1981, p. 372).

In the two preceding chapters, we talked about curriculum development and formulating goals and objectives for teaching and learning. But the success of a curriculum depends upon the skills of the teacher who must plan and carry out the lessons that can bring it to life. One of the skills needed by a teacher is the ability to choose the teaching technique or strategy most suited to the practice of a given behavior. Whatever the technique, the criterion of its choice must always be its ability to elicit the behavior specified in the instructional objective. Moreover, it should be the one with potential for doing so most effectively and in the least time.

METHODS VERSUS TECHNIQUES

What's the difference between a method and a technique? A great many people use the two terms interchangeably. Method has been defined as "the formal structure of the sequence of acts commonly denoted by instruction. . . . [It] covers both the strategy and tactics of teaching and involves the choice of what is to be taught at a given time, the means by which it is to be taught, and the order in which it is to be taught" (Broudy, 1963). Clearly, this implies that *method* involves much more than a specific teaching technique. Means (1973) always speaks of "techniques" in connection with specific strategies, whether they are student centered, teacher oriented, or group, dramatic, or material and equipment focused. We believe that the primary methods of health instruction are problem solving and decision making. Accordingly, for the purposes of this chapter, the techniques that will be described are viewed as subordinate to methods. Such activities as lectures, field trips, debates, role playing, buzz sessions, group projects, simulation games, and the like are ways to involve students in their learning. They, along with materials and teaching devices, make up the kit of tools from which the teacher chooses in designing effective learning opportunities.

PROBLEM SOLVING AND DECISION MAKING

Futurists predict that revisions in the basic cognitive skills now taught will be necessary to match shifting societal needs during the next thirty years. Nevertheless, prominent among the skills perceived as vital to those who will live in the twenty-first century are those needed to carry out the scientific method (Dede and Allen, 1981). *Problem solving* is the more common term describing the process.

Problem solving

A problem in this context is not always a *problem* in the negative sense. Everyone alive solves hundreds of problems every day, most of the time so smoothly and easily that it happens without conscious effort. We don't really think of these kinds of ordinary needs as problems, although they may have seemed so at first encounter. Only when we are faced by a need that *cannot* be easily satisfied or by a dilemma for which no good solution is readily apparent do we term it a problem. As employed in teaching, problem solving is an activity that consists of certain logical steps that lead to the discovery of a workable solution. In that context, the outcome is growth in the ability to solve problems in general, as a specific problem is being solved by practicing the method.

Certain steps are considered typical of problem solving:

1. *Defining the problem.* Health problems may be perceived as primarily physical (e.g., hunger, weight control, disease prevention, dental care), social (e.g., adjusting to divorce, choosing friends, improving parent-child relationships), or emotional (e.g., controlling grief, resolving conflicting feelings, building healthy self-esteem). Whichever of the three dimensions of health is primary relative to the selected problem, the inevitable impact of the other two is taken account of as well.

    Problem-solving skills are more effectively practiced when students are working on problems they have themselves identified. In effect, they have said to themselves, "This is something we want to know." Motivation to find a satisfying solution will be far greater than if they are asked to solve a problem posed for them by others.

2. *Theorizing: proposing tentative solutions.* Before we can begin to work on a problem, we have to give some time to formulating a reasonable

theory about it. Otherwise there is no way to delimit the search for necessary information. Even small children are capable of theorizing if they are encouraged to do so. With every age group, some guidance may be needed in order to get the process started or to avoid blind alley searches. Brainstorming is an excellent way to generate ideas that can lead to promising theories. It allows the students to speculate freely in an accepting classroom environment.

3. *Data gathering.* Depending on the maturity and past learning experiences of the students, the information needed to work on the problem may or may not need to be discovered. If it is known, the information may be outdated or inadequate, in which case more study will be needed. As teacher-facilitator, you will need to help the students channel their search to conform to the problem as stated. In any case, the data-collecting process should be careful and orderly rather than haphazard, and the sources of the information collected must be objective, reliable, and as unbiased as humanly possible.

4. *Proposing solutions.* During this step, the student groups the obtained information in various ways and attempts to formulate promising solutions. Guidance during this sort of analyzing activity helps avoid wasting time on unpromising ideas. The outcome is usually more than one possible solution, and the one that seems most likely to be successful is selected for trial.

5. *Verifying the solution.* This can be the last step if the most favored solution works well when it is tried. It should be tested more than once and in as many ways as practical to be sure of its reliability. In the event that what seemed to be the most likely solution fails, the next best choice is tested, and if necessary another, until the problem is solved.

Actually, the problem-solving method doesn't always proceed so neatly, nor do its steps occur in that exact order. A problem may not need to be defined; it may simply emerge during the process of working on another. It may also arise as an outcome of information gathering. Creative thinking is typically unstructured, even wild. There are often intuitive leaps from problem to solution without any need for data gathering. Theories are really solutions stated first, instead of last. The purpose of data gathering in that event is to support the theory rather than to solve the problem. Sometimes none of the theories works, and the whole process has to be repeated, starting with step one. Nevertheless, the scientific method can be depended upon at every level of need. Once mastered it can be applied for life.

Decision making

Decision making is an innate human behavior. It has been defined for health education as "a process unique to man of consciously deciding to take or not take an action, or of choosing one alternative rather than another" (School Health Education Study, 1967, p. 16). Everybody, everywhere, every day makes hundreds of decisions. Very few of them are made as a consequence of the problem-solving steps just described. Practically speaking, it must be so. Think how much time would be spent if every decision needed to be so carefully explored before any action could be taken. Fortunately, most problems can be solved easily. Yet it must not be forgotten that every decision you make has an impact on health in some way.

The problem-solving method should not be confused with problem solving, however. The scientific method represents a skill, and skills must be learned. Application of that skill dependably gets at feasible ways to solve a problem that is new or for which the answers are outside the present experience of the investigator. The problem-solving method is structured, deliberate, typically a one-time need and end in itself. Decision making that occurs during the several steps is conscious, data based, and intended to be objective.

Problem solving, however, is happening every time a decision is made. The difference is that decision making in that case is ordinarily based upon existing knowledge, beliefs, and values. *Knowledge* as it relates to decision making is defined as a body of facts (gathered by means of observation, other persons, and books) that are accepted as truth. *Beliefs* can be a reflection of knowledge but also often reflect a mix of superstition, wishful thinking, misinformation, and bias. *Values* reflect preferences or standards by which behaviors, objects, or qualities are judged as being worthy or desirable.

Almost all problem solving is influenced by these three variables. Although a specific choice may be more heavily influenced by one of them, the other two are always an influence as well. An exception to this rule is the occasional decision based entirely on impulse. This sometimes results in the kind of action often explained by statements such as "I don't know what made me do that!" We do a lot of impulse buying of products that affect health. Actions motivated by problem-solving decisions are life-style indicators; thus, they describe and in some ways prescribe the quality of an individual's life.

A major goal of health education is to encourage the learner to develop the ability to make responsible and informed decisions that motivate the kinds of actions that make up a healthful life-style. The assumption often has been that if students are given information about health problems along with some good solutions, sound decision making when it is needed will occur. It doesn't work. If you want them to learn how to solve problems and make reasoned decisions, they need to practice solving problems and making decisions. Nothing else will do. Moreover, research indicates that once a decision has been made, there is a tendency for the individual to seek out information that supports the rightness of that choice (Festinger, 1957, p. 50). If this is so, then growth in ability to make difficult decisions also increases interest in discovering new information.

Young people need to become sensitive to the impact of today's decisions on tomorrow's well-being and level of achievement. Health education is the discipline best qualified to help them discover how much control they can have over their lives if they will use it. Problem-solving and decision-making skills are the keys.

DATA SOURCES FOR PLANNING TEACHING ACTIVITIES

Designing a plan for teaching involves a lot more than choosing a suitable technique. Study of the sources of the curriculum is just as important at the classroom level as at the institutional level. Students in every school are different in some ways from those in all others.

Perhaps the first thing to do, and also the simplest inasmuch as the information is quickly available, is to study the curriculum guides and policies established by your school or district. Examine the curriculum plan recommended by your state health education authorities. Any mandates affecting health content will be reflected in its scope. Your teaching plans can take their first cue from any such state level guidelines.

Next, think about the individuals in your classes. Instruction has to begin with the students as they are if it is to meet their needs and interests. Have all the students or only some of them mastered the processes that will be required? Will there need to be some activities that prepare them for the major tasks? What prior knowledge do your students have about the subject matter with which they are expected to work? Ask your students what they would *like* to learn about health and health practices. A good way to find out what your students know, believe, and do in regard to health behavior is to spend some time in pretesting. Let your students score the tests and analyze the results. After class discussion of the results reported by the scoring group, invite them to decide for themselves what the course ought to include and what should be emphasized. Their interest will be captured before you start.

Standardized knowledge, attitude, and behavior inventories can be purchased for testing of this nature (Solleder, 1979). Advantages of using published tests is that their validity and reliability have been established, and norms are available. This allows comparisons between class scores and score averages obtained through wide application of those instruments. Teacher-made tests can also be used if their content validity can be demonstrated, and the vocabulary is appropriate to age group reading experience.

What are the cultural and socioeconomic characteristics of the students in your classes? Don't make plans based on your assumptions about their values or their past experiences. For example, the ghetto youngster tends to learn less from what is heard than what is seen or touched. Which would be the more effective strategy for teaching in that case, lecture or experiential activities? Listening skills can't be taken for granted, especially among urban students who have learned to cope with noise pollution by shutting out unwanted sound. You might find that you are a source of unwanted sound yourself. The youngster whose knowledge of hunger is real will be difficult to interest with lessons that speak of future rewards as related to food selection or any other health behavior beyond his or her control. For some students, lessons may better focus on the immediate and concrete. Instruction may need to be structured as short, developmental steps with prompt reinforcement or rewards. In the same group, however, more advanced learners must be freed to range beyond planned activities whenever this is appropriate. Adaptive measures like these have to be done in such a way that the groupings are perceived as based upon different problems rather than different abilities.

For all children (but particularly among those who are disadvantaged in any way), low self-esteem may make them distrust their own judgment and conclusions. Task setting during the first week of classes ought to be planned so that success is nearly inevitable. Success breeds self-esteem, and self-esteem promotes the kind of confidence that allows the learner to risk failure and try new ways of doing and thinking. Confidence flourishes in a classroom where failure is viewed as a learning experience, and risk taking of this sort is perceived as fun.

The time required to learn certain skills varies among students, too. They learn and develop intellectually, as in all ways, not only at their own rates but also in their own styles.

Students spend much more of their time in a community setting than in a school. Consult public health and other community health authorities, and find out what local needs and problems have implications for your teaching plans. How might health education experiences affect the lives of the students and, through them, the community itself?

Find out what kinds and sources of health teaching aids are available to you within the school and in the community. In-school sources include *places,* such as school and district audiovisual centers and libraries, and *people,* such as the school nurse, physician, librarian, dietician, teachers, students, and the school health council. Two kinds of groups are unique in that they represent both the school *and* the community: the Parent Teacher Association and the various youth groups (Boy Scouts, Girl Scouts, Four-H Clubs, Campfire Girls, and others).

Community sources include voluntary health agencies, public health agencies, service clubs, professional health care organizations, individual professionals, private industry, and the community health council—all of them willing allies of the teacher. In fact, the range of community resources available to provide you with teaching aids is of a richness and quality almost beyond belief. You have only to ask.

CRITERIA FOR SELECTING TEACHING TECHNIQUES

Tyler (1950) proposed five principles to be considered when selecting a teaching-learning technique. First, it must give the students an opportunity to practice the cognitive skills specified in the objective. It must also arrange for the discovery or introduction of the content defined in the same statement. Second, the activities must be satisfying in themselves. Third, the activities must be appropriately matched to the learners' abilities and past experience. Fourth, because there are many possible solutions to the problem of choosing an effective technique, a teacher is free to be innovative. Fifth, because one learning opportunity can bring about several outcomes, those that seem likely to produce more than one positive outcome should be favored.

Goodlad's (1963) criteria for selecting teaching techniques are not dissimilar to Tyler's principles, except that they go beyond them. He refers to lessons as "organizing centers" and as "the instructional flesh on curriculum bones." The good organizing center, he says,

1. encourages the student to practice the behavior sought
2. encourages the simultaneous practice of several behaviors
3. supports learning in other areas of instruction
4. is planned with full awareness of preceding and forthcoming learning for a given group of students
5. reaches both the highest and lowest level of ability in the group
6. is sufficiently comprehensive to provide for a wide range of differences in student interests and learning styles
7. has educational significance in its own right
8. leads beyond itself to other times, other places, and other ideas

That last criterion, "transferability," is an essential for health instruction. Hunter (1971) asserts that the core of creativity and problem solving is the student's ability to transfer past learning to solving present problems. She adds, "the planning of the teacher is probably the most critical element in generating the transfer that yields student productivity and creativity. This planning makes the difference between 'hoping that it will happen' and 'seeing that it does.'" Hunter's small book, *Teach for Transfer,* is highly recommended for its succinctness, clarity, and enjoyable programmed instruction in planning for that kind of learning.

Raths's (1971) criteria for worthwhile activities are proposed in the form of value statements. The following have been adapted from those he lists and explains. A learning activity is worthwhile, he says, if it:

1. permits students to make informed choices in carrying out the activity and to reflect upon the consequences of those choices
2. assigns students to active rather than passive roles in their learning
3. asks students to engage in inquiry into ideas or current problems
4. involves students with the use of real objects or artifacts
5. is feasible for students of several levels of ability
6. asks students to examine a previously studied idea, process, or problem in a new setting
7. requires students to examine sensitive rather than mundane issues
8. involves "risk taking" as it has to do with success or failure
9. requires students to rework and polish initial versions of assigned projects
10. involves students in applying meaningful rules or standards of behavior
11. allows students to share in the planning, carrying out a plan, or the results of an activity
12. relates to expressed purposes and interests of students

Although they have their uses, lecture and recitation would fail many of these criteria. Yet recent research shows that these two techniques dominate teaching in junior and senior high schools today. Goodlad (1984, p. 229) reports:

> We observed that, on the average, about 75% of class time was spent on instruction and that nearly 79% of this was "talk"—usually teacher to students. Teachers out-talked the entire class of students by a ratio of about three to one. If teachers in the talking mode and students in the listening mode is what we want, rest assured that we have it. These findings are so consistent in the schools of our sample that I have difficulty assuming things are much different in schools elsewhere.
>
> Clearly, the bulk of this teacher talk was instructing in the sense of telling. Barely 5% of this instructional time was designed to create

students' anticipation of needing to respond. Not even 1% required some kind of open response involving reasoning or perhaps an opinion from students. Usually when a student was called on to respond, it was to give an informational answer to the teacher's question.

Think about that for a moment. Those statements are taken from a report described as "providing a more comprehensive view of U.S. schools than any previously published" (Tyler, 1983).

No one who is guided by the kinds of criteria listed above will plan lessons limited to lecture and recitation. There *are* classrooms where experiential learning is the mode. There can be more. First there must be a teacher who develops worthwhile objectives. Next, techniques must be chosen for their potential for providing appropriate practice. Choice of the technique is based upon the cognitive skill in the objective. As a consequence of carrying out the activity required by the technique, the student is actively learning or sharpening the specified behavior and usually several more besides. Learning is active, not passive, hence absorbing and stimulating. Skills such as conceptualizing, hypothesizing, interpreting, inferring, generalizing, theorizing, constructing, and concluding are some of those that will be elicited.

Problem solving and decision making are not discrete processes to be learned separately or practiced only at certain levels of education. They should be ongoing so that the full range of cognitive and affective behaviors are being used all the time, from kindergarten through graduate school. You can select from a wide array of techniques and instructional media when planning lessons that actively involve the learner in discovering ways to promote and protect health not just today, but in the future.

ALTERNATIVE TECHNIQUES FOR TEACHING AND LEARNING

It is not intended or appropriate that the techniques selected for consideration here be described in detail, nor is the list exhaustive. Health educators, and particularly school health educators, are usually required to complete a course in teaching methodology. Several good textbooks are concerned entirely with descriptions of teaching methods and techniques. Here we explain specific techniques only briefly and suggest some ways they might be used effectively for health teaching.

Group activities

Whatever the teaching technique chosen, it must actively involve the learner if it is to be effective. Active participation can be direct or vicarious, and it can be experienced as a part of a group or by individual students alone. Direct participation requires that the learner be physically involved in the activity; vicarious participation usually depends on media-facilitated experiences (e.g., the learner is a viewer of a demonstration or activity that is going on in another place or at another time).

Group activities are those in which two or more students participate in the same learning situation, each taking a part and contributing to the total outcome of the activity. Committee work, discussions, dramatizations, field trips, role playing, and simulation games are examples.

Discussion   "Discussion" might be defined as a purposeful interaction among some number of individuals with the intention of verbally exploring an issue or problem of interest. As a procedure basic to productive theorizing or thoughtful analysis of health trends or issues, group discussions have great value. Discussion allows students to practice cognitive skills, formulate concepts and principles in their own words, and gain confidence in their ability to generate and express ideas. Discussion also reveals any areas where further information is needed, and interests that emerge as an outcome provide clues to students' needs.

Discussion can also be used to motivate desired changes in behavior among group members. Considerable research demonstrates that children and adults alike are more readily persuaded to accept new ideas or adopt new practices when they learn about them during group discussions. A resulting publicly announced intention to carry out the health action being discussed tends to reinforce such a decision.

Another factor favoring the use of discussion as a teaching technique is the fact that less able or timid students profit from hearing and observing the interchanges among the others, whether or not they speak out. On the negative side, when the group environment is *not* favorable to new ways of looking at questions and issues, some find it easier to go along with the group rather than risk rejection or derision. Agreement doesn't necessarily mean that a discussion has been worthwhile or successful. Sometimes a student or group of students begins to dominate discussions and literally bullies less aggressive students into agreement.

Discussion activities have to be structured in such a way that all students are able to present their suggestions and thoughts in a climate of uncritical acceptance and mutual respect. Yet enough control must be maintained to avoid wasting time. Generally, if the goals of the discussion are clearly specified in advance, students should be able to differentiate between issues concerning new ideas that are expected and appropriate and those about which comments are inappropriate.

Leading a discussion successfully and fruitfully is not a task for an amateur, and it isn't a talent possessed by all teachers. It can be learned, however, through observation, analysis of results, and practice. Textbooks on teaching and public speaking usually have sections on discussion leading. A recent text on values teaching, *Teaching Strategies for Values Awareness and Decision Making in Health Education* (Dalis and Strasser, 1977), includes sample scenarios for leading discussions. A related problem is the fact that you can't assume that your students know how to discuss an issue productively either. You may have to devote several lessons to establishing ground rules for discussions and demonstrating effective discussions in progress. That so often seen teaching direction, "discuss," is more easily suggested than carried out.

Discussion is not simply a series of leading questions posed by the teacher and satisfied by dutiful parroting of the answer to be found in the textbook. It is not a twenty-second question asked by a student to which the teacher responds with a ten-minute answer. Nor is it a bull session featuring opinion sharing or ignorance swapping. Discussion is a goal-oriented interchange of ideas that spark further ideas, each one building toward the identification of feasible hypotheses, tentative theories, or potential solutions to a problem. Discussion is a learning *activity;* hence, it is learner centered. The teacher must be the facilitator, not the leader. And that is not as easy to manage as you might think. For example, some teachers cannot seem to resist the urge to do most of the talking. Goodlad (1984) found that "teaching" typically consists of "telling" a passive audience of students things it was presumed they ought to know.

Some teachers have difficulty accepting and controlling the relatively unstructured classroom atmosphere necessary if student-to-student dialogue is to be effective. Often only teacher-student interchange is encouraged for that reason. Admittedly, it is difficult to encourage talking and at the same time prevent talkers from taking over the show. For this reason, the most difficult of all formats for discussion is that with the total class. Many of the above difficulties are avoided when the class is divided into small groups, each with its own leader. It may be noisy, but each student has a greater opportunity to be heard. Even in small groups, of course, leadership that ensures each member a chance to be heard with respect is essential. Plan any such group assignments with this in mind.

A good way to initiate discussions, whether with a total class or in small groups, is to introduce the topic of interest by means of a demonstration, film, filmstrip, transparency, audiotape, or other experience that can be shared. After the presentation, everyone has seen or heard the same things and can react to that experience on an equal footing.

Discussion can also be triggered by simply posing a thought-provoking question. Question asking is an art. The query has to be posed in such a way that there is no pat answer, and it should involve an issue or a situation that concerns those students. "What is the penalty for possession of an illicit drug?" may involve relevant information, but it can only elicit a factual answer that is not likely to spark further comment. Better might be, "How can we be sure that an over-the-counter medication is as safe and effective as advertisements say it is?" The question "What is the number one cause of death in the United States today?" may be relevant and important to know about, but a question such as "What is the most effective action one could take today to promote his or her well-being now and in the future?" generates discussion by its nature. Encourage your students to suggest questions of their own. Help them identify those in which the entire class will be interested and for which there may be several good answers, depending on the situation.

Before you begin, if this is the first experience with discussion in your class, establish some rules of order. For example, decide with the students what sign shall be given if someone wishes to speak, how long a speaker may have the floor without interruption, and so forth. Then step out of center stage and into the wings. Let the students do the talking. Limit your role to that of recognizing would-be speakers. Don't be afraid of momentary silences. Give them time to reflect upon what has been said and to prepare a response or take an idea further. Try to listen with interest, but without revealing your own opinion. When the allotted time has been used or the discussion seems to be winding down, avoid taking over as interpreter or summarizer. Instead, urge the students to identify any direction that has emerged as a result and if possible to propose hypotheses that lead to further investigations. Where you go from there depends upon the intended purpose of the discussion and the form in which it has been organized.

Discussion is a technique employed to some degree in almost every lesson, but it dominates in brainstorming, buzz sessions, panel discussions, and lecture-discussion. Each is organized differently from the others. The amount of structure and control varies according to the form.

Brainstorming Possible in small groups or with the total class, brainstorming is a quick means of generating a number of ideas for later consideration. It is particularly effective as an initiating activity. It begins with a posed issue or a problem for which everyone is urged to think of as many possible solutions or resolutions as they can. For example, such an issue might be "Should the sale of marijuana be legalized as a means of controlling its use?" A problem might be "How can the number of traffic accidents among American teenagers and young adults be reduced?"

Every suggestion or idea should be recorded for later consideration without judgment as to its merit. The tenor of the activity has to be free flow of ideas and complete acceptivity. Typically, no one can be sure at the end who thought of the final solutions, for if the technique is working well, these emerge as outcomes of the reactions to a host of earlier suggestions.

When brainstorming is a total class activity, the teacher acts as the facilitator and often as recorder, using the chalkboard or a transparency to note each contribution. If it is carried out in small groups, each is led by an elected leader who also serves as spokesperson. Each group brainstorms and then categorizes its resulting pool of ideas as fits the problem or issue of concern. As a culminating activity, the teacher might poll each group in turn for one suggestion they have developed. As each is reported, it should be recorded and another group polled as long as fresh ideas continue to be offered. Limiting each group to one of their ideas at a time should give every group an equal chance to participate. If the first group were allowed to present its entire list, later groups might have to listen while all the ideas they had prepared were presented before they have their turn.

Brainstorming can be used to define a problem, to determine ways to obtain the information necessary to solve it, and to theorize about solutions. It builds feelings of confidence among the participants as their ideas are given an audience and promotes feelings of rapport among students and between students and teacher.

Buzz sessions Buzz sessions are usually conducted in small groups of five or six given a specified period of time, as a rule no more than six to ten minutes. They are given a specified problem or question for discussion and analysis. The task is to decide quickly upon a promising theory or solution. The activity takes its name from the sounds that result, for it is conducive to active participation of all group members. The same question can be assigned to all groups, or each of them may be given its own.

Unless you can be sure that all the participants are familiar with this procedure, spend time explaining each member's responsibilities in achieving the purposes of the discussions. Then give them freedom to talk and exchange ideas. Move around the room and listen to be sure that each group is on target and is moving along toward a meaningful answer.

The culminating activity should be some means of sharing the results of the discussions with the rest of the class. When the groups have considered individual problems, this might be done by means of reports given by group representatives. If the same problem or issue has been the topic for all groups, the representatives might form an informal panel for joint discussions based on their individual group's viewpoints. The other members of the class become the audience in this situation and should be encouraged to ask questions or talk about any speaker's view with which they disagree or to which they would like to add.

Buzz sessions are also effective techniques for planning demonstrations, dramatizations, role playing, or carrying out any other activity in preparation for major projects.

Panel discussions   In the formally organized sort of panel discussion, members spend considerable advance time preparing their contribution. As a teaching-learning technique, panel discussion is often assigned as a project for which considerable research and reading are expected and necessary. This sort of formal discussion has to be organized in a fairly structured manner. Each panel should be provided a form outlining its responsibilities and detailing suggested procedures for completing the assignment. Class time should be allocated during which a chair is elected, a tentative approach is agreed upon, tasks are assigned as appropriate, and a timetable for each step in completing the project is determined. The chair is responsible for submitting the completed form in advance of the final presentation, indicating the role that each member has played in completing the assignment.

When the presentation is made, usually in the form of a conversational interchange among the panel members following an introductory, stage-setting series of position statements, the chair acts as moderator and summarizer. The discussion may also be presented as a series of brief papers, after which the audience reacts and discusses what has been proposed.

Panel discussions are especially successful in considering issues such as fluoridation, boy-girl relationships, abortion, early marriage, environmental pollution versus nuclear power, and other controversial or especially vital subjects. Successful completion of all the tasks involved requires application and practice of a wide range of cognitive and affective skills.

Lecture-discussion   Often instructors specify that a lesson will feature "lecture-discussion." Although the title suggests a balance between the two activities, lecture often dominates. Ideally, this technique provides some new and essential information in lecture form, after which the students are encouraged to ask questions, express their reactions, and generally talk about what has been told to them. The purpose of the discussion is to clarify what needs further explanation and to reinforce what has been presented.

As a teaching technique, lecture-discussion allows the teacher to set the stage for study of new concepts in a short time. The purpose is to provide a common base of information about the new topic in terms appropriate for a given group of learners. Its success depends upon the instructor's ability to motivate interest by a lecture and to channel the subsequent discussion so skillfully that interest is not only maintained but even fostered.

Whichever discussion technique is being used, the final outcome should be some logical conclusions or decisions. These may not always be clear-cut, but can instead be stated in the form of promising alternatives. The main thing is that the students must make the decision or draw the conclusions rather than have the teacher triumphantly tell them what these outcomes have been. The next steps for them will be to test their conclusions or take action based upon their decisions. These may happen as a part of later assignments.

Committee work or team projects The cooperative participation of a small group of individual students in exploring some selected concern or health interest is sometimes preliminary to the development of other strategies. Committee work can be part of planning a panel presentation. A team project can be its outcome. Committee work may also precede other forms of presentation, such as a drama or a skit, a film, 2-by-2 slides with accompanying live or recorded narration, a debate, or a term report. Committee work helps young people learn how to work effectively with others, to gather and organize relevant data, to generalize from those data, and to apply what has been learned to test or verify their theories as they work to prepare an assignment. Careful structure is essential to the success of this technique, however. You can't just assign a number of students to a project and hope they know how to work as a committee. Everyone has had sad experiences with committee projects in which a few people have done all the work while the others got a free ride. What is perhaps worse is the committee project presentation that leaves its audience bored stiff because the plan was either inept or totally lacking.

One way to avoid that kind of empty outcome is to prepare a series of report forms, each of which considers the specific tasks implicit in committee work. These kinds of forms can be adapted to any project; so once devised, they can be employed whenever the occasion demands. The form appropriate for each step should be filled out by the chairperson and handed in to the instructor according to a posted or specified time schedule. The first such form might require committee members to list library or other resources they will consult during the planning phase of their deliberations. The second might describe current progress, and include an outline of the final plan. The last should name each committee member and explain that person's specific contribution to the work, including a list of references or resources utilized in doing it. It should also specify the format selected for the presentation (dramatization, panel discussion, debate, demonstration, film show, or other medium) and explain how the class will be involved and evaluated to show how well the committee presentations got across.

Committee reports can be a stimulating means of investigating personal or community health issues or health programs of interest. But whatever the focus, the important outcome to be sought is the development of conclusions that tie the committee's work and accomplishments to the overall purposes of the unit or the course.

Role playing Presenting an impromptu dramatization of health-related behaviors or situations is not only fun but at the same time a highly effective teaching-learning technique. Role playing is always ad lib, which means that the participants make up their lines as they go along in reaction to the other players' statements. It can be used to portray a concept or to dramatize a way of preventing or coping with a health problem, whether primarily physical, social, or emotional in effect. Two or more people take part, and a minute or two is ordinarily allowed for preparation. Although informality is always key to the activity, a specific instructional objective should always be recognizably its purpose.

Role playing of a prepared situation can be used to introduce an area of study by dramatizing a related health problem. Or it can be used to give students an opportunity to apply what they have been studying in preventing a problem that concerns them. Role playing can be used to demonstrate the power of tradition, values, beliefs, or social pressure in influencing ways individuals behave. It is useful as a means of providing an outlet for feelings about an issue or to convey ideas that if expressed more directly might be awkward or uncomfortable for the group. For example, a student might be embarrassed to ask about certain health behaviors or unwilling to talk about family practices of some kinds. Role playing in such a situation allows that person to pose an unspoken question in the safe anonymity of the role being played.

Understanding of the other person's point of view and needs can be promoted by having a student play a role from the perspective of self and peers and then switch to the role of parent, teacher, or other adult in the same situation. The fact that differing perceptions often result in different health behaviors can be demonstrated by giving the same situation or problem to two or more groups to role play.

In general, you will need to give your class a clear explanation of the activity itself and the purpose of the role they are to be playing in any particular instance. Whatever the subject of the activity, it should not have direct personal meaning for any class member. For example, if one or more of your students has a weight control problem, it would be wiser to avoid using role playing in that connection. In other words, the situation and resulting reactions must be those of people in general. It probably is better, especially early in the course, to call for volunteers to do role playing rather than to assign students randomly or require everyone to take part.

However you handle such assignments, those who for one reason or another are not playing a role should be given something specific to do while the planning phase is in progress. One way to ensure total participation is to allow the role players to choose and demonstrate some health-related principle, behavior, or concept that the class members are challenged to identify correctly from the action. For example, teams of two or three might select a generalization drawn from the subject matter, such as "Stress can be helpful or harmful in its effect on well-being." Then each team should be allowed at least five minutes to devise a way of presenting its assigned generalization by means of role playing. Those who are too shy to be comfortable with this task might be allowed to serve in nonspeaking roles or assist with planning or stage-setting tasks.

Role playing is an effective summarizing device, with the other students asking questions and commenting on the presentation. For this reason, it needs to be reserved for use only after enough input of information makes it feasible. It is also an effective way of giving students a chance to apply what they have learned and affords the instructor a very good way to discover whether important ideas have been understood or only heard.

Field trips An off-campus visit to a local community health facility or agency or an investigation of a health hazard or problem either on school grounds or in the neighborhood is a dynamic way of linking health instruction to community needs. As is the case with any teaching-learning strategy, this technique should be chosen because it is the best way of achieving a specified objective. It usually involves the total class and is a structured activity. A great deal of preliminary planning is necessary if the trip is to be away from school grounds. All precautions for the safety of the students making the trip must be carried out in accordance with school and district policy as well as state school law. Plans for providing acceptable transportation, teacher aides, parental permission or collaboration, the availability of first aid kits, and other logistic problems must be proposed and worked out in advance.

Class discussion is a good way to decide upon the exact place or resource to be visited, to decide what information is being sought, and to establish the relationship between the trip and course objectives. Depending on students' ages and abilities, students can make some or all of the actual arrangements (arranging for the visit by telephone or interview, setting the date and time for the visit, and providing the hosts with advance information about the number to expect, their age or grade in school, and what they hope to learn about the place they are visiting). Following the visit, a letter of thanks and appreciation should be a responsibility of the class and be signed by all the members. The teacher acts as counselor but stays in the background so that the total experience is one of learning actively rather than passively as mute witnessess of what is prepared for them to see and hear.

The purpose of a field trip should not be to divert, although it will be a diversion. It should be done because it makes possible a unique set of experiences that will demonstrate a health concept more powerfully than any other technique available. This means it cannot be simply a survey of the "look-see" variety but should be focused on data gathering and interpretation of what is revealed. For example, on a field trip to a neighborhood health facility, rather than asking what services are offered and listing them in their notes, the students could be asked to look for evidence of *changing* services as these reflect new community needs. (The concept is that community health programs must be responsive to the many changes in community life-styles, populations, advances in health care, etc.) Rather than questions of simple facts, the focus of a vital field trip should be more meaningful queries, such as "Why are these services or facilities here?" or "Why are certain other services no longer offered?"

Encourage interested students to bring cameras and take pictures of the things they find significant. Afterwards, the pictures can be organized logically and an accompanying commentary written or taped by volunteers as a special project. These can be used later in a number of ways: placed on display on parent nights, used with other classes, or featured during school assemblies. They can be substituted for an actual trip if students in later classes are prevented from repeating that experience. They can also be used as pre–field trip preparation for future students.

To discover how different community groups live, the way they now handle health problems, or how the local community provides for its health needs or to gain an on-the-spot insight into larger social problems related to health, such as the accessibility of health care facilities available to those who can least easily travel to them, provides a richer, more meaningful appreciation of personal and public health responsibilities. Field trip possibilities common to most communities include the following activities:

1. visiting a hospital or clinic to ascertain procedures and facilities for health care
2. visiting a recreational facility in a specified neighborhood in order to assess its adequacy in relation to the needs of the people who live there
3. touring a food-packing plant to investigate what steps are taken to maintain the sanitary processing of the foods

4. visiting a public swimming pool to study the sanitation and safety procedures followed in maintaining the facility and guarding the health of those using it
5. touring the kitchen of a restaurant or fast food facility, if possible in the company of a public health sanitarian, to identify which aspects of their service are controlled by law and how well these laws are obeyed
6. going to a large factory to study its safety equipment and the regulations devised to meet the unique health and safety needs of the employees
7. touring a sewage or waste disposal facility to find out how these problems are handled and what limitations are associated with the present system
8. visiting a dairy to observe procedures followed in the sanitary production of milk and milk products
9. going to a fire station to study fire prevention and control techniques as recommended and practiced by fire fighters
10. touring a power-generating plant to determine what controls are being applied in the prevention of air and water pollutions

Look for other field trip possibilities that may be unique to your own area. There will surely be many, and these may be far more meaningful to your students than any of those listed above.

If for any reason a formal field trip is not feasible, a less structured arrangement can always be worked out. Field experiences such as conducting public-opinion surveys concerning health needs or beliefs, searching out traffic or fire hazards that need to be corrected, investigating health quackery claims, and photographing obvious signs of illegal pollution of the air or water are just a few examples of less structured individual or team projects that could be extra-classroom activities.

Simulation and case study Whether the intent is to give students practice in manipulating a mechanism or dealing with a social problem, simulations are always representative of reality. An example of a mechanical simulation is a driver training mockup that gives the learner an opportunity to practice driving skills in response to filmed driving conditions that appear on the screen just as they would to a driver on the road. Social simulations are often provided in the form of games during which the students assume designated community leadership roles and must work out solutions to hypothetical community health problems from that frame of reference. The case study is a somewhat similar device, being a prepared description of a realistic situation having social, physical, and emotional health implications.* The students read the description and analyze the data they are provided as a basis for developing a tentative plan for the control or elimination of the primary difficulties.

Use of mechanical simulations is straightforward and needs no explanation here. Driver training programs use simulators before putting students into automobiles on the street. Almost too vividly simulated model injuries are available for practice in first aid treatment. Manikins are used to demonstrate procedures such as cardiopulmonary resuscitation. Models of body parts are common simulations.

Games are frequently used as a means of simulating social problems. The values of games as teaching-learning strategies are many. In the first place, games are fun, so students enjoy taking part in them. Learning is no less valuable because it has been gained through play. What is learned through simulation games goes beyond practicing the problem-solving method to applying problem-solving skills. As students play the game, they gain insight into the responsibilities and satisfactions of the adult leadership role.

A disadvantage in using this technique is that it takes so much time to carry out games of this sort. Another is the apparent classroom confusion generated as a consequence. Some teachers may not be able to tolerate the noise or the unstructured atmosphere that goes with freedom to react as seems necessary to the role. Also, because few teachers have the time or the training needed to design such games, they must usually purchase or rent them. Nevertheless, use of simulation games and case studies affords the students practice in decision-making and inquiry skills. They also learn how to work effectively with others. The need to consider possible consequences of an action takes on new significance. The players develop increased sensitivity to and empathy for the problems of the people whose life roles they are playing. It is both a cognitive and affective learning experience.

Individual activities

Individual activities are those in which each student interacts with some form of live communication in class or works alone on an assignment or project. Note taking during a lecture or while listening to a resource person, reading, performing experiments, preparing a demonstration, interviewing, and writing a paper are examples. Individual work often evolves as a part

---

*Many teachers write up short descriptions of situations with which they have had personal experience in or out of school. These, used as case studies, give teaching a relevance not always found in commercially obtained case studies.

of a group activity and contributes to its final outcome in an important way.

Lecture A lecture has been described as a long statement representing the speaker's views concerning what ought to be known about some subject, resulting in a set of notes or mental impressions that reflect the listener's perceptions of what has been said. Those two sets of perceptions are usually very different. Arrange to read the notes that several people have taken while listening to a talk that you have given if you want to see how different they can be. Nevertheless, skillful presentation of essential background information by means of lecture can be an effective way of introducing new content areas. It is particularly useful as an efficient means of transmitting a lot of important information. And if it is carefully planned and delivered, a lecture can be as dynamic an experience as any other teaching technique.

Somehow the word "lecture" has come to be almost synonymous with "dull." The difference between dull and interesting can often be traced more to the speaker's style than to the subject matter. The simple matter of maintaining eye contact with the audience and talking to them rather than reading to them makes a big difference. If you are enthusiastic about your subject, it shows, and your listeners will respond to your enthusiasm. Watch them, and you'll soon learn to tell when they are with you and when some or all of them are lost. Don't be afraid to pause in that case. Ask for questions, and if none are asked, ask some yourself. If no one can answer, or if what emerges is not what you have been trying to say, don't go on until you have clarified the points you wanted them to understand. When students can't tell you in their own words what they have just heard, you have wasted valuable time.

A lecture needs to be carefully planned. It must have a logical beginning, a body of information, and an ending. Rather than assume that your students have well-developed listening skills, do something that will grab their attention and keep it. Highlight key points by revealing each on a prepared transparency or by writing it on the chalkboard. A desirable sequence for a lecture follows:

1. subject: a topic chosen for its significance to a specified unit of study rather than because it's your favorite or because you are used to giving it and won't need to prepare further
2. transition: a sentence or two explaining the relationships between this new material and the just preceding activities or subject matter
3. introduction: a brief presentation in which the topic is looked at from the perspective of the students and society in general (An

overview of the content that will be covered is usually a good lead in.)
4. body of the talk: all the key points, presented in order, with frequent illustrations chosen from life and human needs and occasionally, as appropriate, with humor
5. summary: the main points brought together at the close of the talk as reinforcement and to focus student attention on the primary purpose of the lecture
6. transition: a forecast of what is to follow the lecture and how that will build upon what has been covered so far

As a means of actively involving the learners during your talk, use demonstration or visual aids (transparencies, pictures, graphs, charts, etc.) to illustrate important points and to add a note of informality and change of pace. Another effective device promoting involvement is to begin by asking a question. Then present your material organized so that it flows logically from one point in the outline to the last. Define any terms that may be new to your listeners as you go along. Encourage them to ask questions when they need to and to comment when the lecture is completed. Then ask them to sum up their understanding of what has been said in their own words as a check on your success in communicating and as a means of reinforcing what has been discussed.

Guest speakers Health education encompasses such a wide range of knowledge and concerns that no one can hope to be expert in all its subject areas. It is nearly impossible to keep totally up to date in even one content area. When class interest in a specific health topic is such that the assistance of a guest expert can be justified, a specialist in that subject might be invited to visit the class. That specialist could be a fellow teacher, a health educator from a community health agency, a parent, a paramedic, or anyone whose experience qualifies her or him as expert in a given field of health-related work.

Curriculum guides often suggest, "Invite a doctor (or police officer, fire fighter, or whatever) to visit the class to talk about his/her role in protecting community health." (We will comment later on the adequacy of this kind of one-line suggestion as a guide for teachers.) Success in carrying out so skimpily described an activity depends upon the experience and dedication of the teacher who does the inviting. You need to know the speaker's qualifications, and the speaker needs to know a lot about you and your class. Don't make arrangements based on assumptions about these things.

Several preliminary activities need to be carried out. First, the speaking skills of any such expert should be appraised by some means. Is that person an interesting, well-organized, experienced speaker? Does the individual have the ability to communicate at the vocabulary level of your students? It may not be possible to preview a presentation, but there are ways of checking this point. Many health agencies and official and industrial organizations maintain speakers' bureaus and will furnish you with a list of speakers along with the topics each is qualified to address. You can be reasonably sure that speakers who are identified in this way will be experienced and worth hearing. Recommendations by colleagues or acquaintances who have heard a speaker at another time can be depended upon. Preliminary talks with prospective speakers can help them and you decide whether the proposed presentation is suitable for a class.

Earlier classroom activities should have already generated questions, for they will have motivated the search for a speaker in the first place. These questions should be clearly stated and furnished to the speaker in advance. The amount of time allocated to the presentation and to be reserved for student questions should be stipulated. The presentation might be recorded on tape or, if possible, on videotape for later listening or viewing. Such recordings can be used for reviewing and as an effective substitute for return, time-consuming appearances by a speaker. This is particularly important when a teacher wishes to afford the same experience to each of five or so classes in a day.

The more the students are themselves involved in preparing for the visit, in interacting with the speaker, and in culminating discussions, the more rewarding the experience will be for all. Encourage the class to listen for points of view or statements that seem to need more discussion and to ask questions that will elicit the information they want. Finally, as in the case of field trips, a class-prepared and signed letter of appreciation should be promptly written and sent. One way to prepare such a letter that is heartwarming for the speaker is to ask each student to finish a sentence that begins, "The thing I liked most about your presentation was. . . ." or "As a result of your talk, I learned that. . . . Speakers who have received thank-you letters of this kind find them extremely satisfying.

Use of guest speakers provides information not otherwise easily available to students and gives the class a nice change of pace. Overdependence on this technique would result in loss of continuity, for the course would be a series of unconnected lectures. No one technique can ever serve as the means of carrying out all the goals and objectives of a well-planned health education course.

Values activities Young people are often puzzled by the difference between the values that parents and other adults expect them to accept and those they see reflected in the world around them. What are values, and how should health educators deal with what is essentially a very personal and sensitive area of learning? Values are learned standards of behavior. Like their first cousins, attitudes, they are the product of the wide range of influences each of us experiences from the moment of birth. The most powerful of these influences come from one's family, later from peers and society. What a person believes and does about health is probably more influenced by values than by knowledge. Whether you decide to begin smoking, stop smoking, cut down on calorie intake, jog regularly, or do almost anything, it is your values that tip the choice one way or another. They may not be recognized as such; nevertheless, each of us makes choices based upon these personal standards of worth. Can schools teach values? Dunn (1967, p. 113) observed, "Values which are accepted and stored, but not tried out, are simply declarations of intention. Our sense of surety is achieved only after we ourselves have successfully overcome past difficulties and know that we know how to meet future ones. Knowledge which has not been used is still untried. It has not been assessed. But, when knowledge has been used and found to be acceptable, then it becomes wisdom. Wisdom involves value judgments."

If you believe that health education ought to deal with this powerful influence, does consideration of values belong in the cognitive or the affective domain of objectives? Opinions about this are strong, and they differ. Those who favor the affective approach believe that values are inescapably related to feelings and must be approached by means of activities that stir the emotions. Activities that do this include role playing, discussions generated by inspirational quotations, questions, thought-provoking visual materials, "devil's advocate" arguments, and other affective experiences.

Cognitivists believe that values and moral judgments should be based upon reasoning rather than on opinions or feelings. Activities that are purely affective in intent are viewed as attempts to manipulate rather than to educate. They scorn games and procedures designed to evoke strong emotions as "excitement education" and as lacking in educational value. The primary purpose of a role playing situation should be to promote understanding, they say. An affective experience is valued but planned for as the desired but secondary outcome of any worthwhile cognitive objective.

Whichever point of view seems logical and better to you, it probably is true that there is no cognitive learning without affective outcomes and vice versa. Be sure that both kinds of outcomes of your instruction are those that you *intended*, however. Anticipate and avoid possible negative effects of every lesson you plan. If the activity is boring or seems to be nothing more than busywork, then no matter how important the subject matter, what will be most remembered is that it was boring. A negative affective outcome is nearly unavoidable when the teaching technique requires passive listening rather than active doing.

Surely it is both possible and reasonable to devise lesson plans that can achieve cognitive objectives and at the same time produce desirable affective experiences. Values-clarifying techniques and games have been described in several textbooks intended for preservice and in-service teacher education (Metcalf, 1971; Simon, Howe, and Kirschenbaum, 1972; Howe and Howe, 1975; Dalis and Strasser, 1977). In addition, results of class room application and research have been widely reported in the literature. It is neither necessary nor appropriate that more than a few illustrative examples of values-clarifying procedures be presented here for that reason.

In values education, rather than trying to impose some predetermined set of values or standards of behavior by moralizing or rule setting, the teacher provides students opportunities to become aware of the way that values operate in making choices. Accordingly, they are encouraged to (1) make choices freely, (2) discover and examine available alternatives when faced with choices, (3) weigh the consequences of alternative actions thoughtfully, (4) think about what they prize, (5) make public affirmations of their choices, (6) act accordingly, and (7) examine past choices in order to identify their already established behavior patterns (Dalis and Strasser, 1977).

A basic teaching strategy is the clarifying response. It can be as simple as a teacher's response to a student's remark intended to initiate thinking about the values reflected in what has been said. Statements that are useful in generating clarifying responses often have to do with attitudes, hopes, purposes, interests, and activities. The subsequent question concerns the student alone and is personal. (Was that your own idea? What other choices could you have made? If you do that, what will happen? How strongly do you feel about that? Would you want to tell the rest of us about that? Would you be willing to work to make that happen?) There is no expected right answer, and the student need not answer at all. The purpose is simply to plant a thought about the role that values play in our choices.

Discussion is a major technique employed in value-clarifying activities. Some ways of focusing discussion for this purpose include showing a prepared transparency with a pictured situation to be interpreted, distributing an unfinished story that the students read and then speculate about the ways the story might end most favorably, and posing questions that have to do with current issues or problems and preceded with "How do you feel about. . . ." or "What do you think should be done about. . . ." (Dalis and Strasser, 1977, p. 66).

Ranking and choosing activities are used to get at priorities. They help a person look at alternatives and make choices influenced by personal life needs and experiences. For example, students might be asked to make a list of twenty things that they most like to do, then to rank the twenty activities from most to least favorite, and next to look at their list and put a dollar sign beside each activity that costs money, a circle beside each one that must be done with another or others, a star beside each one that takes place at night, an asterisk beside those that take place outdoors, a square beside those that are passively enjoyed, and so on. The purpose is to help students identify patterns in their choices among possible recreational activities. Do they tend to be activities that require active participation in games or sports? Are they balanced between group and individual activities? Does the individual spend money to watch professional athletes rather than take part in games and sports personally? Compare the results of these kinds of analyses as they are reported by boys and by girls. Are they about the same, or are they different? A number of questions of this sort can serve as the focus of subsequent or culminating discussions.

There has been criticism of certain of the games and activities in some instances. Most of this has been the result of their misuse or overuse, however. Whatever affective strategies you choose as a means of developing awareness of values, take care not to ask your students to engage in activities that could be interpreted as invading personal or family privacy. Also, because some of the games are unstructured and fun to play, their purpose can get lost in the excitement. Be sure that you don't lose sight of your objective, that the strategy you have chosen is the best way to achieve it, and that its achievement is unmistakably related to major course goals. Above all, be sure that your students know *why* they are engaged in the activity. Help them perceive the values involved in the choices they make and reach their own conclusions about the nature of those that presently influence their decisions.

When they are skillfully carried out and based on meaningful objectives, values activities can help youngsters identify and modify, if appropriate, the standards upon which their health behaviors are based. As they do so, they are also sharpening decision-making skills and practicing problem solving.

Textbook use It's easy to forget that the invention of printing made a dramatic change in education. Before the printing press, teaching depended almost entirely on lecture and the slate. Since then, the textbook has been the dominant classroom aid, whatever the discipline. American education remains very much textbook centered, albeit today a host of electronic media is also used. Everybody—teachers, students, and parents—seems to be uneasy in the absence of a textbook in the apparent belief that if there is no text, nothing worthwhile can be happening. The principal work in a typical classroom has been, and continues to be, study and recitation from assigned, daily textbook reading (Goodlad, 1984, p. 215).

Effective health teaching uses textbooks as a resource, not as the sole source of course substance and sequence. Many school districts prefer, or are required by state law, to adopt textbooks from an approved list for each grade in which a given subject is offered. There are a number of health education textbooks available for grades K–8 and middle and high school levels. They vary in their approach and emphasis, however. Some are physiology and anatomy oriented; some are outdated or contain inaccuracies; some focus on study of diseases and disorders and their treatment; some stress study of health-enhancing choices and behaviors. The first step in selecting a health textbook should be to determine whether it fits the pattern of needs and interests of the students for whom it is intended. Does the chapter organization permit revision of the sequence to match course plans? Are the authors recognized authorities in school health education with experience in the schoolroom? Other criteria that may be useful in evaluating textbook choices include the following:

1. Is the primary emphasis of the content upon health enhancement and promotion of health-related skills and behaviors?
2. Has the text been subjected to extensive review by content specialists?
3. Is the vocabulary suitable for the reading skills of the students with whom it will be used?
4. Is a glossary of terms included in the text or an appendix?
5. Is there a detailed index of topics?
6. Does the teacher's edition provide teaching ideas, evaluation activities, and other aids?
7. Is there an instructor's guide or test manual?
8. Is the paper of good quality and the print large enough to avoid causing eyestrain?
9. Are the illustrations, charts, graphs, statistics, and other graphic devices meaningful, current, and easily understood?
10. Are the references current, authoritative, comprehensive, and appealing to student interests?

Any textbook has certain drawbacks. One may be too easy for some students and too difficult for others. The content is always vulnerable to the rapid changes taking place in health knowledge. A text published today is already two years old because it takes that long to get it from manuscript form to the printed and distributed copy. In addition, publishers are interested in what will sell, which is not necessarily what is the best of health education.

Nevertheless, a well-written textbook that provides comprehensive discussion of what is currently perceived as up-to-date and scientifically correct information about health and healthful life-style choices can be a vital component of a course. It will not suffice by itself, however.

Students should be encouraged to seek out new material to supplement what is afforded them in the book. One way to help them do this is to establish a reading center in your classroom. A filing system can be organized by concept or subject area with current articles (either originals or photocopies) stapled into file folders for easy student access and use. Students could be challenged to discover new articles or newspaper stories as additions to the file. (Warn them not to cut out parts of magazines or newspapers either at home or anywhere else without first obtaining permission.) Current health-related pamphlets and booklets can be added as well. Such a reading center can be used in several ways. It can be used to give students a newer view of health content than the text can provide. It gives students who have completed an assignment or test ahead of the others a chance to pick out and read something that interests them. It serves as an ever-ready source of information available for research or preparation of projects or papers.

Individual learning tasks Within recent years, packaged health curriculum modules have been developed and widely disseminated by commercial organizations. Because the development of most of them has been financed by public funds, the material has been subject to some amount of accountability. Packaged curriculums are characterized by emphasis on individual instruction, are generally conceived of as "programs," are accompanied by a system of instructional media and materials, and have been field tested before being offered for sale.

The independent learning units focus on a specified task, which in turn is based upon a measurable objective, usually made known to the learner. Each student can work at his or her own pace. There are enough alternative tasks set up in separate work spaces or stations so that one or two students can work at each of them independently. The tasks need not be completed in any particular order, but every student is expected to complete all of them. Each station is self-sufficient in that full directions and all the materials needed to complete the work are provided. The task may be to perform an experiment or demonstrate competence in some skill. It may also be concerned with a response sheet of some sort. Frequently, several media are employed and designed to be a part of the activity. For example, taped instructions, short lectures, film loops, slide-sound presentations, or models and other such artifacts to be assembled or examined are ready for the learner's guidance or manipulation.

There are some disadvantages to adopting packaged curriculums. The cost of purchasing the materials and providing in-service training in their use can be considerable. Another disadvantage often encountered is the inflexibility of the curriculum modules. Many are so detailed that neither teachers nor students have any options for change. Some are so weighty and long that it may take more time to figure out what to use or exclude than can be saved by using the plans that have been so carefully worked out. Nevertheless, their use can promote the ability to work efficiently without close supervision, add to the learners' satisfaction by letting them work and achieve at their own pace, stimulate practice of inquiry skills, and promote active participation in learning. Teachers are then free to be diagnosticians and facilitators rather than information and direction givers. They have more time to help individual students and provide appropriate enriching experiences.

Curriculum modules are limited in scope and not intended as a substitute for a total course. If you decide to use such a teaching module, choose one that supplements your own areas of expertise. Study the whole program and ask questions as recommended by Unruh (1970): "Will it motivate individual learning?" "Does the package provide for self-direction, self-teaching on the part of the student?" "Does it lead him out of the package into real life?" If the answers are "yes," and it meets your students' needs and is consistent with your beliefs about the goals of health education, it should work well as a teaching tool to be included among the others you use.

Individual projects Special student interests or abilities can be given expression and at the same time learning skills can be increased by assigning or encouraging the development of individual projects. This kind of activity provides practice in research, synthesizing, evaluating, organizing, and a host of other high-level cognitive skills. Appropriate projects might be creating collages that promote some health-enhancing action such as preventive dental care procedures, use of seat belts, and making sound diet choices; constructing artifacts such as smoking machines, dioramas, or exhibits; designing charts, graphs, bulletins, or other means of presenting health statistics; putting together media-assisted presentations using slides or films depicting community health needs or facilities; developing a research paper to be delivered orally or submitted as a term paper; planning and carrying out a community survey to identify and locate health services and facilities available to those who are economically unable to secure private medical care; or any other long-term investigation relevant to the health of individuals or the community.

The key to success with this technique is to allow your students freedom to choose their own topic and design the plan for its exploration and presentation. Motivation is greater when students are allowed to experiment and create a unique product than when they are assigned a topic and must adhere to a certain format. It also creates interest in sharing the results of the individual endeavors. There is no competition for grades such as goes with assigning the same task to all students. Rather than having to compete with every project, students have an opportunity to choose what they are most apt to do well because it suits their interest and their talents. Each unique project is evaluated according to its own objectives and purposes.

Independent work does not mean that guidance will not be needed or provided, however. What it does mean is that you will be helping each student according to his or her special needs. Unquestionably, it makes the teacher's task more difficult than when all the students have the same assignment. The other side of the coin is the pride that both you and your students are sure to feel when the finished projects are shared and displayed.

Experiential learning activities No listing of teaching-learning strategies is complete without some discussion of those proposed as uniquely experiential in intent and outcome. The problem is that "experiential learning" doesn't always mean the same thing in every educational context. What are we talking about in health education when we speak of experiential activities?

Experiential learning has been defined as "learning which comes as close as possible to direct experience of the subject under study—at least a step closer than reading a book or hearing a lecture" (Association for Experiential Education, 1982). The second part of that definition excludes only those two activities and by inference includes everything else. Experiential *education,* although surely intended to result in learning, is spoken of in reference to specific curriculum units. Conrad and Hedin (1981) use the term to describe special programs that are offered as an integral part of the general school program but take place outside the conventional classroom. Such experiential programs are categorized as volunteer service, career internships, outdoor adventure (Outward Bound), and community/political action.

Of course, in the final analysis, *all* learning is experiential. Combs (1981, p. 372) says: "People learn most and best from personal experience. To prepare for a future dependent upon successful human interaction, therefore, calls for schools that confront students daily with significant human problems, where students and faculty are continuously exploring effective interrelationships, where humanistic goals have high priority, and all school personnel are actively seeking to model good human relationships."

Reynolds (1981) suggests that, rather than antithetical to the back-to-basics goals of competency-based education, experiential learning is the logical and most meaningful means of achieving them. This is because experience-based instruction arranges for learning within a framework of meaning. Students are actively practicing skills, rather than simply reading about them. However, they are concerned with those competencies as means to an end, not as ends in themselves. She points to the much greater potential for mastery when learning activities are based on applications that are reality based, carried out in cooperation with others, and occur in a more comprehensive setting than a schoolroom (i.e., typically community rather than school based).

Health educators usually think of experiential activities as what are called "hands-on" learning opportunities, which means that students are working with materials or procedures that are real or close approximations of reality. These kinds of teaching strategies are most apt to develop an affective as well as a cognitive outcome. For example, students might be given an opportunity to discover some of the problems that the blind, the deaf, or the crippled must solve in meeting their everyday needs. Rather than learn about them by reading or hearing a lecture given by someone who has one such problem, they are asked to try doing a number of commonplace things, such as using the telephone, getting across the street, or buying groceries, without the aid of a specified sense or ability. They analyze social situations that reflect issues or problems that are significant in their lives and the lives of their friends and families and role play their perceptions. As a result, they gain insight into the needs and motives of others in a way that could never be accomplished by reading about interpersonal communication. They visit community facilities, talk with community workers, and find out firsthand what their responsibilities are and what rewards and problems go with the job. They may spend an evening with groups such as Alcoholics Anonymous or volunteer to work in a drive to clean up a blighted community area.

One high school health educator organized a club for students called YGAD (Youth Gives a Damn) whose members gave countless hours of community service and willingly spent many weekends and vacations actively promoting community health. They staged frequent clever anti-smoking campaigns, and produced award-winning television shows and films dramatizing the harmfulness of alcohol abuse. They assisted voluntary health agencies in conducting community surveys and appraisal activities. For example, trained and supervised by medical personnel, YGAD club members conducted over five thousand blood pressure readings and more than five hundred hearing tests. These were done at health fairs and at free clinics provided for senior citizens. YGADers raised money for health programs by washing cars and participating in sponsored runs for donations linked to the distance covered and helped in many small ways as needed by community health agencies.

Annually, short-term YGAD health camps drew overflow registrations of youngsters at both junior high and senior high school levels who came to learn more about ways to enhance their own health and that of others. They came not because attendance was a condition of membership or satisfied graduation requirements, but because they were keenly interested and enjoyed being part of a group whose motivation was unabashedly health promotion. Before long the YGAD philosophy and purpose were picked up by teachers and students in other schools and cities, and new chapters were established.

There is much more to starting an YGAD club than recruiting a lot of members. If you believe that an YGAD club could be a worthwhile experience for your students, remember that it takes a lot of time and effort on the part of the sponsoring health teacher to generate and maintain this kind of enthusiasm and student participation. First there must be the kind of health teaching that emphasizes thinking and decision making, not just health information. And you must be willing and able to guide without running the show. YGAD is a club for kids, and they must be the planners and the doers if it is to work. And it does work.*

Experiential learning is the hallmark of effective health education. It is not necessarily tied to the classroom but happens in the community as well. Simulations and demonstrations are obvious experiential activities, but any of the teaching strategies we have been discussing can be experiential, depending on how they are used and for what purpose.

The purpose matters more than the activity. Know *why* you are involving your students in any particular experience, and be sure that *they* know why they are doing it, too. Don't let your purpose get lost in the excitement and fun of it. And never use experiential activities merely to entertain or even to motivate. Always focus first and last on the concept you intend for your students to learn. Health education does not depend upon the assumption that its content has been learned elsewhere but accepts full responsibility for the cognitive growth of students. As Jernstedt (1980, p. 15) emphasizes: "The power of a demonstration to improve intellectul performance lies with its intellectual content and with the necessity for the ex-

---

*Those wishing more information about YGAD may wirte Ric Loya, 6020 Miles Avenue, Huntington Park, CA 90255.

perience." James (1980, p. 188) says something of the same sort in these words: "Schools do have communities around them where all manner of journeys into other lives are possible and there is no shortage of opportunities for genuine small group-experience and worthwhile service to others. The things schools teach need not be abstracted into a coercive culture of duty and performance when there are ways of teaching through a shared life of experience, ultimately rooted in freedom and self-reliance. Cognitive learning and experiential learning need not be viewed as adversaries. Students allowed to make allies of them will form a lasting attachment to education and social life."

INSTRUCTIONAL MEDIA FOR HEALTH TEACHING

Teachers who depend upon *telling* as the principal means of communicating the information their students need are denying them the enrichment potential of a multisensory experience and reducing themselves to the role of a tape playback. Fortunately, few teachers are either so enchanted by the sound of their own voice or possess the stamina needed to talk all the time. Moreover, health information is so widely diverse and changes so frequently that even were it possible for an instructor to keep up with it, there would not be time enough to tell it.

Schools are built and teachers are provided for the purpose of educating the young. The learners, not the teachers, are the stars of the classroom, or ought to be. The effective teacher provides them with an array of information sources and learning materials of all kinds. Some students learn most readily by listening, some by observing, others by reading, still others by touching things. *All* students learn best when a variety of sensory experiences is provided in every learning opportunity. Today's health educator is not limited to the lecture or textbook readings, but uses a wide range of instructional media and materials ranging from the chalkboard to computer-assisted educational programs.

Courseware: computerized teaching aids

It's easy to think of computer-assisted instruction (CAI) as a teaching technique, but it's not. It's a tool. Clark (1983, p. 455) suggests that media used in instruction are simply "vehicles that deliver instruction but do not influence student achievement any more than the truck that delivers our groceries causes changes in our nutrition." He concludes that any currently reported differences in learning rates between teacher-assisted learning and CAI can be attributed simply to its novelty. Furthermore, students tend to view computer use as difficult, so they work harder to accomplish the assigned tasks.

Chen and Cornett (1983) suggest that although health knowledge and attitudes can be influenced by computer-assisted instruction, there is little evidence that health behavior is modified as a result. McDermott and Belcastro (1983) caution against too quick acceptance of computer-assisted teaching as the easy solution to teaching-learning problems. They pose and discuss seven questions that ought to be answered prior to a decision to invest in the hardware and software needed for CAI. These include questions of access, software generation, piracy, controlling educational software, teacher in-service training, negative side effects, and stability of schooling.

Unquestionably, there are problems associated with the adoption and use of microcomputer-based instruction. But their use is increasing, students enjoy using them, and learning is happening. It looks very much as if CAI is here to stay. That is not to say that there are no problems that must be considered before investing in equipment and programs.

Expense is a problem. Both the hardware and the software are costly to buy and to maintain. Keeping up to date is a problem. Computer technology is evolving so fast that both equipment and programs are being outdated almost while they are being installed. Access is a problem. Health classes must vie for computer use with all the other subject areas in a school. Even if every classroom had its own terminal, it would be difficult to arrange a schedule that gave every student access to the same program. The lack of good courseware for health education is a major problem. Health education is less easily computerized than some other disciplines (e.g., mathematics and science). Software currently available for health teaching is limited to storing factual information, basic drill, practice, and storing and retrieving various types of questions for quick construction of test instruments. Only low level cognitive processes are engaged in these programs.

On the positive side, CAI can motivate otherwise uninterested students and in the process enhance their self-esteem as they achieve program objectives. The responses generated by the computer's commands allow the student to participate actively, thus increasing the likelihood that learning will result. Use of computerized instruction saves teacher time. Students can work unassisted most of the time, more information can be transmitted, and teachers have more time to interact with individual students as they require. The activity is self-paced, and the learner gets immediate feedback at every step (Chen and Cornett, 1983). Authoring systems (computer programs that let teachers create a lesson framework that best suits the needs of the teachers and students) can be used by teachers to prepare tutorial lessons (Beall, 1983, p. 94). Health risk appraisal programs can be used as a needs assessment tool, to motivate risk-reducing changes in certain behaviors, and to serve as baseline data in evaluating the impact of health instruction programs.

Health education software is currently limited, but there is great potential for the development of programs involving simulation, health promotion games, problem solving, and interactive video. A video disc is a twelve-inch brass disc on which several types of information can be stored and used in interaction with a microcomputer. The amount of information that can be stored on just one side of such a disc is enormous. An entire textbook or up to fifty-four thousand pictures can be accommodated easily. Other media such as motion pictures, stereo sound, slides, and diagrams can be loaded on a disc as well.

The National Health Information Clearing House (NHIC) has a list of all health-related software. It can be obtained by writing or calling that office. Another valuable resource for health educators wishing more information about the selection and use of microcomputerized courseware for health education is the special issue of *Health Education,* "Microcomputers and Health Education" (1983). This is probably the best and most comprehensive set of articles concerning current and future uses of this newest teaching aid. Included is a set of criteria for evaluating software specific to health education. If worthwhile courseware is to be developed for health education, it probably will need to be created by health educators. Whether you will be a programmer or not, you need to be knowledgeable about microcomputers and their uses.

Educational television

Although television as an educational tool has never achieved the level of use once envisioned, it does work well as a means of health instruction. Students *can* learn from television as well as from the classroom teacher; the success of *Sesame Street* attests to that fact. However the cost of equipment has been a limiting factor in some places. Another problem has been the lack of programs appropriate for health teaching or scheduled during school hours. Where closed circuit television systems are available (means of sending and receiving programs that originate and end within school walls), the potential for more effective presentation of demonstrations, experiments, and other visual experiences is obvious. Just as the television audience of sports often has a better view of the players and the activities, each student can observe a procedure as closely as the individual performing it.

Some large school systems (as in Los Angeles, California, KLCS) have their own television channel and broadcast programs intended not just for the schools but also for the general public. In that situation, a classroom teacher can tune in desired programs using an ordinary television set.

Use of videocassettes makes it possible to record demonstrations and experiments or presentations by specialists for future use. These can be viewed by means of closed circuit presentations, broadcast by public television channels, or presented by individual teachers using a video tape recorder in connection with a television set. Many classes can view a single demonstration or experiment at the same time, or at different times, thus saving both time in setting it up and the energy it takes to replicate the experience when needed.

Many teachers assign home viewing of commercially sponsored documentaries as supplementary health education material. Documentaries are usually scheduled with considerable advance publicity and can be easily identified as relevant to health teaching and coordinated with a course objective. It may be feasible to tape either the audio portion alone or videotape the entire program for classroom use.

Overhead projection transparencies

You can buy or make transparencies that can add interest and clarity to your presentations or explanations. Professionally prepared materials are available for every aspect of health instruction, whether it deals with the physical, social, or mental/emotional dimensions of the concept of interest. When the subject is anatomical or physiological, the illustrations are usually simple line drawings with little distracting shading or detail. Research has shown that the simpler the representation, the more effective the sketch is in promoting learning and comprehension of structure and function.

Prepared transparencies can be used to initiate a new topic or to stimulate discussion. Blank film can be used instead of the chalkboard to record ideas generated by the class (or any other data that need to be emphasized or stored temporarily), to provide supplementary information, to give directions for an activity, to provide pre–field trip instructions, or to present a quiz or a test. They have all the adaptability of the chalkboard and some advantages that the board lacks. For one thing, if you have a good test, a good illustration, or anything that works well, you can store it and reuse it. You don't have to erase it, and it doesn't fade with time. Yet a handwritten transparency *can* be erased and used over and over again if you choose. You don't have to turn off the lights in order to use it, as you must with other projectors. Perhaps most important, you don't have to turn your back on your students while you are using it. They can thus hear you better, and you can respond to their reactions more effectively because you can see them.

The development of original transparencies by students gives them a chance to express their own ideas and present them to the class illustrated by their own visual product. This opportunity fosters creativity and promotes communication skill development. Furthermore, speaking skills can be practiced with far less stress when the presenter can focus the audience's attention on the screen.

Films, slides, and filmstrips

A vicariously experienced field trip, long-term experiment, or elaborate demonstration that otherwise would be difficult if not impossible to arrange can be provided to students through use of films. A field trip involves a great deal of time, expense, and effort. Yet a fifteen-minute film can communicate as much or more information and with nearly as much emotional impact. In addition, a film enables each student to see exactly the same things and from the same angle, hear the explanation just as clearly, and see the details of every illustration equally sharply. This is not to say that a motion picture is always better than a field trip. The flexibility and stimulation of experiencing real-life situations and the opportunity to ask questions and get answers on site make a combination difficult to simulate. But we can't very often take a field trip, and distance can be a problem. An educational film can be a very satisfactory substitute.

The effectiveness of filmed presentations depends as much upon the way they are used as upon the expertise with which they were planned and developed. The more interesting the film, the more your students will need to be prepared for viewing it because the action and the actors may be so beguiling that the message gets lost in the entertainment. Few films can be shown without comment. Preview a film, and tell the students in advance what points to look for while they are enjoying the presentation. Encourage them to evaluate the effectiveness of the film in illustrating the concepts or principles being studied. Knowledge that they are to participate in decisions affecting its use with other classes not only ensures closer attention but gives the teacher a very sound basis for later choosing among available films.

Research shows that learning is enhanced when a film is shown, discussed, and then shown for a second time, perhaps without the sound. It takes time, but the better the film, the more you pick up from it the second time around.

If slides and filmstrips don't have quite the dynamic realism of motion pictures, they have the advantage of greater versatility. Individual frames can more logically be viewed one at a time and for as long as necessary if closer attention to details is desired. A filmstrip can easily be shown in part when this is appropriate. Slide-film presentations are the most flexible of them all. New pictures can be added, old ones deleted, and the sequence changed in moments. When combined with a taped commentary, a slide show rivals the dynamic quality of a film.

Creation of a slide presentation relative to a selected health issue, concern, or concept can be a valuable individual or class project. Every student can have a part in such a project. Even young children can use a camera well enough to create usable slides. Others can be working on a script to accompany the pictures. Some or all of the students can participate in recording the commentary that goes with it.

When completed, such film projects have many uses. They can be exhibited at parent-teacher meetings or school assemblies; they can be used to introduce the subject area to new classes and to review or summarize what has been learned in connection with the content depicted. The most important outcome is perhaps the teamwork experience and the satisfaction each student finds in contributing to the production of such a film show.

Professionally developed educational films specific to health education can be purchased, rented, or borrowed. Those available only by purchase or rental will usually be sent for preview, after which a teacher can either recommend its purchase for continuing use or request that it be rented for a specific period of time. A great many films can be borrowed with advanced booking from certain voluntary and public health agencies, major insurance companies, service clubs, private industries and councils, local libraries, and sometimes departments of health education in community colleges and nearby universities. Your school and district audiovisual center will be likely to have catalogs of films, and other sources can be contacted directly. Take time to check on the films already owned by the school. What health topics are covered and which are lacking? Is the date when each film was produced given? Is the running time specified in each case? Read the description of the content. Is it appropriate for use with your students? Once you know what is available in your school audiovisual library, you have a starting point from which to begin a search for films that are current both in subject matter and approach.

Teaching aids

In addition to those discussed earlier, there is a wealth of free or inexpensive teaching aids such as health-related booklets, pamphlets, and health article reprints. Many such printed materials can be obtained from local voluntary and public health agencies for the asking. See appendix A for addresses of national and government agencies from whom a list of available publications can be obtained by writing a request on your school stationery. Usually at least one copy of those you would like to have can be obtained without charge.

Professional journals published by health and other educational organizations are a source of many articles with health information important to the teacher, students, or both. Watch your local newspaper for news stories about advances in health information. Encourage your students to watch for and bring in related articles as well. Sources of information and printed matter concerning health are virtually unlimited.

Learn how to make and use artifacts such as posters, exhibits, flannel boards and the stick-on materials to be displayed on them, graphs, charts, models, puppets, crossword puzzles, and recordings, any and all of which can provide sensory experiences that enrich learning activities. Any good audiovisual textbook contains descriptions and directions for construction and use of these and more.

Purely visual artifacts may lack motion and sound, but they can reach and pique interest at times and places where more dynamic presentations are impossible to arrange. To show films, you must have equipment in working order, you must have electricity, and ideally you must have a captured audience. Maps, duplicated handouts, photographs, cartoons, diagrams, exhibits, pamphlets, bulletin boards, and other such artifacts that do not depend on these conditions can reach passersby and community audiences as well as students enrolled in a class. Sometimes these kinds of silent attention getters are more effective than what must be heard. We don't always listen to what we hear.

Human resources

People are resources, too. Many who would be willing to serve as consultants, speakers, or providers of various kinds of health-related services can be found both within and outside school walls. Human resources include adult professionals of many kinds, as well as students at various levels of maturity. Among the adults, within schools or a school district, there are nurses, dieticians, physical educators, home economists, guidance counselors, school bus drivers, custodians, speech therapists, and teachers of other disciplines who have some unique specialty and interest in the health education program.

In the community, there are even more kinds of professionals who are concerned with the promotion and protection of health and therefore are involved in health education. The list is long (for example, physicians of every kind, dentists, hygienists, paramedics, firefighters, police officers, safety engineers, public health educators, sanitarians, lifeguards, psychologists, social workers, and physical therapists). All of them have a contribution to make to the health education program and are willing to make it, if invited. Don't be afraid to ask, but make certain that you use their time sparingly, effectively, and with good purpose.

Finally, let students serve as teaching aides, for they can often teach their less able peers more effectively than their instructors are able to do. Studies show that not only do children who need special help make better progress when tutored by older students, but their tutors' achievement rate is accelerated as a consequence. There is a Spanish proverb that seems to explain this, "¡El que enseñe, aprende!" or "He who teaches learns!" University students, as part of their teacher training program, often serve as tutors or part-time classroom teachers in nearby public schools. High school students act as tutors or present special health education units (for example, antismoking programs) for middle school or younger students. Actually, no one ever got through school without having depended on classmates for explanations and help in understanding an assignment or concepts. It is so common that it's easy to forget that.

Edgar Dale (1969) places teaching aids in a cone-shaped hierarchy with a verbal symbol at its apex representing the most abstract aid and the direct, fact-oriented approaches at the base representing the most concrete experience. No one teaching aid is better than the others; there are too many variables operating in the learning process for that to be the case. Each of them has a contribution to make, often in concert with others. Any of them can involve the learner emotionally if it is used wisely and well. You must be skilled in using all of them, but always choose the one that will do best what needs to be done to achieve the instructional objective.

SUMMARY

1. Teaching strategies for effective health education focus on process, with content as the vehicle for practicing intellectual skills.
2. The primary methods of health teaching are problem solving and decision making. The specific strategies selected as means of practicing the steps involved are techniques.
3. The problem-solving method, often also called the scientific method, involves certain logical steps that lead to the discovery of one or more promising solutions.
    a. The scientific method, once mastered, can be applied lifelong in every aspect of living.
    b. Solving problems in the classroom builds competence in rational decision making.
4. Decision making is a process of choosing one alternative over another and taking action accordingly.
    a. Problem solving is happening when a decision is made.
    b. Decision making is usually influenced by knowledge, beliefs, and values.
    c. Health education can be effective in shaping the quality of all three.
    d. Actions based upon an individual's decisions are life-style indicators.

5. Teaching strategies should be selected on the basis of careful investigation of the sources of any curriculum.
   a. Study of curriculum guides, school and district policy, and recommendations of state and local educational authorities
   b. Needs, interests, past experience, and present abilities of the students for whom they will be planned
   c. Analysis of the needs, concerns, and characteristics of the community in which the school is located
6. Principles or criteria suggested by curriculum authorities for the selection of teaching techniques can be applied to choice of techniques.
   a. Tyler's five principles in selecting learning experiences
   b. Goodlad's eight criteria for the selection of "organizing centers" or learning opportunities
   c. Raths's twelve criteria or value statements describing worthwhile teaching activities
7. Teaching techniques are used with groups or with individuals.
   a. Teaching strategies usually involving groups are those such as lecture-discussion, brainstorming, buzz sessions, panel discussions, committee or team work projects, role playing, field trips, simulations, and case studies.
   b. Activities typically carried out by individuals either reacting or working alone, are attending lectures, engaging in values activities, studying and researching, working on packaged learning tasks or modules, and developing original projects.
8. Experiential learning activities attempt to engage the learner cognitively, physically, and emotionally in situations as close to reality as possible.
   a. Mastery of basic cognitive skills is facilitated when activities are practical and require application of knowledge in real or simulated situations, rather than in isolation and as ends in themselves.
   b. Experiential activities combine cognitive with affective outcomes, hence are uniquely effective in health instruction.
9. Use of instructional media increases the experiential quality of teaching-learning strategies.
10. Teachers need to familiarize themselves with a wide range of sources of teaching aids.
11. Teaching aids may be technological (computer courseware, television, radio, overhead projected transparencies, films, filmstrips, or slides), printed materials (pamphlets, booklets, articles), purely visual aids (posters, models), electronic (audio or video tapes and cassettes), or human (consultants, speakers, contributors, colleagues, students).

12. Every health teacher needs to know how to create both audio and visual teaching aids, as well as being skilled in matching the right technique and aids to a given instructional objective.

QUESTIONS AND EXERCISES

Questions
1. What is the relationship between the action word specified by an instructional objective and the choice of a teaching technique?
2. In what significant ways do Tyler's principles, Goodlad's criteria, and Raths's value statements differ as guidelines for the selection of effective teaching strategies?
3. Explain the concept of transferability as it pertains to worthwhile learning outcomes.
4. If teaching strategies focus most importantly on process, what happens to the subject matter that is to be learned?
5. What is the connection between health behavior and problem solving?
6. Explain the difference between decision making and the scientific method.
7. Comment on this statement: "Any college graduate can teach health if he or she keeps up to date and has a current health textbook available." Do you agree or disagree? List the reasons for your answer.
8. Explain the principal advantages of a packaged health curriculum module over teacher-made curriculum plans. What would you say are the advantages of a teacher's own plans over packaged materials?
9. Which techniques are best suited to the direct communication of information? Which are more directly concerned with practicing cognitive skills?
10. What government agency should be contacted for listings of health-related computer software?

Exercises
1. Based on the scope of health education as it is defined by your state board of education, develop a filing system of envelopes or folders. Begin a collection of related pamphlets, news clippings, pictures, cartoons, teaching ideas, and any other materials that could be resources for future lesson planning.

2. Analyze the similarities and differences among Tyler's principles, Goodlad's criteria, and Raths's value statements. Prepare a set of guidelines that represents a synthesis of all three.
3. Choose one cognitive behavior from each of the six Bloom categories and list as many group and individual techniques as you can that would allow the student to practice that behavior.
4. Analyze a health textbook designed for elementary, middle, or high school students and in current use in your state. Evaluate its worth on the basis of the criteria suggested in your text. What are its strengths and weaknesses? Would you recommend that book to a school board interested in adopting a new health text?
5. Select and study a software program designed for health education. Write a review discussing the content with which it is concerned and the cognitive processes the user must exhibit in completing the program. Conclude with your evaluation of its potential contribution to health education and the ease with which it could be used by students.
6. Choose one teaching aid or artifact for investigation and construction. Write a short paper explaining (a) how it is constructed, and (b) how it is most effectively employed and for what purpose, and (c) list the references that were most useful to you in preparing this report.

REFERENCES

Association for the Advancement of Health Education, "Microcomputers and health education." *Health Education* 14:6, Oct. 1983, whole issue.

Association for Experiential Education, *Journal for Experiential Education* 5:2, Summer 1982.

Beall, Sue, "Pilot programs." *Health Education,* Oct. 1983, p. 94.

Broudy, H. S., "Historic exemplars of teaching methods." In *Handbook of Research on Teaching,* edited by N. L. Gage. Chicago: Rand McNally, 1963, pp. 1–43.

Chen, M. S., and Cornett, B., "How effective are microcomputer-based programs for health education: a prospective view." *Health Education* 14:6, Oct. 1983, pp. 88–89.

Clark, R. L., "Reconsidering research on learning from media." *Review of Educational Research* 53:4, Winter 1983, pp. 445–457.

Combs, A. W., "What the future demands of education." *Phi Delta Kappan* 62:5, Jan. 1981, p. 372.

Conrad, D., and Hedin, D., "National assessment of experiential education: summary and implications." *Journal of Experiential Education* 4:2, Feb. 1981.

Dale, E., *Audio-Visual Methods in Teaching.* New York: Dryden Press, 1969.

Dalis, G., and Strasser, B., *Teaching Strategies for Value Awareness and Decision Making in Health Education.* Thorofare, NJ: Charles B. Slack, 1977.

Dede, C., and Allen, D., "Education in the 21st century: scenarios as a tool for strategic planning." *Phi Delta Kappan* 62:5, Jan. 1981.

Dunn, H. L., *High Level Wellness.* Arlington, VA: Beatty, 1967.

Festinger, L., *A Theory of Cognitive Dissonance.* Stanford, CA: Stanford University Press, 1957.

Goodlad, J. I., *Planning and Organizing for Teaching.* Washington, DC: National Education Association, 1963.

Goodlad, J. I., *A Place Called School: Prospects for the Future.* New York: Mcgraw-Hill, 1984.

Howe, L. W., and Howe, M. M., *Personalizing Education: Values Clarification and Beyond.* New York: Hart, 1975.

Hunter, M., *Teach for Transfer.* El Segundo, CA: TIP, 1971.

James, T., "Learning as practice into theory." *Phi Delta Kappan* 62:3, Nov. 1980, pp. 185–188.

Jernstedt, G. C., "Experiential components in academic courses." *Journal of Experiential Education* 3:2, Feb. 1980, pp. 11–19.

McDermott, R. J., and Belcastro, P. A., "The microcomputer bandwagon is here—but watch your step!" *Health Education,* Oct. 1983, pp. 76–78.

Means, R. K., *Teaching Health Today.* Portland, ME: Walch, 1973.

Metcalf, L. E., ed., *Values Education: Rationale, Strategies, and Procedures, Forty-first Yearbook.* Washington, DC: National Council for the Social Studies, 1971.

Raths, J. D., "Teaching without specific objectives." *Educational Leadership,* April 1971, p. 715.

Reynolds, S., "A marriage proposal: competency based education and experiential learning." *Journal of Experiential Education* 4:2, Feb. 1981, pp. 34–37.

School Health Education Study, *Health Education: A Conceptual Approach to Curriculum Design.* St. Paul, MN: 3M, 1967.

Simon, S. S., Howe, L. W., and Kirschenbaum, H., *Values Clarification.* New York: Hart, 1972.

Solleder, M. K., *Evaluation Instruments in Health Education.* Washington, DC: Alliance for Health, Physical Education, Recreation, and Dance, 1979.

Tyler, R. W., *Basic Principles of Curriculum and Instruction.* Chicago: University of Chicago Press, 1950.

Tyler, R. W., "A place called school." *Phi Delta Kappan* 64:7, March 1983, p. 463.

Unruh, G. G., "Can I be replaced by a package?" *Educational Leadership* 27:8, Aug. 1970.

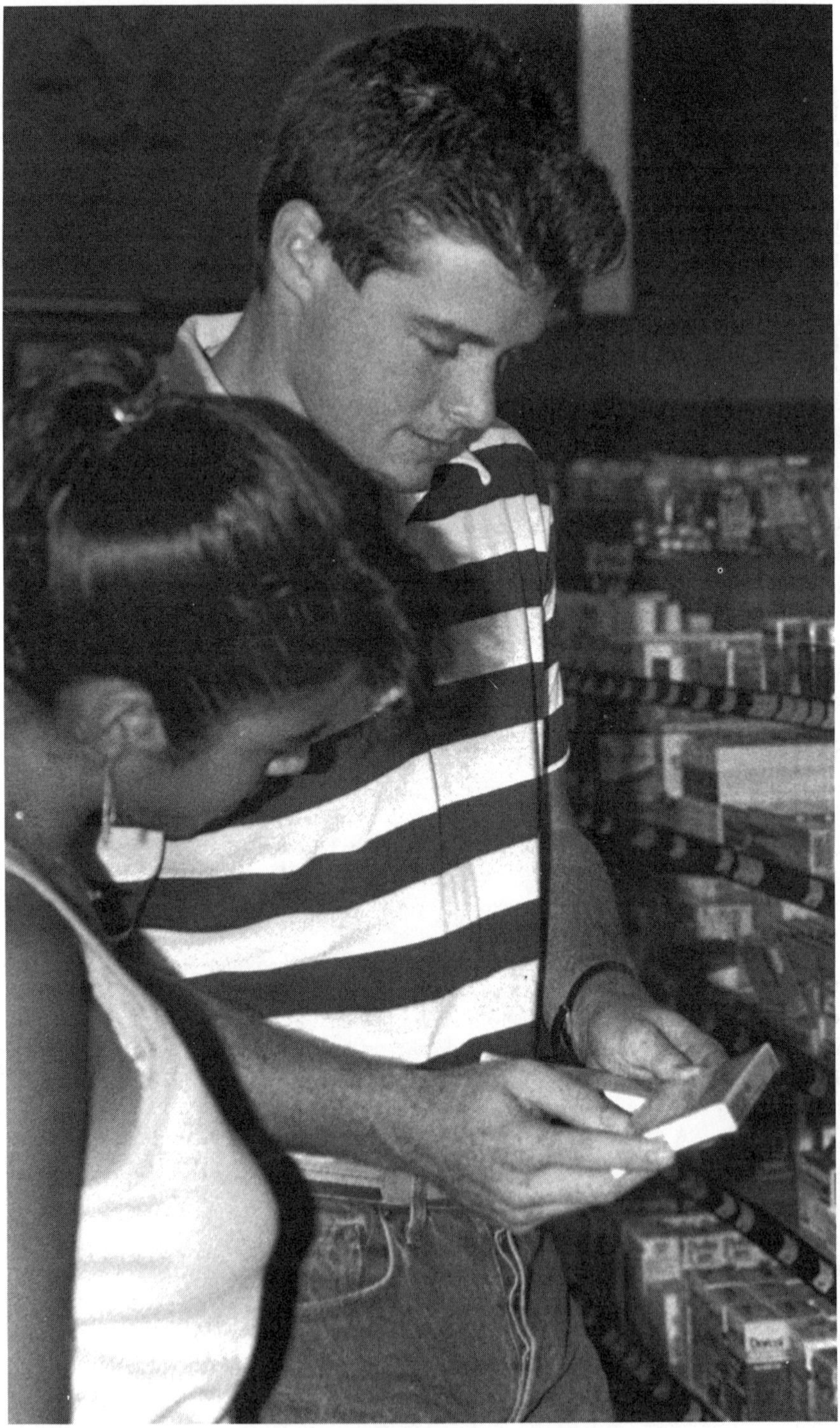

6
Avoiding controversy and criticism in health teaching

A Classroom Case Study

In a seventh grade classroom, students have been asked to make a report on reproductive anatomy. This is the lesson plan that is part of a broader unit on human reproduction extending over a five-day period. This unit, in turn, is part of the health education curriculum that deals with the larger subject of sexual development and responsibility. The following is an excerpt from a case study of the classroom experience when the lesson plan on reproductive anatomy was being implemented.

The teacher divided the class into groups of five (boys and girls randomly chosen), assigning them the task of researching and describing a particular reproductive anatomical area and including further information on its function and its meaning to them as male and female. One group was to describe the uterus, ovaries, and fallopian tubes, another the testicles, vas deferens, prostate, and semen. Others had similar related areas. Each group was to report to the whole class about its findings. They were to use the library resource reading lists as well as the slides and cassettes on their topic on reserve for their research.

The group reporting on the uterus, fallopian tubes, and ovaries is now reporting to the class.

One student has just described the uterus and ovaries in her own words, based on the combined research of her group: "And that's what happens when the egg pops from the ovary, but I forget the name of the tube that carries it from the ovary to the uterus." A male classmate from another group chides her: "You ought to know the name and how it works . . . that's *your* function." The reporting student answers defensively: "I'll remember it better when I menstruate, but I haven't started yet!" Whereupon he responds: "Hey, I'm never gonna menstruate, but I think we should *all* know what parts of our bodies are involved in making us boys or girls." The class then became involved in a wider discussion of their roles as future men and women and possible parents.

The teacher states that she could not have been more pleased with the approach she had taken to the topic. The students had to become involved in a process and a series of experiences that included doing research as teams and taking responsibility for synthesizing the material specific to their area in order to report clearly to their classmates. The need to relate anatomy to function and personal meaning led them into a discussion of social and health ramifications inherent in the topic.

How did the teacher incorporate sexual development and responsibility into the health curriculum? Was this an overall commitment of the long-range goals of health education in the school district? Had the administration and other teachers been advised about these units and lesson plans? Had it required approval of the school board or the parents? Were there repercussions from any sector? Were the students required to have permission to attend these sexuality classes? Did anyone, other than the students, know that the teacher was conducting classes on the topic? Why would these questions even arise? This chapter will focus on the origins of such questions and how they might be answered, but preferably how they may be avoided.

Chapter 4 emphasized that effective curriculum guides and lesson plans require attention to process-oriented versus content-oriented learning. The goal is for the student to become engaged cognitively and affectively in the subject. In no other area of the curriculum will these educational skills be more critical than in implementing the content of sensitive, personal, and private health behaviors unique to each individual. Our eating habits are personal and unique, and nutrition health topics are now traditional in schools. But they are also public, acquired through imitative behavior (parents, peers) and influenced by expressed preference of the family and its culture. Information, education, and learning about our sexuality, in contrast, are the result of the accumulation of nonpublic experiences and feelings that most often are not addressed by the family and almost never enacted (in the case of sexual intercourse) deliberately by parents for imitation by their children. In addition, *nonverbal* cues of family sexual beliefs, either restrictive *or* approving, also influence children's sexuality.

Other subjects besides sexuality and its related areas are also intimate, personal, and private. Preventive approaches to such topics, intended to promote health and well-being, frequently run into opposition from parents, community, and some school personnel. Why would this be so in a nation that is so committed to staying healthy? The most pragmatic reasons appear to be that most people do not think about their health until they become ill, and that financial and governmental support is committed to treating, rather than preventing, disease. Even though there is now ample evidence to demonstrate that support of preventive services can be beneficial to a large number of people and can eventually help reduce the numbers of those who require the most expensive therapies, the situation on funding has changed very little (Department of Health, Education and Welfare, 1979).

One other reason that the concepts of prevention, and/or health promotion have not been widely accepted is that many people consider personal health to be solely a private matter, and they perceive education or information about health as an intrusion in their health practices and an invasion of their privacy. These individuals or groups often find health topics in general, from nutrition and safety to all or any references to reproduction or to sexuality, to be controversial. It is for this reason that current and past health education textbooks contain chapters like this one, which focus on specific, controversial subjects.

BRIEF HISTORY OF THE CONTROVERSY

Over the years, debate and disagreement have centered on the same or similar subjects: sex education, addictive behavior, suicide of children and youth, sexual assault and abuse including rape and incest, sexually transmitted diseases, death and dying, and any courses considered to be "humanistic" (i.e., those that refer to a mind/body interaction that might influence human behavior and that bring a wide variety of viewpoints to the ethical issues involved).

The intensity of the opposition to these subjects and the addition or deletion of specific topics appear to be the major elements that change over time. These changes are usually predicated on social and cultural shifts in values for the particular period in which a person lives. This historical perspective is important for teachers to recognize, for it is useful in helping alleviate previous teaching and administrative patterns that may have precipitated dissension and opposition by some members of the community. "Those who do not remember the past are condemned to relive it" (George Santayana) best summarizes the cyclical nature of resistance to teaching in certain areas.

There is documentation to illustrate that opposition to sex education, however defined, appears to be stronger at some periods than others. Just after World War I, when the American Social Health Association attempted to educate the public about venereal diseases (now labelled sexually transmitted diseases or STDs), their efforts were met with strong dissenting opinions from various groups that believed "only promiscuous, bad" people contracted such diseases; therefore, others need not be worried. They also believed that words referring to sex would lead to a breakdown in sexual mores, causing havoc with family life and law and order. Similar opposition was heard with the publication of the Kinsey reports, *Sexual Behavior in the Human Male* (1948) and *Sexual Behavior in the Human Female* (1954) (Bullough 1976), and with the publication of the Masters and Johnson book *Human Sexual Response* (1966).

These public outcries were mirrored in the schools in those same years with an absence of curriculum content on human reproduction and normal growth and development or any reference to sexuality. In cases where attempts were made to provide such programs, teachers were often fired and principals and administrators removed or relocated. During the middle and late 1950s and 1960s, as parents who favored sex education helped back administrators and teachers, there was a gradual expansion of courses. By the late 1960s, many courses flourished. Some covered only one topic, such as menstruation; others combined a number of related topics about sexual function and behavior. Some states such as California and Colorado listed sex education as an important factor in health education and called for required courses. Some schools in many states still maintain such programs, but their struggles with a minority of parents and community opposition are the subject of numerous articles published over the last twenty-five years that are being closely reexamined today (Calderone, 1966; Hilu, 1967; Brown, 1981).

Although the history of the development of sex education in the schools is not the topic of this chapter, teachers and other professionals involved in health education are urged to consult some of these references so they can better appreciate the persistence of the issues and the nature of the opposing groups. The cyclic nature of the controversy over this period underscores the absence of any consistent progress. The AIDS epidemic of the 1980s has caused new confusion and panic, not only about the condition but also about how public and school education should address it.

CONTROVERSIAL SUBJECTS

Sex education is used in this chapter as one of the major examples of a controversial subject because it encompasses most of the objections raised to any controversial area and most frequently receives popular media attention. However, other sensitive topics have undergone similar cyclic periods of approval and opposition (Block, 1979). The following is not an exhaustive inventory of what might be included in each of the subjects in question. It is presented to emphasize that whether a curriculum includes only one, some, or all of these areas, it can become controversial whenever there is some objection to any one of them.

Sex education

The following subtopics may be included in sex education:

- human reproduction: fertilization, gestation, birth, delivery, anatomy of the reproductive tract, discussion of embryonic development, responsibilities of parenthood
- fertility and infertility: contraception, abortion, sterilization, artificial insemination, ovum implantation, discussions of problems and/or opportunities that cause people to seek help in having or preventing pregnancies
- sexuality: gender, gender roles, sex roles, sexual development, menstruation, masturbation, sexual orientation (homosexuality, bisexuality), sexual intercourse, sexual hormones, pornography, obscenity, discussion of social and ethical issues related to any of these
- sexually transmitted diseases: syphilis, gonorrhea, herpes, chlamydia, Acquired Immune Deficiency Syndrome (AIDS), the background and health implications of any or all of them
- sexual assault and abuse of children and adults: rape, incest, their impact on families and individuals
- family living: couple interaction, child rearing, premarital sexual activity, marriage, divorce, separation, discussions pertaining to them

Sexual development may be seen as only one aspect of total physical, intellectual, and social development. Many parents, students, teachers, health organizations, and other professionals in education and health support a course or a related health topic that provides students with information about sexual function, about human interaction, and about the opportunity to learn more about themselves as developing individuals. In this context, it relates to a number of other subjects in the health curriculum. Major opinion polls over the last three decades, both local and national, even in intense times of opposition to the subject, continue to reflect this support (National School Boards . . ., 1968; Reis, 1968; Scales, 1980).

The major benefits cited in these polls were the opportunity for the learner to explore with peers and responsible adults the role of sexuality as one aspect of being human and to open up discussions with parents about sexuality and sexual questions. This positive response from parents and the public was partially stimulated by the policies and position statements issued by health, medical, and educational professional associations supporting and/or advocating sex education as part of a health curriculum. In general, these policies did not suggest that sex education is a panacea for the sociosexual problems of society, but rather that information, exploration of attitudes, and discussion might help students understand their own sexual growth and recognize their responsibilities connected to sexual choices and might stimulate communication about sexual issues with their families. Some groups, no doubt, believed that sex education *would* help decrease sexually transmitted diseases, unwanted pregnancies, premarital sex, and a host of other sexual problems. For a brief period in the mid 1970s in some locales where teenage unwed pregnancy was being carefully studied in relation to sex education programs, the number of these pregnancies decreased. These controlled matched studies were encouraging. However, as financial support to schools decreased and nonbasic subjects (including sex education) were dropped, this trend ceased. The results of such studies were not pursued over time in large number, so current data give only limited information.

Opposition to sex education centers around a number of beliefs:

- that the school will usurp the natural role of parents to be the sex educators of their children
- that these courses teach children how to have sex; that information about reproduction, sexuality, or genital anatomy stimulates sexual experimentation
- that sex education promotes "irresponsible behavior"
- that students become more liberal following sex education courses (in all ways, not just sexually)
- that learning about sexuality promotes sex crimes
- that if information about sexually transmitted diseases is presented, students will no longer fear them (because they will know how to avoid or cure them) and therefore will become more promiscuous (In the case of AIDS, where no known cure or prevention is known, the stance has been to banish the people who have AIDS—once more not providing information.)
- that sex education will always include birth control methods and provide another way to promote promiscuity
- that students will be taught that abortion is a primary method of birth control

6 Avoiding Controversy and Criticism in Health Teaching 195

- that teachers will indoctrinate students with sexual ideas that are contrary to their family's values
- that homosexuality will be discussed and advocated as a way of life

These beliefs may originate in the parents's religious backgrounds, politics, or concern for parental rights. These rights must be respected while educational attempts are made to change the basic misinformation that perpetuates concern.

No one is neutral about the subject of sex. Most individuals have strong personal feelings about this subject that account for the intensity of emotions surrounding it. These beliefs and the questions they generate can be answered from available research from both prospective and retrospective studies now encompassing the past two decades. Although they do not show startling results that can be directly linked to the outcome of sex education, they do show some significant data reflecting the increase in responsible behavior on the part of teenagers and younger and older adults. Some of the findings include:

- Information and knowledge about sexuality, whether provided by the school, the family, or both, has not been shown to increase sexual experimentation. Basic and moral values and standards appear to be formed before children reach school age. Sexual behavior that violates values learned from one's family (positive or negative) does not change dramatically because of teaching meant to augment the family's expressed and nonexpressed attitudes toward sexuality (Hilu, 1967).
- Sex crimes do not increase in populations where sex education was part of the learning process. A large percentage of sex offenses are committed by persons with backgrounds lacking in sexual information and where ignorance about sex and sexual repression have been predominant (President's Commission on Obscenity and Pornography, 1970).
- A new commission on obscenity and pornography appointed by President Reagan has just completed its report. The findings and the text of the report are not available at the time of this writing. Advance newspaper items provide few reliable details.
- Students do not become more "liberal" in their thinking about sexual conduct following sex education courses. They do become more tolerant of the behavior of others and more responsible for their own.
- Following sex education courses in which contraception has been included as a topic, young people have demonstrated a high level of responsible sexual attitudes and behaviors; for example, unmarried

pregnancy rates in the communities analyzed have decreased. Studies indicate that this is due to (1) a *somewhat* increased use of contraception and (2) a reduction of sexual activity in general as students more openly discuss their sexual desires and resist peer pressure. These findings contradict the idea that increased irresponsible sexual activity will occur.
- A 1986 report of a controlled study of sex education in the Baltimore schools replicates these findings. It is to be published in detail in a forthcoming issue of the *Guttmacher Institute Journal*.

Abortion and sterilization can be discussed also. They are not alternative or substitute contraceptive measures, but options that people in this society may choose to end a pregnancy if the woman so wishes to prevent pregnancy. Frequently, the controversy that arises around these topics is that parents or the public believe that such information is equivalent to telling students what to do rather than describing what exists. If students were learning about choices patients have about their medical care, there would probably be no disagreement that they should have this information. A similar viewpoint about reproduction is usually not forthcoming because it is more highly charged emotionally for most people.

Studies show that racial differences in premarital pregnancy rates are lessening. Black and nonwhite pregnancy rates have consistently been higher statistically than white rates. As the overall educational level of minority students has increased, including sex education, the pregnancy rates in these groups have decreased (Furstenberg, Lincoln, and Menken, 1981; Cancila, 1985).

Students involved in sex education open up communication channels about sexuality with their parents. Parents and students who develop such dialogue have a more positive approach to their own sexuality, exhibit more self-respect, and limit impulsive sexual behavior (Albee, Gordon, and Leitenberg, 1983).

These studies are not as widely publicized as they might be, but even when they are, those in opposition do not accept them. Even in the mid 1980s, increasing numbers of school districts are dropping what little sex education they have whenever vocal objections of even a few parents are registered. In-depth integrative programs are being altered or diminished as disputes arise. The current spotlight on the nation's schools relating to student literacy, mathematical competency, and science skills allows minimal energy for many school administrators to cope with further criticism.

School and community health administrators must also consider other areas (i.e., child sexual abuse, assault, rape, incest, and the sexually transmitted diseases) as separate or inclusive topics of sex education. For many years, they were addressed only minimally or omitted, but with public attention focused on them, some parents who object to sex education demand that these areas be addressed. Others continue to want all information withheld. But a majority of parents and much of the general population feel they are important aspects of a health program (1983; Finkelhor, 1984a).

Child sexual assault and abuse, rape, and incest Although most parents agree that they want their 3- to 18-year-olds to be able to avoid situations where these problems may occur, they are suspicious about what should be conveyed about them. Health personnel whose personal and family lives have included these experiences, as well as students or parents of whom this has been true, do not feel less violated, but often appreciate the chance for it to be a health topic that might help others. Recently, child sexual abuse was a cover story for many U.S. newsmagazines. Television programs have covered father-daughter incest. Mailings have been made nationwide to encourage families to see such programs together in order to discuss their content. Previously, these topics were buried in health, medical, and social science literature, useful to the educator and scientist, but not very helpful to parents and children.

This is only one way for young people to learn about these problems. There are parents who do not watch TV specials or read magazines, or who refuse to do so with their children. There are families who do not talk even though they view such material. This kind of "one-shot" exposure to a subject does not constitute learning about it. Discussion, however, can become more open following such events, resulting in a truly positive benefit. Public figures have spoken out in newspapers, magazines, and even before a public Senate hearing about personal experiences of being sexually abused as a child and the dangers inherent in not reporting these happenings. Education about this subject requires a context in which learners can create internally an understanding of their own body privacy, the importance of talking about adult behavior that makes them uncomfortable or frightens them can be impressed on them, and they can be made aware of their own personal integrity (Sanford, 1980; Goodwin, 1982; Schlesinger, 1982; Finkelhor, 1984b; Hyde, 1984).

Sexually transmitted diseases The problem of sexually transmitted diseases (STDs) requires a discussion of various sexual behaviors in order for students to know how they are contracted and how they may be prevented. Their impact on their own lives and those of others are an equally important aspect of the learning process. Discussing *Acquired Immune Deficiency Syndrome (AIDS)* means that the subject of sexual preference or orientation (homosexuality and bisexuality) has to be addressed if it has not been included elsewhere in a course.

In many programs (either on human sexuality or STDs), the topic of sexual orientation is frequently omitted. Because questions about sexual identity are at their most intense between the ages of 10 and 18, this is one area that needs to be addressed, not only about its relationship to the spread of disease through sexual contact, but also in another context more suitably related to sexual development. In education about AIDS, its heterosexual spread through sexual contact with intravenous drug users and through blood transfusions (to contrast with sexual contact) must also be stressed. The further movement of this condition through the general population will most likely be through the I-V drug-using group. For school-age children and young adults, sexual contact with their peers who use IV drugs poses their highest risk of getting the disease. IV drug users are found in all age groups, from 10 to 70. Any of them can be sexual contacts.

Chlamydia, a vaginal viral infection especially prevalent in teenage and young adult women and infecting their partners as well, is now the leading worldwide sexually transmitted disease. Only recently has it begun to be diagnosed accurately. Its long-range complications are infertility in males and females. Ten percent of adult men and women experiencing fertility problems have been found to have been infected with chlamydia, which causes tissue destruction in the reproductive tract. This infection can be cured quite easily if detected early enough so that infertility does not occur. However, no preventive or curative measures can be taken unless the most susceptible population knows it exists and what its complications mean (Barlow, 1979; Cahill, 1983; Mayer and Pizer, 1983).

Herpes, a viral disease estimated as affecting more than 3 million people in this country, also causes infertility and can produce birth defects in children of mothers who have the disease. Currently there is no cure. However, couples are dealing with it by limiting their sexual interaction to periods when the infection is in remission. They must also learn as much as possible about how their bodies react to the virus and how to manage their sexual lives so as not to infect a noninfected partner or spouse. When both partners are infected, they have to consider in advance their decision to have children and/or recognize that a surgical caesarian delivery may be necessary to give their child the best chance of being free of birth defects.

Gonorrhea is currently a worldwide epidemic that is frequently found in conjunction with other STDs. It is detectable and treatable. There is no vaccine to prevent it, and no immunity is bestowed once a person has been infected and treated. They can become reinfected. Unlike the diseases previously mentioned, this one does not have the same life-threatening or fertility-damaging consequences. Although sterility *can* occur in both males and females as the result of infection, it occurs less frequently because treatment can be instituted when a person has the symptoms. Gonorrhea is a frequent infection associated with child and adult sexual abuse, assault, and rape.

Syphilis is one of the earliest sexually transmitted diseases in medical history. It is a life-threatening disease that over time, if untreated, will be fatal. It is readily diagnosed, and there is effective treatment. As with gonorrhea, there is no preventive innoculation, and there is no immunity conferred even when a person has been infected and treated. They can again become infected through sexual contact. Public health measures have greatly diminished this once plaguelike disease through routine blood testing, notification of the sexual contacts of infected persons, and specific treatment of individuals involved.

Although these are highly charged areas, if students' needs are to be met, information and discussion of all these aspects of sexuality bear analysis and better understanding. If they are ignored, more newborns will suffer unnecessary birth and delivery defects, increased infertility will occur, and sexual ignorance in general will continue to escalate.

Teachers must recognize and be familiar with the above array of topics that may be included in sex education so that they will be more aware of the intense reactions of even a few parents. Only with this broad base from which to work can they treat the subject with respect and responsibility, whether in the curriculum planning stages, in their own preparation for teaching, or in the classroom. Their ability then to meet and cope with individual or group objections will be greatly enhanced (Gendel and Green, 1971; Jenkinson, 1979; Ryan and Dunn, 1979).

Addictive behavior

Alcohol and drug use appears to be occurring at earlier ages (Milkman and Shaffer, 1985). Experimentation with beer, wine, and whiskey has increased as the adults whom school-age children emulate have increased their own drinking, as well as continuing their use of recreational drugs. Children as young as 8 years old have been identified as "drinkers" in primary school classrooms. Junior high school students in particular appear to be especially vulnerable. Despite the adult health movement toward more exercise and fewer stimulants, only a small proportion of the U.S. population (about 25 million people) is involved in exercise. In addition to family members, students' "idols" of music and film are frequently heavy users of stimulants. Front page stories about athletes and other public figures being arrested for trafficking and/or using drugs or driving while intoxicated do not diminish these heroes in their admirers' eyes. Many parents themselves are also avid fans of these same figures.

Addictive behavior does not contain as many subtopics as those subsumed under sex education. It deserves, however, to be examined in its most comprehensive scope in order to alert teachers and administrators to the areas about which opposition occurs (Croskeg, 1979; Mills, Neal, and Peed-Neal, 1983).

- alcohol use—social uses; history of beer, wine, and whiskey use (ceremonial, celebratory); chemical nature of alcohol addiction and its definition as a disease and not a moral aberration
- psychological features of alcohol abuse, influence of addiction on work, family, and personal development
- public drunkenness, legal consequences, death and disability from accidents caused by intoxication, as well as family disruption and child abuse
- physical effects of alcohol and its relationship to chronic disease, death, and suicide (Finn and O'Gorman, 1981; Grant and Ritson, 1983).
- illegal drugs—marijuana, LSD, amphetamines, cocaine, and heroin
- chemical addiction, psychological dependence, and serious diseases including AIDS (spread by use of contaminated needles), death, and suicide.

Care must be given to the sensitivities, fears, and guilt of students whose parents or other close family members are alcoholic. Some students may be witness to or subjects of abuse and exposure to quarrels and violence. Many times opposition to teaching in this area comes from just such families, especially when the problems are being denied or ignored.

Because the initial response to drug use is a pleasant or "high" experience (except for individuals who are allergic to some of the ingredients), teaching about the consequences of starting drug use frequently has little meaning for students (Huber and Bentler, 1980). This information is central to the topic, just as it is with alcohol use. However, the heroes of young children and some of their parents are athletes and TV and movie personalities whose drug exploits also receive national attention. Their popularity, however, does not decrease. Those parents who are horrified by these activities have only a small impact on their children's continuing idolization.

"Pushers" and the sale of drugs are generally not shown in a positive light in movie and TV scripts. However, the theme of drug trafficking is frequently featured in these media as adventuring, in "cops and robbers" fictional story lines, or on the news as matters of financial gains involving the "rich and famous."

Intravenous use of drugs with exchange of needles is the second major means of spreading AIDS. Frequently, young people (as well as adults) wishing to experiment are either unaware of this complication or choose to believe "it can't happen to me." Everyone who is an IV drug user is not a "doped out" drop-out from society. Individuals of any age and socioeconomic group can be intravenous users, hiding their habit and continuing to function at school or at work.

Adequate attention has not been given to the criminal focus in the movement of drugs in neighborhoods, across the country, and internationally. The overall human harm of drugs to users and nonusers has not been stressed. What needs to be more clearly demonstrated is the association between specific drug ring assassinations and of deaths of family members, including children of drug dealers and their associates. These innocent groups are engulfed through violence, blackmail, graft, and petty theft (Anderson, 1981).

Teachers need to be aware of these ramifications as some of their students become caught up in loyalties to family members and friends who may use drugs. Just as intense are the reactions of such families to what they perceive as slanders against their own behavior, especially if social use of drugs is a significant part of their life-style. Including addictive behaviors in a health curriculum and the approaches used require consideration, not only of the topic itself, but of the characteristics and demographics of the local community (Jessor, Chase, and Donovan, 1980; Mayer and Filstead, 1980; Miller and Nerinberg, 1984). Prescription drugs and their addictive side effects, their casual use by other than the patient, and the borrowing of pills and capsules from parents or relatives raise similar family and peer issues.

It is around such questions that the guilt, shame, or anger of some parents are concentrated. For the majority of opposition forces, the following beliefs seem to be voiced most often:

- Teaching about addictive behavior will cause it to occur
- Discussion of drugs and alcohol and their effects will stimulate students to experiment with them
- Experimentation with any one drug or with alcohol will lead to increased and multiple drug use
- Exposure to discussion of social and cultural uses of alcohol (including customs of many religious denominations) is a form of approval of use of alcohol
- Teachers and/or administrators (schools) have more permissive attitudes toward alcohol/drug life-styles and are therefore telling students that they can choose their own options

Many parents and communities support education about addictive behavior. Sometimes they expect results from teaching that are unrealistic (i.e., that information alone will prevent addictive behavior). However, the majority believes that education will assist their children in understanding the problems so that they are more likely to avoid them. Their expectations reflect what has been found in the few studies conducted on behavior and attitude changes:

- Information and education permit students to take a more critical view of their own and their peers' behaviors
- Public drunkenness and drug-induced violent or destructive behavior is not supported by the peer group
- Some students with drug and alcohol problems seek counseling and/or other treatment in order to break their addictive habits
- Drug dealers on school grounds move on because they are unable to recruit new users
- Students themselves are no longer tolerant of drug dealing activities and are more prone to identify and report them

As in other areas of controversy and dispute, there is little publicity about such studies, if indeed they are known to local communities (Cornacchia, Smith, and Bentel, 1978; Huber and Bentler, 1980; McAlister et al., 1980; Nahas and Frick, 1981; Grant and Ritson, 1983).

Death and dying (including suicide)

Ordinarily, discussion of suicide in a school begins after a student suicide has occurred. Curriculum topics focused on the causes, prevention, and consequences of suicide are generally not part of a general health curriculum.

Because of the sharp increase in adolescent suicide over the past three decades, some individual school districts and/or teachers have attempted to review the question in order to prevent imitative behavior by other students within the district and to help students cope with their own feelings of perplexity, their own depression and fears over the loss of a peer. The Center for Disease Control of the United States Public Health Service, as well as local and state suicide prevention centers, have been aware of the problem for many years. Large segments of the public have been involved in suicide prevention units, assisting families where youth suicides have occurred, helping identify high risk youthful populations, and responding to suicide hot lines (Hendin, 1982; Husain and Vandiver, 1984; Mandle, 1984; Mercy et al., 1984).

Although much information has been collected, no strong conclusions have been reached concerning suicide prevention (Sudak, Ford, and Rushforth, 1984). Many people still consider suicide of a family member a family failure or family disgrace. The social stigma associated with suicide has not lessened. Thus, the currently available statistics may be only a small reflection of the true number in this country. Parents tend to report as accidental deaths that may have been suicide. The suicide rate for white males 15 to 24 years of age has increased by 50 percent from 1970 to 1980, while the rate in females and nonwhite males in the same age group remained relatively stable (Hendin, 1982).

The low suicide reporting rate reflects that one aspect of the opposition (to include suicide topics in a health education program) is the negative social attitude it evokes. Most religious teachings and many ethical and philosophical positions strongly condemn suicide. Attempts to analyze suicide deaths or to institute methodologies for developing profiles of high risk children and their families are frequently perceived as an invasion of privacy of the dead child's life and the lives of the survivors, as well as an attack on a family's religious and/or ethical values.

Studies of death and dying and courses designed to help children examine this part of life in their school years appear to fall into a similar trap. Opposition centers on the taboo nature of the subject in society at large, on religious convictions, on privacy issues, and on the "humanistic" characteristics attributed to these subjects. Conflict centers most frequently on the latter concept. Some groups believe that examining philosophical and ethical issues from the standpoint of the varying worldviews on the subject is the same as overriding their own family values. This so-called open approach to a topic appears to be threatening on these grounds to some parents and to be unnecessary and frivolous to others (Green and Irish, 1971).

Those parents who support this educational effort tend to want their children to explore areas that may be pertinent to their overall development. They frequently believe that students' exposure to death of their own friends or family members or through media coverage of deaths of familiar figures can be overwhelming in their impact. If there has been some previous preparation for a more realistic, less violent, and less mystifying approach to the subject, through education, students' reactions might be less devastating.

When high schools offer units on death and dying, they are oversubscribed. Students appear to have a keen interest in a subject about which they all have thoughts and fears, but about which they have little opportunity to express themselves. A number of the articles on this subject compare the controversy about education about death to education about sexuality. Since the death of a teacher-astronaut, more parents appear to favor implementation of topics dealing with loss and grief following death.

COMMON THEMES UNDERLYING CONTROVERSY

The roots of disagreement about each of the subjects reviewed appear to have a number of common themes where parents and the community are concerned.

Loss of control over children's behavior

Examining specific subjects in a factual way, providing an overview of varying cultural and ethical beliefs, and encouraging peer discussion in a classroom setting translates to some parents and community groups as a loss of control over their children's lives. There is a segment of the parent population that ignores, denies, or avoids the subjects altogether. Facts alone become a frightening encroachment on their right to protect their children from these topics.

If control of their children's behavior is predicated on instilling fear or guilt in them, the parent's wish is to eliminate the chances that the child will learn that there are solutions and preventive measures that can result in less frightening consequences of particular behaviors. A "worldview" of a particular topic is anathema to those families that do not want children to learn about other beliefs and cultures and hope to keep children who are "different" out of the circle of their children's friends.

Either/or beliefs about education: by the family versus the school

With parents who *do* wish to educate their children in the home on all these subjects, their objection to courses in school are based on an either/or belief. They do not wish family-oriented teaching to be usurped by classroom treatment of the subject. They do not view school-based curriculum as adjunctive or complementary to their own efforts and as a way of expanding their children's breadth of understanding. Instead, they see it as competitive and perhaps contradictory to home teaching.

Secondary political gain

A small percentage of parents opposes teaching all the subjects listed in this chapter. Their motives are politically inspired and do not represent religious or personal views, although they will frequently mask the purpose of their opposition by joining with other opposing groups. In the 1960s and 1970s, the John Birch Society and other radical right-wing groups represented the major political agitators. In the 1980s, similar fringe right-wing groups are the major groups seeking secondary political gain by keeping dissension and opposition alive and visible in the community and in the media. These groups are skillfully organized and sophisticated in their techniques. Their strength lies in building lists of parents and community groups that already express fears and genuine concern about sensitive subjects. These parents are then sent material quoted out of context about curriculum content, about goals to subvert their children's morals, as well as highly charged propaganda implying that teachers, administrators, and school board members may be part of a communist conspiracy (see figures 1 and 2, pages 206–211). It has been estimated that approximately 1 percent of the total number of people involved in disputes about curriculum content belong in this agitator/political category. Their tactics exacerbate the fears of parents at all levels.

Ignoring the issues prevents the "problems"

For many parents, data supporting the need for students to be informed about critical issues affecting their lives as a means of demystifying them and reducing the physical and psychological damage that ignorance frequently promotes appear never to be adequate. The belief that "ignorance is bliss" or that "ignorance preserves innocence" continues to be prevalent among those parents who fear loss of control over their children's behavior. For example, from the time of World War I into the late 1940s and 1950s, sexually transmitted diseases, teenage pregnancy, and use of drugs were believed to be "under control" by being associated with only certain segments of the population. Only uneducated, underprivileged children and adults were considered subject to such problems. This gave parents a feeling of security for their children and less of a need to feel they were vulnerable. We know now, however, that it was simply a way of ignoring more widespread behavior that involved all socioeconomic groups and educational levels. When it became known that drug use, increased unwed pregnancy, or other negatively regarded behaviors were also prevalent across broader demographic dimensions (meaning that middle- and upper-class children and adults were involved), panic and further reaction resulted. At this point, families in these expanded population groups produced enough pressure to galvanize interest by federal health and research agencies to make funds available for special programs to address these problems (Milkman and Shaffer, 1985).

Parent's fears of discovery of prior or current behaviors

There are emotional overtones to all the controversial topics. Parents who currently, or in the past, have personally experienced drug or alcohol addiction, sexual abuse, unwanted pregnancy, or other problem behavior feel particularly threatened. Unresolved psychological trauma resulting from these experiences will frequently intensify these feelings.

Loss of trust in school administration and teachers

Active "opposition groups" can undermine the trust that parents often normally have for the school's educational endeavors. These groups distort

FIGURE 1
Example of "opposition" material sent to parents in Kansas in 1969

We are forced to make up a form letter to keep up with requests for literature and directives on combatting "FAMILY LIFE EDUCATION" and "SENSITIVITY TRAINING". For further details or special requests, please specify "Research Department."

Dear

Almost all of the FAMILY LIFE EDUCATION programs are produced from material outlined in the *Teacher's Resource Guide* K through 12th Grades. This means that such material as "Time of Your Life" TV and "How Babies Are Made" slides (as well as other described evidence) may or may not be included in your particular program. These are just *two* of the visual aids out of *over 500 books, pamphlets, tapes, movies, etc.* that have been prepared for the wholesale indoctrination of our children. Therefore, our research department has been working on an in-depth investigation of all materials listed in the "over-all" Teacher's Resource Guides, and has come to the following conclusions:

1. That this program is intended as a national method of influencing the "think patterns" of our children away from the traditional Judaic-Christian ethical culture formulated by our Nation's Founding Fathers, towards a Humanist and Socialist approach in matters of Faith and Morals, as well as Political Science.

2. That the new political "activists" now controlling the National Education Association are largely responsible for the *dissemination and acceptance* of this controversial program through all of their associated school organizations, both public and parochial, thereby influencing local educators and school boards excessively.

3. That S.I.E.C.U.S. (Sex Information and Education Council of the U.S.) is the promotional agency, as well as the influencing "brain-trust" comprising most of the writers or dictating their material. Its directors determine the philosophy and "indoctrinating" procedures, both from a sexual and sociological standpoint, as well as enforcing "sensitivity" training in psychological techniques on teachers in order to manipulate the attitudes of their students. They actually boast in their own literature that this "revolutionary" material is based on the philosophy of Humanism (defined constitutionally as an "Anti-God Religion") as well as the political philosophy of Socialism, which is the antithesis of our free-enterprise system. "Indoctrination" (day-by-day "brainwashing" from infancy to maturity) replaces academic education. For instance, sex

FIGURE 1 (*continued*)

education would not be limited to scheduled class hours; it would be integrated into all classes.

We are basing our campaign on the judgment that most educators are too "involved" because of their positions to be trusted to sacrifice expediency for principle. Unfortunately, many of our clergy and religious in the educational field have fallen into this same category . . . in order to qualify for the federal subsidies dangled before them for the first time. We must rely on the PARENTS, and those responsible citizens who are willing to challenge this intolerable program.

We suggest you SAVE YOURSELF THE FRUSTRATION OF APPEALING TO THE SCHOOL BOARDS—*GO DIRECTLY TO THE PEOPLE!*—TO THE PARENTS WHO CARE ABOUT THE MORALITY OF THEIR CHILDREN AND THE CONSTITUTIONAL AS WELL AS GOD-GIVEN DUTY TO UPHOLD IT! It is unfortunate, but NECESSARY that we must SUBJECT THEM TO THIS "SHOCK THERAPY" . . . IF ONLY TO PREVENT OUR CHILDREN FROM BEING INOCULATED WITH IT INSTEAD.

WE SUGGEST:

1. PASS OUT WHATEVER LITERATURE YOU FEEL MOST EFFECTIVE FOR YOUR PARTICULAR SCHOOL OR DISTRICT.
2. DISTRIBUTE IT AT *EVERY* SCHOOL MEETING AND *EVERY* OPPORTUNITY.
3. HAND IT OUT DOOR-TO-DOOR. (DO *NOT* PUT IN MAIL BOXES—It is against postal regulations to put *anything* in mail boxes.)

WE PROMISE YOU, THEY WILL DO THE REST. We've proved this in many cities, starting with our own and using Redwood City (The County School Board and headquarters for the Teacher's Resource Guide) as a "Test" city of our own. YOUNG PARENTS RESPONDED MAGNIFICENTLY . . . OVER 2,000 DEMANDED AND *GOT* ACTION. NOW THEY ARE WORKING ON "RECALLS" AND OTHER SCHOOL REFORMS.

SAN LUIS OBISPO DISTRIBUTED 1,000 PIECES OF LITERATURE FIRST AND THEN 10,000 MORE WHEN THEY DISCOVERED THE

FIGURE 1 (concluded)

REACTION! ANAHEIM DID THE SAME—RICHMOND CREATED AN UPROAR IN *2 WEEKS* BY FOLLOWING THESE SUGGESTIONS. YOU CAN DO THE SAME!

    All of our literature is available at $12.00 per 1,000, mixed or matched (except the documentary booklets—they are 3 for $1.00). You have our permission to reprint it yourself if you can do it more cheaply, but we doubt you can unless you have a machine of your own. Most of our time and research is donated, and *NO ONE PROFITS—EXCEPT OUR CHILDREN,* WE HOPE. We also have the advice of our *Attorney* . . . for our concerted State effort . . . and eventually, we expect a SUPREME COURT TEST. Therefore, we desperately need legal contributions at all times. We found that a RUMMAGE SALE and GARAGE SALES help get us "off the ground" in handling some of the expenses. We suggest that each town who feels they have benefited by our original action have a similar rummage sale or garage sale to help us enlarge our legal fund to fight this in the Courts and through research and legislative activity. CITIZENS FOR PARENTAL RIGHTS was formed *solely* for these purposes . . . to research and disseminate information . . . to correlate ideas and activities of other concerned parental groups . . . to collect funds for court actions that benefit all of our children . . . and to be able to sue if necessary.

    Please stipulate if contributions are for "literature" or "legal fund".

                                            Thank you, and God bless our efforts.

CITIZENS FOR PARENTAL RIGHTS
P.O. BOX 593
Belmont, Calif. 94002

                                            Margaret Scott, Publicity Chairman

---

or sensationalize the subject material to promote their own causes. These are often politically motivated operations directed toward establishing a power base to attack education in general by discrediting part of it. The community at large may also enter the debate (city and county commissioners, other legislative bodies, newspapers), thereby directing disproportionate attention to the subjects in question (Scales, 1980).

    Generally, teachers are trusted to teach most subjects. When the topic is controversial, however, both the training and the background of the teacher

FIGURE 2
Support for the Hatch Amendment, 1984

Hatch Amendment regulation advocates urge parents to demand school compliance

- You probably remember the Hatch Amendment. Last year an assortment of Far Right groups advocated that the Administration adopt regulations for the enforcement of a Privacy Rights piece of legislation known as the Hatch Amendment. The strict regulations these groups wanted would have had the effect of prohibiting many federally-funded projects—including D/D programs—from ever being used in classrooms.
- The actual regulations adopted were considerably better than those the Far Right groups had proposed. Which may mean all is right (no pun intended) with the world. Or maybe not. The letter below has been sent nationwide to parents by Phyllis Schlafly's Eagle Forum, which has been consistently pro-strict Hatch regulations, anti-NDN, and anti-Education Department. For your information. Don't be surprised if teachers in classrooms where you work begin receiving letters that look a lot like this one.

PARENTS: HOW TO PROTECT YOUR RIGHTS—Here is a sample letter (prepared by the Maryland Coalition of Concerned Parents on Privacy Rights in Public Schools) which you can copy and send to the president of your local School Board (with copy to your child's school principal) in order to protect parental and student rights under the Hatch Amendment Regulations effective Nov. 12, 1984. This letter does NOT ask for the removal of any course or material; it merely demands that the schools obey the law and secure written parental consent before subjecting children to any of the following. Parents are NOT required to explain their reasons for denying consent.

To: School Board President _____ Date: _____

Dear _____.

I am the parent of _____ who attends _____ School. Under U.S. legislation and court decisions, parents have the primary responsibility for their children's education, and pupils have certain rights which the schools may not deny. Parents have the right to assure that their children's beliefs and moral values are not undermined by the schools. Pupils have the right to have and to hold their values and moral standards without direct or indirect manipulation by the schools through curricula, textbooks, audio-visual materials, or supplementary assignments.

FIGURE 2 (*continued*)

Accordingly, I hereby request that my child be involved in NO school activities or materials listed below unless I have first reviewed all the relevant materials and have given my written consent for their use:

Psychological and psychiatric examinations, tests, or surveys that are designed to elicit information about attitudes, habits, traits, opinions, beliefs, or feelings of an individual or group;

Psychological and psychiatric treatment that is designed to affect behavioral, emotional, or attitudinal characteristics of an individual or group;

Values clarification, use of moral dilemmas, discussion of religious or moral standards, role-playing or open-ended discussions of situations involving moral issues, and survival games including life/death decision exercises;

Death education including abortion, euthanasia, suicide, use of violence, and discussions of death and dying;

Curricula pertaining to alcohol and drugs;

Instruction in nuclear war, nuclear policy, and nuclear classroom games;

Anti-nationalistic, one-world government or globalism curricula;

Discussion and testing on inter-personal relationships; discussions of attitudes toward parents and parenting;

Education in human sexuality, including premarital sex, extra-marital sex, contraception, abortion, homosexuality, group sex and marriages, prostitution, incest, masturbation, bestiality, divorce, population control, and roles of males and females; sex behavior and attitudes of student and family;

Pornography and any materials containing profanity and/or sexual explicitness;

Guided fantasy techniques; hypnotic techniques; imagery and suggestology;

Organic evolution, including the idea that man has developed from previous or lower types of living things;

Discussions of witchcraft, occultism, the supernatural, and Eastern mysticism;

Political affiliations and beliefs of student and family; personal religious beliefs and practices;

Mental and psychological problems and self-incriminating behavior potentially embarrassing to the student or family;

Critical appraisals of other individuals with whom the child has family relationships;

Legally recognized privileged and analogous relationships, such as those of lawyers, physicians, and ministers;

Income, including the student's role in family activities and finances;

Non-academic personality tests; questionnaires on personal and family life and attitudes;

Autobiography assignments; log books, diaries, and personal journals;

Contrived incidents for self-revelation; sensitivity training, group encounter sessions, talk-ins, magic circle techniques, self-evaluation and auto-criticism; strategies designed for self-disclosure (e.g., zig-zag);

Sociograms; sociodrama, psychodrama; blindfold walks; isolation techniques.

The purpose of this letter is to preserve my child's rights under the Protection of Pupil Rights Amendment (the Hatch Amendment) to the General Education Provisions Act, and under its regulations as published in the *Federal Register* of

FIGURE 2 (concluded)

> Sept. 6, 1984, which became effective Nov. 12, 1984. These regulations provide a procedure for filing complaints first at the local level, and then with the U.S. Department of Education. If a voluntary remedy fails, federal funds can be withdrawn from those in violation of the law. I respectfully ask you to send me a substantive response to this letter attaching a copy of your policy statement on procedures for parental permission requirements, to notify all my child's teachers, and to keep a copy of this letter in my child's permanent file. Thank you for your cooperation.

are often questioned. Parents will demand more than the usual character references. English or math teachers are expected to be qualified in these teachable subjects, and their characters are assumed to be above reproach because all teachers must meet certain standards in both areas. Trained health teachers who include sex education in their programs will suddenly become objects of particular investigation into their private lives (Ryan and Dunn, 1979).

Demands for proof that courses will solve social and health problems

There are expectations that if a topic deals with personal problem behavior, the problem will be "cured" once the course is completed. The school may be requested to show "proof" that this is the case. Teachers of American government cannot prove that their former students are active voters, which would "prove" that at least one expected outcome of their learning could be measured. The fact that voter registration over the past twenty-five years has diminished has not caused removal of these courses. There is no methodology to "prove" that courses about controversial topics change behaviors because outcomes cannot be measured, except over a lifetime of experiences. The short-term studies on unwed pregnancy and other areas have not been amply evaluated over time to provide long-term results (Hilu, 1967).

COMMON CONCERNS OF TEACHERS AND ADMINISTRATORS ABOUT CONTROVERSIAL SUBJECTS

Educators in schools and communities want to be as fully prepared as possible in all of their work. When topics become labeled "controversial," reactions vary. Some teachers do not wish to be associated with the topic or the person who will teach it. Some of their reasons include feeling unprepared, reacting to their own life experiences (the same as parents), objecting to subjects being taught separately, and wanting to help establish for the topics a context that fits children's needs.

Conflicts on policy

There are conflicts over how to manage controversial material and how to develop policy, with whom, during what school years. How will the school maintain its leadership and facilitating role with parents and the community in the face of opposition? How can controversy about subjects be prevented?

Teachers particularly find themselves the victims in disputes about what sensitive subjects will be covered in health promotion. The principal, the administrator, and the school board often assign the subject to competent teachers but then do not provide the necessary in-service training or suitable resources. Those teachers are left on their own.

Current administrative pressures

Administrators know that the schools are being scrutinized by numerous private and governmental institutions. They are not rushing to seek the spotlight over causes that conceivably will hurt the perception of the important role of education in our society. They may be sincerely dedicated to the needs of students for learning about critical issues, but may be unable to risk the loss of funds or personnel in defense of a specific subject.

Framing educational goals

Meeting students' health needs relevant to their sexual and social behavior is a more difficult goal in curriculum planning. It includes consideration of the attitudes and behaviors of students' families and friends, the media focus on these behavioral/health topics, and the values of these groups based on societal changes.

How can these goals be made clear to parents? Although most authorities and a majority of the public believe these goals can be reached most appropriately by the schools, the strident nature of opposition groups continues to inhibit their continuation and development.

Why should this be so? Most administrators, teachers, and school board members find the greatest obstacle to be the increased time and energy necessary to avoid controversy or to refute it once subjects are in place. Those who begin including any of these topics in health education without knowing that controversy is likely to occur are surprised, angry, and often disillusioned by such responses. Assuming defensive positions can be demoralizing and inappropriate. Several school districts in the past won suits brought against them by opposition groups to delete sex education, for instance, from the curriculum. But these victories were gained only by disrupting the overall school program and caused continuing concern for the feelings of the students whose parents were involved in dissent.

Preventing controversy and teaching students what they need to know

The following suggestions can be useful both to those who currently include some of the disputed subjects in the health curriculum and to those who contemplate doing so.

Development of a health promotion policy Students and teachers alike function best in a human and physical environment that enhances personal interaction. In this sense, the school serves as a prototype of the home and the community. Attaining an overreaching health instruction goal requires planning, teamwork, and safe physical surroundings in which to work. Development of a health promotion policy is a major step in this process. It will not bring instant solutions to those problems related to sensitive teaching areas—but without a policy, or framework in which to operate, a number of school endeavors will be unsuccessful.

Health policy encompasses defining the goal of the total health promotion program to provide a baseline for all members of the school and community to establish communication about the purpose of health education. Particular subjects (controversial or otherwise) will vary from district to district. The objective, however, is to involve those who will be affected by the policy.

Involvement of school personnel Involving all school personnel in the orientation about health promotion helps avoid major misunderstandings. Administrators, students, the health teacher, and the health team (nurse, counselor, health aides, physician) not only contribute to planning, but provide the links to those not involved directly in health education tasks. Clerks, custodians, and teachers of other subjects need to know that health instruction is part of the curriculum and to understand the relationship of the topics they teach to health education, especially to the controversial subjects. Developing this kind of understanding among teachers may avoid school rumors and disagreements typified by a remark by one teacher about another: "*She* teaches sex education—nobody *else* would."

Evolution of an integrated approach There is no isolated "unit" on addictive behaviors or sex education in an integrated program. Thoughtful planning by teachers can make specific connections to the long-range goal of health education in a continuum that is applicable to the life experiences of the students. This approach is not a device for "hiding the subject" (i.e., sex education hidden under the guise of "family life" or a facet of "community responsibility," sexual assault and abuse being depersonalized as a "social ill"). It does require applying the principles of curriculum development to topics that have often been isolated from the rest of the health curriculum by special treatment.

Engagement of parents and the community Some schools have determined that parents and the public should have an opportunity to decide what their children will do about participating in health education classes that include sensitive topics. This kind of action is likely to imply that the educational system is not sure about what it is doing.

More useful is a statement to parents that critical issues will be dealt with in the context of overall health teaching. Parents would then be informed about the topics to be included and invited to review the content and offer suggestions to the curriculum planners. To accomplish this, several approaches have been used, ranging from a series of small group meetings between interested parents who respond to the initial statement and teachers to arranging larger assemblies. The organization depends on *an assessment of community attitudes.* Some school districts conduct polls about parents' positions on various subjects, whether or not they are controversial. Others hold a series of lectures or orientations for parents about new or different curriculum material (e.g., computer instruction, intramural varsity sports, sex education).

One example of an initial announcement is "Behavioral patterns relating to sexuality, drug and alcohol use, etc. are part of the health education curriculum. The outline of the goals and objectives is contained in the health policy statement. Please don't hesitate to contact us (teacher, board, administration) if you have comments or questions about particular subjects." Sending consent forms to parents or convening special parent meetings to discuss only particularly sensitive subjects just takes them out of context. Informing parents about the general direction of health education, health, and health services is consistent with the patterns used for other subjects. The parents are informed, they are free to request more information, but their "permission" or "consent" is not solicited. Parents and the community at large are thereby invited to learn more about all aspects of the school program and to receive additional information as desired.

Another approach involves using a "model" to demonstrate an integrated health promotion program where controversial topics are integral to the total health curriculum. Selecting one school in which the teacher, students, members of the health team, and community organizations have been involved in designing the health teaching must first take place. As an example, the health team may be offering a service or screening related to the particular topic, such as role playing in counseling a student who has contracted herpes or providing an ongoing display table with literature from self-help groups (articles about recent research for treatment and cure and a series of "tips" on prevention). Concurrently, the community health educator or nurse may be conducting discussions on the "life-style" impact of sexually transmitted diseases (STDs) in general to various community groups. Students are encouraged or arrangements are made for small classroom groups to visit these programs, where former patients or self-help leaders will talk about their own experiences. The teachers, meanwhile, are presenting an ongoing program on the positive social and psychological factors connected with understanding one's own sexuality as one facet of one's total health. The STDs are being used as one example of upsetting a health balance, whether or not the student is sexually active. The concept for a non–sexually active student will be descriptive and instructive; for a sexually active student, it may raise awareness of the need for an examination or for informing a partner. The physical, social, and emotional factors will impact differently on each student.

This "model" class can serve as a pilot or laboratory for other teachers. They can observe or meet with the teacher conducting the ongoing model to discuss her or his methods, feelings, feedback from students, and so forth. An in-service program for other interested teachers can be based on the model. Administrators can have a chance to evaluate the feedback, if any, and students can contribute their reactions. The system can proceed from this pilot program to expanding throughout the district. The principles that have worked well become incorporated into the ongoing planning for health education. The community is familiar with the model and has had a chance to comment and make suggestions.

FORMULATING PRINCIPLES THAT ARE CRUCIAL TO INITIATING NEW PROGRAMS OR CONTINUING OLD ONES

No matter what procedure is used to introduce controversial subjects, there are some general principles to be kept in mind:

- Curriculum and/or services must always be as current as possible. The knowledge of today (about alcohol, drugs, sexual problems, etc.) may become the myths of tomorrow.
- Respect for the integrity of each student must be maintained. Too often health problems are "blamed" on teenage behavior. Students will some-

times express feelings that "everyone believes you're into dope, sex, and booze—so why not?"

- All health promotion materials in an integrated program should stress the ability to choose and to discriminate what individuals will do for themselves. Informed personal action versus following the crowd can be encouraged by stimulating classroom problem-solving sessions and open participation in debate.
- Activities that can be reality tested in classroom or community settings (coordinating health service experiences in school/community settings, etc.) can be useful in perceptions of health promotion.

Teacher training through in-service programs and other educational efforts (i.e., seminars, advanced college courses) must be encouraged or required for controversial subjects, just as they are for other topics in the general curriculum.

All responsible participants in the educational system are involved in implementing the overall school curriculum. It is the controversial subjects, however, that cause each participant to examine his or her role in this process. Each should be aware of the principles previously outlined so no one person in the system is feeling uneasy or uncertain about what and how subjects are being taught. Each person is essentially helping to create a common ground for communication and trust with the community.

Members of the board of education or other legal bodies to whom the superintendent is responsible are elected officials representing the school district. Together with the superintendent, they develop policies that determine the general operation of the schools in the district. Health education curriculum planning represents one aspect of those policies. The board may have questions or suggestions. Their role is to help develop the policies and to approve them before they are implemented.

The *superintendent's* role is to inform and instruct the board about various items and to listen to their concerns when they arise. The superintendent may wish to present illustrative material to assist in informing board members, in which case, students, parents, nurses, physicians, or anyone connected with the health program may be asked to define the scope and purposes of a subject area.

The *principal's* role is to implement the health education policy utilizing a management systems (or other) approach that allows for shared information and creative use of the classroom teacher and other health team members. Their methods and concepts may differ from those of another school in the district, but with a policy framework in which to work, they should more easily accomplish the stated goals and objectives.

Teachers have the most pivotal role. As educators, they are the major communicators. Teachers must be able to contribute ideas, demonstrate leadership, and raise questions at all levels of implementation. Teaching sensitive topics requires being knowledgeable about school health policies and sure of administrative support. If there should be controversy, teachers need to know that they will not be left "on their own" in a defensive position. Consistent, thoughtful curriculum and policy development in which they have participated ensures against such occurrences.

The *student* is also a central figure in implementation. From the outset of policy development and program design, student needs must be assessed. This is an ongoing process. The status of biological, psychological, and social knowledge at any one point may be increasing or may be in a rediscovery phase, but it is always changing. The students' role is to interpret to those who teach and set policy what these changes mean to them. Each generation must discover its own equivalent, or lack thereof, of a "human potential movement" or "personal growth event." It is similar to students liking their own music and their own politics, whether or not they resemble those of the adults around them. The updating process requires their participation.

Health team personnel, whether school or community based and however constituted (from one school nurse to a team of doctors, nurses, counselors, social workers, etc.), must serve in many capacities. Their expertise can be utilized in health policies about use of services, on-site school treatment, referral source, or consultant capacity. They may serve as adjunctive educators. What experiences can they offer for students to observe preventive measures, learning life-saving methods, or reporting their own symptoms? Their role is determined by their operation as part of the learning program and their participation in planning.

Community educators and institutions have a role in keeping school personnel current in how health promotion policy can be more comprehensive. What goes on in the community affects the school and vice versa. Developing a cooperative partnership can make the difference between a workable health education program and one based on unrealistic expectations of what the community offers.

Parents and the public are interested in the health of their children. The teenage years are the most uncertain and threatening ones for many parents. They see their role as doing the best they can to maintain the health of the family. They may do this well or extremely poorly, but most see themselves as making the best decisions they can at any given time. Parental understanding and support of health education can generally be elicited when parents are kept informed and encouraged, regardless of the level at which they are functioning. Too often, parents feel that they are being viewed as the source of problem behavior in their children. Just as often, this is the attitude of the educators. The parents' contributions to development of health education can enrich the structure of a health promotion program.

The public's role parallels that of the parents, in many ways, except that the intensity of interest may be less. Their support of education in general, as taxpayers, is reflected in their selection of school board members and their attention to exemplary educational efforts.

The subjects discussed in this chapter—sex education, addictive behaviors, death and dying, and suicide education—are the most obvious objects of current opposition. Teachers should not be surprised, however, to find that in a particular school district (theirs), any of the following subjects might also be the center of debate. The list is being limited to health topics, but there are many more in other areas (e.g., creationism versus evolution):

- smoking education (primarily rights of smokers versus nonsmokers)
- fluoridation of water
- pornography (as a separate mental health subject)
- masturbation (as a separate mental health subject)

Frequently it is believed that schools must take on these topics because parents and the community are not capable of doing so. Yet in no area of education other than these sensitive, health-related behaviors does the education system claim to educate by default.

The controversy surrounding education about any sensitive topic in school is only one aspect of education. Teachers, school officials, parents, the community, and students should be aware of other strong "educations." These include the five Ps:

- *Parent education.* Whether or not parents ever say a word about sex, drugs, suicide, or any other health behavior, they are educating their children by their attitudes, beliefs, and behaviors, which provide both verbal and nonverbal learning experiences.
- *Peer education.* This is probably the most authentic and authoritative education that individuals between 10 and 20 years of age receive (and probably the most significant throughout people's lives). Eighty percent of the college-age population will volunteer that most of their sex, alcohol, and drug information was learned from their friends before or during junior high school years. The most powerful learning experiences occur within this peer group.
- *Public media education.* There are almost no subjects of a controversial nature that have not been seen and/or discussed via radio, TV, newspapers, books, or magazines. These exposures vary from the most thoughtful, research-backed presentations to the most blatant manipulative, commercial ones. Such words and images permeate the learning atmosphere for most young people throughout the early years.

This, too, is a powerful teaching-learning influence, both positive and negative.
- *Public school education.* Like parents, the school system teaches whether it wants to or not and whether or not the subjects are ever presented in school. Silence through absent subjects in the health curriculum conveys its own message to students that the system in which they are being taught does not know their concerns and interests, does not care, or finds the subjects too shameful or unfit for classroom discussion.
- *Planned public health education.* The basic fifth P for which education should strive, this allows all the above-named educations to continue (because they will), but indicates the interest of educators in meeting the students' needs through planning and implementing a health education curriculum encompassing all health behaviors.

SUMMARY

1. Teachers must recognize that most people are oriented to treating disease and illness rather than focusing on preventing problems and promoting health. When subjects stimulate controversy, the educational approach, preventive or otherwise, may be a cause for dissent.
2. Health education is a preventive approach to health problems and, as such, requires that teachers of health education include subjects that deal with areas of sensitive human behaviors affecting health.
3. These areas usually involve behaviors that some people consider to be too private for public instruction.
    a. How and what one eats is considered private behavior. Some people believe that teaching about nutrition is an invasion of privacy.
    b. Beliefs (religious, social, political) about more sensitive activities are more likely to provoke stronger reactions.
4. Controversy is not new, and its cyclic history should be familiar to teachers in order to help them understand the similarities to current controversy and how not to repeat prior mistakes.
5. The most frequently controversial topics concern sexual and addictive behaviors and "humanistic" subjects such as suicide and death and dying.
    a. When ethical, social, and legal aspects of behavior converge with health considerations, "humanistic" labels are apt to be applied.
    b. Some people believe that humanistic considerations and/or a worldview of a subject are "liberal" or "communistic."

220 Planning and Implementing Health Education in Schools

6. Sex education may include an array of topics, including reproductive biology, use of contraception and abortion, sexually transmitted diseases, sexual assault and abuse, sex roles, and sexual orientation (homosexuality, bisexuality).
   a. Teachers need to know that opposition may be focused on any one item or on all of them, but the goal of those opposed is usually to remove the subject altogether.
   b. The majority of parents would like to have these topics as part of the curriculum. However, until they hear that it may be eliminated, they are not likely to demonstrate or write letters in favor of a subject.
   c. Teachers must recognize that some parents, for political reasons, wish to raise opposition to sex education in order to discredit all educational endeavors. Teachers should not confuse them with parents who are sincerely concerned about how and what their children will learn.
7. Addictive behaviors include a wide array of topics that precipitate controversy. These usually include alcohol and illegal and prescription drugs, about which teachers must learn to be objective as well as empathetic to students whose "ideal" adults may use all of them.
8. Suicide and death and dying have raised similar types of opposition. However, experience with both teaching about these subjects and the intensity of opposition are currently not well documented.
   a. Teachers should be prepared to use the principles contained in this chapter to deal with preparation of materials for these topics.
   b. Acknowledgment of parents' fears about previously "taboo" subjects can be useful in applying these principles.
9. Parents' concerns about any controversial subject center on common themes that threaten what they believe to be loss of control over their children's lives.
10. Teachers and administrators also share concerns about these subjects focused on attaining health education goals and objectives that will enhance students' health and well-being.
11. Preventing controversy on important subjects while attaining the goals of health education requires a series of steps that are not considerably different from those of any other curriculum planning. It also requires some additional steps to preserve the time and energy otherwise expended once controversy arises.
    a. There must be a school health policy with which teachers and all other school personnel are familiar, within which health curric-

ulum and adjunctive health services can be planned. Within this framework, sensitive topics can be included in a consistent manner.
b. The utilization of parents, as well as community resources when incorporated into this planning process, can assure the most comprehensive learning experience for the student. Teachers must serve as leaders, as well as questioners of this practice, in order not to be "left on their own" without administrative support when controversy does occur.
c. Teachers must also recognize that they need not "prove" that teaching about health behaviors will necessarily influence what students will do about them. The principle that knowledge is preferable to ignorance about a subject provides a basis for decision making.
d. Most students, however, appear to learn more about themselves and their responsibility for choosing their own behaviors when the subject matter does pertain to the privately meaningful events for their lives. Awareness of these factors can increase a teacher's effectiveness.
e. Teachers must also understand that teaching about a "sensitive" area does not necessarily make it a problem or a subject for controversy.
f. Informing parents and the public about the inclusion of sex education, addictive behaviors, and such in the overall health curriculum (when students first enter primary, secondary, and high school years) allows them to have an overview of school policy without surprises.
g. Inviting parents and the community to comment or inquire about material for these subjects and making them available demonstrates the school's commitment to the topics, the policy, and parents' possible concerns.
h. Recognizing that many parents expect the school to provide complementary and adjunctive learning to the family's education can help counteract the attitudes that some parents have of "parent *versus* school instruction" and also support those parents who trust the school's educational goals and welcome the input to subjects they would otherwise ignore. Respecting all these attitudes can help prevent a "federal case" being made about controversial topics.
i. Being prepared to teach and requiring in-service and continuing education for controversial topics can demonstrate that the school administration takes these sensitive topics just as seriously as any other area of teaching.

12. Controversial and sensitive subject matter is frequently dramatically related to students' lives. A single school-age suicide, a cocaine death, a fatal alcohol-related accident, an unplanned pregnancy, an infection with a sexually transmitted disease are examples of conditions that produce morbidity and mortality in thousands of junior high and high school students. They represent a larger pool of young people who are also affected by these events physically and emotionally, whose numbers are impossible to calculate.

    If teachers are aware of the myriad sources of information available to young people—public media, peers, parents, public education based on fear, or planned public education—they can understand better their own contribution to the latter.

    Most health educators have not considered that the major thrust of their work would focus on controversial topics. They will need to be the supporters and advocates for increased quality of this critical group of subjects in an active way. This means helping to bring administrators, colleagues, parents, and the community together in a joint effort.

QUESTIONS AND EXERCISES

Questions

1. What are the common themes underlying parental concerns about controversial topics?
2. How would an understanding of the history of the sex education controversy be useful to a teacher currently facing objections to a health topic on sexual development that he or she is teaching?
3. What sex education topics would have to be included in a lesson plan about Acquired Immune Deficiency Syndrome (AIDS)? Why?
4. List and describe two ways in which all parents in a school district can receive information about a new health curriculum that encompasses several controversial topics.
5. What steps should health teachers and others in the school system take to prevent controversy while promoting a health curriculum that includes major sensitive topics?
6. What conflicts do health teachers and school administrators face when they are deciding whether or not to begin or continue controversial health education topics?

Exercises

1. The health education teacher has agreed to serve on an interdisciplinary health education policy development team. Controversial subjects are to be included in this policy. Outline what steps the teacher needs to take to participate in this activity. What would he or she want to know?
2. The health education teacher is designing a "model" health education program and has been asked to describe a lesson plan on birth control encompassing contraception, abortion, and sterilization. Indicate where you believe this aspect of sexual behavior is most effectively situated in an overall sex education curriculum, and put this in a written statement to the school administrator.
3. A group of parents who have been objecting to the books recommended in conjunction with learning about sexuality is visiting the school at the invitation of the principal. The health teacher has been asked to explain the relationship of the readings to the course. Write down the steps the teacher might take to help the parents with their concerns.
4. The health education teacher wishes to plan a visit to a community agency that he believes would best help students to understand resources that treat drug addiction. Describe how the teacher might enlist the support of the people and/or the agencies involved.
5. A community health agency has sent flyers to the school about a public broadcast TV program on child sexual abuse. Teachers and administrators have been asked to circulate these notices to students and their parents in hopes they will watch the program. Write a short paragraph on the pros and cons of such a suggestion from the viewpoint of a health education teacher.
6. The health teacher needs a resource person to assist her in bringing together a panel of people who have had a member of their family die from a protracted chronic illness. What major available resources can the teacher contact first? Outline a plan for arranging such a panel that the teacher could follow.

REFERENCES

Albee, G., Gordon, S., and Leitenberg, H., eds., *Promoting Sexual Responsibility and Preventing Sexual Problems.* Hanover, NH: University Press of New England, 1983.

Anderson, P., *High in America: The True Story behind NORML and the Politics of Marijuana.* New York: Viking Press, 1981.

Bakalor, J. B., and Grinspoon, L., *Drug Control in a Free Society*. New York: Cambridge University Press, 1984.

Barlow, D., *Sexually Transmitted Diseases: The Facts*. Oxford, England: Oxford University Press, 1979.

Berent, I., *The Algebra of Suicide*. New York: Human Sciences Press, 1981.

Block, D., "Attitudes of mothers toward sex education." *American Journal of Public Health* 69, 1979, pp. 911–915.

Brown, L. ed., *Sex Education in the Eighties: The Challenge of Healthy Sexual Evolution*. New York: Plenum Press, 1981.

Bullough, Vern L., *Sexual Variance in Society and History*. New York: Wiley, 1976.

Cahill, K. M., ed., *The AIDS Epidemic*. New York: St. Martin's Press, 1983.

Calderone, M. S., "The development of healthy sexuality." *Journal of Health, Physical Education—Recreation* 37, Sept. 1966, pp. 23–27.

Cancila, C., "Teen pregnancy, abortion rates highest in U.S." *American Medical News*, March 29, 1985, p. 15.

Coates, T., and Perry, C., eds., *Promoting Adolescent Health: A Dialogue in Research and Practice*. New York: Academic Press, 1983.

Cook, A., Kirby, D., Wilson, P., and Alter, J., *Sexuality Education: A Guide to Developing and Implementing Programs*. Santa Cruz, CA: Network Publications, 1984.

Cornacchia, H. J., Smith, D. E., and Bentel, D. J., *Drugs in the Classroom: A Conceptual Model for School Programs*, 2nd ed. St. Louis: Mosby, 1978.

Croskey, B. F., *Death Education: Attitudes of Teachers, School Board Members and Clergy*. Palo Alto, CA: R & E Associates, 1979.

Department of Health, Education and Welfare, *Healthy People: The Surgeon General's Report on Health Promotion and Disease Prevention*. Washington, DC: U.S. Government Printing Office, 1979.

Department of Health and Human Services, *Promoting Health, Preventing Disease: Objectives for the Nation*. Washington, DC: U.S. Government Printing Office, 1980.

Eddy, J. M., and Alles, W. F., *Death Education*. St. Louis: Mosby, 1983.

Finkelhor, D., *Child Sexual Abuse: Theory and Research*. New York: Free Press, 1984a.

Finkelhor, D., "The prevention of child sexual abuse: an overview of needs and problems." SIECUS Report 13:1, Sept. 1984b, pp. 1–5.

Finn, P., and O'Gorman, P. A., *Teaching About Alcohol: Concepts, Methods and Classroom Activities*. Boston: Allyn & Bacon, 1981.

Furstenberg, F. F., Jr., Lincoln, R., and Menken, J., eds., *Teenage Sexuality, Pregnancy, and Childbearing*. Philadelphia: University of Pennsylvania Press, 1981.

Gendel, E. S., and Green, P. B., "Sex education controversy—a boost to new and better programs." *Journal of School Health* 41, 1971, pp. 24–28.

Goodwin, J., *Sexual Abuse: Incest Victims and Their Families*. Boston: PSG Publishing, 1982.

Grant, M., and Ritson, B., *Alcohol: The Prevention Debate*. London: Croom Helm, 1983.

Green, B. R., and Irish, D. P., eds., *Death Education: Preparation for Living*. Cambridge, MA: Schenkman, 1971.

Hendin, H., *Suicide in America*. New York: Norton, 1982.

Hilu, V., ed., *Sex Education and the Schools*. New York: Harper and Row, 1967.

Huber, G. J., and Bentler, P. M., "The role of peer and adult models for drug taking at different stages in adolescence." *Journal of Youth and Adolescence* 9, 1980, pp. 449–465.

Husain, S. A., and Vandiver, T., *Suicide in Children and Adolescents*. New York: SP Medical and Scientific Books, 1984.

Hyde, M. O., *Sexual Abuse: Let's Talk About It*. Philadelphia: Westminster Press, 1984.

Jenkinson, E. B., *Censors in the Classroom*. Carbondale: Southern Illinois University Press, 1979.

Jessor, R., Chase, J. A., and Donovan, J. E., "Psychosocial correlates of marijuana use and problem drinking in a national sample of adolescents." *American Journal of Public Health* 70, 1980, pp. 604–613.

Koblinsky, S., and Atkinson, J., "Parental plans for sex education." *Family Relations* 31, 1982, pp. 29–35.

Mandle, C. L., "Suicide: a human problem." *Educational Horizons* 62, Summer 1984, pp. 119–123.

Mayer, J. E., and Filstead, W. J., eds., *Adolescence and Alcohol*. Cambridge, MA: Ballinger, 1980.

Mayer, K., and Pizer, H., *The AIDS Fact Book*. New York: Bantam Books, 1983.

McAlister, A. L., Perry, C., Killen, J., and Maccoby, N., "Pilot study of smoking alcohol and drug abuse prevention." *American Journal of Public Health* 70, July 1980, pp. 719–721.

McCormack, W. M., ed., *Diagnosis and Treatment of Sexually Transmitted Diseases*. Boston: PSG Publishing, 1983.

Mercy, J. A., Tolsma, D. D., Smith, J. C., and Conn, J. M., "Patterns of youth suicide in the United States." *Educational Horizons* 62, Summer 1984, pp. 124–127.

Milkman, H. B., and Shaffer, H. J., eds., *The Addictions: Multidisciplinary Perspectives and Treatments*. Lexington, MA: D. C. Heath, 1985.

Miller, P. M., and Nerinberg, T. D., eds., *Prevention of Alcohol Abuse*. New York: Plenum Press, 1984.

Mills, K. C., Neal, E. M., and Peed-Neal, I., *A Handbook for Alcohol Education: The Community Approach*. Cambridge, MA: Ballinger, 1983.

Nahas, G. G., and Frick, H. C., eds., *Drug Abuse in the Modern World: A Perspective for the Eighties*. New York: Pergamon Press, 1981.

National School Boards Association and American Association of School Administrators, Joint Committee, "Health education and sex/family life education." Washington, DC: American Association of School Administrators, 1968.

North, R., and Orange, R., Jr., *Teenage Drinking: The #1 Drug Threat to Young People Today*. New York: MacMillan, 1980.

Ooms, T., ed., *Teenage Pregnancy in a Family Context: Implications for Policy*. Philadelphia: Temple University Press, 1981.

Oriel, J. D., and Ridgway, G. L., *Genital Infection by Chlamydia Trachomatis*. New York: Elsevier, 1982.

Ostrow, D. G., Sandholzer, T. A., and Fleman, Y. M., eds., *Sexually Transmitted Diseases in Homosexual Men: Diagnosis, Treatment and Research.* New York: Plenum, 1983.

Reis, I. L., "Sex education in the public schools: problem or solution?" *Phi Delta Kappan* 59, Sept. 1968, pp. 52–56.

Report of the Commission on Obscenity and Pornography. New York: Random House, 1970.

Ryan, I. J., and Dunn, P. C., "Sex education from a prospective teacher's view poses a dilemma." *Journal of School Health* 49, Dec. 1979, pp. 573–575.

Sanford, L. T., *The Silent Children: A Parent's Guide to the Prevention of Child Sexual Abuse.* New York: McGraw-Hill, 1980.

Scales, P., "Barriers to sex education." *Journal of School Health* 50, June 1980, pp. 337–341.

Schlesinger, B., *Sexual Abuse of Children: A Resource Guide and Bibliography.* Toronto: University of Toronto Press, 1982.

School Health Education Study, *Health Education: A Conceptual Approach to Curriculum Design.* St. Paul, MN: 3M, 1967.

Storz, J., *Chlamydia and Chlamydia-Induced Diseases.* Springfield, IL: C. C. Thomas, 1971.

Sudak, H. S., Ford, A. B., and Rushforth, N. B., eds., *Suicide in the Young.* Boston: PSG Publishing, 1984.

Troyer, R. J., and Markle, G. E., *Cigarettes, the Battle over Smoking.* New Brunswick, NJ: Rutgers University Press, 1983.

Ulin, R. O., *Death and Dying Education.* Washington, DC: National Education Association, 1977.

U.S. Department of Health and Human Services (DHHS), Public Health Service, *Smoking, Tobacco and Health: A Fact Book.* DHHS Publication No. PHS80-50150, 1981.

Zalaznik, P. W., *Dimensions of Loss and Death Education: A Resource and Curriculum Guide.* Minneapolis, MN: Eden Poe, 1981.

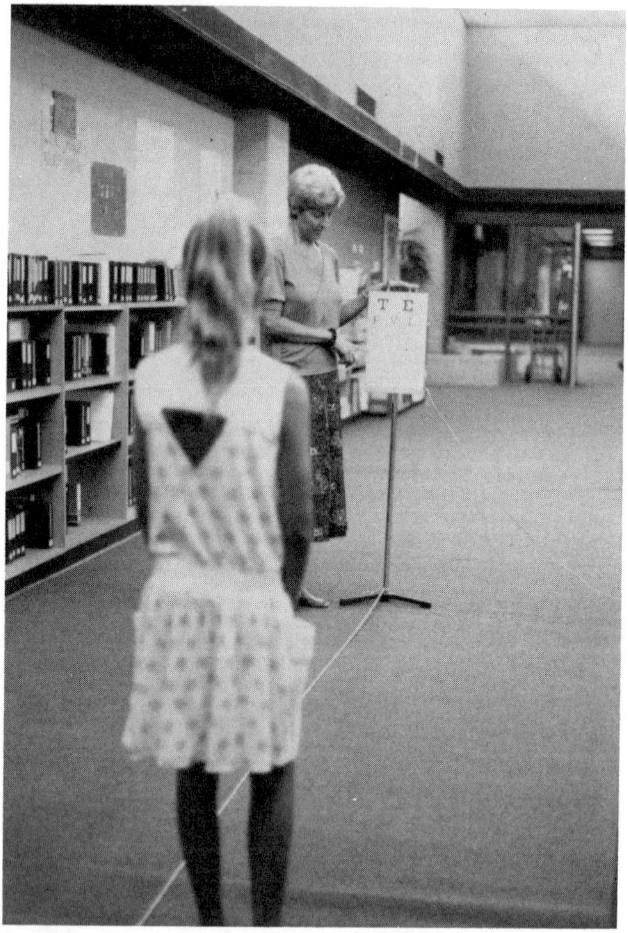
T E

7
Evaluating school health education

Although evaluation has almost always been given consideration in books concerned with the school health program, discussion has tended to focus more on *what* to evaluate than on methodology. Development of evaluation skills has necessarily depended on the assumption that they would be learned elsewhere during the professional preparation of health teachers. Typically, an evaluation section is either completely lacking or is the weakest element in an otherwise nicely developed health curriculum guide. Evaluation of health curriculums or methodology has been the exception rather than the rule (Green et al., 1980). In the classroom, evaluation has largely been limited to the use of tests and measurements as a means of assigning grades.

All of this is changing rapidly. No longer does lip service suffice, nor do fuzzily proposed evaluation schemes satisfy accountability requirements or justify continuing support of health education programs. School health educators, like all health educators, must know the language of evaluation, understand and be skilled in applying its methodology in appropriate ways, and be able to interpret the results of evaluation, whether their own or as reported by others.

WHAT IS EVALUATION?

Educational evaluation has become an academic specialization. Related textbooks and professional journals have introduced new terminology as they describe a broader and more rigorous approach to the development and application of evaluative instruments and strategies. And because the field of evaluation is evolving so swiftly, many of those terms have yet to be widely applied or accepted. As a result, words such as "measurement," "assessment," "appraisal," and "grading" are often used interchangeably with "evaluation" itself. The word "evaluation" is also commonly used as an umbrella term referring to educational research. Therefore, in order to avoid the confusion or misunderstanding that can occur when two people use the same word to mean different things, key words should be defined in advance of their use in evaluative statements or reports.

EVALUATION TERMINOLOGY DEFINED

Discussion of evaluation theory and methodology is necessarily limited in this chapter to school health education. However, the following terms, as defined here in order to clarify and establish their meaning in that context, should be just as appropriate as applied to evaluation of health education programs in general.

Evaluation

What do we mean by "evaluation"? In general terms, it is a process of determining the value of things. That is something that everybody does, all of the time. Most of the everyday choices a person makes are based upon valuing, whether this is done consciously or subconsciously. However, these are judgments heavily influenced by attitudes, past experience, social and economic forces, education, and a host of other often unrecognized variables.

Evaluation, as a process employed in determining the worth or merit of aspects of health education programs, is formal and systematic. Its primary purpose is to gather information for use in making informed decisions about a phenomenon of interest. What is evaluated relative to a health education program may include a wide range of things such as the methodology employed, its effectiveness in changing behavior (whether in knowledge, attitudes, or practice), the curriculum, its goals and objectives, the outcomes, and even the evaluation activities themselves.

Current definitions of the term vary little, whatever the health education setting with which its authors identify. For example, Green et al. (1980) say, "evaluation is the comparison of an object of interest against a standard of acceptability." Others say, "The concept of evaluation has been defined to mean the act of placing a value, positive or negative, on something" (Windsor et al., 1984). The process has been described in greater detail as "a continuous, systematic process of directly or indirectly observing, keeping a record of, and objectively judging the extent to which a target behavior has changed so that the new behavior can be supported and reinforced and its future trend predicted" (Ross and Mico, 1980). Specific to school health, it has been defined as "a process of determining the effectiveness of the program and its several phases by measuring the degree to which the health objectives of the school are being achieved" (Anderson and Creswell, 1980). Evaluation is defined for health educators in *all* settings as "a process by which we seek to determine if the objectives of a program have been achieved" (National Task Force, 1985, p. 84). In essence, all those statements describe the determination of the value of something as measured by comparisons with accepted standards of worth.

Measurement

Measurement usually focuses on specific behaviors or subject matter and seeks to determine the present status of some phenomenon. Independent of value judgments, it is descriptive only, employing tests and other procedures appropriate for the identification and orderly recording of quantitative data. The data yielded by measurement are used as one kind of evidence useful in making evaluations. Hence, although measurement is a tool of evaluation, it is not in itself an evaluation activity.

When a teacher uses a pretest in order to find out what students need to learn about health-affecting practices or after instruction to find out how much they have learned, that is measurement. But when that same information is used to judge the effectiveness of a teaching unit designed to teach them what they need to know, that is evaluation.

Appraisal

"Appraisal" is a word often acceptably used interchangeably with evaluation because to appraise something is to make a judgment regarding its quality. Scrutiny of this nature is often carried out by experts or professionals whose qualifications as judges in a given situation are considered unquestionable. Usually, a rating is given, either verbally or in writing, in such a way as to assign an index of the worth of what was to be appraised, along with comments in support of that rating. The word is often also used simply as an alternative to "evaluation" (Popham, 1975).

Assessment

Assessment is a process involving value-free measurement; therefore, it can be used only to describe activities that can just as aptly be titled measurement. It is status determination, not quality determination, even though it is often employed improperly in the latter meaning. For some, the word is less threatening than "measurement," especially when it is one's own performance that is to be measured. The term may also be appealing simply because it sounds more profound than measurement, and one gets tired of using the same word all the time, however correct it may be.

Evaluative research

It's easy to confuse evaluation activities with what is happening when evaluative research is being conducted. Both evaluators and researchers use measurement techniques, they both analyze the data they obtain with statistics procedures, both are required to write reports of their results, both engage in systematic, formal inquiry. It is the difference in their goals that sets them apart.

Researchers study the obtained data for the purpose of drawing conclusions. The finding of interest is one that is usefully generalizable to similar situations in other places and times. Research seeks to discover new scientific truth, and determination of the relative worth of that information is not a question. Evaluators gather data for the purpose of making decisions about a particular program or question. They must estimate the worth of the object or activity of interest to help make decisions about it. Is it worth keeping, or ought it to be modified or abandoned? Evaluators need estimates of worth if they are to make the decisions that are the purpose of their analyses. Such decisions always involve comparisons between alternative courses of action.

School health educators have sometimes been criticized for an apparent neglect of program evaluation. Very often what is actually meant is that less evaluative *research* is reported relative to school health programs than seems appropriate to other health educators. Evaluation, in the sense in which it has been defined above, is very much a part of school health education.

However, in 1985, the final report of a four-year research project evaluating the effectiveness of school health education curriculums provided evidence that health education works, that it works better when there is more of it, and that it works best when it is implemented with broad-scale administrative and pedagogic support for teacher training, integrated materials, and continuity across grades.

In brief, the primary purpose of the School Health Education Evaluation (SHEE) was to evaluate the School Health Curriculum Project (SHCP) curriculum as compared with three other approaches to school health education. The SHCP was deemed an ideal candidate for such a study because it contained a comprehensive program for grades 4–7, was more widely disseminated than any other health education curriculum, and had received substantial federal support, having been sponsored by the public health service since 1967 (Gunn, Iverson, and Katz, 1985, p. 301).

The design of the SHEE was divided into two parts. One was a representative study of the SHCP and three other health education curriculums. The objectives were to measure the effects of these curriculums on students, teachers, and parents and to assess average costs per pupil. The other part was to conduct an experimental study of the SHCP program at new sites to evaluate the effects when implemented in an exemplary way. At the end of the first year, because no significant differences between the experimental and representative groups could be identified, data obtained from the two samples were combined for analysis.

The test instruments developed for the evaluation were not tied to any particular health instruction course, but addressed objectives that by consensus of experts constituted those most important for children in grades 4–7. Parcel (1985, p. 345) summarizes the major SHEE results in these words:

> The SHEE provides clear evidence that school health education curricula, which is [sic] carefully designed to involve active student participation and includes extensive in-service teacher training, are likely to significantly increase students' health knowledge. The findings also suggest that these programs may have a limited effect on health attitudes and practices, but the evidence is not nearly so strong as for knowledge. . . .
>
> The results . . . provide evidence that the effects of school health education programs are related to the resources committed to preparing and implementing the program. In-service training and preparation of teachers seems to be a critical factor in making school health education programs effective.
>
> Allocating sufficient time for instruction also is related to effectiveness. The study suggests that merely providing time for instruction is not by itself sufficient. There is a leveling-off effect of the relationship between time of instruction and observed effects. This suggests that other inputs besides class instruction may be needed within a school health education program to obtain additional effects on knowledge, attitude, or health practice. The results suggest that a curriculum guide used as the major structure for a school health education intervention is likely to be inadequate in obtaining significant effects.

Validity and reliability

Any discussion of evaluation and measurement is sure to refer to validity and reliability. These are the characteristics of a useful test or measurement technique that must be established if the results are to be dependable in making evaluations. "Validity" refers to the extent to which an instrument or procedure measures what the evaluator wants it to measure. "Reliability" refers to the results obtained through administration of such instruments, not to the instrument itself. It is a gauge of the consistency with which an instrument measures what is being measured.

Reliability is usually expressed in terms of a statistic (as in r. = .90, where 1.00 would show perfect reliability). Such a statistic, called a "reliability coefficient," is calculated on the basis of test scores or other results treated according to certain mathematical formulas. Of the two qualities, validity is the more important. If an instrument does not or cannot measure what it is supposed or required to measure, then reliability is irrelevant. No matter how perfect a test is at measuring what you don't want to know, it's a waste of time. But there is no such thing as a valid test that is not reliable. Both characteristics are essential in a valid instrument.

CURRENT FORCES AFFECTING EVALUATION

Evaluation of health education can no longer be limited to tests and measurements of learner success in recalling factual material relative to health, if ever that was acceptable. Combined community, economic, professional, and other pressures and changing educational standards have forced changes in both the range of things evaluated and the ways they are appraised. Examples of some of these external forces include accountability demands, the minimum competency movement, federal and private agency funding requirements, and the Role Delineation Project.

Accountability demands

Public education costs a lot of money. In some communities, the school budget is larger than that of any other business in town. Taxpayers have begun to question the value of certain school courses and activities. For example, there is a general feeling among parents and adults that public education is not as good as it needs to be. There are complaints that the curriculum is overemphasizing frill courses and that the schools are taking over the teaching of information and behaviors that are traditionally a responsibility of the home. "Back to basics" has become a rallying cry among those who believe that will solve all the problems that keep Johnny and Jane from reading as well as they should. In the case of health education, people ask to be shown that it does what it is supposed to do. Critics demand to know why children and adolescents smoke or use other dangerous drugs if health education is effective. Some claim that units dealing with drug abuse problems and sex education have actually contributed to related problems. One result of these kinds of complaints is that, in many states, teachers are now required to reveal their goals and objectives in advance and to demonstrate that their teaching accomplished exactly what was proposed. Knowledge of the techniques of program evaluation is a must for health teaching specialists, just as it is for every health educator.

The minimum competency movement

As a direct consequence of the back-to-basics, accountability furor, competency-based education became the bandwagon of the 1970s. Within a very few years, more than two-thirds of the state legislatures had mandated minimum competency for elementary and secondary school graduation. Emphasis thus passed from educational achievement as determined by completion of specified courses to competency as defined by successful performance on related proficiency tests. Overnight, evaluation had become an equal partner with instruction instead of an end-of-course ritual.

Teachers had to be able to select or construct tests capable of assessing competency relative to their stated objectives. There was a dramatic shift from norm-referenced to criterion- or objective-based testing. Norm-referenced tests are designed to reveal a student's standing relative to all others taking that test. Criterion-referenced tests are designed to ascertain what a student can or cannot do relative to specified objectives or skills. New skills and greater rigor were required to construct tests that were valid measures of proficiency or mastery.

Federal and private agency funding requirements

Millions of dollars in support of health education in all of its settings have been awarded by federal agencies such as the Center for Health Promotion and Education (CHPE-CDC) or its predecessor, the Bureau of Health Education, and other health-concerned institutes and offices. Voluntary health agencies and philanthropies interested in promoting the health of the nation are also major sources of funds supporting health education. Whatever the source, in order to obtain grants or contracts for health education research or development, a proposal must be prepared and submitted. Every such proposal must include a carefully designed evaluation plan. Not every health educator will be involved in conducting research or expected to prepare grant-winning proposals. Nevertheless, every health educator needs at a minimum to be able to interpret the information provided in the evaluation reports written by those who do conduct such research.

The Role Delineation Project

It seems likely that the Role Delineation Project curriculum framework will have a major influence on evaluation of school health education programs in several ways. First, if it is adopted by health education professional preparation programs, the responsibilities and competencies identified as essential to health education practice become the standard against which individual curricula will be evaluated. Second, evaluation has been identified as one of the seven primary areas of responsibility for which all health educators must be prepared. (see appendix F). As a consequence, future preparation programs will require far more time given to the practice and study of evaluation than has been the case in the past.

FORMATIVE AND SUMMATIVE ROLES OF EVALUATION

So far we have been talking about evaluation as a goal. That goal is always the same: to appraise something according to a specified set of values. The roles of evaluation vary, depending on the function they serve in any instance. The role of an evaluation activity depends on what is being evaluated and whose standards are being applied. A great many kinds of evaluation are possible in any particular educational setting. Evaluation can be part of a teacher preparation program, in which case a student-teacher's performance is being appraised, and standards of professional practice are being applied. Evaluation is a vital component of curriculum development. The success or failure of every aspect of the plan is constantly being appraised and the obtained results employed in making necessary revisions. Whatever the educational activity (research, lesson planning, or selecting effective teaching materials), evaluation plays a vital role in its development and refinement.

As originated by Scriven (1967), the roles of evaluation were categorized as either formative or summative in function. *Formative* evaluation refers to judgments of worth based upon information gathered during the developmental stages of a program. The object of interest can be the learner, the course, the curriculum, the choice of instructional materials, the kinds of interventions, or any other aspect of a health education program. The purpose is to identify areas of needed improvement or modification. *Summative* evaluation refers to assessments of the effectiveness or merit of the completed educational programs. The summative evaluator gathers information about and judges the worth of an overall program as a basis for decisions regarding its retention or adoption.

Bloom, Hastings, and Madaus (1971) have applied the notion of formative and summative evaluation to determinations of merit particular to teaching and student learning. They explain the distinction between formative and summative evaluation in that context in these words: "The main purpose of formative observations . . . is to determine the degree of mastery of a given task and to pinpoint the part of the task not mastered. . . . The purpose is not to grade or certify the learner; it is to help both the learner and the teacher to focus upon the particular learning necessary for movement toward mastery. On the other hand, summative evaluation is directed toward a much more general assessment of the degree to which the larger outcomes have been attained over the entire course or some substantial part of it" (Bloom, Hastings, and Madaus, 1971, p. 61).

In health education, instead of formative, the term "process evaluation" is often used. Summative evaluation in that case is differentiated into "impact" and "outcome" evaluations.

Process evaluation is described as helping to explain the causes of a program's strengths or weaknesses and to indicate the modifications that are needed to improve the program (National Task Force, 1985, p. 85). It in no way differs from the functions or roles of formative evaluation as described above. *Impact* evaluation is concerned with measurement of immediate changes occurring as the final effect of a health education program. For example, have the cognitive, affective, and behavioral objectives of an instructional program been achieved?

Outcome evaluation requires data obtained over a long period of time from large population samples. Seldom are there sufficient resources or follow-up time available for this purpose. But these are not the only difficulties. As Hochbaum (1982, p. 17) observes: "Such problems stem from 1) the usual inability to observe and measure behavioral outcomes when these do not manifest themselves until long after the program has ceased, for example in school health education, and, 2) the difficulty of identifying the role played by health education in producing behavioral outcomes when other interventions, conditions, or events may have influenced such outcomes as much or more, either by adding to or by counteracting the educational efforts." For these reasons, evaluation efforts in health education usually give greatest emphasis to process and impact levels of analysis.

PURPOSES OF EVALUATION IN SCHOOLS

In general, evaluation in school health education seeks to appraise the effectiveness of the program in (1) favorably influencing the knowledge, attitudes, and practices of its students and (2) protecting and maintaining the health of both students and staff. Probably the most significant purposes of evaluation are formative in their role.

Specific purposes of evaluation of school health programs include but are not limited to the following:

1. to obtain baseline data about student health information, attitudes, beliefs, and practices
2. to identify curriculum strengths or weaknesses
3. to assess the effectiveness of particular teaching materials and strategies in achieving course objectives
4. to appraise the worth and feasibility of stated instructional goals and objectives
5. to improve student counseling effectiveness
6. to appraise the relevance and worth of the evaluation procedures themselves
7. to provide a basis for constructive curriculum revisions as needed
8. to measure changes in student knowledge, behaviors, and problem-solving abilities effected by the program
9. to assess the quality of the total environment of the school as it affects student well-being and ability to learn
10. to determine the effectiveness of school health services in meeting the needs of both students and staff of the school

WHAT CAN BE EVALUATED?

In principle, the primary goal of health education in schools is to change behavior, just as it is in its other settings. However, there are many kinds of behavioral changes. Behavioral change in the sense of modification or adoption of specified health habits or practices is often an immediate goal of community-based health education programs. As used in education, however, the term refers more broadly to mental, emotional, and physical reactions to instruction. An increase in an individual's knowledge, growth in cognitive or psychomotor skills and abilities, a favorable shift in attitude—all of these are classified as changes in behavior. School health educators are required by the community to apply the latter criteria of behavior change to evaluation of their educational programs. Yet they are also committed to the long-range goal that students will apply what they have learned to the prevention of future health problems and the promotion of a healthful life-style.

In community or clinical settings, for example, a program or intervention focuses on a specific behavioral change, and the target population is defined by a shared need for that change. Such a health education program might focus on teaching older adults how dietary changes can help control or avoid the bone loss that can lead to osteoporosis or loss of teeth. In a clinical setting, instruction in breast or testicular self-examination techniques might be provided patients at special risk of cancer. Evaluation in those situations is intended to appraise the effectiveness of the program in motivating the desired behaviors.

School health education has a broader mission. Rather than prevention of specific problems, the scope of its curriculum includes all the content areas commonly considered part of the body of knowledge of health instruction. The target population is not limited to individuals who need to change their behaviors (indeed, there are often those whose already established health behaviors need sustaining rather than changing), but includes all school-age youngsters. Subject matter alone is not the focus of instruction so much as skill in problem solving and critical thinking. Selection of subject matter and teaching techniques is based upon meaningful and measurable course objectives. Hence, growth in knowledge is a desired but not the only outcome.

When health instruction is provided in schools as a separate subject, that course is but one component of the general education curriculum. Few of the disciplines commonly taught in the public schools are expected to effect changes in students' personal behavior as a consequence of instruction. For example, no one suggests that appraisal of the worth of a civics course rests upon later evidence that as adults those students exhibited exemplary voting records. What is required of courses whose subject matter might also influence future actions affecting health (such as biology, physical education, psychology, home economics, and sociology) is that desirable gains in knowledge, interests, and ability to apply the acquired information can be measured and reported.

School health educators are first of all teachers, but they are also concerned with the health of students as it is affected outside the classroom. All teachers are expected to be skilled in evaluating instruction, if for no other purpose than to determine grades. School health educators must also be knowledgeable about standards for the evaluation of the total program (which includes health services and measures taken to maintain a healthful school environment) as well as skilled in the development and administration of appropriate evaluation techniques and instruments.

In essence, appraisal of the total school health program examines two principal sources of data. These are (1) the learners and (2) the school. Among the categories of change expected in the learners are the following:

1. knowledge
2. attitudes
3. behavior or practices
4. cognitive skills and abilities

Student health status is often also evaluated as a part of health services, but with the purpose of ascertaining and protecting the learner's ability to learn. Evaluation of the school (which covers learning experiences provided directly by teachers and other school personnel and indirectly as a consequence of its physical, social, and emotional environment) includes

1. the effectiveness and quality of teaching aids that are used
2. the appropriateness and effectiveness of the teaching strategies employed to implement the objectives
3. the relevance of the evaluation strategies to the objectives as stated
4. the quality of the services and environment provided for the protection and promotion of the health of both learners and school personnel

LEARNER-FOCUSED EVALUATION

Evaluation of the individual learner probably receives greater emphasis in connection with health education in schools than in other settings. The reasons for this should be obvious. The business of schools is educating young people. Evaluation is the means by which the success or failure of the teacher, the teaching, and the student can be measured and reported. Formative evaluation is necessary if lesson planning is to be responsive to student needs. Immediate knowledge of results not only increases student satisfaction and sustains motivation, but also helps the student identify areas needing extra work. Summative evaluation provides a broad view of a student's performance that facilitates preparation of final grades more fairly descriptive of a semester's work than an accumulation of data generated by a succession of formative evaluations.

To speak of cognitive, affective, and psychomotor or action domains of learning as separate categories for evaluation is not to say that it is often possible to measure growth of one in isolation from the others. Information is never independent of affective elements, and affective learning is always in some ways based upon knowledge. Certainly, psychomotor skills depend upon knowledge, which in turn reflects attitudes about the worth or value of what has been learned. Just as it might be said that it is the whole person who learns, so evaluation appraises the total change that has occurred as a result of instruction. Measurement seeks to quantify change, typically in one domain at a time.

Evaluating health knowledge: the cognitive domain

Growth in knowledge is probably the instructional outcome most apt to be appraised by teachers, whatever the discipline. Health education encompasses a great deal of factual information, and evaluation logically seeks to find out how much of it has been learned as a result of instruction. It is comparatively easier to devise measures of knowledge than of cognitive skills, especially if the kinds of questions are limited to recognition or regurgitation of facts or statements directly derived from the textbook. However, when successful coping with or preventing of a health problem depends upon possession of relevant background information, or when an evaluation activity requires the learner to predict consequences of alternative health actions, then knowledge becomes a tool rather than an end in itself.

Possession of knowledge does not assure us that the learner will apply it appropriately when it is needed. But if students are given an opportunity to practice its application in the classroom, the chances are better that what has been learned will transfer to a real situation. As Ebel (1973) has said, "I do not believe that we need tests of critical thinking ability. What we do need is subject matter tests that call for understanding and application, or demonstration of command of knowledge. Only those who are accustomed to thinking critically are likely to have solid and enduring structures of knowledge."

Evaluating health attitudes and values: the affective domain

Affective behaviors refer to the sort of learned reactions, such as attitudes, interests, values, and beliefs, that predispose the individual to act in certain ways. All of them are in some part cognitive, particularly beliefs, which are considered more cognitive than affective. Most important, all of them have strong emotional or feeling components. They are difficult to evaluate, and the obtained results of related tests, although significant, are least reliable among health education measurements.

The best source of information about an individual's attitudes, values, or beliefs is that same individual. This means that self-report is most often the means chosen for identifying and recording these kinds of data. However, we don't always realize what our true feelings are regarding a given issue, concept, or concern. The respondent may decide either consciously or unconsciously not to respond in a way that might seem negative or unpopular. The result can be a "fake good" or a "fake bad" set of answers.

Other ways of assessing attitudes or values, which have been defined as "bundles or clusters of attitudes toward an object, person, or situation" (Green et al., 1980), include interviews with people who know the person being appraised well enough to report any actions that corroborate self-reported attitudes or other affective behaviors, interviews with the respondent that add another dimension to the analysis, and observation of the respondent's actual behavior to check the validity of what has been reported by that individual in writing.

Tyler (1973) cautions evaluators to remember that human beings exhibit many more affective behaviors than should be the concern of the schools. Therefore, only those reflecting widely accepted social values should be assessed for achievement. Specific to health education, he says: "Curriculum guides in the field of health education mention such goals as Places high priority on maintaining personal health, Values good health more than having a good time, Seeks to contribute to the health of the community in general as well as his own. . . .the strong endorsement of public health programs by citizen groups indicates the high value placed on health by the lay public and suggests that objectives like the foregoing would be acceptable as goals for the public schools" (Tyler, 1973, p. 6).

Evaluating health behavior: the action domain

So far we have discussed evaluation of the cognitive domain, which asks the question "What does the learner know about health and ways to promote it?" We have considered evaluation of the affective domain, which seeks to discover what the learner believes or values relative to health. The action domain is concerned with what the learner does or will do that influences personal or community health.

The third domain of educational objectives ordinarily includes those that emphasize muscular and motor skills, manipulation of material or objects, or some act requiring neuromuscular coordination. These activities or skills are classified as belonging to the psychomotor domain. However, there is very little in health instruction that fits within this category of learning. Cardiopulmonary resuscitation and dental brushing and flossing are all that come readily to mind. For this reason, the term "action domain" seems more appropriate in classifying the goals of health education in schools. It was first used by the School Health Education Study writing group as an alternative to the psychomotor title. The long-range goals proposed relative to that category were described as "those observable, non-observable, or delayed health behaviors in which the individual actually applies knowledge and attitudes to a life situation" (SHES, 1967, p. 31).

What do we mean when we say "health behavior"? Oddly enough, it isn't easy to find any definition at all, let alone one that is appropriate to every health education setting. There is some agreement that it can be defined in general terms as a typical behavior taken by an individual under normal circumstances that may influence her or his present or future well-being and sometimes also that of others. Some also speak of health practices interchangeably with health behavior. However, the term "practice" often refers rather specifically to the personal health care habits developed during early years as a part of the socialization process—practices such as brushing teeth after meals; maintaining clean nails, hair, and skin; balancing sleep, rest, and activity; and the like. Thus, health practices of this kind are not ordinarily the result of conscious or deliberate decisions but are done routinely. They are typically positive in effect, and when circumstances prevent their being carried out, the individual is apt to feel guilty or uncomfortable about it.

What we think of as a health action is usually the outcome of deliberate decision making. Health, or its promotion, is seldom the primary factor influencing a decision to take or not to take any particular health action. Instead, most behaviors affecting health are based upon a complex of knowledge, beliefs, attitudes and values, hopes or fears, personal aspirations, peer pressure, and other social forces. Which of these may be operating to explain the fact that so many who perceive themselves as healthy, and who are well educated, freely choose to abuse alcohol on occasion, smoke cigarettes, overeat, or systematically starve themselves? When an overweight teenager takes up jogging on a regular basis, which of those forces would be most likely to have motivated that behavior?

It is necessary to distinguish behavioral changes in the context of the action domain from those sought as an outcome of instruction based upon a measurable behavioral objective. In the latter case, the term "behavioral" refers to the intellectual skill or process being practiced or learned, such as "interprets," "identifies," "analyzes," or "compares." Behavioral objectives have to do with *means;* behavioral changes are the desired *ends* sought as the outcome of their achievement.

Evaluating customary health behaviors is far from easy. Behavior can be assessed at only one point in time, however valid the instrument employed, and it is never safe to generalize from one set of observations unless they have been obtained from large numbers of respondents. Even then, it is necessary to use caution when drawing any conclusions about what is typical. Then there is the difficulty involved in observing or discovering what an individual actually does with regard to health behaviors. If the only feasible means of obtaining information about an individual's typical health behaviors consists of self-report questionnaires, behavior inventories, or personal interview, responses are often biased in several ways. For example, a student may report practices that reflect knowledge of what is healthful rather than actual behaviors. Or the response may reflect beliefs about desirable health behavior as the student perceives it or thinks the teacher perceives it to be. Conversely, some students like to "fake bad" just for the fun of it.

Even if the responses to a self-report survey were completely honest, unbiased, and reliable, information obtained from a single source can be misleading. Ideally, two or more independent measures of the same practice should be obtained. When one measure of a behavior is consistent with another or others, the dependability of each is far greater than for any one of them alone.

A weakness inherent in some techniques or scales used to assess behavior is their dependence on verbal descriptions of behavior frequency. Words don't mean the same thing to all people. The respondent is often asked to indicate the frequency of a practice as "always," "usually," "seldom," "sometimes," or "never." One can place considerable faith in the validity of the first and last response modes, assuming that the answer is true, but the middle three depend totally on the individual's interpretation of the words. Let us assume that the behavior being assessed is alcoholic beverage consumption. One drinker's "usually" may mean exactly the same as somebody else's "always" in that both mean that they use alcohol every day. And that may mean any amount, from one drink every night before dinner to the amount it takes to render the drinker unconscious. "Sometimes" may mean once or twice a week to one person and may mean only on holidays or special occasions to another. What differentiates one person's "seldom" from the "sometimes" drinker? In the absence of anything more specific than those three words, the respondent does the best she or he can, and the evaluator has to assume that everybody interpreted the ratings in about the same way. However, unless the directions carefully and unmistakably define the meaning to be attached to each option, the generalizability of the resulting data is limited.

Unfortunately, some behaviors cannot be evaluated by health instructors because most health behaviors are not, and some cannot be, manifested in the classroom. Kreuter (1984) concludes that "in the case of school health education, healthful behavior is the long range goal. Teachers and schools should be held accountable for students' command of health knowledge and skills, not their behavior." For example, a smoker's actual practices and beliefs about the potential harmfulness of smoking may not change for twenty years following a health course. The reasons for that eventual change may not be directly traceable to what was learned in that class, but who is to say that what was learned played no part in it at all?

Surely it cannot be denied that knowledge of ways to promote health, or counteract the effects of a harmful behavior, transfers to present needs when the decision to change behavior is made, whatever its motivation? Hochbaum (1982) suggests:

> Health educators need to take a firm stand and educate others to the self-evident fact that health education can only affect conditions that are likely to affect, in turn, what behavioral decisions people will make and how they will follow up on these. It cannot affect decisions and behaviors directly. . . . Health education, specifically, faces also the fact that people do make their own personal choices, to some de-

gree independent of any influences that may be exerted on them. This is in human nature. It is also a right of any individual in a democratic society, a right that is granted with only certain restrictions. It is acknowledged in the concept of "informed consent" which clearly implies that people may also respond to educational efforts with "informed refusal."

If changes in behaviors are long-range goals, and evaluation of long-range goals is beyond the power of the classroom teacher, why talk about it at all? Why assess present practice, for that matter? We should assess present practice because we need to know what it is before we can sensibly propose long-range goals. It would be nonsensical for schools to plan a curriculum based solely upon assumptions about student health behaviors. Curriculums must be based on what is known, not assumed, about the learner if either the teaching or learning is to be valued or valuable. Moreover, the notion of "change" depends on knowledge of where you were before instruction began. Evaluation of present practice is the pretest of a curriculum that seeks to effect change in the learner, whether as increased knowledge, shifts in attitude, or modification of behavior.

Evaluating student health status

Most tests of student health status are not the responsibility of teachers, but of health care professionals, physicians, nurses, dentists, and certain paramedical personnel. Only a few simple screening tests for visual or hearing acuity, or measurement of height and weight, are ever appropriate or expected of school health educators. However, every teacher must be alert to signs of ill health or a change in ability to participate in school activities that differs from what has been usual for a given youngster. Not only should signs such as an unusual pallor or flushed face, marked weight loss or gain, or obvious distress be noted, but straining to see or hear or atypical inattention as well. Abrupt negative shifts in personality or emotional balance or changes in achievement and study patterns are clues to health problems as well.

A conference with the school nurse or with parents can help explain or lead to remedial measures that can have a dramatic effect on a learner's immediate and future potential for learning. A health care professional sees a student too seldom to be sensitive to subtle changes that may be early symptoms of a health problem. Next to a student's parents, teachers who work with him or her every day are most able to observe early signs of trouble. For example, it is entirely possible for a student's visual acuity test score to change from 20/30 to 20/200 Snellen in a single year. School health programs do not ordinarily schedule vision screening on an annual basis. Unless someone notices behavior changes that would result from that much loss of vision, the student must try to adapt to the problem without understanding that what has happened is far from normal. Evaluation of any aspect of student behavior must look at the whole performance, not just cognitive and affective growth or their lack.

General procedures in planning for evaluation in schools

Evaluation, as a part of the teaching process, represents one side of a theoretical triangle. The other two are the objective and the teaching plan for implementing its study. These three basic aspects of instruction might be expressed simply as three questions:

1. Where do we intend to go (the objective)?
2. What is the best way to get there (the learning opportunity)?
3. Where are we now (the evaluation results)?

Specification of measurable objectives not only facilitates evaluation but helps to assure the validity of the procedures designed to test their achievement. Accordingly, the first step in planning evaluation is to study the objectives upon which instruction was to have been based. We will assume that the stated objectives are measurable, desirable, and achievable by the students concerned. Each such objective delimits the scope of the subject matter involved and describes the cognitive or affective skill or behavior with which the learner has been working. In sum, the objectives represent a blueprint of the total plan for teaching and learning.

The fundamental assumption of evaluation procedures designed to appraise achievement is that the learner now knows the subject matter and has learned to deal with it competently, employing the specified behavior. Whatever the evaluation technique, it should elicit the competency described by the objective it purports to evaluate. That is to say, if an objective were to stipulate that students should be able to identify causal relationships between specified social problems and drug abuse behaviors, then a case study describing a social environment and drug abuse problems occurring in that situation might be presented, and the task would be to identify which social conditions might have been contributing factors. It could also be done in several other ways. Whatever the means, the evaluation procedure must give the student a chance to exhibit mastery of the stated objective.

SCHOOL-FOCUSED EVALUATION

Evaluating learners is only half the job. The quality of student learning is directly affected by the nature and quality of the teaching, teaching aids used, and every aspect of the physical, social, and emotional environment of the school and the services it provides.

Evaluating teaching aids

Printed matter A wealth of written materials produced by federal, state, and local health agencies; pharmaceutical, insurance, and food companies; voluntary health associations; and other such organizations with certain health interests is available for classroom use. Many of them are either free or inexpensive.

The federal government is the largest single producer and distributor of health education materials. Single copies are distributed free or at a minimal cost from clearinghouses and information centers such as the National Diabetes Information Clearinghouse. Although more than one health organization may distribute the same materials, it is best to contact the subject clearinghouse directly to be sure of getting the latest version. See appendix A for an annotated list of federal health information clearinghouses and information centers.

Obtaining abundant supplies of current pamphlets, booklets, and other relevant printed matter for health teaching is not a problem. The problem is how to select those that are appropriate to your needs and acceptable for use in the schoolroom and to school administrators.

Very often a school or district will have an established policy that teachers must follow in choosing and using supplementary printed materials. In the event that no such guidelines exist in a district, the following criteria could be adopted and applied with confidence. The statements below are adapted from a document developed by the School Health Activities Committee of the Tuberculosis and Respiratory Disease Association of Los Angeles County in 1964.

PREMISE
Health education materials are appropriate when they:
1. are scientifically accurate and free from bias.
2. contribute to the development of critical thinking and use logic rather than emotional or propaganda techniques.
3. are directed toward positive health practices.
4. stimulate interest in the topic or lesson and provoke desirable student activity.
5. reinforce other materials, and the time involved in their use is justified.

General Criteria

	Yes	No
1. appropriate to the course of study.	___	___
2. a reinforcement of other materials.	___	___
3. significantly different.	___	___
4. impartial, factual, and accurate.	___	___
5. up-to-date.	___	___
6. non-sectarian, non-partisan, and unbiased.	___	___
7. free from undesirable propaganda	___	___
8. free from excessive or objectionable advertising.	___	___
9. free or inexpensive and readily available.	___	___

Specific Criteria	Excellent	Good	Fair	Poor

Pamphlets

	Excellent	Good	Fair	Poor
1. Type is easily readable.	___	___	___	___
2. Illustrations are appropriate.	___	___	___	___
3. Organization of content is logical.	___	___	___	___
4. Concepts are developed sequentially.	___	___	___	___
5. Important aspects of topic stand out.	___	___	___	___
6. For students, teachers, or parents.	___	___	___	___
7. Reading level is appropriate.	___	___	___	___
8. Based on interests and needs of intended group.	___	___	___	___
9. Positive in emphasis.	___	___	___	___
10. Promotes desirable health practices.	___	___	___	___
11. Minimal use of fear techniques.	___	___	___	___
12. In good taste, avoiding stereotypes or ridicule.	___	___	___	___
Total rating	___	___	___	___

Posters

	Excellent	Good	Fair	Poor
1. Realistic and within experience level	___	___	___	___
2. Appeals to interest	___	___	___	___
3. Emphasizes positive behavior and attitudes	___	___	___	___

Specific Criteria	Excellent	Good	Fair	Poor
4. Message easily perceived	___	___	___	___
5. Little or no conflicting detail	___	___	___	___
6. In good taste	___	___	___	___
7. Attractive and in pleasing colors	___	___	___	___
Total rating	___	___	___	___

Recommended

1. For use by:
   Students _____ Teachers _____ Parents _____ Adults _____
2. Appropriate grade level:
   primary _____ elementary _____ junior high or middle school _____
   secondary _____ college _____ adult _____

Not Recommended

Why not? _____
Date: _____ Evaluator: _____

Audiovisual media Films, filmstrips, slides, videotapes or cassettes, transparencies, records, and tape recordings should always be previewed by the teacher before they are used in the classroom. Factors or qualities essential to consider include the length of time required for effective presentation of the medium involved, its appropriateness for the students for whom it is intended (vocabulary level, subject matter, relationship to the needs and interests of this age group, currentness of the treatment and information it provides, and so forth), its special relevance to the instructional objective, its scientific accuracy, and what major points are made or emphasized in its message. Be sure that a presentation does not use up all of a day's class meeting time. If it is so long that no time will be available for discussion, then find a shorter way of presenting that material. Alternatively, devise some means of dividing the presentation so that part is used as introduction the first day, and the rest is offered the following day. Always allow some time for discussion before and after the use of instructional media.

Evaluating teaching effectiveness

For a long time, it was believed that there was such a thing as "the effective teacher." Hundreds of researchers worked hard to isolate some index of teaching skill that could dependably be used to evaluate the competence of a teacher. They never found one. Popham (1975) confides that some have concluded that the search for a defensible index of teaching skill ranks third behind two other equally elusive phenomena: the Holy Grail and the Fountain of Youth.

Currently, the position taken by educational researchers is more realistic. Instead of the simplistic view of teaching competence as an identifiable learned or innate skill, a multidimensional concept has evolved. Now it is accepted that different instructional techniques work for different teachers in different settings, with different learners in efforts to achieve different educational objectives (Popham, 1975, p. 286). This leads to the conclusion that if you want to assess teaching competence, don't look to see what the instructor does about teaching. Instead, look at the students to see what they have learned.

Millman (1973) defines teaching as the ability to change the knowledges, skills, and attitudes of students in prespecified ways. If we can agree that the teaching effectiveness of greatest interest to you is your own, then evidence of change in those dimensions of learning is what you want to be able to show. Here are the steps. If we may assume that pretesting has shown that the instructional objectives upon which your teaching is to be based are appropriate to the needs and interests of the students in your class, and

1. those objectives are relevant to and supportive of the prespecified general objectives or course goals, and
2. your students are provided a variety of learning activities that
3. require application of the subject matter and practice of the skills described in the objectives, and
4. the evaluation plan you devise matches the instructional purpose defined by your objectives, and
5. your students are able to demonstrate the competencies that were the objective of your teaching, then

you can with considerable confidence describe your teaching as effective. Moreover, you should have nothing to fear from those who ask for accountability.

Evaluating the course of study

The process of evaluation is essentially the same whether what is being appraised is a student's progress, a lesson, a unit, a course, or an entire curriculum. The only real difference depends upon *what* is being evaluated and whose values determine the criteria being applied. All the techniques already described for appraising these elements of an education can be used in analyzing the quality and effectiveness of a course of study.

Evaluation of the *quality* of a course of study focuses on the clarity and the internal consistency with which the plan is developed and reported. Appraisal of the *effectiveness* of a course of study has to do with how well it produces desired changes in the learner.

Appraising the quality of the plan Formative evaluation is probably the only valid purpose for appraising a plan for instruction at the course or curriculum level. No course should be regarded as fixed over time. Changes in student needs and interests, legislation, knowledge about human health, advances in teaching techniques and instruction media, and the unending production of new resources for teaching require that teachers and other school personnel be continually reviewing course plans to ensure their continued relevance and currency.

A curriculum document is a means of communicating what the district views as what and how that subject ought to be taught. Local curriculum guides are usually developed by a small group of teachers and curriculum specialists assigned to do so for a district in relation to a specified subject area. In some cases, curriculum guides are produced by agencies outside the schools and adopted by the district as supplementary to or in lieu of locally produced plans. Such plans need to be just as carefully reviewed as do those developed internally. That reviewing has to be done by the teachers whose teaching is supposed to be guided by them.

Payne (1969) suggests the following guideline questions for the evaluation of course plans or guides:

1. Does the plan provide the outline for organization and sequence of the course or curriculum area?
2. How specific is the treatment of subject matter (unit topics, daily topics, specific examples, etc.)?
3. Does the plan include specific activities for students? If so, are the activities described in sufficient detail to suggest what the student is actually to do and the related cognitive process? What is the general emphasis in types of activities described?
4. Does the plan give specific activities or methods for teachers? What is the general emphasis in types of activities?
5. Does the plan specify the materials to be used in instruction? Are there descriptions of what is to be done with the materials?
6. Are there any explicit statements about the nature of learning and the conditions under which it occurs (e.g., statements about motivation, learning environment, maturation and capacity, cognitive processes)?

7. Are there any explicit views on the structure of the subject matter? Are the criteria for selecting and organizing subject matter and materials given?
8. Is there a statement of objectives or desired results of instruction? To what degree of specificity have these been developed (course, unit, or activity)?
9. What are the suggested purposes for evaluating students? What evaluation methods are recommended? Are the specific procedures given? Is there a proposed schedule for evaluation? What suggestions are provided for the analysis and the use of the results of evaluation?

Answers to those questions actually represent all the decisions that should have been made in developing the course of study. The final questions that should be asked have to do with the form in which those decisions are presented. It's important to note whether they are given as directives or as suggestions. If as suggestions, are there options indicated? If there are options, are there circumstances specified in which certain options are preferred?

Finally, Payne describes two evaluative criteria that are essential to analyzing all curriculum plans. These are clarity of meaning and internal consistency. Primary and most often neglected is clarity, which depends upon the care with which key terms are defined and used. Internal consistency is determined by examining the separate parts of the plan (philosophy, objectives, learning opportunities, evaluation, etc.) to see that each is congruent with the others.

Appraising the effectiveness of a course of study Course effectiveness has been described earlier as its success in producing desired changes in the learner. Remember that changes of this sort include growth in knowledge and understanding and shifts or reinforcement of attitudes favorable to health-promoting decisions and actions. In appraising the effectiveness of a health education course, you must first define the scope of your appraisals. If you want to know how well your own course or any particular course is achieving, you write a test or devise evaluation procedures that fit the curriculum. If you want to know how well that curriculum serves national health education needs and interests, you plan and administer a test that surveys student abilities and understandings relative to all worthwhile outcomes of health instruction. The closer the resulting ratings relative to what is, as compared with what the course ought to be, the more valid the claim for course effectiveness.

How do you devise a test that can evaluate the effectiveness of a course? The need is for questions that can discriminate between students who have experienced the course and those who have not. Husek (1969), although admitting that it certainly isn't easy to write or obtain those kinds of items, suggests the following criteria for selecting those that might do the job: "They should be related to the objectives of the course; they should be items that few if any of the students answer correctly at the beginning of the course; and they should be items not dependent on knowledge of special language unless the learning of the language is part of the objectives of the course."

Evaluating classroom evaluation procedures

If we view measurement of desired student growth in abilities and understandings as one aspect of evaluation, then classroom tests are evaluation instruments. Moreover, results of either written or performance testing probably constitute the basis of most decisions affecting curriculum and grading. Thus, evaluation of the worth and relevance of the assessment procedures being applied needs to be continual and careful.

Let us assume that you have carefully constructed a final examination covering expected learning outcomes of a semester-long course in health education. It is composed of multiple-choice questions, based upon descriptions of personal, family, or community health needs or responsibilities. Each item is written in such a way that the student is required to apply what has been learned in choosing the best answer from among those provided. Because the test has been developed in accordance with a district-provided table of specifications, its relevance seems assured. In addition, you have read and carefully edited each item to remove any obvious flaws, such as grammatical, syntactical, factual, spelling, or typographical errors. The directions are clearly written, and the test has been pretested to be sure that it can be completed within one class period.

What else might you do before using this test to assess student achievement and in essence your own success in teaching? A very good last check on such a test is to ask several of your colleagues in health education to read it for errors or weaknesses such as unintended bias, ambiguity, or any other source of confusion or misinterpretation you may have missed. Often another instructor will see at once a possible problem with an item that you as its author will have missed. In such a case, rewrite the item if possible, and, if not, delete it.

Once you have administered a test, you have a wider audience of judges of its validity. Find out what they think of each item. Encourage your students to challenge any answers that you have specified as correct or best with which they differ. They may be right, especially if the item as written is in any way ambiguous. If they are right, let them know that you accept their criticism. Give them credit for the item, and either delete or revise it before using the test again. Remember that there is no good reason why a test should not be used more than once *if* it has been modified as necessary after each administration.

Teachers are often criticized because they do not attempt even the simplest statistical analysis of the results of a test. Most schools today have access to computer analysis of test scores. Find out what the mean score was. If a test is criterion referenced and teaching has been effective, the mean should be very high. If the test is norm referenced, the mean will instead permit analysis of individual performance relative to that of others taking the test. Find out how many students selected each of the alternative responses offered them. If more of them picked the same wrong answer than chose the best answer, find out why, and do what needs to be done to change that. If no one picked some alternatives, you must rewrite them and check once they have been included in a testing to see if they now are functioning well.

The basic principle in evaluating evaluation procedures is that the goal behavior elicited by each task or item must be that specified in the matching objective. This means that evaluation of student achievement of some learning outcomes cannot be determined by paper and pencil tests but must be done by observation and judgment of actual performance.

Whatever the results of any test, remember that even the most carefully constructed instrument is prone to measurement error. Don't base a course grade on a final examination score. Don't base a semester grade on *any* one measurement or appraisal. It has often happened that a student whose semester's work has been A in quality ends up with a B because the final test score fell a few points below some arbitrarily determined standard. Look at the whole performance. At the very least, try to find out why that slight drop in achievement occurred. It might have been the test itself.

Evaluating school health services and the school environment

Although this book emphasizes health instruction, that is only one part of the school health program. The others—school health services and a healthy school environment—are no less important. The activities and purposes of each of the three aspects of the total program are integrated with and complement those of the others.

Health services in schools include health appraisals, vision and hearing screening, continuous observation on the part of *all* teachers, referrals as necessary, teacher–school nurse conferences, health counseling and guidance, communicable disease control, and emergency care.

A healthful school environment encompasses all the efforts made to protect the health and safety of students, teachers, and staff. Resulting decisions and actions taken with this in mind determine selection of the building site; building construction; appropriate attention to the quality of lighting, heating, ventilation, and acoustics; plans for the sanitary maintenance of facilities, grounds, and food services; provision for the safety of the playgrounds or athletic fields and equipment; fire prevention; disaster preparedness; care of the handicapped; and promotion of the sort of mental-emotional school climate that is beneficial both to student learning and the morale of school personnel.

Appraisal of the quality of school health services and provisions for a healthful school environment are usually based upon comparisons between an actual program and established standards of excellence. State departments of education or departments of health often publish official checklists or questionnaires covering all or parts of a school health program. State education and health and safety codes contain mandatory or permissive legislation concerning school health. Professional education and medical groups such as the National Education Association and the American Medical Association have studied health problems in schools and published detailed texts categorized by the three aspects just described (Joint Committee of the NEA and AMA on Health Problems in Schools, 1964, 1969).

Appendices B and C present examples of state-developed instruments for the evaluation of a school health program. In the event that a school district wished to develop its own evaluation form, reference to these or other state forms would provide a good starting point. In addition, study of legislation in that state, along with the texts cited above, should provide valuable assistance to anyone responsible for developing such an instrument locally.

SUMMARY

1. Evaluation is defined for all health education settings as a process, the purpose of which is to determine if program objectives have been achieved.
2. Terms such as "measurement," "assessment," "appraisal," "evaluation," and "evaluative research" are frequently improperly used interchangeably and need to be defined and employed consistent with those meanings.
3. The current recognition of evaluation as a process and skill essential in the repertoire of school health educators reflects certain trends in public and professional expectations:
    a. public demands for accountability of schools relative to their worth and achievement
    b. state-mandated minimum competency focused curriculums and testing

c. federal and private agency funding requirements for prestated evaluation plans
d. the Role Delineation Project, which identifies evaluation as one of seven primary areas of responsibility for which health educators need to be qualified

4. The roles of evaluation are today often categorized as either formative or summative in function.
    a. Formative evaluation is ongoing and carried out during the developmental stages of a program or curriculum.
    b. Summative evaluation refers to appraisals of the effectiveness of a completed program or instructional unit.
    c. "Process evaluation" is a term used by some in health education in place of "formative." In that case, summative evaluation is differentiated into "impact" (immediate effects) and "outcome" (long-range effects) evaluation.

5. Most purposes of evaluation in schools are formative in their role.

6. Appraisal of the total school health program examines two principal sources of data.
    a. the learners (changes in knowledge, attitudes, actions, and cognitive skills and abilities)
    b. the school itself (learning experiences provided, effectiveness and quality of the teaching, relevance of evaluation strategies employed, and the quality and quantity of provided health services and beneficial environmental factors)

7. Three primary domains of learning structure learner-focused evaluation.
    a. The cognitive domain of learning is most often appraised because growth in knowledge is easiest to assess and because it is a primary public charge and a principal professional purpose of education.
    b. The affective domain seeks to assess positive changes in attitudes, values, interests, and beliefs as effected by instruction.
    c. The action domain is observable, nonobservable, or delayed health actions in which people reveal whether they apply what they have learned in coping with health problems and whether they choose wisely when confronted with a decision affecting the quality of life.

8. School-focused evaluation is concerned with the quality of teaching aids used, teaching effectiveness, the course of study, the evaluation procedures, and the total school health program.
    a. Printed matter and audiovisual media should be appraised to see that those selected for use in instruction are acceptably up to date,

relevant, accurate, and unbiased in their treatment of the subject matter presented.
   b. Evaluation of teaching competence is complicated by the fact that it is not a single skill, but a multidimensional concept, perhaps more efficiently judged in relation to observable success in achieving prestated objectives designed for typical students.
   c. Evaluation of the *quality* of a course of study looks at its clarity and consistency. *Effectiveness* of a course has to do with how well it produces desired changes in the learner.
9. The worth and relevance of the procedures or tests used to evaluate the learner of the school need to be appraised carefully and frequently so that conclusions continue to be valid.
10. The quality and effectiveness of each aspect of the total program affect the quality and effectiveness of the curriculum and instruction.
11. Health teaching specialists as well as all teachers should be sensitive to indicators of change in the health of their students.

QUESTIONS AND EXERCISES

Questions

1. Contrast the purposes of educational research with those of educational evaluation.
2. How would you distinguish between health behavior, health practices, and health actions as your first step in planning means of evaluating changes effected in each by health instruction?
3. What is the relationship between test validity and test reliability? Which is more important and why?
4. Explain the difference between formative and summative roles of evaluation. What would be some formative roles of evaluation in health education?
5. "Changing behavior" is the goal of all health educators. In what ways is this goal interpreted differently for school health education than for health education in other settings?
6. Why is growth in health knowledge most often the focus of evaluation by teachers?
7. Differentiate between the uses of impact versus outcome evaluation data.

8. What is the principal weakness of attitude measurement procedures or instruments? In what ways could corroborating information be gathered to support the reliability of self-report instruments?
9. If the fundamental assumption of an instructional objective is that the learner does not know the specified content or have the ability to deal with it as proposed by the behavioral word, in the same way, what must be the assumption of a valid evaluation procedure?
10. Why is it so difficult to assess teacher effectiveness? If you were asked to appraise the effectiveness of a health teacher, what measures would you consider appropriate and valid?
11. What is the meaning of "behavioral change" as used in education? How does this differ from the concept of behavior change as perceived by health educators in other settings?
12. Explain the significance of Hochbaum's statement relative to the ability of health education to change anybody's behavior—that the concept of informed consent . . . clearly implies that people may also respond to educational efforts with informed refusal.

Exercises

1. Apply the criteria suggested for the analysis of pamphlets presenting health information to one distributed by any commercial or professional health-interested group. Which criteria does it fail, if any? Would it be acceptable for use with elementary students? With secondary students?
2. Arrange to preview a health education film, filmstrip, or videotape. If you find that it would be effective and acceptable for classroom use, prepare a list of the points you would want students to focus on as they watched the presentation.
3. Propose an instructional objective for a junior high school health class. Next describe a learning opportunity that clearly communicates how the students would be practicing the behavior and obtaining the stipulated information. Ask yourself what you would accept as evidence that your students had accomplished the objective. Would the lesson that you have in mind equip them to provide that evidence in that way? If not, what would be the remedy?
4. Write or phone the appropriate federal health information clearinghouse for a single copy of the most relevant material available relative to a health concern of special interest to today's adolescent. Using that information and more obtained from the literature, prepare a

brief message or pamphlet that could be distributed to students for their reference and education.

REFERENCES

Anderson, C. L., and Creswell, W. H., *School Health Practice*. St. Louis: C. V. Mosby, 1980.

Bloom, B. S., "Some theoretical issues relating to educational evaluation." In *Educational Evaluation, New roles, New Means*, edited by R. W. Tyler. Chicago: University of Chicago Press, 1969.

Bloom, B. S., Hastings, J. T., and Madaus, G. F., *Handbook on Formative and Summative Evaluation of Student Learning*. New York: McGraw-Hill, 1971.

Ebel, R. L., "The future of measurements of abilities II." *Educational Research* 5:12, March 1973, pp. 5–12.

Green, L. W., Kreuter, M. W., Deeds, S. G., and Partridge, K. B., *Health Education Planning: A Diagnostic Approach*. Palo Alto, CA: Mayfield, 1980.

Gunn, W. J., Iverson, D. C., and Katz, M., "Design of the School Health Education Evaluation." *Journal of School Health*, Oct. 1985, pp. 301–304.

Hochbaum, Godfrey, "Certain problems in evaluating health education." *Health Values* 6:1, Jan.–Feb. 1982, pp. 14–21.

Husek, T. R., "Different kinds of evaluation and their implications for test development." *Evaluation Comment* 2:1, Oct. 1969, Los Angeles, UCLA, pp. 8–10.

Joint Committee of the NEA and AMA on Health Problems in Schools, *Health Services*. Washington, DC: NEA-AMA, 1964.

Joint Committee of the NEA and AMA on Health Problems in Schools, *Healthful School Environment*. Washington, DC: NEA-AMA, 1969.

Kreuter, M. W., Health promotion: the public health role in the community of free exchange. Fourth Annual Colloquium in Health Promotion, Teacher's College, Columbia University, New York, March 21, 1984 (mimeographed draft).

Millman, J., "Teaching effectiveness: new indicators for an old problem." *Educational Horizons Bloomington, Pi Lambda Theta,* Winter 1973.

Moss, B. R., Southworth, W. H., and Reichert, J. L., eds., *Health Education*, 5th ed. Washington, DC: NEA, 1968.

National Task Force for the Preparation and Practice of Health Educators, *A Guide for the Development of Competency-Based Curricula for Entry-Level Health Educators*. New York, 1985.

Osborn, B., and Sutton, W., "Evaluation of health educational materials." *Journal of School Health* 34:2, Feb. 1964.

Parcel, G., "Comments from the field. Results of the school health education evaluation." *Journal of School Health,* Oct. 1985, pp. 343–345.

Payne, A., *The Study of Curriculum Plans*. Washington, DC: NEA, 1969.

Popham, W. J., *Educational Evaluation*. Englewood Cliffs, NJ: Prentice-Hall, 1975.

"Results of the school health education evaluation." *Journal of School Health* 55:8, Oct. 1985, whole issue.

Ross, H. S., and Mico, P. R., *Theory and Practice in Health Education*. Palo Alto, CA: Mayfield, 1980.

School Health Education Study, *Health Education: A Conceptual Approach to Curriculum Development Design*. St. Paul, MN: 3M, 1967.

Scriven, M., "The methodology of evaluation." *Perspectives of Curriculum Evaluation*, edited by Robert E. Stare. Chicago: Rand McNally, 1967.

Tyler, R. W., "Assessing educational achievement in the affective domain." *NCME Measurement in Education* 4:3, Spring 1973, whole issue.

Windsor, R. A., Baranowski, T., Clark, N., and Cutter, G., *Evaluation of Health Promotion and Education Programs*. Palo Alto, CA: Mayfield, 1984.

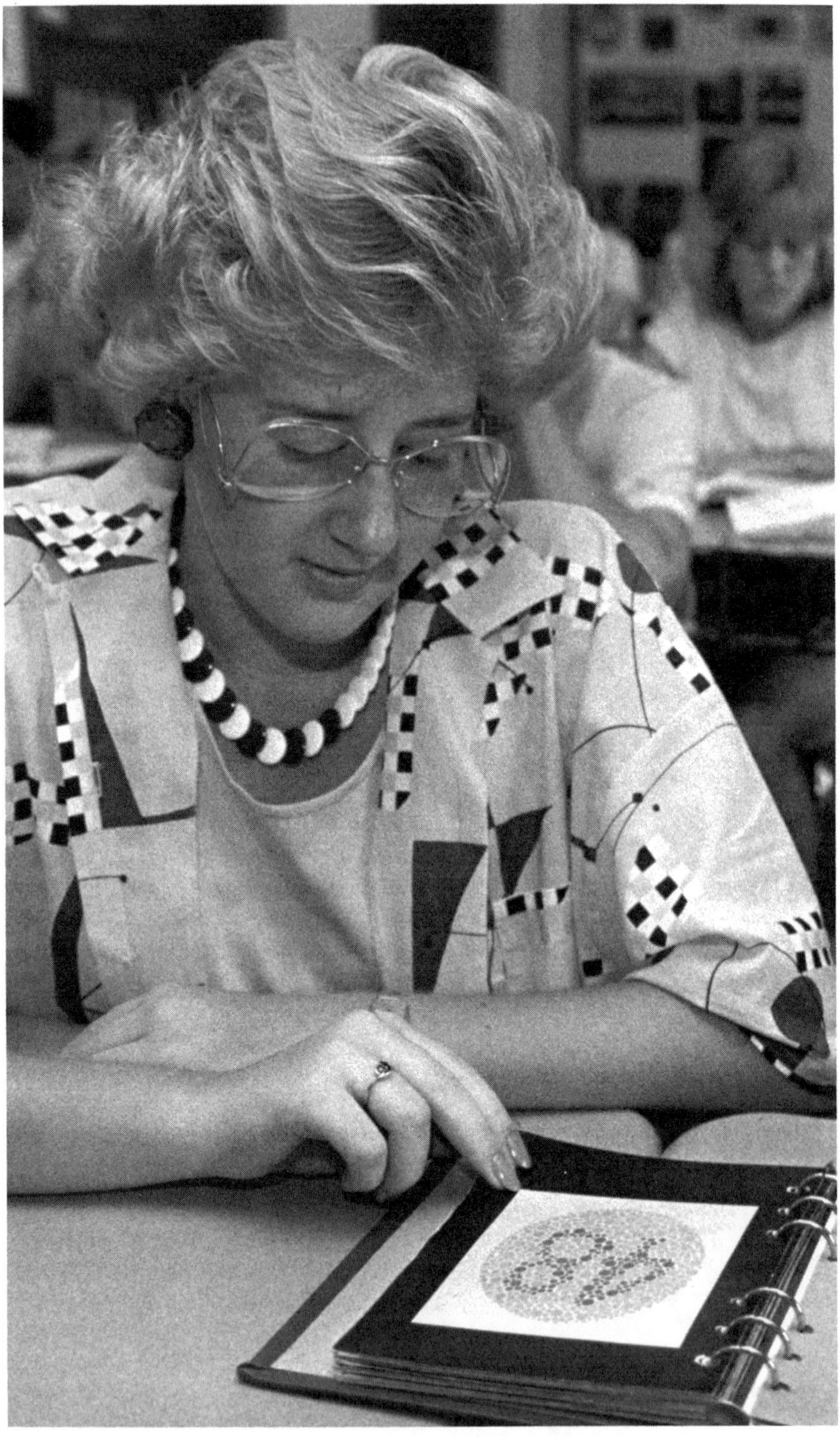

8
Constructing and using evaluation tools and measures

Most people think of evaluation as testing, but tests are just one kind of evaluation tool. A test may be limited to measurement alone and its results expressed by a numerical score. It can also be constructed in such a way as to elicit qualitative data as well. The important thing to remember is that the process of evaluation necessarily uses a wide range of methods and instruments in the search for information about the person or program of interest.

Health education in schools is concerned with summative evaluation of the achievement of course objectives and increases in abilities and knowledge, but also with formative evaluation of present beliefs, interests, attitudes, values, and typical health behaviors and practices. Tests can be used to gather information about some of these; others require instruments such as questionnaires, checklists, interview forms, behavior inventories, self-reports, and rating scales.

Necessarily brief descriptions of the principal forms of tests and other information-gathering instruments or procedures used by health educators follow. Common weaknesses or faults in item construction are illustrated, and suggestions regarding appropriate applications and interpretation of results are provided.

WHAT IS A TEST?

A test is essentially a series of tasks used to measure a sample of a person's abilities or behavior at a given time (Gronlund, 1976, p. 10). Paper and pencil tests are most commonly used to measure abilities, which in turn are categorized as either aptitude or achievement. Aptitude tests predict success in some future learning situation, and achievement tests are designed to assess the degree of success resulting from some past learning activity. The difference between the two is often largely a matter of emphasis because some tests can be used for both purposes. The tests prepared and used by teachers are most often achievement tests. Some refer to these as mastery tests inasmuch as they measure the knowledge, skills, and other learning outcomes the learners were expected to acquire. Typically, they are summative in purpose, administered at the end of a unit of study and at the end of a course.

Self-report devices such as interest or behavior inventories, questionnaires, interview schedules, and attitude scales seek to ascertain what the learner typically will do rather than what she or he can do. These kinds of instruments don't test anything at all and therefore should not be referred to as "tests." The purpose of a self-report survey is simply to find out how the respondent feels or behaves relative to some activity, object, or practice, and what is wanted is the truth, not what the learner knows.

No test can measure all that has been encompassed in any course of study. Any test is only a sample of the many questions that could have been asked. It is always possible that a different set of items might have yielded a markedly different score, either better or worse than that obtained in a particular testing situation. Test items must be based on a representative sample of the course content and objectives. There should be several test items for each objective, as many as possible without making the test too long. Generally speaking, the greater the number of items, the more reliable the test.

A learner's ability to perform well on a test is always influenced by a great many variables. The list of possible such influences is almost endless (for example, a person's physical or emotional status at the moment, whether the test is taken in the morning or afternoon, what else is happening at school or at home, or whether the student ate a nourishing breakfast or none at all). But the kinds of questions asked have the most significant effect upon a test score. A test that is overloaded with simple, fact-oriented questions measures just what it appears to measure—the ability to recall bits of information. Unfortunately, those are the easiest questions to write. But as soon as students learn that a teacher's tests will be fact oriented, they begin to prepare for them by memorizing. They never get a chance to show whether they have achieved any higher levels of competence, and they quickly forget most of what they have memorized.

STANDARDIZED VERSUS TEACHER-MADE TESTS

Strictly speaking, a standardized test is one that has been prepared by measurement specialists and published for general use. The term is also often applied to any instrument that has been carefully developed and validated and for which some norms have been established. In health education, most tests of the latter kind are constructed either as the primary purpose of a thesis or dissertation or secondarily as a means of gathering data needed to test the hypothesis of a degree-related study. In this chapter, the term "standardized" will be used to refer to a published or unpublished test for which research-based validation data have been established.

A published test is ordinarily accompanied by a manual that provides information to be used in evaluating its quality and appropriateness for a given purpose. A good manual explains the uses for which the test is recommended, describes any special qualifications needed to administer the test or interpret its scores, provides evidence of its validity and reliability for a given use, gives clear directions for administering and scoring the test, reports the norms that have been established, and explains the procedures used in obtaining them.

Manuals of this sort are not required for tests published as part of a thesis or dissertation. Nevertheless, explanations of the procedures and results of the total investigation typically provide much of the same information. Descriptions of health education–related research can be obtained through searches of Dissertation Abstracts. ERIC, AAHE publications such as *Health Education Completed Research* and *Evaluation Instruments in Health Education,* and other such compendiums. However, don't assume that if a test has been developed as part of an academic investigation, it is as valid as it claims to be or that it is appropriate for other uses. Because it is probably copyrighted, be sure that you have permission to make any use of it at all.

Standardized achievement tests and well-constructed teacher-made tests are alike in many ways. Both are based upon a carefully designed table of specifications, use the same kinds of test items, and provide clear directions for the learner (Gronlund, 1982, p. 26). A table of specifications is often presented in the form of a matrix in which health content areas make up one axis and general objectives or skills and abilities, the other. A plan for balance in allocating items in terms of content and skills is thus easily plotted.

The differences between teacher-made and standardized tests in health education include these. A classroom test is usually developed by a teacher or teachers of the same subject in the same school. Standardized tests are typically developed through the collaborative efforts of evaluation and subject matter specialists or by graduate students under the supervision of qualified university faculty. Teacher-made tests tend to focus on specific subject matter and skills. Standardized tests more often probe for comprehension of concepts and principles and elicit problem-solving and decision-making skills. The quality of the individual items may be somewhat lower in classroom tests because teachers seldom have either the time or the expertise required to refine and validate the many items they must generate and use during a semester. Reliability, difficulty, and validity ratings are available in the case of standardized tests, but unknown relative to teacher-made tests. Standard scoring and administration procedures established for standardized tests make it possible to pool scores obtained from many geographical areas to add to the data upon which norms are based. Teacher-made tests at best permit comparisons with other classes, past or present, at the same school.

Standardized tests are useful as pretests or for defining areas of need for health instruction in a particular school, as a means of conducting state or national health education status studies, and as posttests to assess a given health education program or teaching strategy as compared with others.

The weakness of standardized tests is that they are not likely to be appropriate measures of the objectives of any particular teacher for a given group of students. Reliability and validity do not transfer to all possible uses of an instrument. When selecting or using a standardized test, remember that although it may be highly reliable for one purpose, it can also be totally unreliable for others. Standardized tests are no substitute for the teacher-made test. Both have their uses, each serving purposes complementary to the other. A teacher needs to be skilled in test construction and also wise to the uses and limitations of standardized tests.

FREE RESPONSE VERSUS STRUCTURED RESPONSE TESTS

Free response tests require recall of information in order to prepare an answer; structured response items appear to depend primarily upon a student's ability to recognize the best or correct answer from among those offered. Tests developed by teachers for their own students are often categorized as either *free response* or *structured response*. Tests with structured responses are those in which students select their answer to an item from a limited number of alternatives provided by the test writer. Each student indicates an answer to as many of the items as possible within the allotted time and receives points or a score based on the number shown as correct by comparison with a standard answer key.

When skillfully constructed, both kinds of test require recall and thinking. Whether a given response represents rote recall or ability to think depends a lot on how the student has been taught, not solely upon the question itself. When facts are the focus of instruction, knowledge of facts will be the outcome of that instruction. This is perpetuated in evaluation by the use of textbook-specific statements. This is especially so in the case of completion items. Often the missing words cannot possibly be filled in unless the student has memorized or learned the exact sentence as it was printed in the textbook. An example of this kind of an item is "A balanced diet provides the ____, ____, ____, and ____ necessary for good nutrition." Even a student who knows the information needed to fill in those blanks is apt to be baffled by that one. A lot of words could be used that might make sense. Yet chances are good that its author wanted and accepted only those used in the book or emphasized in class discussion or lecture. This same sort of dependence on exact quotations is also often seen in true-false items. The correct answer is almost always taken verbatim from the text. The wrong answer usually has the word "not" or some other negative inserted in the original statement.

Free response tests

A free response test is one in which students use their own words, organize their own answers, and respond in writing to a relatively small number of questions. The quality of those answers is judged more or less subjectively by the teacher. The least structured test, and that given the most subjective judgment of them all, is the essay test.

Essay tests Essay questions provide a means of measuring complex learning outcomes that can't be measured by objectively scored tests. The student must recall, rather than recognize information, then organize, integrate, and synthesize that information in preparing the answer or required discussion. The emphasis is on cognitive skills such as application, reasoning, and problem solving.

It takes less time to prepare an essay test than to construct a structured response test, but it takes a lot longer to score or appraise the results. Good essay questions are based upon a table of specifications, just as any test should be, and they must be faithful to the purposes defined by the instructional objectives they purport to measure. First, they must ask the students to exhibit the cognitive skills or process stipulated in the objective. If it was "compares," then the essay question must ask them to compare—not list, describe, or any other behavior. The question must be written in such a way that it can't be answered by reiterating what the book said about the subject. Thorndike and Hagen (1974) suggest that words or phrases such as "contrast," "give the reasons for," "explain how," "predict what would happen if," "differentiate," or "illustrate" help to present tasks requiring students to select, organize, and use their knowledge. Words like "what," "how many," "list," and "who," lead to tasks requiring only recitation.

A poorly or thoughtlessly constructed essay item is more apt to measure students' ability to figure out what it means than what they know about the matter. A question such as "Discuss the importance of various locations of accidents" is impossibly ambiguous. Is the student expected to itemize locations and describe the importance of each as a factor in the occurrence of accidents? What does "importance" mean in this context? Are they to rank all possible locations with respect to the probability of an accident's occurrence? How many is "various"? Is there a location where an accident could *not* occur? What cognitive ability is implied in "discuss"? That question has not been devised to illustrate a poor essay question but taken from the teacher's manual of a college health textbook. Suggestions for its improvement are difficult to offer short of tossing it out and writing a new one.

One way to ensure that every student will interpret the task in the same way is to pose a problem situation and ask a series of questions based upon that situation. For example: "Automobile accidents claim more lives than all other accidental causes combined. Of these deaths, five of six occur among males, most of them between the ages of 15 and 24. Describe in a short paragraph how each of the following factors might contribute to those statistics: (1) age, (2) fatigue, (3) emotional state, (4) alcohol consumption, (5) the environment (weather, vehicle design or fault, traffic, etc.), (6) social forces." An essay question structured thus is more easily scored because the potential for misunderstanding is less and the range of required answers is defined exactly. Yet the students are free to compose their own answers to each of them, and the requirement that knowledge about safe driving be used to explain the statistics of accident occurrence makes it meaningful and relevant to the needs and concerns of young adults.

Other examples of simply developed but clearly posed essay questions are:

- "There are five times as many deaths per mile due to motorcycle than to automobile accidents. Explain why this difference exists. Describe ways the potential for accidents could be lessened for motorcyclists."
- "A married couple and their three small children have just moved to a large city in a state where they have no relatives or friends. They wish to locate a family physician and a pediatrician. Suggest at least

four sources of reliable information about medical doctors that could be contacted. Describe criteria by which physicians could be evaluated in making a selection among those recommended as qualified."

The essay test is notoriously difficult to score fairly and consistently. Many biasing factors influence the judgment process—whether a particular paper is read before or after one that is good or poor, whether the handwriting is legible and neat, how tired the reader is when it is read, how competent the respondent is at writing, whether the rater perceives the question in the same way as the respondent or has any prior experience with the kind of work done by the respondent. All of these and more can bias the scoring of an essay test.

Some students are so skilled at putting down words that *sound* good that they are able to disguise how little they really know. Judges tend to vary in their evaluation of the same paper from one time to another in any case. Research has shown that the same paper, reviewed by a series of judges, can be given every grade from A to F. And, even though it is wearisome to read a great number of essay tests, so few questions can be asked that the obtained sample of achievement may not fairly represent the individual's abilities and knowledge. There are many such sources of error in scoring essay tests. Awareness of the factors contributing to unreliability is a first step toward improving the reliability of a teacher's essay tests (Coffman, 1972, p. 7).

Scoring is facilitated when criteria for each item are set at the same time as it is written. Another way is to prepare a model answer to each item for comparison with those received. Papers should be read without knowledge of their authorship in order to avoid any subjective "set" on the part of the teacher reading them. All answers to each item should be read at the same time and evaluated independently rather than in the context of all the other answers to the test. This avoids the temptation to generalize rather than give credit for item successes. Another technique is to read through all of the papers quickly, sorting them roughly into piles of what seem to be very good, good, average, fair, and unacceptable work. Then reread each paper carefully in terms of the preliminary sorting, making shifts to other rating levels as appropriate. This helps ensure that the quality of a paper is really equal to, less than, or better than the others in a particular category.

Thorndike and Hagen (1974) offer the following suggestions to help make the most of the essay questions as indicators of student achievement:

1. Be sure that the test does not include too many or too lengthy questions for completion in the time available.

2. When several essay questions are to be given, try to have a range of complexity and difficulty represented in the items.
3. In most classroom tests, require all students to answer the same questions. Otherwise in effect they are taking different tests, and there is no way of fairly equating performances.
4. Write a set of general directions for the test, including the time that each item should be given.
5. Specify the point value for each question on the test and the criteria that will be applied to its evaluation.

Short answer and completion tests The short answer test item is a more restricted form of the essay or free answer test. It may be composed of very specific questions that can be answered with a word, phrase, number, or symbol. Sometimes the answer is more nearly a brief discussion. The shorter the required answer, the more easily it is scored, for example:

- Amino acids are components of which class of nutrients?_____.
- Name the major voluntary health agencies concerned with the two leading causes of death in the United States._____.

Completion items are similar to the short answer question but written as incomplete statements. The student is to supply the missing words. An example of the completion item is "When a person is frightened or angry, the adrenal glands produce a special hormone called _____."

Advantages of the short answer item include the fact that it is one of the easiest to write; yet the student must supply an answer. The item does not give any clue that makes a guess possible, nor does it trigger recognition by offering alternate answers. Because it takes very little time to fill in the missing words, a wider sample of the respondent's knowledge can be assessed.

Disadvantages include its inability to assess anything more than knowledge of specific facts, dates, definitions, and terminology. Moreover, if more than one answer could be just as correct, scoring becomes time-consuming and complex. It cannot be done solely by key but must be done, item by item, by a person competent to judge whether alternative answers may be equally correct.

Scoring reliability depends a lot upon the way the items are stated. Teachers sometimes unintentionally reward and encourage memorization instead of comprehension when they accept as correct only the statement exactly as it appeared in the book. Other weaknesses common to all test items include overemphasis on trivialities, such as "The first year that manufacturers made seat belts available to new car buyers was *(1949)*.", omission of inconsequential words like this: "The first teeth to *(erupt)* usually are lower incisors.", or items written so that the desired answer is factually wrong, such as "Insulin is a hormone manufactured by the *(pancreas)*." A more accurate item would be "Insulin is a hormone manufactured by the islets of Langerhans, which are located in the *(pancreas)*."

No item should omit so many words that what is left of the statement is incomprehensible, for example, "The disease that causes _____ and is characterized by increased _____ within the _____ is called _____." The missing words are "blindness," "pressure," "eye," and "glaucoma," but as it stands without them, it's anybody's guess what is wanted. A better statement would be "The leading cause of blindness among adults in the United States is a disease called _____."

In general, write these kinds of items in such a way that only one word or phrase could possibly be correct. In completion items, omit only one or a few *key* words. Place the blank spaces near the end rather than at the beginning of the statement so that the respondent knows what you're after when the blank occurs. Finally, score each item as either right or wrong. Don't try to assign partial credit corresponding to the number of blanks in an item that are completed correctly. If the word needed to fill in each of the blanks is significant enough to deserve separate credit, then write more items as needed to deal with every point on its own.

Structured response tests

Tests that ask the student to choose among already prepared alternative responses to questions are usually spoken of as "objective." No test is objective, of course. What is objective in this case is the scoring procedure. In other words, a standard key is used to score the answers, and every answer sheet is treated exactly according to that key. Otherwise every test is subjective inasmuch as judgments function at every level of teaching and evaluation decision making. Somebody decides that those are the important questions, and somebody decides which is the best or correct answer. The most commonly used objectively scored tests are the true-false, multiple-choice, and matching item tests.

True-false tests A true-false item is simply a statement that a student is to read and indicate a response to in one way or the other. Such a test is usually referred to as true-false, although often the response may be "yes-no," "agree-disagree," "fact-opinion," "right-wrong," and so forth. The more general term is "alternate response," sometimes "binary choice" item. Whatever the response mode, the distinguishing characteristic is that there are always just two possible answers.

True-false items appear more frequently than other objective forms in teacher-made tests in part at least because they appear to be so easy to write. But it isn't easy to write good true-false items. For one thing, it isn't easy to identify statements that are unqualifiedly and without exception either true or false. Those kinds of statements are apt to be trivial or have to be so specific that it takes a great many of them to add up to a comprehensive assessment of student achievement. Another problem stems from the fact that the truth or falsity of an item often depends to some degree on the context of a larger statement from which it has been lifted. Ironically, the more able the student, the more difficult it is to decide on an answer in that situation.

Thorndike and Hagen (1981) suggest some guidelines to writing good true-false items.

1. Be sure that the item as written is unquestionably true or false.
   Example
   Poor: *T* F   The adrenal glands are located above the kidneys. (That could be anywhere between the kidneys and the head.)
   Better: *T* F   The adrenal glands are located on top of the kidneys.
2. Avoid the use of words, termed "specific determiners," that provide clues to the answer. Statements containing words such as "all," "always," "never," and "no" are likely to be false, as you probably learned yourself long ago. Conversely, statements qualified with words such as "usually," "may be," and "ordinarily" are likely to be true.
   Example
   Poor: T *F*   All blue-eyed children have blue-eyed parents.
   Better: *T* F   Some blue-eyed children have brown-eyed parents.
3. Avoid ambiguous or indefinite terms referring to an amount or degree of something. Words like "frequently," "in most cases," and "sometimes" don't mean the same thing to all people, and the respondent shouldn't have to guess what the test writer had in mind.
   Example
   Poor: *T* F   In most cases infectious diseases today are caused by viruses.
   Better: *T* F   Viruses are responsible for more infections than any other pathogen.
4. Avoid the use of negatives and especially double negatives. Their use increases the time it takes to read and interpret an item and can lead students to miss the item even though they know the answer.
   Examples
   Poor: T *F*   Plaque buildup is not a major cause of tooth damage among children and youth.
   Better: *T* F   Failure to remove dental plaque every day is a major factor in tooth decay.
   Poor: *T* F   Noninfectious diseases are not communicable.

Better: *T F* Some diseases are functional or hereditary rather than caused by pathogens.
5. Limit the true-false item to a single idea in most cases. Deciding whether both together are either true or false complicates the student's task and increases the time required to read long, complex statements and judge the truth or falsity of the whole.
Example
Poor: *T F* Gamma globulin is that portion of human blood that contains antibodies that can prevent or minimize the effect of certain infectious diseases.
Better: *T F* Gamma globulin injections provide short-term immunity against certain infectious diseases.
6. Keep true and false statements about the same length. In the attempt to make a statement unequivocally true, many make it so long that its length becomes a specific determiner. The experienced test taker knows that a statement that is much longer than average is probably true. This is not a problem if there are several longer statements, either true or false, intermixed with shorter ones.

An advantage of the true-false test is that it is possible to test knowledge of all the important factual information relative to a given outcome more quickly and efficiently than with more complex test forms. In addition, the two-alternative response mode makes it possible to read the test aloud to those who for one reason or another cannot read it themselves. It is far easier to answer either "true" or "false" relative to a single statement than to try to follow the many alternatives considered in multiple-choice and matching items.

A common fear expressed relative to true-false tests is that the student who simply guesses has a 50 percent chance of getting the right answer. Those who worry about that forget that there is exactly the same chance of getting it wrong. Moreover, those odds have to do with single items. The greater the number of items, the less the likelihood that guessing will have much influence on a student's score. For example, the odds that anyone could correctly guess ten out of ten items are less than one in a thousand (IOX, 1983, p. 41). With as many as twenty items, the potential influence of guessing is insignificant. If the test has enough items and all the students have time enough to read and respond to them, alternative response tests work as well as more complicated forms of achievement testing.

An easy variation in test directions helps diminish the effect of guessing even further and diminishes the possibility that the answer has been based upon misinformation or misunderstandings. For each item marked *false*, the respondents are asked to supply either a corrected version or to explain *why* it is false. This of course increases both the time needed by the students to complete the test and the time it takes to score the results. And the objective nature of the scoring procedures is altered, at least in regard to the items judged false, for the justifications or corrections have to be read and evaluated separately.

Multiple-choice tests The multiple-choice item is the most flexible of those that can be scored by key. It is also the most versatile in that so wide a range of cognitive behaviors can be assessed. It is especially adaptable to measurement of the more complex learning outcomes such as comprehension, application, analysis, and synthesis. As is true of other selection kinds of test items, multiple-choice questions cannot be used to measure writing skills. Further, only the quality and amount of a student's learning *about* health and health behavior can be measured. Actual behaviors or applications of what is known cannot be measured or predicted on the basis of multiple-choice knowledge tests.

An advantage of the multiple-choice tests comes from the fact that so many more alternatives are available to the respondents. In a sense, each item represents four or five questions of the true-false type. A twenty-item multiple-choice, five-option test is the equivalent of one hundred alternate response items. This factor adds to the reliability. The more choices offered by an item, the greater the reliability of its results as evidence of whatever is being measured. Moreover, analysis of the number of students selecting each of the distracters tells the teacher much more than how many each student got right. Knowing how many picked each of the wrong answers is important in many ways. A particular option may need revision or removal. Perhaps better or different learning opportunities need to be devised in order to remove misconceptions. It may be that the item is testing abilities or material that have not been effectively taught or perhaps not taught at all. It might be said that the number right is what matters most to the student, but the number wrong should matter most to the instructor.

The multiple-choice item consists of two parts: a stem and a set of four or five alternate responses or distracters from which the student is to select the one correct or best answer.

The stem should pose a clearly defined problem. It can be stated in the form of a question, as in "Which of the following hormones is released as a result of extreme stress"?, or as an incomplete statement: "The hormone associated with the 'fight or flight' reaction is _____."

The question or problem posed by the stem should be short but complete and clear enough to make sense as it stands. One or two words do not suffice as a stem. For example, here is an item taken from a published list of multiple-choice questions:

Aspirin
a. is harmless even in large amounts
b. can be addictive
c. can cause ulcers
d. cures headaches
e. is rarely overused.

Although the item is presented in multiple-choice form, it is not a multiple-choice item. It is a set of five true-false items, each of which begins with the word "aspirin." The supposed stem standing alone means nothing except as the name of a popular over-the-counter-drug. All the respondent knows is that presumably all of the options will have some connection with that word.

In addition to clarifying the task the respondent is to address, clearly written stems favorably influence the homogeneity and quality of the options provided the respondent. This is because the item writer is helped to focus on a specific problem, generating a set of more closely related, hence more discriminating, options.

The most challenging task is to devise three or four alternatives that sound just as plausible as the desired answer. A distracter so unreasonable that not even someone guessing would choose it is termed "nonfunctioning." If the test writer is not careful, so many distracters may be nonfunctioning that the real choices dwindle to but two or three, for example:

During the last ten years, automobile accidents:
a. caused over a million deaths
b. decreased
c. increased
d. were entirely due to drinking drivers
e. were more frequent on four-lane than on three-lane highways

The first, fourth, and fifth are not plausible, which leaves just two choices. Which would you choose? In addition, the stem is incomplete, and the five options are unevenly constructed and so unrelated in substance that the two options that are left stand out at once, whether they are right or wrong.

Recommendations regarding the construction of the multiple-choice item are too many to discuss in this chapter. You are urged to obtain and read one or more of the excellent texts on evaluation and measurement listed among the references. Briefly, other guidelines include:

- Avoid the use of negative terms in the stem, unless it is important that students know a particular exception or can detect errors in statements.

- If using a negative, underline or capitalize it so that the student doesn't miss it by accident.
- Keep the responses short and about the same length.
- Include in the stem any introductory words common to them all.
- Be sure that the grammar in the options matches that in the stem. Otherwise the respondent may avoid or choose an answer only because it fits or does not fit.
- Avoid the use of "none of the above" and "all of the above" as alternatives. These are frequently employed as a device to hide the fact that the test writer ran out of ideas for any more distracters. Moreover, unless these answers are absolutely correct or incorrect, they cannot be used at all. Neither option works with answers that are chosen as "best" of the lot.

Here is an item that illustrates several of the weaknesses mentioned above.

Evaluation of health education:
a. should be left to paper and pencil tests.
b. should not be left to paper and pencil tests.
c. should be formative but not summative.
d. should be summative but not formative.
e. should be neither formative nor summative.

How many weaknesses do you see? (The stem does not present the problem. The word "should" could have been included in the stem rather than restated in every option. The options are too heterogeneous, the last three having nothing much to do with the first two except in the broadest sense. Actually, it is unlikely that the first and the last would be selected by anyone at all, even one who had not read the material on which the item was based.)

Finally, when preparing the key for a test, be sure that the answer to each item is defensibly the best or the correct answer, not just arguably so.

Matching item tests The matching item test is a variation of the multiple-choice instrument. It consists of two parallel columns of terms, words, or phrases that are to be matched on some specified basis. The items in the left column for which a match is to be made are called *premises*. The items in the column to the right, and from which the choices are to be made, are called *responses*. All premises should be homogeneous in nature (i.e., closely related to the same topic or problem). Each of the responses must be equally plausible as matches for all of the premises. Responses that apply only to certain premises provide clues to the correct match, hence make guessing easier and reduce the number of possible choices for the others.

There should be an unequal number of items in each list, normally more responses than premises. The directions should specify how the matching is to be done and whether any response can be used only once or more than once. When the student is free to use a response more than once, the effect of guessing is further minimized.

Place the list of response items on the right, if possible using some logical order such as alphabetical. This cuts down on searching time because the student is able to focus on one premise at a time, then scan the opposite list more rapidly. The total number of premises should be kept short, say four to seven items, and in no case more than ten, again to minimize reading time. An example of a matching test follows:

Directions: On the line to the left of each hormone function in Column A, place the letter from Column B that names the related hormone. Each item in Column B may be used once, more than once, or not at all.

Column A *Function*	Column B *Hormone*
1. ____ Controls rate of metabolism	A. Adrenalin
2. ____ Affects skeletal growth	B. Androgens
3. ____ Controls reaction to stress	C. Cortisone
4. ____ Stimulates development of female secondary sex characteristics	D. Estrogen
	E. GSH
	F. Insulin
5. ____ Controls sugar metabolism	G. Thyroxin
6. ____ Stimulates development of male secondary sex characteristics	

Matching tests are limited to the assessment of factual information concerning a relationship between two things. Their principal advantage is the compact format, which facilitates quick measurement of knowledge about sets of things logically related one to another.

CRITERION-REFERENCED TESTS

Tests that focus on measurement of achievement in terms of actual proficiency rather than relative standing in a group are most commonly referred to as criterion referenced. "Domain referenced," "objectives referenced," "competency based," "proficiency," and "mastery" are other terms used interchangeably to describe such tests (Berk, 1980, p. 4.). A distinction between the then-existing emphasis on relative achievement (norm referenced) and absolute achievement (criterion referenced) was first clearly defined by Glaser (cited in Popham, 1971, pp. 6–7) in these words:

The scores obtained from an achievement test provide primarily two kinds of information. One is the degree to which the student has attained criterion performance, for example, whether he [sic] can satisfactorily prepare an experimental report, or solve certain kinds of word problems in arithmetic. The second type of information that an achievement score provides is the relative ordering of individuals with respect to their test performance, for example, whether Student A can solve his problems more quickly than Student B. The principal difference between these two kinds of information lies in the standard used as a reference. What I shall call criterion-referenced measures depend upon an absolute standard of quality, while what I term norm-referenced measures depend upon a relative standard.

This means that it is possible to interpret scores yielded by an achievement test in both ways. To put it simply, the same test can be used to find out what students can or can't do and at the same time how well each of them performs compared to the others. Nevertheless, the results are more meaningful if a test is specifically designed for one purpose or the other.

The meaning of a norm-referenced test depends upon the relative position of each student in comparison with all students taking the test. The more variability among scores, the better. Items are constructed with this in mind. Those that are too easy or too hard are discarded in favor of those of average difficulty. The test is comprised of samples of questions representative of a theoretical universe of all the items that could be written relative to the objectives of a course. Although the test is based upon a carefully defined table of specifications, it usually covers a broad area of achievement.

A criterion-referenced test looks very much the same as a norm-referenced test in form. The major difference stems from the rigor with which the table of specifications describes the attributes the test claims to measure. The number of attributes or outcomes being assessed is kept to a manageable few, as opposed to the broadly based norm-referenced instrument. A minimum of five to ten items is needed in order to measure competence required for most important health outcomes. Because criterion-referenced items are absolute indicators of proficiency, the meaning of the scores is not dependent on comparison with other scores. The chief rule in writing a criterion-referenced item is that it accurately reflects the criterion behavior. Theoretically, such items are those that most students could not answer at the beginning of instruction and will be able to answer easily following instruction.

Berk argues that the most important item characteristic is the congruence between what the item measures and the objective it purports to measure. Three elements of the objective and the item must match: (1) the skill or behavior, (2) the content or subject matter, and (3) the level of cognition. The last of these is that most likely to be neglected. He notes that teachers tend to construct items at lower levels of cognition than indicated by test specifications or objectives (Berk, 1980, p. 51).

It is beyond the scope of this chapter to provide more than this brief description of the essential elements of a criterion-referenced test worthy of the name. However, two excellent resources are recommended to the reader for further information and study. The first is by W. J. Popham (1978), probably the best known among those who have pioneered criterion-referenced measurement. Second is the set of seven handbooks developed for the evaluation of health education programs relative to the following six health problems and physical fitness programs (IOX Associates, 1983):

1. smoking
2. immunization
3. stress management
4. nutrition
5. alcohol and substance abuse
6. diabetes
7. a handbook to evaluate physical fitness programs

Each of the handbooks contains information on basic concepts regarding the evaluation of health education programs; a set of newly devised assessment instruments focused on knowledge, attitudes, skills, or behavior; test specifications for each of the instruments (see appendix E for an example), and a collection of existing measures that have been used for evaluation of related health education programs. For the newly developed instruments (tests, questionnaires, attitude scales, self-reports, etc.), one form is provided for adults and older adolescents. Where appropriate, a simplified version of the same instrument is provided for elementary grade children. High face validity of these materials is assumed at present, but extensive validation studies are planned. In the meantime, copies of these handbooks are available for duplication and use of the tests as developed.

Not only are the instruments ready for application, but the test specifications for each represent the best practice known. In effect, the procedures followed and described in these handbooks can serve as a model for the construction of criterion-referenced tests intended for classroom use or evaluation of school health programs in general.

EVALUATION ACTIVITIES

Tests are almost always paper and pencil instruments, and they are efficient tools for the assessment or measurement of student learning outcomes that can be scored objectively. Results are limited to written responses to questions or markings on an answer sheet indicating choices among possible responses. What is assessed tends to focus on factual information, and the required outcome seldom goes beyond evidence of ability to recall what has been learned or to recognize right or best answers among those provided as alternatives.

An evaluation activity is a postinstruction task or exercise planned to appraise student competence relative to a given course objective. It is designed to provide students an opportunity to demonstrate the competency they have been practicing during the learning opportunities just experienced.

The most valid sort of evaluation activity poses a real-life health-related problem, issue, or situation for the learners to consider. In order to resolve or deal with it successfully, they must apply the skill and the information they have gained rather than simply regurgitate the information that has been provided. An evaluation activity cannot be similar to or just another version of the problem or situation dealt with during the learning phase. Instead, it should be an entirely new situation to which the new ability logically transfers. Using a skill even as limited to what can be done in the classroom is more satisfying and meaningful than taking a paper and pencil test. First of all, it's more fun. There can be a feeling of elation as the student discovers that what has been learned really does work. You don't get that same lift out of a test score.

Tests are planned according to objectives and so are evaluation activities. We've been exploring test construction techniques. How do you describe an evaluation activity? It is done almost exactly the same as is a learning opportunity, but the expectations are different. An evaluation activity and a learning opportunity represent opposite views of an objective of interest. One is a plan for learning; the other is a plan for appraising competence. The same techniques (role playing, small group discussion, projects, use of audiovisual media, debate, case study, problem solving, or any activity that elicits an objective-centered performance or product) can be employed.

It's easier to develop and describe an evaluation activity because you know that the students have been working with the objective. They are assumed to know the subject matter and have some competence in doing what the objective proposes. Hence, the plan simply arranges a situation that allows them to show what they have learned to do. And they *do* it; they don't write about it.

Suppose that the objective were "identifies commercial appeals used to promote the sale and use of health products and services." One way to appraise the success of the just completed learning opportunities designed to develop that competence would be as follows: Prior to the activity, the students are asked to clip out and bring to class two or three advertisements urging purchase of specific health products. Then working in small groups of four or five, they are given time to share their materials, make a list of the kinds of appeals employed, and classify each appeal according to type (e.g., testimonials, flattery, exaggeration, or however described in the learning opportunities they have just experienced). As soon as all their advertisements have been examined and the appeals noted, the group is to tally how many times each kind of appeal appeared and determine which two were most often used. When this has been done, an elected member shares the group's findings with the total class. Once all the groups have reported and their data have been combined, it should be easy to discover which appeals are used most often and whether different appeals dominate, depending on the nature of the product. At this point, the students should be able to draw some conclusions on their own. Such an activity enables the teacher to assess the success of the instruction. The students learn more about the strategies of advertising. They are learning to generalize as well. They have generated new information about the frequency and targeting of certain kinds of appeals by their own investigations. Ability to distinguish sales appeals from factual information provided by advertising copy should be a concomitant learning.

Achievement of another objective, "explains that needs and interests shift with changes in stages of the family life cycle," could be appraised in several ways. One way would be to divide the class into nine groups and assign one stage of the cycle to each. The groups are to devise a short skit that illustrates the needs and interests that typify a family during that stage of its development. After a specified amount of time spent in discussion, planning, and preparing their skit (perhaps ten minutes), each group is called upon in random order to make its presentation. The rest of the class, as audience, should be able to name the stage being dramatized without difficulty, assuming everyone has grasped the concept of the family life cycle. Another way would be to ask each student to construct and present a poster, chart, or other artifact that portrays the total cycle, highlighting the stage now typical of his or her own family and himself or herself as part of it. The products thus created should be shared with the class and explained as need be. The criteria of success should be accuracy and the effectiveness with which the life cycle is illustrated, rather than quality of artistry.

Objectives that intend to promote health-related interests, attitudes, and values can often be assessed more reliably by means of evaluation activities than by paper and pencil tests. Values clarification has often been the focus of learning opportunities in health education. Frequently, the success of these procedures has been an assumption based upon the students' enjoyment of the novelty and informality of the games. Seldom has measurement of any cognitive or affective change been attempted. Part of that problem stems from the fact that values games are typically conducted without any specific objective in mind.

Let us assume in this case that the following affective objective has been the object of several sessions: "values the lifesaving potential of automobile seat belt use." It would be easy to ask the students to state whether they agree that seat belts should always be fastened now that they have learned how effective they can be in minimizing injuries. Most will say that they agree and mean what they say, although in practice they don't do it. People who really value the use of seat belts buckle up as soon as they are seated in the car and urge others to use them, too.

How can an evaluation activity distinguish between knowing and valuing? One way is by indicating signs of commitment. Actions taken in behalf of a value imply commitment (Krathwohl, Bloom, and Masia, 1964, p. 150). Ask students who believe that seat belt use should be mandated to write a letter to a local newspaper or their senators and members of the House of Representatives urging the enactment of a national law requiring seat belt use. Alternatively, have them write to a special friend to describe the potential benefits of habitual seat belt use. A copy of their letter, along with any resulting responses, is submitted to the teacher as evidence of the writer's conviction and willingness to support it publicly.

Another way to elicit evidence that something more than information is involved is to ask students to devise a motto or saying that persuades as it promotes some health-related action. Supply each student or pair of students with a strip of transparency plastic and a suitable pen or some other means of preparing and presenting their idea. In this instance, explain that they are to devise and present a one-word or short phrase slogan that promotes seat belt use. Start them off with an example of your own, such as "Don't Bet Your Life: Buckle Up!" or "Reach for the Buckle Before the Key."

Remember that the purpose of these kinds of activities is not so much to measure knowledge as to tease out feelings about its impact on value systems. It is one's values that form the bridge between information and positive health actions. Don't worry about determining a grade, but look for indications of student convictions or at least beginnings of convictions. Those already convinced will be reinforced in their beliefs, and that is important. But there is also an interesting effect upon those not so committed: the well-known human tendency to shift existing beliefs and behaviors to fit what one has publicly supported in any way (Festinger, 1962).

A psychomotor skill such as "demonstrates ability to administer cardiopulmonary resuscitation" is probably *best* assessed by means of an evaluation activity. Even though there is as much knowledge as manipulation involved, the skilled application of that knowledge is what matters most. There is no range of acceptability in this kind of evaluation. The student is competent or not. If not, there must be more instruction and more practice until competence can be demonstrated.

Sometimes, instead of a test assessing what students have learned about nutrition and meal planning, offer them an evaluation activity. If the objective was that students should be able to select daily meals that meet personal needs, ask them to analyze and compute their present energy expenditures and devise a model diet that would satisfy those needs. If some of them are more interested in weight control than maintenance, let them work out a plan that would safely result in a weight loss not to exceed a pound a week. Another approach would be to prepare and give the students a work sheet describing a hypothetical person of a specified age, sex, and activity pattern and ask them to plan a week-long regimen for that individual. The diets may vary in detail, so long as the calories are adequate for the needs of that person and the meals provide a desirable balance among all the nutrients.

Evaluation activities, even though primarily focused on measuring cognitive outcomes, also often indicate change in related attitudes and feelings. This is especially true in the case of role playing and dramatizations when the role puts students in another person's shoes. When students are asked to devise a poster, picture, or other visual artifact that illustrates some aspect of health behavior, almost inevitably feelings about what is depicted are reflected. Inasmuch as affective outcomes constitute a valued aspect of health instruction, evaluation activities clearly facilitate their measurement in ways that scores on tests or scales may not.

Theoretically, an evaluation activity can be inferred from any measurable objective. However, not every measurable objective is most efficiently measured by means of an evaluation activity. Testing works best when the objectives of interest are fact oriented and narrowly focused. But when the objective describes a skill or performance that has lifelong application and utility, evaluation activities are far more effective than paper and pencil tests in determining whether it has been mastered or not.

Whatever the required activity, it should be as clearly related to the behavior and the subject matter specified in the objective as was the learning opportunity. The focus should be on application, with emphasis on problem solving and decision making as much as possible. Evaluation activities can play either a formative or a summative role in appraising performances, depending on whether progress or outcome is of interest. They are not necessarily the best or most desirable way of appraising achievement in health education. They are simply another way of doing it.

Classroom evaluation should be based upon observable changes in the learner. There are many ways to measure change. Administration of objectively scored tests and analysis of the results of evaluation activity assignments are just two of them. Each provides a special and significant view of the students' achievement. Neither is adequate by itself; each complements the evidence provided by the other.

AFFECTIVE MEASURES

The affective domain of behaviors is a construct commonly considered to include those reactions or behaviors having significant emotional or feeling components. *Attitudes*, defined as a person's learned favorable or unfavorable evaluation of an object, person, issue, or event, are viewed as the purest manifestation of affect. Although attitudes cannot be measured directly, they can be inferred on the basis of responses obtained by various kinds of scales, questionnaires, and other self-report instruments. A major weakness of *all* attitude measurement methods is that they involve solely a verbal response. They can record only what a person *says* he or she believes or intends to do about health or health behavior. Generally speaking, all the major attitude-scaling methods (Guttman, Thurstone, Likert, and semantic differential) base inferences about attitudes on respondents' reported beliefs or intentions and their associated evaluations.

The terms "attitude," "belief," and "intention" have been defined in relation to attitude measurement in these words: "Attitude" is appropriate when the measure used places the respondent on a bi-polar affective dimension. The concept includes such things as value, interest, and utility that can be judged either as good or bad, worthy or worthless, and so forth. When the measure relates an object (person, group of people, institution, behavior, policy, event, etc.) to an attribute (trait, characteristic, property, quality, outcome), the term "belief" is used—for example, "health education should be a requirement for high school graduation." Opinions, knowledge, information, and stereotype statements are classified as beliefs. And when the measure links the person to a behavior, it is referred to as an "intention," as in "I intend to become a health teacher."

Of the four major scaling methods named above, the Likert and the semantic differential are easiest to construct and most familiar. According to Fishbein and Ajzen (1975, p. 76), the semantic differential is probably the most widely used attitude-measuring instrument, whatever the purpose. Research shows that whatever Guttman and Thurstone scales measure, the evaluative factor of the semantic differential measures just as well (Osgood, Suci, and Tannenbaum, 1964, p. 194). Given that attitudes play so important a role in predicting health behavior, teachers need to be able to interpret attitude scores and differentiate among attitudes, beliefs, and intentions as elements of affective behavior. Accordingly, a brief discussion of the Likert and semantic differential techniques follows.

Likert scales

Likert scales consist of twenty or so carefully devised statements in the form of opinions, beliefs, or intentions. Each of them unambiguously indicates either a favorable or unfavorable attitude toward the object in question. Typically, the respondent is asked to check one of five alternative reactions to each item, stipulated as *agree strongly, agree, undecided, disagree,* and *disagree strongly*.

Responses are scored from 1 to 5. Strong agreement with favorable items is given a score of 5, and strong disagreement with the same items is given a score of 1. For unfavorable items, scoring is reversed so that strong disagreement results in the high score (5), and strong agreement gets only one point. All the item scores are summed. Assuming a list of twenty items, the highest possible score would be 100, and the lowest would be 20. The higher the total score, the more favorable the attitude.

Semantic differential scales

The semantic differential technique was developed as an instrument to measure the meaning of words. Its use today as a means of revealing attitude is based upon the research carried out by Osgood and his associates. It was shown that a person's attitude toward an object is equivalent to the object's meaning for that person.

Application of this scale involves providing the respondent with one or more concepts (person, issue, or other stimulus) to differentiate and a set of bi-polar adjectives against which to do so. The task is to rate each concept on the basis of each of the adjective sets in the scale. In essence, the procedure represents a variation of the familiar parlor game "Twenty Questions." In that game, questions such as "Is it something new or something old?" and "Is it something you use or something you wear?" are asked, and the object of interest is identified by a process of elimination. In the same way, selection among the pairs of bi-polar adjectives gradually reveals the respondent's attitude toward the specified concept.

A seven-point scale inserted between each pair of adjectives allows the respondent to indicate both the *direction* (i.e., positive or negative) and the intensity of that judgment (i.e., whether what is felt about the concept is very closely, quite closely, or only slightly related to the selected adjective. Seven-alternative scales seem to work best for adolescents and adults because they elicit roughly equal frequencies of choice. Grade school students seem to work better with just five-step scales (Osgood, Suci, and Tannenbaum, 1964, p. 85).

The following example of a semantic differential scale employs a set of bi-polar adjectives established by Osgood's research as most highly loaded on the general evaluative factor.

Family Planning

Interesting	____ : ____ : ____ : ____ : ____ : ____ : ____	Boring
Unimportant	____ : ____ : ____ : ____ : ____ : ____ : ____	Important
Fair	____ : ____ : ____ : ____ : ____ : ____ : ____	Unfair
Worthless	____ : ____ : ____ : ____ : ____ : ____ : ____	Worthy
Pleasant	____ : ____ : ____ : ____ : ____ : ____ : ____	Unpleasant
Dirty	____ : ____ : ____ : ____ : ____ : ____ : ____	Clean
Good	____ : ____ : ____ : ____ : ____ : ____ : ____	Bad
Meaningless	____ : ____ : ____ : ____ : ____ : ____ : ____	Meaningful
Strong	____ : ____ : ____ : ____ : ____ : ____ : ____	Weak
Dark	____ : ____ : ____ : ____ : ____ : ____ : ____	Light

In constructing a semantic differential inventory, evaluative adjective pairs are alternated or randomized in polarity in order to prevent the formation of position preferences. For purposes of consistency in scoring, the most favorable pole receives seven points, and the most unfavorable is given only one. A neutral attitude is given four points, and the remaining positions make it possible for the respondent to indicate how closely the selected adjective represents his or her belief. There is no correct answer, but there is a desired direction.

Scores on each concept rated are obtained by summing all the responses given relative to each of the paired adjectives. The maximum and most positive score on the above example would be 70, and the lowest and most negative attitude would be reflected in a score of 10. Absolute neutrality would be indicated by a score of 40.

Attitudes are not easily influenced or changed. It takes a lot of experiences over a long period of time, and school health education so far has not enjoyed the kind of community support that would be necessary if this were to be a possibility. Even so, it has been demonstrated, especially in the case of younger students, that health education can effect some amount of change in specific attitudes. And it has been argued that attitudes predict behavior better as the specificity of the attitude increases (Stainbrook and Green, 1982, p. 17).

It may be that attitude measurement is most useful as a pretest strategy. If you know what a group's attitude relative to an important health concept is today, you can plan instruction to reinforce that system of beliefs if it is positive or to modify it if it is negative. Then posttests, using the same scales, indicate what the impact of the instructional program has been. Research indicates that a shift in group ratings as small as half a scale unit is significant at the 5 percent level of confidence (Osgood, Suci, and Tannenbaum, 1964, p. 132).

Whatever the purpose of attitude measurement, anonymity of the respondent should be provided. If it is important that individual scores be identified, then the students should be assured that grading is not the purpose. Attention to these two considerations help ensure the honesty of the answers given.

Unobtrusive measures

There are many indicators of health behavior that do not require the cooperation of the person being investigated. Alternative methods of obtaining information about human behavior termed "unobtrusive measures" (Webb et al., 1966) include data obtained or inferred from physical traces, archives, and observation. An absence of ashtrays or odor of tobacco smoke in the rooms of an individual who claimed to be a nonsmoker would be an example of the first kind of measure. Examination of student health records maintained over a period of years would provide a great deal of information that would corroborate or not support statements on a questionnaire about individual health status and certain practices. These kinds of sources are classified as archival. Observation of food choices or eating habits in the school cafeteria or lunch areas, of personal health practices such as grooming, care of the teeth, and body cleanliness, of qualities such as friendliness and ability to get along with peers and adults, and a host of other characteristics illustrate the third category. The observant health teacher begins to know much more about the students in a class than can be gleaned from their self-reports alone. These kinds of data can be recorded as anecdotes or as descriptions of critical incidents and placed in a student's health records folder. A prepared checklist or other form can be used as an efficient means of recording observations regarding common health practices needing to be fostered.

POSITIVE AND NEGATIVE EFFECTS OF EVALUATION

Even the most carefully constructed and administered evaluation procedures can have negative effects. Some of them are predictable. In fact, the more crucial the outcome of an examination, the greater the associated stress, anxiety, and agonies of self-doubt one experiences. It may not be possible to avoid these kinds of immediate negative reactions. It's the unanticipated and potentially destructive effects that must concern the evaluator.

Bloom (1969) suggests that the basic questions to ask about evaluation procedures are

1. Will they have a positive effect on students and learning?
2. Will they leave both teachers and students with a positive view of themselves, the subject, and the learning processes employed?

The task is to design tests and measurement so that they will in the long run have these positive effects.

It's highly unlikely that anybody ever designs a test for the purpose of discouraging further effort or to add names to the list of school dropouts. Nevertheless, tests designed and used with the best of intentions can have negative outcomes like those. A current case in point is the minimum competency testing (MCT) going on in nearly forty states. Students are obliged to take paper and pencil tests of the so-called basic skills (i.e., reading, writing, and mathematics). Those who perform poorly on these tests receive additional instruction or in some states are denied high school diplomas. Although it is conceded that few state programs of this nature are yet as good as they need to be, it is claimed that high quality MCT programs will have decisively positive effects on students, on the curriculum, and on teaching (Popham, 1981).

Nobody can quarrel with the assertion that the business of the schools and of teaching is to turn out graduates who are competent in the basic skills. Certainly students whose competency has been demonstrated by this means must find this public recognition not just satisfying but the source of increased self-esteem. But what about those students who *don't* pass the test? Even supposing such a student is allowed to try again and later succeeds, some amount of negative labeling has occurred.

Madaus (1981) comments, "Everyone has taken tests, some are good at it, some are not. We all know how easy it is to lose concentration, become nervous, have other things on our mind, make a silly blunder that costs a few points. . . . On a minimum competency test, because of an arbitrary passing score, the loss of a few points can be particularly harmful and costly. You are publicly labeled an incompetent, a functional illiterate. You are pulled out of your regular classes. You may be denied a diploma or kept back to repeat a grade."

If the principal purpose of evaluation is to decide whether a student passes or fails, or whether a performance is good or poor, the person being evaluated feels threatened before it is begun. The teacher is perceived as a judge, the examination as a trial, and the experience is stressful and unpleasant. Under such circumstances, few students perform as well as they might. And if they fail or their performance is perceived as mediocre, they begin to view themselves as failures. Few are motivated to work harder in that situation.

A good evaluation procedure is as much a learning opportunity as it is a measurement. It asks students to show that they have mastered the competencies proposed by course objectives. It requires conceptualizing and integrating information rather than regurgitating facts. It elicits application, not recitation. It covers aspects of learning that are regarded as important. Finally, a worthwhile evaluation requires students to combine elements of information learned separately into a new and meaningful whole.

When students know that an evaluation activity will be relevant and fair, motivation to prepare for it will be high. To pass or do well on examinations that meet the above description is likely to be perceived by students as worthwhile, and success in doing so is the source of pride and satisfaction. Those who do less well must not be made to feel they have failed, but that they have discovered areas that will need some added study in order to equalize the competence they have already demonstrated in their areas of strength. This point emphasizes the importance of formative evaluation in promoting learning.

Evaluation instruments and procedures need to be designed with a clear awareness of possible negative effects. Be sensitive to ways that certain items or an entire instrument might be misinterpreted by your students, their parents, or other adults who might be interested.

SUMMARY

1. Evaluation is a process involving judgments based upon data obtained by means of a wide variety of instruments and procedures.
2. Interest, attitude, and behavior inventories are not tests, but are tools of evaluation nevertheless.
3. Valid tests and other evaluation procedures employed in school health education are based as directly as possible on curriculum objectives.
4. Paper and pencil tests are composed of a series of problems or tasks intended to measure a sample of the learner's understandings and abilities.
    a. Standardized tests are those prepared by measurement specialists and published for general use.
    b. Teacher-made tests are ordinarily developed by a single teacher to evaluate the achievement of his or her own students.
    c. Each kind of test has its limitations and strengths. Both should be viewed and used as complementary to the other.
5. Generally speaking, tests are categorized as either *free response* or *structured* response.

6. Evaluation activities pose realistic health-related issues, problems, or situations that require the student to apply what has been learned in order to demonstrate the competence of interest.
7. Criterion-referenced tests are designed to indicate actual proficiency rather than relative standing among all those taking the same test.
8. Affective measurement methods generally facilitate inferences about feelings rather than provide concrete or specific information about them.
9. Evaluation instruments and procedures should be designed with clear awareness of possible negative effects so that these can be avoided to the extent possible.

QUESTIONS AND EXERCISES

Questions

1. What would be the advantages of using standardized tests to assess student growth in knowledge? Discuss any corresponding disadvantages.
2. Why is a short test apt to less reliably sample achievement than one composed of many items?
3. What is the effect on the score of a matching test when there are the same number of responses as premises?
4. What are some physical traces, archival data, and observations that could be identified within a school or about the grounds and used in the evaluation of typical student health behavior?
5. Are there any disadvantages associated with the use of subjectively scored tests such as the essay form? What are the advantages? How could any disadvantages be offset?
6. Why does the number of attributes assessed by a competency-oriented test need to be fewer than for a norm-referenced instrument? What is the fundamental difference that distinguishes the purpose of each sort of test?
7. Probably no one undergoes formal evaluation without experiencing some amount of stress. Stress can be positive or negative in its effect. What are some ways to minimize the possibility of negative outcomes of testing?
8. Why is it so difficult to evaluate teaching effectiveness? If you were asked to evaluate the effectiveness of a health teacher, what qualities

would you consider most important? What measurement procedures would you consider most valid as a means of appraising those qualities?

Exercises

1. Interview a minimum of five individuals in order to discover and record how each of them perceives the meaning of the words "usually," "sometimes," and "seldom" as descriptors of frequency of a given health behavior. Do the words mean the same thing to all of your interviewees? If not, what differences did you find? Add your conclusions to those found by the others in your class. Would other words more dependably convey the meaning intended?
2. Obtain a manual prepared for a standardized health education test. Review the data presented for the test user's guidance in administering the test and interpreting its scores. For example, what are the reliability and validity statistics? What procedures were employed in determining these data? What was the nature and size of the normative sample? Are there special recommendations relative to its administration? Cite any unanswered questions or data that you would need if you were to use the test in a secondary school classroom.
3. For a selected health content area, develop a measurable instructional objective for either junior or senior high school students. Then devise an example of each of the objective test forms discussed in the text (i.e., essay, short answer, completion, true-false, multiple-choice, and matching items). Supply the answers for each. Which of the forms is more difficult or time-consuming to write? What would be a good way to test the clarity and relevance of each item to the objective of interest?
4. Write a second measurable objective, mastery of which could most effectively be demonstrated by means of an evaluation activity or performance test. Next, prepare or obtain a case study describing a realistic health problem or need typically faced by young people in our society. Carefully describe both the activity students would be asked to carry out and the criteria by which the product of that activity would be appraised. Such criteria cannot simply specify *what* is to be evaluated. The objective tells us that. What is needed is clear specifications of the standards of performance to be applied. For example, it is no help to say "Look for understanding" unless we know how one is to evaluate "understanding" in this situation.
5. Study the table of specifications in appendix E. Then select at least one statement from each of the categories of information as outlined in the supplement and devise an inaccurate test item created by means of paraphrase that meets all of the other specified criteria possible.

REFERENCES

Berk, R. A., *Criterion-Referenced Measurement: The State of the Art*. Baltimore: Johns Hopkins University Press, 1980.

Bloom, B. S., "Some theoretical issues relating to educational evaluation." In *Educational Evaluation: New Roles, New Means*, edited by R. W. Tyler. Chicago: University of Chicago Press, 1969.

Coffman, W. E., "On the reliability of ratings of essay examinations." *NCME Measurement in Education* 3:3, March 1972, pp. 1–7.

Festinger, Leon, *A Theory of Cognitive Dissonance*. Stanford, CA: Stanford University Press, 1962.

Fishbein, M., and Ajzen, I., *Belief, Attitudes, Intentions, and Behavior*. Reading, MA: Addison-Wesley, 1975.

Gronlund, N. E., *Measurement and Evaluation in Teaching*. New York: Macmillan, 1971.

Gronlund, N. E., *Measurement and Evaluation in Teaching*. New York: Macmillan, 1976.

Gronlund, N. E., *Measurement and Evaluation in Teaching*. Englewood Cliffs, NJ: Prentice-Hall, 1982.

IOX Associates, *Evaluation Handbooks for Health Education Programs*. Culver City, CA: 1983.

Krathwohl, D., Bloom, B., and Masia, B., *Taxonomy of Educational Objectives II: Affective Domain*. New York: McKay, 1964.

Madaus, G. F., "NIE clarification hearing: the negative team's case." *Phi Delta Kappan* 68:2, Oct. 1981, pp. 92–94.

Osgood, C. E., Suci, G. J., and Tannenbaum, P. H., *The Measurement of Meaning*. Urbana: University of Illinois Press, 1964.

Popham, W. J., ed., *Criterion-Referenced Measurement*. Englewood Cliffs, NJ: Educational Technology Publications, 1971.

Popham, W. J., *Criterion-Referenced Measurement*. Englewood Cliffs, NJ: Prentice-Hall, 1971.

Popham, W. J., *Criterion-Referenced Measurement*. Englewood Cliffs, NJ: Prentice-Hall, 1978.

Popham, W. J., "The case for minimum competency testing." *Phi Delta Kappan* 63:2, Oct. 1981.

Solleder, Marian, *Evaluation Instruments in Health Education*. Reston, VA: AAHE-AAHPERD, 1979.

Stainbrook, G., and Green, L. W., "Behavior and behaviorism in health education." *Health Education* 13:6, Nov.-Dec. 1982, pp. 14–19.

Thorndike, R. L., and Hagen, E., *Measurement and Evaluation in Psychology and Education*. New York: Wiley, 1974.

Thorndike, R. L., and Hagen, E., *Measurement and Evaluation in Psychology and Education*. New York: Wiley, 1981.

Tyler, R. W., ed., *Educational Evaluation: New Roles, New Means*. Chicago: University of Chicago Press, 1969.

Webb, E. J., Campbell, D. T., Schwartz, R. D., and Sechrest, L., *Unobtrusive Measures: Non-Reactive Research in the Social Sciences*. Chicago: Rand-McNally, 1966.

USE
of
Alcoholic Beverages
Arises From A Variety of
MOTIVATIONS
Physical
Mental
Social
ENX

9
Administration and management of school health programs

What is a school health program and how is it different from the health education program as described in the foregoing chapters? First, a school health program is broader in scope, involving every teacher and all of the school health personnel in some way and encompassing many health services, healthful school environment arrangements, and health instruction. Second, the school health program is designed to provide optimum learning environments and to maintain, protect, and promote the health and ability of students and staff to work together harmoniously and effectively. The quality and quantity of the procedures and activities may vary among schools and districts, and especially between states, because what is offered must be either mandated or permitted by state law or established by local policy.

LEGAL ASPECTS OF THE SCHOOL HEALTH PROGRAM
The public schools are tax supported, and that means that monies allocated for education may not be spent in the absence of specific enabling laws.

Beyond that, local ordinances concerned with the public health and safety and school board-established policies must be adhered to in the administration and management of school health programs. Another set of laws, termed "tort" laws, having to do with the responsibility of schools or school personnel for the health and safety of students while in the care of the school, have an important bearing on the administration of the school's health program.

State level legislation

State legislatures pass laws and appropriate money for local school health programs. Once a law is passed, the development of regulations and policies to guide and monitor its implementation are the responsibility of the state department of education, where such bodies exist. State education agencies are often governed by a state board of education, which is charged with developing rules, regulations, and policy in relation to new laws. In connection with health education, on rare occasions, the state public health agency may oversee these same functions. Even more rarely, the education and public health agencies may be required to work together to the same purpose. Usually these two agencies compete with each other for the power and money to control school health programs. By the time bills are introduced, legislators have been heavily lobbied by the various constituencies and persuaded to place the authority and money with one agency alone. That may be good or bad, but it is a reality of politics.

Some state educational agencies designate an office of school health staffed by consultants who serve a major function in providing technical assistance to local school districts in planning and implementing school health programs. They also assist local schools in interpreting the law and gather data that can be useful to the state office of education and the legislature in creating new laws or establishing policies. Often state health education consultants provide local districts with help in developing curriculum guides, in directing them to valuable resources for their programs, and in conducting continuing education programs for health teachers.

It does little good if laws are passed when implementing and conducting the specified program require large sums of money, and the legislature fails to *allocate* the necessary funds. For example, millions of dollars may be authorized for a program under the law, but when that item comes up for discussion at budget time, it may not rank high enough on the priority list to receive any money at all. In such a case, it is virtually impossible for a state or local educational agency to act on the law. This is exactly what has happened in most states that have enacted laws requiring or permitting the development of programs of comprehensive school education. An exception is section 115-204.1 of the North Carolina Education Code (1978), which established resources, the structure, and the process for implementing their health education program. The code establishes a ten-year phase-in period for the development of health education in grades K–9, places responsibility for the development and administration of the program with specific state and local offices, appraises local education agencies of eligibility criteria for funding, defines the role of the state department of public instruction, and establishes a state school health advisory committee and describes its charge and membership. Some may argue that this is an example of a state imposing too many rules on local school districts, but as of this writing, eight years since the law was passed, North Carolina along with Florida leads the nation in implementing a comprehensive school health program throughout the state.

In many states, the collection of laws governing education is termed the "education code." Laws affecting health services and the school environment can also be found in a state's health and safety codes. Regulations for implementing state laws are developed by state boards of education and their staff. Following that step, local school boards usually develop related policies as guidelines for their staff so as to be certain they are meeting the intent of the laws.

Local policy

The American system of education is based upon the concept of local control over the public schools. State departments of education lead, encourage, and enforce minimum standards based on the law. Departments of health can enforce state laws stipulating minimum standards of performance with regard to sanitation, safety, and disease control. But by and large, determination of the quality and scope of the school health program is a local decision and dependent almost entirely upon the convictions, commitment, and managerial skills of school administrators, teachers, and nurses. Whether health instruction is excellent, poor, or nearly nonexistent is in most states entirely a local matter. To employ a physician, to organize special education programs for the handicapped, to provide full-time school nurses or health coordinators are local decisions. School health programs are comprehensive or minimal according to the extent to which local school and municipal authorities exercise their prerogatives under the law. The responsibility falls most heavily upon the local superintendent of schools. The nature of the school health program in a district reflects that person's professional attitudes toward and skill in developing effective programs focused on the promotion of wellness of the students. Others share this responsibility, but final authority rests with the chief administrator working within the framework of the laws and standards established by the state legislature and board of education. School principals are secondarily authorized to make the necessary decisions and take appropriate action in individual schools.

If state laws gives local boards the right to require a physical examination of school employees without describing in detail what that examination should include, then the board may specify whatever health standards it wishes. Further, if public funds may be expended for such a program (a right usually reserved for legislatures to establish), then local boards may or may not require that examination as they see fit. Local boards have autonomy in deciding what the curriculum shall include as long as it meets state standards. They can if they wish prohibit the teaching of certain aspects of health education curriculums, such as sex education, or require that other aspects be offered, for example, a unit of study on drug and alcohol use and abuse.

This is why local policy and regulations in health education are so important in planning and implementing the school health program. Who is liable for injuries incurred as a result of high school athletics? How much sick leave may teachers have without loss of pay? What kinds of excuses from required physical education are acceptable? Is health instruction to be offered in sexually segregated classes or mixed classes? Shall it be provided at the ninth or tenth grade? Are parents required to give permission for the participation of their youngster in athletics? How much freedom does the health teacher have in dealing with controversial subjects?

The answers to questions like these are matters of policy. They require some predetermined judgment and decision. Once the policy is set and full notice is given to school personnel and appropriate community people, such problems as may be covered by the policies are usually handled without difficulty.

How are local policies developed? Sometimes policy comes from the top down. The board of education can formulate a policy without consultation or public hearing. More often the board will ask a committee of interested personnel or community experts to study a problem and make a recommendation regarding needed policy. Sometimes a committee of teachers or the school administrator will propose a policy to the board for approval.

Perhaps the best way to have policy evolve is to have it come upon the recommendation of a formally or informally organized school or community alliance, council, or coalition. Some communities have established standing coalitions of this sort (Metropolitan Life Foundation, 1986, p. 117–119). In other places, they may simply be ad hoc to advocate the need for formal policies with regard to some aspect of the program. There should be a policy to cover any possible problem affecting the efficiency, efficacy, and quality of the total program. Who shall be responsible for giving first aid? Who shall be permitted to teach health education? How shall working parents be notified in case of injury to their child? How shall students who are ill be transported to their home? How will latch-key children be handled in the event of their illness until parents return home? There are hundreds of such questions the answers to which cannot be left to spur of the moment decisions.

Tort laws

The answers to some of those last questions are tied to the concept of liability. A tort is an act or absence of an act by which someone causes an injury to a person, property, or reputation, either directly or indirectly. In every state of the union, teachers are liable for their own torts. A few states, such as California, New York, and Washington, have enacted legislation making the district liable, but in most places, under common law the district can do no wrong. Therefore, the teacher or other school staff member concerned is the only one who can be sued for damages when an accident occurs or a reputation is damaged. In general, tort is considered to be an act of negligence (defined as failure to do what a reasonable person would do) or doing something that a prudent or reasonable person would *not* do. So negligence can be an act of commission or omission.

Examples of how a school employee could get into difficulty include the following: Under California law, a teacher or school administrator is required to report suspected child abuse. Failure to do so within thirty-six hours is a misdemeanor punishable by six months in jail or a $500 fine or both. Some states have various laws that require that a person must take certain action if confronted with a case of serious bleeding, lack of consciousness, stoppage of breathing. There are laws regarding administrators' right to search student lockers or for dealing with students who appear to be under the influence of alcohol or other drugs. Accidental injury to students that could have been prevented had the teacher acted responsibly; failure of a teacher to be present as assigned to supervise a playground, lunch areas, or classrooms during which time an injury occurred; even providing the wrong kind of first aid can render the provider liable for damages. Most states have regulations regarding the necessity of obtaining parental permission in writing before taking students on field trips requiring travel off school grounds. Some require written permission for students to participate in class discussions of human sexuality.

All teachers should be informed in general about the criteria defining a tort, and in particular about those school-related activities with special potential for errors in judgment that might lead to a suit for liability. A careful administrator will see to it that new employees are provided with information explaining school policies on all matters involving the health and safety of both students and staff.

Unfortunately, the laws mandating health services and standards of school sanitation and safety are far more specific and numerous than for health instruction. Hence, it is the health education element of the total school health program that is most dependent for its existence and effectiveness on support and decisions made by the principal administrator of the school district and of each school.

What has not been stressed before is the fact that health instruction is not limited to the planned curriculum and learning experiences typical of a functional program of health education. Thoughtfully administered health services, efficient and nutritious food services, and exemplary standards of cleanliness and safety protection are educational in impact as well as protective in outcome. So far, all of the emphasis of this book has been on the health instruction aspect of the program. As the other two parts of the program are described, think about some ways you might logically build upon the opportunities implicit in these procedures for the enrichment of health teaching and learning or for reinforcement of past learning experiences.

Health services

School health services have been defined as the procedures carried out by physicians, nurses, dentists, teachers, and other health-related professionals and workers to appraise, protect, and promote the health of students and school personnel. These procedures are designed to do the following (Joint Committee . . . , 1964):

1. appraise the health status of both students and staff
2. counsel students, teachers, parents, and other concerned persons for the purpose of helping students obtain needed health care or for arranging school programs in keeping with their needs and abilities
3. help prevent or control communicable diseases
4. provide emergency care for injury, sudden sickness, or disaster victims
5. promote optimum sanitary conditions and provide sanitary facilities
6. promote the health of school personnel

Health services may be provided on an individual school basis or by district personnel. Large school districts frequently employ a central health services staff that has responsibility for establishing policy for and overseeing services provided by individual schools. It is not uncommon that a physician is the director of such a central unit. Working with that physician will be school nurses, dental hygienists, sometimes dentists as well, and other health care specialists. These specialists, in addition to setting policy, supervise the health program at individual schools, provide technical assistance to the staff of such schools, coordinate the assignment of health personnel to schools, and in some instances assist with curriculum development.

In other cities and towns, there may be written contracts between local school systems and the local health agency that detail a plan for the health agency to provide school health services (and sometimes school health instruction) either on a fee-for-service or some sort of prepaid plan. The kinds of services generally provided under such an arrangement include health screening (e.g., dental, vision, hearing), immunization services, emergency health care, and sometimes health examinations.

Partially because of rising health care costs, more and more school systems urge students to see their own physicians for health examinations. However, many systems employ nurse-practitioners in order to offer some of the services that might otherwise have to be provided by physicians at greater expense. These nurses have had training in addition to that usually required of school nurses, which qualifies them under the preceptorship of a physician to diagnose and treat certain kinds of complaints. Studies indicate that they do an excellent job of identifying previously undiagnosed medical problems in children (The Robert Wood Johnson Foundation, 1985).

Today there are many working mothers who find it difficult to accompany their children during the day to obtain health care services. In 1983, 59 percent of children aged 6 to 17 had working mothers. Almost 13 million U.S. children (one in five) live with their mothers only. The median family income of this group was only $11,787 in 1983. Poverty level for a family of four at that time was $10,178. It is thus understandable that in many places the school is being viewed as a venue for providing expanded health services to school-age children.

In a few cities, support has been provided for the establishment of clinics that provide direct health care to students on the school campus. In most of these situations, private funding has been secured for demonstration projects testing such an innovation. They have proved most successful so far in schools where the majority of the students are children of medicaid-eligible parents. In more affluent neighborhoods or communities, the complexities of the many privately held insurance programs have made maintenance of these clinics less feasible. Given the very rapidly changing developments affecting reimbursement for health services, many new concepts for providing health services through the schools will probably emerge in the next few years.

One administrative pattern for providing health education and health services gives total jurisdiction to the school system while still complying with local health agency mandates. Another gives jurisdiction for the total school health program (environment, services, and instruction) to the local health department. A third pattern divides this jurisdiction. In this case, there is a sharing of responsibility. For example, the schools may oversee all health instruction while the health department provides all the health services. Accurate data regarding which pattern prevails today are hard to come by, but knowledgeable school health experts would agree that the pattern most frequently found in the nation's schools is one in which the school district maintains full control over the administration of these programs although complying with local health department mandates. For example, in the event that health department policy stipulates criteria for readmission to school of students who have suffered certain diseases, schools may be required to report cases of specified diseases. If the policy is to deny admission to students lacking certain immunizations, the school administrator must comply.

Whatever model a school system employs, one is most likely to find a quality school health program where good working relationships exist between the schools and the local health agency. Both agencies need to be involved at the very earliest stages of planning health services intended for students. It would be foolish for a local health officer to hand a school superintendent a package that has been completely planned. The classic example of this mistake occurred in the late 1970s when the health establishment imposed an immunization program on the nation's schools without ever having involved educators in the planning stage. The health agency personnel responsible were pleased with what they viewed as a highly successful immunization program. They soon discovered, however, that in many parts of the country considered fully immunized, measles epidemics were occurring. What had happened? In those places, school administrators had found it impossible to implement the plan or to report its outcome accurately. The health agency, having learned its lesson, came back a few years later to do something about these outbreaks. This time they involved the school administrators from the first day of planning, and the outcome was a successful program.

The federal government frequently offers grants and contracts to either a school or a health agency to carry out portions of the school health program. The recipients of these programs are supposed to be school-age children. Good working relationships are necessary to avoid the possibility of ego problems threatening the intended goal of such programs, which is to promote the health of students.

Healthful school environment
The third aspect of the school health program includes all the provisions made for the safety, protection, and promotion of the health of all those students and staff members who spend their days in the school and on its

grounds. The notion of environment in this case is not limited to its physical aspects, but includes social and emotional dimensions as well. Even every curriculum experience is carried out with concern for its possible negative impact on student health. Consideration of the quality of the building and the grounds on which it is situated, the safety of access streets and entrances, noise pollution in the area of the school, the lighting, heating, and ventilation, school food services, sanitation, fire prevention and safety, good housekeeping, and the health of school personnel (e.g., provisions made for sick leave, health insurance, retirement, rest periods, sabbatical leave, etc.) are examples of the kinds of environmental factors that are involved.

Most of the requirements for the physical environment are set by law, and current safety and sanitation aspects are checked by the appropriate community agency (e.g., fire department inspectors, sanitation inspectors, safety experts, building inspectors). Responsibility for the social, emotional, and intellectual quality of the school rests primarily with the administrator. Organization of the curriculum, assignment of qualified personnel to the right job, and plans to promote the emotional tone of the school and provide safe transportation to and from schools are just a few of the elements of a healthful school environment for which a principal or superintendent of schools has responsibility.

It is easy to take all of this careful planning for a school health program for granted because ordinarily it works so smoothly. It is never a one-person job, but depends upon the leadership of qualified personnel and the interested cooperation and participation of every other member of the school's staff, along with key members of the community as needed.

The school health team Many people contribute to the development and provision of a school health program. Some participate in leadership, decision-making roles, such as school principals, health teachers, and health coordinators. Some are health care or health-concerned specialists such as school nurses, school physicians (whether part- or full-time), speech therapists, and guidance counselors. Some are more directly responsible for protecting the health and safety of students and staff, such as custodians, school bus drivers, and street crossing guards. Others, drawn from the community as consultants, health aides, or advisers, participate as requested or on an ad hoc basis. It is not possible in these few pages to discuss the separate contributions of all of these school health team members. Those most closely associated with the administration of the program are the principal, the health coordinator, health teachers, and the school nurse.

Administrative roles The term *principal,* usually applied to the individual serving as school administrator, is a descendant of the original "principal teacher." Today principals seldom, if ever, do any teaching but are usually qualified to do so by professional preparation and past experience. The principal is given authority to administer the school's affairs by the district school superintendent, who in turn is given authority by the local school board. Though principals are involved in many activities during the school year, they generally perform at least the following six major roles.

First, the principal is a *manager*. That means that all of the usual managerial functions (*planning*—deciding on goals and objectives and on the activities needed to accomplish them; *controlling*—measuring performance to determine how well goals are being met, determining causes of any roadblocks or changes in direction, and implementing actions needed to bring the program back on course; *organizing*—grouping and assigning activities and providing the means and authority to carry them out; *staffing*—determining staff needs, recruiting, selecting, training, and providing for continuing development; and *motivating*—directing staff in a manner that will lead them to accomplish organization goals) are special responsibilities (Rue and Byars, 1983, p. 11).

Principals play a decisive role in determining the nature and quality of the instructional and health services programs of a school. Yet the professional preparation of principals does not include any health courses at all. Moreover, if the principal's experience with health education during school days was poor, a lot of convincing may be needed if the kind of administrative support that a quality program needs is to be given it.

Second, a school administrator is a *supervisor* who nevertheless understands that most teachers know their subject matter and the methodology for teaching it far better than does a principal. A school principal who wants to revise the curriculum or improve instruction organizes teams of teachers of the same or related subjects, along with appropriate community resource persons, to work together to that purpose. Often the principal's supervisory role is not so much overseeing individual teacher performance as initiating and directing in-service and development programs where needed. Effective supervision requires the principal to be skilled in curriculum development, teaching methodology, and evaluation. It also requires that the school administrator know the community well enough to be able to identify those with health and health education expertise who could be helpful. Parents and other interested adults are obvious sources of this kind of information.

Third, a principal is the final authority in maintaining school *discipline*. No longer are students expected to sit quietly listening to teacher talk, reading textbooks, or filling out workbooks at their desks. Health classes, in particular, often participate in hands-on, experiential activities that are noisy and may seem disorganized. A school administrator is sensitive to the difference between meaningful experiences and out-of-control fun and games. Further, responsibility for maintaining discipline necessitates ability to apply measures that are both appropriate and applied to the right person, whether it be student or teacher who deserves it.

Fourth, as a *facilitator* of good human relations, the school principal is responsible for meeting the needs of students and school employees and promoting cooperative and harmonious relationships between them (Gorton, 1976, pp. 67–68).

Fifth, the school administrator serves as a *change agent* to the extent that change is introduced as a means of better meeting students' needs. The role of change agent involves the following (Gorton, 1976, pp. 68–69):

1. diagnosing a need for change
2. developing or selecting an innovative action
3. orienting those to be changed (i.e., the students) to the proposed change
4. anticipating problems and resistance to the change
5. developing and carrying out a plan that can introduce the change in a way that can overcome obstacles and resistance to it
6. evaluating the results of the change and making any needed refinements.

Sixth, the school principal is increasingly being placed in the position of *conflict mediator*. The role requires securing all the facts and perceptions surrounding issues of concern and working with both sides to seek compromise (Gorton, 1976, p. 69). In many school systems today, very complex bargaining agreements detail who may do what, when, where, and how. It may be necessary for the principal to become involved in the bargaining process in order to negotiate time in the curriculum for health classes or to require that those who are assigned to teach health have been professionally prepared to do so.

School health coordinators may be employed at the district level, serving in this role for all the schools, especially at the secondary level, in the system. Such an assignment may be given to a health education specialist as a part-time responsibility along with teaching. The major responsibilities of the district level coordinator include:

1. administering board of education policies as related to health education
2. supervising and training coordinators responsible for specific schools
3. planning and conducting in-service workshops, conferences, seminars, and meetings for all district school health personnel
4. guiding health curriculum development
5. establishing and maintaining a central instructional materials and resources center
6. supervising the distribution of such teaching aids to schools

7. assisting health service and environment staff as appropriate
8. planning and implementing evaluation of the total school health program or specific parts of the program as needed
9. assisting the administrator in budget planning
10. serving as liaison to college and university health education professional preparation programs
11. actively participating in professional health education associations
12. assisting the administrator in handling controversy related to health instruction if it occurs
13. planning educational programs in cooperation with health service and environment control personnel
14. advocating for health education with media representatives

Schools lucky enough to have a coordinator assigned full-time to the job should expect that person to help the district coordinator carry out the above tasks as needed and to perform the following tasks:

1. planning and coordinating the scope and sequence of curriculum units where more than one teacher is assigned to teach health education, whether full-time or part-time.
2. continuous upgrading and updating the content of the course
3. working with the faculty in integrating and correlating health education with other disciplines as appropriate
4. communicating and working with various individuals and groups in the community (e.g., voluntary, professional, official health agencies, and industry) to promote community understanding of health education and facilitate their effective involvement in school health programs
5. identifying and reviewing health education literature, curriculum materials, and teaching aids for recommendation and possible use to health education faculty
6. evaluating new teaching materials for their appropriateness and accuracy
7. informing faculty of available health education–related workshops, seminars, conferences, and so forth that are to be offered in the immediate area of the school
8. chairing the school health council or committee
9. working with health-related student organizations

Those employed as health coordinators should have earned a master's degree in school health education from an accredited college or university offering professional preparation in health education and have at least two (and preferably five) years of classroom experience as a health teacher.

Every teacher is a *health educator,* a part of the school health team, and has a leadership role in the school health program. There are three reasons for this. First, a teacher is an authority figure and inevitably a role model. Students are observing the health-related behaviors of their teachers perhaps more closely than teachers observe their students. Health teachers, in particular, are expected to exemplify what they teach. Second, even at the secondary level, a teacher is in a better position in some ways to observe significant changes in a student's health than are parents or any other adult. That is because no other professional sees a youngster every school day at the same time and in a context of thirty or so others of the same age and level of development. Having noted an unexplained alteration in physical, social, or mental well-being, a teacher is uniquely able to take the first necessary step in doing something about it. Third, teachers are liable under the law for the safety and health of their students.

Health education specialists are well qualified to take a leadership role in the school health program. They know that comprehensive school health education is not limited to teaching facts about human health and are quick to see ways to integrate health service procedures with their health teaching. The educational potential implicit in a fire drill or in selecting foods at the school cafeteria is not ignored or unnoticed. Many of the health coordinator's activities depend upon the competence, knowledge, and enthusiasm of those responsible for health teaching.

It is entirely possible that health education taught by nonspecialists can be effective; yet unquestionably, the health teaching specialist is better equipped to assist the principal in planning and implementing the school health program. The specialist knows the subject matter and methodology of health teaching so well that the textbook is employed as a supplement rather than as a crutch. Moreover, the specialist considers health teaching a primary assignment, not a minor responsibility tacked onto a teaching load in another discipline.

The *school nurse* is an integral part of the school health team. Relatively few schools have the services of a full-time nurse. More often, and especially in small schools or districts, a nurse is assigned to serve several schools on a regularly scheduled basis. In some private schools, public health nurses provide needed service occasionally or for special needs. Perceptions of the role of the school nurse are more often based on stereotypes than reality today. This is supported by a recent study of high school students' perceptions of school nurse performance. Many students viewed school nurses primarily as validators of student illness, wound bandagers, temperature takers, shot givers, and people who could easily be conned. Asked what the job of school nurse *should* be, the majority of students recommended that the role be expanded, made full-time, and strengthened with more authority to provide preventive and general medical care (Resnick, Blum, and Hector, 1980, p. 551).

And that just about describes what is happening as nurses are increasingly completing professional programs preparing them to use the title "school nurse-practitioner" and to assume additional responsibility for the health care of students. A joint statement issued by major professional organizations concerned with nursing practice and standards details guidelines for the professional preparation of school nurse-practitioners. The functions and responsibilities of the traditional school nurse as described in that statement include:

- obtaining a relevant health history
- aid in obtaining a physical appraisal
- participating in evaluating of developmental status
- advising and counseling children, parents, and others
- helping in the management of technologic, economic, and social influences affecting child health
- participating in appropriate health screening programs
- assessing and managing certain minor illnesses and accidents of children
- planning to meet the health needs of children in cooperation with physicians and other members of the health team

The description continues with "school nurses may also serve as health consultants to administrators, teachers, and the community. In association with physicians and others, school nurses may participate in the formulation, implementation, and coordination of standards, policies, and procedures for school health services and health education programs . . . and engage in defining their role with other members of the school health team."

The expanded role enables school nurse-practitioners to identify and assess factors that may contribute to learning disorders, psychosocial-educational problems, perceptive cognitive difficulties, and behavior problems as well as those causing physical disease. They may assume a major role in health education and counseling and work collaboratively with physicians and other health professionals, educators, and parents to provide comprehensive assessment and remediation of problems ("Guidelines on educational preparation . . . ," 1978, p. 265).

Educators, administrators, and parents need to understand the role the school nurse plays in providing for the health maintenance, preventive health care, and education of students. It is argued that the education of the public and administrators in this regard is a responsibility that school nurses need to assume today (McNab and Canida, 1980, p. 90).

The school health council/committee

The participation of a school health council is a time-tested aid in the administration and management of school health program. Such a council is an excellent mechanism for gaining support for the adoption or revision of curriculum plans, provision of services, or improvement of facilities. There is strength in numbers, and the more people involved or represented in decisions for change, the better the chances for a program's acceptance and success.

Such a council is a problem-solving, coordinating, recommending body only. It has no regulatory powers but can only study the situation, gather facts, and finally by consensus arrive at a recommendation to be presented to the administrator.

Membership is drawn from the school administration, faculty, and staff and includes parents and school representatives as well. Typically, there will be the school principal or designee, the school nurse, dietitian, custodian, health educator, faculty with special interest in health education, parents who may be health care specialists such as physicians, dentists, or sanitarians, and student leaders such as class presidents. The school health coordinator, if there is one, or the district coordinator, if not, would be the logical chair of such a council.

People, and especially the students who will be most directly affected by the deliberations of this body, are better able to accept new rules or programs when they have been analyzed and recommended by their peers.

Such an organization can assist the school administrator in solving many kinds of problems. For example, the members might do the following:

1. assist in determining school health needs
2. serve as an advocate for the school health program
3. assist in locating and securing required health resources, materials, or funds
4. recommend needed new policies and programs
5. identify sources of requisite professional expertise
6. support the school or district in coping with controversy over health-related issues
7. assist in evaluating the total program

The most successful of such groups recognize that they are not organized to administer the school health program, but only to offer consultation and assistance. Knowing that volunteers are seldom able to meet more often than several times during a semester, leadership of a council wisely limits its considerations to priority issues and programs most appropriate to their role.

SELECTING THE INSTRUCTIONAL PLAN FOR HEALTH INSTRUCTION

Whether health instruction is to be scheduled as a separate course, integrated throughout the entire school curriculum, or correlated with designated host subjects is an administrative decision. A teacher is hired or given responsibility for instruction accordingly, whatever the chosen pattern may be. The assumption of this book is that you are interested in becoming a health education specialist. Whether that role is to be carried out in a school or any other setting, you need to know something about the different patterns employed in schools. Some schools use only one, some use two, and in some places, all three patterns are in operation to some degree because the three are not mutually exclusive. Each of them has certain advantages and disadvantages, but the trend is toward offering direct teaching as the most effective single plan. Direct teaching is the only plan for teaching a basic health course at the college level.

Some school administrators believe strongly that it is essential that specified areas of health content, based on study of the sources of the curriculum, be offered every year during the elementary grades. Careful planning is done to ensure the match between curriculum emphasis and student abilities as well as needs and interests. Some school districts organize the teaching of health education so that students have a full semester's study during the tenth or eleventh year of high school. Still other administrators limit any health instruction to those few areas mandated by state law or demanded by community pressure groups who seek to promote study or specific health topics (usually problems or diseases) or to incidental teaching done voluntarily by various teachers in response to momentary peaks in student interest. What are the special characteristics of the three major patterns of organized health instructions, and what are the strengths and weaknesses of each?

Direct teaching

The most familiar pattern of health instruction is as a separate subject provided equal time and facilities with other regularly scheduled courses in the school curriculum, usually as a requirement for graduation. What is taught varies according to state and local guides and often also to the textbook selected by the school and authorized for adoption by a state board of education commission. In the event that a teacher depends entirely upon the textbook, what is taught becomes whatever the textbook's authors decided was important for that age group. Most health teaching specialists will select a text from among those authorized that best matches local curriculum guides as well as their own beliefs about health and health behavior.

When direct teaching is provided is again an administrative decision and varies with the philosophy of the school and district. The Education Commission of the States proposes a model policy statement for school health education that includes the following recommendations: "During the middle school or junior high school years, the minimal time allocation shall not be less than one semester or its equivalent. One semester is required during the senior high school experience. Health education at this level should be in the form of direct instruction, but should be supplemented by correlation, integration, and incidental teaching" (Education Commission, 1981, p. 18).

When the administrative commitment is to provide health education through direct teaching, the program must be of high quality and coordinated by qualified health education specialists. Without such competent faculty, it is hardly likely that supplemental correlation, integration, and incidental teaching will occur in other disciplines. In direct teaching, the subject must be given time, space, and material support equal to that provided other basic subjects. Its teachers should be qualified by professional preparation and interest in teaching health.

The strength of direct teaching can be traced to several factors. First, teachers are most comfortable with it because it is the way they themselves have been taught. Second, health textbooks are written to fit the direct teaching pattern. The teacher's edition is supplemented with good suggestions for lessons and practical teaching aids to go with them. This is particularly helpful inasmuch as teachers who are not health majors and have had little or no preparation in either the content or techniques used in health education are often assigned on short notice to teach health classes.

Another advantage of direct teaching is that because there is a set amount of class time regularly allocated, the teacher can be far more responsive to current student and community needs than when health instruction has to be wiggled in among all the things that must be accomplished for the host courses (e.g., biology, social studies, home economics). In addition, interest and motivation to investigate and solve problems are far more easily maintained when a day-by-day program can be provided. In that case, both teacher and students have time enough to follow through on projects in sufficient depth and breadth that health behavior can be studied in all of its dimensions and implications.

A weakness of direct teaching is that, where it exists, administrators and other teachers tend to view the subject as completely taken care of, and planned enrichment by means of integrating experiences in other subjects is neglected. Also, if assigned teachers have had little or no preservice or in-service preparation in health teaching, they may perceive its subject matter more narrowly than desirable and not give it the comprehensive study it should have. When a teacher is not qualified as a health teacher, necessary dependence on the textbook leads to lockstep trudging through the chapters with little attempt to give priority to the topics most relevant to the needs of a given group of students. And where teaching is equated with *telling,* lecture becomes the primary technique, and health education becomes a series of health rules and warnings rather than an opportunity to investigate and solve health problems concerned with realities of life.

Still, direct teaching seems to many to be the best way to promote the goals of health education. Learnings resulting from comprehensive health education can enrich students' lives and reinforce related concepts gained in other subject areas. School health education seeks to develop the student who has learned to generalize and has mastered problem-solving skills that will be useful long after specific facts will have been forgotten or made obsolete. Direct health teaching under the direction of a competent instructor is potentially health education at its best.

Integrated teaching

To integrate is to relate the parts of something to the whole. To use integration as the pattern for teaching health education is to focus on relationships, generalizations, or concepts that tie facts or experiences together in meaningful ways. Integration can be employed as reinforcement at any level of education, but as a pattern for instruction, it is most typical of the elementary school.

As a process, integration functions as part of any effective teaching program, however it may be organized. In traditional educational patterns, from elementary grades onward, instruction is often compartmentalized and specialized. The relevance of what is learned in one subject area to that considered in others is seldom clear to the student given no help in grasping the essential relationships. Organization of learning opportunities as it is done in integrated curriculums promotes this kind of understanding as concepts gathered from other disciplines are pulled together in studying a health problem or issue of interest. Emphasis on process, rather than subject matter, is an added integrating force in curriculum. Cognitive processes are universals that link learnings in one field to those in all others. The desirability of giving process major emphasis in education has been urged in these words: "The world is changing at an exponential rate. If our society is to meet the dizzying changes in science, technology, communications, and social relationships, we cannot rest on the *answers* provided in the past. We must put our trust in the *processes* by which new problems are met. For so quickly does change overtake us that answers, 'knowledge,' methods, skills become obsolete almost at the moment of their achievement" (Rogers, 1969). Toffler (1974) believes that it is the prime task of education to help make the individual more sensitively responsive to change. Integration may be the method with the richest potential for doing that today.

Concepts are excellent means of integrating health instruction into the total curriculum. Because concepts are ideas of great vitality and power, they seem to demand learning activities that stress action and involvement rather than passive listening or recitation. For example, teaching toward the concept "Utilization of health information, products, and services is guided by values and perceptions" (School Health Education Study, 1967), or any other similarly powerful generalization, engages learners in activities requiring application of the whole range of cognitive skills commonly taught in schools. In this case, integration of other courses is being accomplished within the health curriculum. As the students work with the learning opportunities, they are using mathematics, adding new words to their vocabulary, mastering the spelling of those words, practicing research and literary skills, composing written materials, developing poise in speaking before groups, creating art works, and more. Most important, they are led to participate actively in investigations relevant to personal needs and those of family or community. They learn about living rather than about topics, and they discover ways of processing the unending floods of data that pour in upon us daily. They learn skills they will need if they are to live in the twenty-first century effectively and with assurance.

The strength of the integration pattern of instruction is its appropriateness to this kind of education. Integration is implicit in the current renewed emphasis on general education. In health education, the necessary use of data and techniques of other subject areas as they relate to health issues of interest reinforces what has been learned in general education courses. Promotion of self-acceptance, acceptance of others who may be different in certain ways, learning how to solve health-related problems, and learning how to choose sensibly among alternative health behaviors are among the outcomes particular to the thoughtfully designed, integrated health curriculum.

A weakness of the integration pattern for health instruction is that its success depends so utterly on the teacher's perception of natural relationships between health and life-styles. If the teacher lacks understanding of the scope of comprehensive health education, true integration probably won't happen. In elementary schools, where integration is most apt to be the curriculum pattern, teachers have been prepared to be generalists, and they do a remarkable job of teaching the many subject areas for which they are responsible. However, few teachers at any level who are not health teaching specialists have had even one course in health education. What is offered in health teaching in such a situation may be biased by the instructor's past experience. For example, the biologist may emphasize anatomy and physiology. The physical educator may focus on posture and physical fitness. The home economics teacher may be most interested in nutrients, and so forth. Moreover, in the absence of a qualified health coordinator, health education that depends on integration is often fragmented, repetitive, or missing.

Correlated teaching

As a means of organizing the curriculum for health education, correlation is the planned or proposed interweaving of health instruction throughout specified parts of the school curriculum. Correlation has rich possibilities. There is such a close relationship between biological science and the science of living that correlation is virtually unavoidable. In many science textbooks, human biology and health are combined for this reason. There are limitless opportunities to explore health material within the study of the traditional subject areas. Health instruction can draw upon all the other disciplines as sources of information required for the investigation of health issues and concerns.

What is stressed in a correlated health education curriculum should be the outcome of decisions made and adhered to by all those whose responsibility it is to implement the plan. Ideally, a curriculum committee made up of representative teachers should plan the scope of the program as well as the assignment of specific content areas to host disciplines (e.g., biology, social studies, physical education, home economics). Only when there is cooperation between administration and these teachers can there be comprehensive health education through the use of correlation as the primary or only pattern of instruction.

A strength of the correlation pattern is considered to be its planned reinforcement of prior and parallel learnings about health. Because it is considered in so many subject areas, health becomes more clearly related to all aspects of living. Many teachers participate and have responsibility in their own area of expertise rather than limiting health instruction to a single instructor. Obviously, this pattern is possible only where there are separate subjects offered.

The weakness of correlation lies in its total dependence on the host teacher's willingness and ability to organize teaching economically and effectively enough to achieve personal teaching objectives and still have time to include those proposed for health education. Not just ability but special interest in health education is crucial to the success of this pattern. Whatever the host area, however, health education is by design left in the hands of a teacher whose primary qualifications and interests are not in teaching health, but something else entirely.

Attempts to provide health instruction by correlation alone are not likely to be comprehensive or evenly effective. Even in science, teachers are not likely to spend much time stressing the social and mental/emotional forces influencing health and health behavior. In social science, a teacher may be more inclined to examine social aspects but less concerned or knowledgeable about physical and mental dimensions. Suppose the correlation plan expects nutrition to be studied as a part of home economics. What could be more logical? Is it likely that many boys would elect a course in home economics? Unless the course is required of all students, it isn't even safe to assume that every girl would take the course.

Correlation plans are imperfect at best and can never cover the area of healthful living as it needs to be. They are probably best employed as a supplemental plan for direct instruction. Yet, if this is the only way possible or feasible for a school, it is better than nothing at all. In such a situation, the following suggestions may be helpful in managing such a program so that it will be reasonably effective.

1. Every teacher as well as the administrator must be committed to the idea of correlation and willing to do what is needed to make it work.
2. One individual or a small committee of teachers must become familiar enough with the scope of comprehensive health education to be able to identify the most appropriate host discipline for each health content area.
3. A program of in-service training should be provided for the teachers to be involved in order to familiarize them with the techniques and materials of health education.
4. Conferences should be scheduled at regular intervals so that teachers can exchange ideas, agree on purposes, evaluate progress, review films and other resources, and replan as necessary.
5. A health education specialist from the district office or health educators employed by community health agencies should be invited to consult at frequent intervals during the school year. The purpose would be to obtain new ideas and new health concepts, and explore fresh ap-

proaches to teaching and leads to current resources and materials. Note that this assumes that the community health educator is qualified by training and experience to fulfill these needs.

Unquestionably, it takes dedication, hard work, and valuable time. But if everybody works at it, correlating health with other subjects, if not the best way to implement health education, can at least be a profitable one.

Incidental teaching

The potential for incidental health teaching exists in every classroom every day. A so-called "teachable moment" occurs, and, depending on how a teacher handles it, the effect on student knowledge, values, and health behavior can be significant one way or another. This kind of unplanned experience ranges in impact from a fleeting interchange between a teacher and one student to full class involvement in an absorbing project temporarily superseding previous instructional plans. Incidental teaching and learning can arise in extraclass experiences such as during hearing or vision screening, as an outcome of a teacher's sensitivity to a particular student's health need, or as a consequence of a community crisis or issue such as a sudden need for a specific immunization or the battles over the admission of children identified as having antibodies to AIDS in their blood.

It can happen in any class, but incidental teaching can be especially dynamic and absorbing in a health class. Never hesitate to allow students to focus on a health issue of immediate interest just because it doesn't coincide with scheduled plans or topics. Actually, health and health behavior are so interrelated that there is little difficulty establishing linkages and getting back to where you were when the issue arose. If the learning outcome was worthwhile, and chances are it was, you will have increased interest in the health course, satisfied student needs to know and grow, and earned their appreciation for your flexibility and understanding.

The trick is to demonstrate the sure ability to use incidental teaching productively but without losing control of your teaching. Don't let your students run your class with "excitement of the week" discussions. Keep your eye on the objectives of your instructional plan, and remember that is what is to be accomplished.

Whatever instruction pattern is implemented in a school or school district, it must be authorized by the administration. It is essential that the school principal accept the goals and the potential for achieving them relative to the pattern that is selected, that evaluation of its effectiveness be an ongoing process, and that changes be effected in a timely manner as needed.

PERSONNEL MANAGEMENT CONSIDERATIONS

However carefully the physical environment of a school is planned and administered, it must never be forgotten that an environment is made up of people, too. The health of faculty and staff is fully as important an influence on student health and ability to learn as are the provisions for sanitation, safety, and the adequacy of school facilities for teaching. The following provisions are recommended as essential if the health of teachers is to be maintained and protected:

- a healthful and attractive physical environment
- the absence of excessive mental-emotional pressure
- rational teaching load and extended day assignments
- a healthful school-community social climate
- adequate sick leave provisions
- sabbatical and retirement provisions
- appropriate insurance programs
- pupil-teacher-parent-administrator interaction
- community recognition and respect (Bauer, cited in Oberteuffer et al., 1972, p. 408)

Most states have legal provisions that empower boards of education to establish and implement regulations concerned with the health of school employees. Most of these emphasize freedom from communicable disease and certain disabling conditions. There are great variations across the country in terms of the frequency of health examinations required, but there is most consistency in standards for the health of food handlers and bus drivers.

Some states have very specific preemployment requirements that certified personnel must meet (e.g., California, Delaware, Georgia, North Carolina, Kansas, and Maryland). New York goes further than others by giving boards of education the authority to require any employee to submit to a medical examination at any time to determine current physical or mental capacity to perform the duties for which that person was hired.

School board policy statements should detail health standards for initial and continued employment, procedures for dealing with physical or mental illness or injury of faculty or staff, provisions for health insurance and disability retirement, and procedures for dealing with grievances related to other health policies and procedures.

Preemployment health evaluation

State requirements for preemployment health assessment vary widely. Very few states require a complete physical examination. Some require proof that the candidate does not have tuberculosis nor is dependent on alcohol or other drugs. At the very least, a medical history generally includes a record of previous serious illnesses, injuries, operations, immunization status, and personal data such as height and weight.

Certain applicants must be disqualified for employment by public health law. Health departments usually specify reasons for disqualifying food handlers (e.g., carriers of certain communicable diseases and those with contagious skin disease). Transportation, safety, or education departments have special criteria disqualifying bus driver applicants (e.g., vision or hearing disabilities, epilepsy, and heart disease). Chronic illness that limits mobility to the degree that the individual cannot carry out the duties of the position also prohibit hiring. Other conditions disqualifying individuals include serious hypertension and obvious emotional illness.

Employment of the handicapped

Physical handicap does not per se disqualify a person for employment in the schools. If an applicant can meet the hiring standards set for a job, that person must be considered for employment without bias. In fact, if a school district wishes to receive federal funds for its program, it must not discriminate against the handicapped. A district should establish policies that permit individualized attention to the unique needs and circumstances, and whenever possible special work adaptations should be arranged. This includes giving consideration to individuals with serious health problems such as diabetes, progressive vision and hearing problems, paraplegia, or other disability. Decisions to hire should depend upon the candidate's potential for regular attendance, level of energy, and other factors such as the age and needs of the group to be served.

Postemployment health evaluation

Schools should establish plans for periodic postemployment health examinations considering the regulations for certain employees (i.e., school bus drivers and food handlers). Such examinations can be helpful in the early detection of conditions that can be corrected or minimized, preventing future disease or disability, and maintaining the health of all employees.

There should be a plan for helping teachers cope with severe stress. Stress responses that have been identified include headache, dizziness, abdominal pain, sleeplessness, fatigue, job dissatisfaction, anxiety, tension, irritability, depression, use of medication, alcohol, cigarettes, and other harmful behaviors. Associations between job stress, coronary heart disease, mental illness, and alcoholism have been reported (Needle et al., 1980, p. 98).

Many school districts have excellent employee assistance programs for staff or faculty with alcohol or drug-abuse problems. Employees are helped to locate health advisers and resources appropriate to their needs.

Safety protection and occupational health

Schools have a legal responsibility to protect the health and safety of all students and staff. This requires that the physical environment of the school be checked regularly to see that it meets established standards of safety. There should be written policies and procedures regarding first aid and emergency care on file and well known to all school employees. Periodically, these procedures need to be reviewed and revised as necessary and changes communicated to all concerned. Key employees, such as coaches, health teachers, athletic trainers, and other teachers, should be required to qualify by formal training in first aid, CPR, and disaster handling. Fire drills must be held at stipulated intervals, and students and teachers should know what they are to do and where they are to go in the event of fire or other disaster.

Sick leave

The necessity and justification for sick leave allowance is well established; however, there is no one accepted way of handling its administration. Some systems allow a certain number of days per month or year, which may be used as necessary. Some permit unused sick leave to be carried over from year to year. Other systems stipulate that it must be used during a fiscal year or lost. Many schools allow unused sick leave to be accumulated and counted as service in calculating retirement payments. There are advantages and disadvantages to every plan. When unused sick leave cannot be accumulated, some employees abuse the privilege or use sick leave days for other purposes. When sick leave can be accumulated, some individuals come to school when they are ill and should have stayed at home to facilitate recovery and to protect students and others from exposure to the illness. No solution to that dilemma has yet been identified.

Collective bargaining and employee health

In many school districts, a bargaining team representing faculty and staff negotiates with the school board to define the policies regarding many of the above programs. Negotiable items commonly considered include insurance costs and coverage, disability and retirement plans, sick leave, personal and other types of leave, policies for returning to work after serious physical or emotional illness, and alcoholism treatment, pre- and postemployment health examinations, and the quality of the school environment (American Public Health Association, 1980).

The cost of school health programs

Determining the cost of a school health program is a complex task. So many factors are involved that one can create just about any scenario. How do you measure what never happened because health education was successful in preventing risk behaviors and promoting health behaviors? That is, if school health educators are successful, then the risk behaviors, currently the targets of community health interventions, might be minimized or even prevented. Further complicating the problem, school health educators might be justified in saying that specified risk behaviors are at least being prevented among young people now. How do you measure future success today? The Department of Health and Human Services stated in 1980 that, if school health efforts led to only a modest 10 percent reduction in the costs associated with certain risk-taking behaviors, the saving would equal billions of dollars each year.

In 1983, health care costs in the United States totaled $355 billion, or $1,459 per person. It would seem logical to expect that an education program that could actually change life-styles would result in enormous dollar savings. It is estimated that four hundred thousand lives and approximately $20 billion could be saved annually if only five risk behaviors are properly addressed (diet, smoking, lack of exercise, alcohol abuse, and failure to use antihypertensive medications).

Can the schools neglect their part in promoting health and preventing disease and disability among the American people? Community values will determine the answer to that question. Do the people value having a competent teacher in the classroom? Do they value having a health coordinator, school physician, or school nurse? Do they support the inclusion of a health course in the curriculum? Do they value good health for their children and for their community? If the answer to these questions is "no," then for them, the cost is too high. If the answer is "yes," then they will find the necessary funds to implement a quality program (O'Rourke, 1985, pp. 121–24).

SUMMARY

1. A school health program includes formal, scheduled instruction, the provision of specified health services, and arrangements and procedures designed to maintain an environment that is safe, sanitary, and healthful.

2. State legislatures write the laws either mandating or permitting the activities carried out to this end in the schools and authorize the expenditure of tax money to support school health programs. Local policies focus on specific rules and policies pursuant to developing a program that is faithful to the laws and fulfills community and student needs. Tort laws have to do with liability.

3. Determination of the quality and scope of school health programs is set by local decision makers authorized to act for the board of education (i.e., the superintendent of schools and, by extension, school principals).
4. Local policies are developed by boards of education and administrators within the framework of mandated and permissive laws.
5. Policy statements clearly defining responsibilities and acceptable procedures minimize problems that may be encountered in administering and managing a school and its health program.
6. Health services are those activities carried out by health care specialists to appraise, protect, and promote the health of students and school personnel.
7. Healthful school living is the intention of all the provisions defining standards of design and maintenance of the environment of a school, including its physical, social, emotional, and mental dimensions.
8. A school health team is composed of representatives of the administration, faculty, health care personnel, and staff of a school. Ideally, parents and students are also represented.
9. Ultimate responsibility for the school health program rests with the local superintendent. School principals are delegated authority by the superintendent to administer the program in their schools.
10. Health coordinators, health teachers, and nurses (increasingly school nurse-practitioners by training) implement the teaching-learning aspect of the instructional program, which may and usually does interact with activities occurring in association with those carried out by the other two program components.
11. A school health council is a problem-solving, coordinating, recommending body that serves the school administrator in an advisory capacity only.
12. Health teaching is usually organized in one or more principal patterns: a separate course with direct teaching, integrated throughout the total school curriculum, or correlated by content area with designated host subjects as appropriate and feasible.
13. Faculty and staff constitute an important aspect of the school's environment, and the quality of those people greatly influences the quality of the learning experience for the students.
14. The cost of effective school health programs is minimal compared with the potential for promoting health and preventing disease and disability.

QUESTIONS AND EXERCISES

Questions

1. Why should teachers of subject areas unrelated to health education be responsible for any part of the school health program?
2. What is the relationship between a state superintendent of education and a district superintendent of schools?
3. To what extent would failure to allocate funds authorized by the legislature affect implementation of enacted laws mandating comprehensive school health education?
4. Why is it essential that teachers and other educators be involved in designing health service programs intended for implementation in the schools?
5. How could the location of a school enhance or detract from the ability of students to learn, the serenity of faculty and staff, and the prevention of accidents or injuries?
6. What would be the advantages and disadvantages of having a health coordinator serving half-time as a teacher?
7. Why would parental and student body representation on a school health council facilitate acceptance of innovative school health procedures?
8. If you were asked to recommend selection of only one pattern of health instruction, which would it be, and what would you cite as justification for that decision?
9. How would the provision of sabbatical leaves for teachers enhance the environmental health of a school?

Exercises

1. Arrange for an interview with a school administrator with the purpose of discovering (1) how that person would rank the listed managerial functions in terms of (a) importance to school administration and (b) time spent in carrying out each function; (2) what pattern of health instruction is in operation in the school curriculum; and (3) what courses or teaching experience in health education that person has had prior to appointment as school administrator. Does there seem to be any relationship among these three sets of data as revealed by the answers to these questions?
2. Most community libraries will have or can arrange to have copies of your state education and health and safety codes. Examine these documents and find out what the law requires relative to health instruc-

tion, and select some examples of laws affecting health services and the school's environment that interest you because you think that school personnel ought to know about them. Prepare a brief written list of these laws to be shared with the class.
3. Together with a group of interested classmates, plan a simulated school health council meeting. Identify a school health problem that reflects the need for a statement of policy or demands a solution by action. Assign roles to correspond with the recommended membership of a council, and ask each participant to contribute to the discussion as that school or community representative might be expected to do. Encourage the rest of the class to offer suggestions or ask questions that seem important. Prepare the policy statement or recommended solution in written form for class distribution and acceptance.

REFERENCES

American Public Health Association/School Health Education and Services Section, *Health of School Personnel*. Washington, DC: APHA, 1980.

Education Commission of the States, *Recommendations for School Health Education*. Denver, CO: Education Commission of the States, 1981.

Gilbert, G., et al., "Current federal activities in school health education." *Public Health Reports,* Sept.-Oct. 1985, pp. 499–505.

Gorton, R. A., *School Administration: Challenge and Opportunity for Leadership*. Dubuque, IA: W.C. Brown, 1976.

"Guidelines on educational preparation and competencies of the school nurse practitioner." *Journal of School Health* 48:5, May 1978, p. 265.

Joint Committee on Health Problems in Education of the NEA and AMA, *Healthful School Environment*. Washington, DC: NEA, 1969.

Joint Committee on Health Problems in Education of the NEA and AMA, *School Health Services*. Washington, DC: NEA, 1964.

McNab, W. L., and Canida, E. U., "The need for nurse educators." *Journal of School Health* 50:2, Feb. 1980, p. 90.

Metropolitan Life Foundation, "Healthy me awards." *Journal of School Health* 56:3, March 1986, pp. 117–119.

Needle, R. H., Griffin, T., Svendsen, R., and Berney, C., "Teacher stress: sources and consequences." *Journal of School Health* 50:2, Feb. 1980, pp. 96–99.

Oberteuffer, D., et al., *School Health Education*. New York. Harper and Row, 1972.

O'Rourke, T., "Why school health education? The economical point of view." *Health Education,* Apr.-May 1985, pp. 122–124.

Resnick, M. D., Blum, R. W., and Hector, J., "Adolescent perceptions of the school nurse." *Journal of School Health* 48:10, Dec. 1980, pp. 551–554.

The Robert Wood Johnson Foundation, *National School Health Services Program* (special report). Princeton, NJ: Number One, 1985.

Rogers, Carl, *Freedom to Learn*. Columbus, OH: Merrill, 1969.

Rue, L. W., and Byars, L. L., *Management Theory and Application*. Homewood, IL: Irwin, 1983.

School Health Education Study, *Health Education: A Conceptual Approach to Curriculum*. St. Paul, MN: 3M, 1967.

Toffler, Alvin, ed., *Learning for Tomorrow*. New York: Vintage Books, 1974.

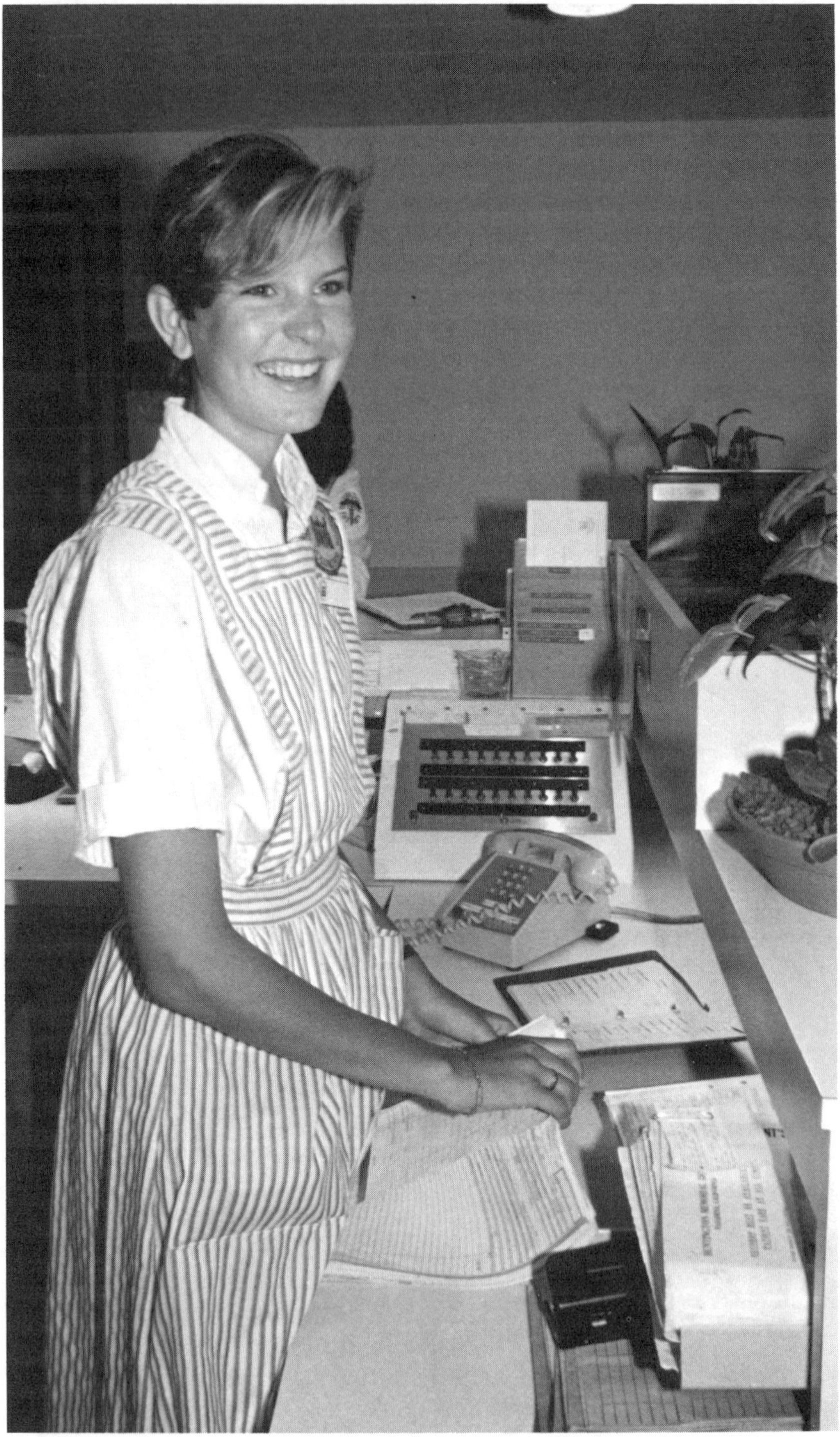

10
Community relationships with school health programs

What is a community? In its broadest sense, it is any group of people who share the same or similar needs, concerns, values, and organizations. Theoretically that might cover any grouping beyond two people. Most commonly we think of a community as a political entity such as a village, town, city, county, nation, even the world, which is a community of nations. But it would not be that simple even if those were the only kinds of communities, which they are not. For example, as of 1986, Los Angeles County in California encompassed within its boundaries eighty-four cities, one of which, Los Angeles, has more inhabitants than some states. The city of New York is made up of five boroughs, each of which is a county of New York State. In fact, Metropolitan New York includes part of New Jersey and the state of Connecticut. In that case, you have a city composed of counties and in its largest view including parts of two other states.

However, the concept of community goes beyond these kinds of political jurisdiction. There are also, and importantly, socially defined communities (e.g., families, neighborhoods, schools, clubs of many kinds, ethnic populations, religious groups, professional groups). There are also what have been titled "communities of solution" (National Commission . . ., 1966). The boundaries of a community of solution are defined by the existence of a health problem of common concern. Air pollution does not begin or end at the borders of one city, county, state, or any other level of political jurisdiction. The 1986 Chernobyl disaster in the Soviet Union demonstrated the potential impact of such a nuclear accident and resulting air pollution on the health and safety of most of the Western world. Certain communicable diseases are rarely limited in incidence to one area. Influenza frequently spreads worldwide in a matter of weeks or months. AIDS, virtually unknown until recently, is now a universal concern of epidemiologists and medical specialists.

Clearly, when health educators speak of community health, it is in the global sense of the word. *Community* is an abstraction in that case. However, few health problems, if any, can be solved in the abstract. Specific populations living in specified areas are in need of certain health services, health education, or other interventions. Hence, for the purposes of this book, community involvement is delimited to the contributions made by individuals, organizations, and agencies outside the schools for the purpose of promoting school health programs and the health of students, as well as ways that school health activities and instruction directly or indirectly help fulfill the goals of those community people and of community health in general.

WHY INVOLVE THE COMMUNITY?

Learning about ways to protect one's health and establishing the kinds of health behaviors likely to achieve that goal are not processes that end when students walk out the classroom door. Secondary school students will soon be the adults with whom community health programs are concerned. Health-educated high school graduates are less likely to adopt unhealthful life-styles and more likely to accept and support community health programs. Nor can school health programs developed in isolation from the community be as meaningful and effective as they need to be. No school health program can claim success if it is not extending its program into the community and if it is not bringing the community into the school. As Kreuter, Christenson, and Davis (1983, p. 32) have declared: "We are not likely to influence schools without first understanding and involving the community. Nationwide implementation of health education in schools appears now to be less dependent on policy statements than it is on an activated community system that turns policy into reality."

Just as school administrators need to know and work with the community in which their schools are situated, so do all those who work in the school health program. Who are the people who live in the community? How many are parents of school-age children? How many children live in single-parent homes? What is the racial and cultural mix of the students? What are the groups or organizations to which most of the heads of families belong? What is the method of communication preferred by the residents? (An effective school health program uses the best lines of communication a community has to offer.) Finally, it is essential to identify the expectations and attitudes of the people because these reflect standards by which the school will be evaluated (Gorton, 1976, pp. 343–346). Once these assessments are complete, the next step is to choose a balanced representation of individuals and groups whose collaborative efforts give promise of producing the best school health program possible.

INDIVIDUAL AND GROUP COMMUNITY RESOURCES

A successful school health program depends not only on the dedication and efforts of all school personnel, but also upon the support and involvement, to some degree, of every member of the community. Frequently, the same individual may be participating in more than one role (e.g., as a parent of a schoolchild, as a private health care professional donating some service, and as a representative of an interested community organization or agency). Community resources upon which the school can and does depend and draw assistance and support for its health program include the following.

Individual parents and parent groups

A school health program is not likely to achieve its goals if planned communication with and involvement of parents is lacking. It is essential to keep parents informed about existing and new policies that affect the care and education of their children. For example, there are explicit policies in most schools regarding procedures for obtaining parental approval for immunization requirements, for providing emergency health care beyond lifesaving measures, for notifying parents or guardians in the event of accident or sudden illness, and regarding health screening programs.

In the absence of parental consultation and cooperation, needed corrective measures identified by the school screening program or other physical examinations may not be obtained. Parents ought to be informed about the school health curriculum and allowed to review materials used in the classroom if desired. Some states require that parents be informed about proposed sex education programs and invited to view related films and other materials if they wish. Written parental permission is sometimes a proviso for each student's participation in that portion of the curriculum.

Parent groups, such as a local Parent Teacher Association, can be most helpful in promoting the school health program. Their meetings also provide excellent opportunities for those involved in the program to inform parents of recent activities and new policies. Those who direct health programs must remember that many homes today are headed by single parents, and even when there are two parents, both may be working. Either way, attendance at PTA meetings or conferring with teachers may be difficult or impossible unless special arrangements are made.

Community health care professionals

A school needs to maintain a close working relationship with the local official health agency or health department. There are certain public health ordinances that schools are required to enforce (particularly in connection with communicable disease prevention and control). Most official health agencies employ a variety of health professionals, many of whom have skills and information that have great interest and utility for both health teachers and students. For example, the public health educator, nutritionist, sanitarian, and social worker can serve as consultants, or they can be brought into the classroom to provide students with firsthand information about their function in maintaining community health. Public Health agencies are dedicated to serving the health needs of *all* the people of the community. Beyond legal requirements, they may not feel welcome in the schools unless invited specifically to do more. Public health workers are usually very willing to participate in the school health program if they are asked to do so and told exactly what is wanted. A good health teacher will enrich a school program by taking advantage of this resource often.

Other health care professionals who work in the private sector include individual physicians, dentists, dental hygienists, nurses, health technicians of many kinds, nutritionists, psychologists, and social workers. They constitute a special pool of talents and expertise for those administering a school health program to tap. Among the kinds of things these professionals often volunteer to do for schools are the following:

1. serving on school health councils or ad hoc committees
2. assisting schools in developing health screening policies and guidelines and helping to implement screening programs
3. teaching dental hygiene and carrying out fluoridation programs (in the case of dentists or dental hygienists)
4. speaking to classes or parent groups (e.g., on alcohol or drug abuse problems, suicide prevention, accident prevention, unwanted pregnancy)

5. assisting those involved in school health services in obtaining needed health care for children whose parents are unable to provide recommended treatment
6. assisting the school in establishing health employment standards and procedures for application in hiring staff and faculty
7. aiding in determining essential standards for student physical examinations
8. providing consultation and volunteer services to the school athletic program as a means of minimizing the effects of injuries
9. providing expert consultation to those engaged in curriculum development
10. serving as advocates and effective lobbyists for the school health program

Private health agencies and organizations

Numerous private health organizations, civic, and social groups have an interest in promoting school health. Some (e.g., voluntary health agencies) focus on a particular disease, disability, or group of related health problems. Still other groups, such as service clubs (e.g., Lions Club, Elks Club, Shriners), take on specific health projects as ways to serve their community. Many of these organizations develop materials and allocate funds for both health instruction and services. In the case of voluntary health agencies, a great many teaching materials are prepared specifically for use with health education classes, and school administrators are pressed to include them in the health curriculum. Although many of these materials are excellent in quality, there is not enough time in an entire school year to use them all. Moreover, some of them are so extensive that, were a teacher to fully carry out even one of them, the possibility of completing the expected scope and sequence plan for comprehensive health teaching would be diminished. This is where competent school health coordinators or teachers prove their value. Such individuals know what is appropriate for a given group of students and how to choose the best of what is offered to fit and enrich existing plans.

In order to help teachers and coordinators in this task, several health education leaders who are employed in national voluntary health agencies have worked together to construct a chart that lists all their materials combined and categorized by generally accepted major health education concepts or content areas. A teacher seeking reliably accurate instructional materials can identify every one of them (pamphlet, booklet, film, filmstrip, audio or video tape, curriculum guide, etc.) relevant to each of the content areas available from the participating organizations.

However, health education in schools has been promoted by private sector organizations in a host of other ways. Some agencies have speakers bureaus, and even those who don't can often be counted on to provide a representative to talk with health classes or other school groups when the topic is germane to their area of expertise. They have contributed funds for continuing education programs for teachers and school nurses and sponsored conferences, seminars, and workshops to advocate comprehensive school health programs. They have funded immunization programs as required by school laws or policy and arranged for health screening for students. Schools have been provided with needed equipment and with money in support of worthy health projects. Some civic groups specialize in providing specific kinds of assistance to children (e.g., the Lions Club purchases glasses for needy children, the Shriners support hospitals for crippled and severely burned children, PTA groups often help to clothe children whose clothing or shoes are inadequate). Some private sector organizations carry out valuable research related to children's health problems.

Many voluntary health organizations operate at local, state, and national levels of jurisdiction. School health educators should familiarize themselves with the goals and activities of these important organizations in their own communities. If possible, establish contact with health educators employed at the other levels of the organizations most frequently consulted at the local level. At the very least, find out who is in charge of health education at state or national levels, and make a note of the address. Many times it is possible to obtain materials that are not available locally from these higher level offices.

Professional associations

A wide range of professional health associations have school health as a special or at least a secondary interest. Their primary goal is the furthering of the named profession or discipline and the skills and knowledge of the membership. They are often strong advocates for school health. A few of those most actively involved and supportive of school health programs include:

   *The Association for the Advancement of Health Education
    The American Medical Association
    The American Public Health Association
   *Public Health Education Section
   *School Health Education and Services Section
   *The American School Health Association
   *The Society for Public Health Education

*The American College Health Association
*Society of State Directors of Health, Physical Education, and Recreation
*Conference of State and Territorial Directors of Public Health Education
The American Nurses Association
The National League for Nursing
The National Association of School Nurses
The American Dental Association

Those organizations marked with an asterisk have joined together to form the Coalition of National Health Education Organizations (discussed in chapter 1). The coalition can speak as one voice on matters concerning health education, which gives health education as a profession more clout than if each of the eight groups were to speak out individually on important issues.

Commercial organizations

There are virtually thousands of commercial organizations that produce materials or provide services that have relevance to or are intended for use in schools. The publishing and advertising world has flooded the schools with health-related materials. The problem for the health teacher or coordinator is not how to locate enough good supplementary teaching material, but how to sift through it all in order to choose the best and most accurate of what is offered. Many schools use curriculum materials developed by the National Dairy Council, which is a cooperative or combine representing and supported by the industry as a whole. Certain pharmaceutical companies provide slide series and curriculum guides on skin care and the treatment of pediculosis. Kimberly-Clark, Tambrands, and other companies have excellent curricula and teaching aids for use in teaching about menstruation. Cooperative groups such as the Cereal Institute and the National Livestock and Meat Board produce informative newsletters and teaching aids concerned with nutrition. Toothpaste manufacturers offer dental hygiene kits complete with classroom sets of brushes, toothpaste samples, and tablets containing a harmless food dye that clings to and discloses plaque deposits. The Metropolitan Life Insurance Company has produced and distributed films, pamphlets and booklets for use in schools for over sixty years. The Equitable, Prudential, and other life insurance companies also provide materials for use in schools. In short, the community is a vast source of free and inexpensive teaching aids—more than you could ever use. All you have to do is look at the lists, ask for those that sound interesting, and make sure that what you decide to use is acceptable to your school administrator. It must also be consistent with state law and district policy governing the use of materials prepared by individuals and organizations outside school jurisdiction and therefore not authorized for use without permission.

Recently, a manual titled *Wellness at the Worksite"* (1985) has been made available for school use. It was produced by the Health Insurance Association of America, American Council of Life Insurance. The purpose of the manual is to help school administrators develop and implement wellness programs for school personnel. There are also video tapes that can be purchased to go along with the manual (which is free). The association points out that in 1984, there were 4,167,608 public school employees (including teachers). If the health of a substantial number of those people could be improved, not only would it many ways positively influence the health of students, but it would lessen national health care costs and help schools make better use of the tax dollars they receive.

The largest single private contribution in support of comprehensive school health programs, a four-year, $4 million initiative entitled "Healthy Me," was provided in 1985 by the Metropolitan Life Foundation. The announced objectives were simple: "To stimulate more involvement in health education by schools and communities, to motivate teachers to provide better health education, and to encourage students to recognize that their future health is strongly influenced by what they do today." The following are the means to be supported to that end:

- awards for excellent programs
- matching grants for community health coalitions
- matching stipends for professional preparation
- orientation sessions for school superintendents
- high-quality materials to enhance school programs
- a promotion campaign to heighten awareness of the importance of comprehensive school health education (*Center,* 1985, p. 38)

School-community liaison groups

All of the community-based groups just discussed are invaluable sources of assistance or counsel to those administering school health programs. The efficient coordination of the kind of help that each can provide can best be organized and coordinated by representative bodies such as community and school health coalitions.

Community health councils A community health council draws its membership from all the key community health-concerned agencies, organizations, and professions. In urban areas, total representation may be impractical, but it can be achieved over time on a rotating basis. Such a group might also be augmented by ad hoc subcommittees as needed.

A community health council provides an orderly procedure for mobilizing community resources to assist the school in protecting and promoting the health and learning abilities of its students. Other community representatives are frequently those such as clergymen; any interested civic leaders; specialists from contributing fields such as law, medicine, social work, and psychology; and school district health service and education personnel.

When such a council exists and is functioning well, rather than force an administrator to spend long hours meeting with each kind of agency or group singly, it is far more effective to work instead with such a council—not just for efficiency in solving school health problems or school-community problems, but for *any* community health problem. Whatever the problem brought to the council, each member can consult with the parent group and return with its suggestions or offers, which are then shared with those offered by the others. Communication is facilitated, and tentative solutions are refined until by consensus a workable and acceptable solution is defined.

School health coalitions By definition, a coalition is an alliance, especially a temporary one, of factions, groups, or individuals for a common purpose or goal. School health coalitions have become an effective mechanism whereby members of health-concerned community-based groups seek to promote comprehensive health education for students at all school levels. Whether national, state, or local in organization, their primary goal is much the same, although their programs may vary widely in scope and complexity.

An example of a state level coalition is the California School Health Alliance, which is comprised of representatives of state level voluntary health agencies; the California Association of Health, Physical Education, and Recreation (CAHPER); the California Association of School Health Educators (CASHE); the California Association of School Administrators; the Parent Teacher Association (PTA); and the California School Board Association. The quarterly meetings of this group are supported by the parent agencies or organizations. Their purpose is to serve as state level advocates for comprehensive school health education, to promote and support enactment of legislation mandating comprehensive school health education in California schools, and to stimulate formation of local coalitions with related interests.

Another large coalition of private organizations in New York City is headed by the New York Academy of Medicine. It was founded in 1979 with twenty-two members and now includes nearly forty individuals and agencies (corporations, banks, foundations, voluntary agencies, and professional groups). A five-year demonstration project, Growing Healthy, trained teachers and administrators in five school districts and reached twenty-five thousand children. Now the New York school district will make the project a regular part of *all* elementary school programs. Future collaboration by the coalition is planned, and fund-raising efforts will continue (*Center,* 1984, p. 19).

MESHEC, the Maine School Health Education Coalition, has moved the state closer to the goal of "comprehensive school health education for every Maine student." For the first time, Maine has a half-credit requirement in health education for both elementary and secondary programs. Formed in September 1984, the coalition now includes forty-three organizations. Two task forces, The Community Advocacy Task Force and the Preservice/Inservice Task Force, meet separately and jointly every month. The advocacy group has conducted training sessions for more than forty local advocates for school health who give presentations on school health education to their local organizations. The Preservice/Inservice Task Force is examining health education preparation programs in Maine to assess how or if they address the standards, skills, and competencies developed by the National Role Delineation Project. Depending on the results, recommendations will be made regarding these preparation programs. Future plans will deal with in-service programs in health education for elementary and special education teachers (NASHEC *Newsline,* 1986).

Local coalitions recognized as worthy of support by the Metropolitan Life Foundation "Healthy Me" awards program in 1985 included twenty groups located in eighteen states. Each of the selected groups proposed actions or programs designed to promote comprehensive school health education in one way or another and received a $5000 matching grant in support of its plan. Examples of plans proposed include those to assist districts wishing to apply for drug abuse prevention funds; to provide training sessions for faculty, administrators, and other school personnel in the "Growing Healthy" curriculum; to expand in-service programs for health teachers; to develop accessible, updatable, computerized resource guides for health education teacher use; and to organize regional coalitions, which in turn would generate grassroots support and demand for comprehensive school health education (Metropolitan Life Foundation, 1986, p. 117).

The National School Health Education Coalition   The National School Health Education Coalition (NaSHEC) was founded in May 1982 when representatives from a widely diversified group of private sector organizations united to form it. Its primary goal is to assure that every student, K–12, receives a comprehensive school health experience. Its purposes include the following:

1. encouraging the creation of state and/or local school health education coalitions in the private sector and providing strategic and tactical support to such coalitions

2. elevating the public perception of health education as a basic component of education at all levels
3. assisting appropriate decision makers at all levels in aiding the provision of comprehensive school health education experiences to all students
4. supporting comprehensive school health education programs by aiding the coordination of research, materials development, and dissemination of training and services
5. providing a forum for the identification, discussion, and resolution of school health education issues
6. facilitating national level coordination, collaboration, and communication among the NaSHEC member organizations
7. identifying and discussing the opportunities, sensitivities, and appropriate roles of private sector organizations in school health
8. encouraging the NaSHEC member organizations to take actions that facilitate the accomplishment of these purposes (NaSHEC *Newsletter,* 1983)

Membership is open to any national private sector organization that has an interest in school health education. Voluntary agencies, educational professional groups, health care professional groups, businesses, organizations, and corporations are encouraged to join. Government agencies with an interest in school health education may designate nonvoting representatives to the coalition. The following groups were represented at the first meeting: The National Health Council; American Red Cross; Eta Sigma Gamma, American Medical Association; American Academy of Ophthalmology; National Task Force on the Preparation and Practice of Health Educators; National Center for Health Education; National School Board Association; Equitable Life Assurance Society of the United States; American Council of Life Insurance; March of Dimes; Health Insurance of America; National Association of State Boards of Education; American College of Preventive Medicine; Center for Corporate Public Involvement; American Council of Life Insurance; Blue Cross/Blue Shield Association; United Way Health Foundation; American Heart Association; American Optometric Association; American Cancer Society; National Mental Health Association; National Society to Prevent Blindness; American Lung Association; Coalition of National Health Education Organizations; Educational Development Center; American Dental Association; National Dairy Council; and Washington Business Group on Health.

A survey funded by a $5000 Exxon Corporation grant, reported by the coalition (NaSHEC *Newsline,* 1986), reveals that of forty-seven local and state school health coalitions identified, 73 percent said that their most significant accomplishments included the recruitment of dedicated personnel, networking, and dissolvement of territoriality. Ironically, 47 percent reported that lack of support for health education was the most frequent problem. Eighty-two percent of the forty-seven coalitions contacted mentioned that teacher attitude, lack of commitment, and lack of cooperation between the fields of education and health were problems. Financial dilemmas were the second most mentioned problem.

Another coalition project is the development of file folder charts of available health education materials categorized by ten content areas representative of a comprehensive curriculum.

Community organization of this sort is most effective in promoting the cause of school health education for two reasons. First, it reaches into the offices of the gatekeepers and power structure of the community and simultaneously talks to the people at the grass roots of our society. Second, the motives of such diverse groups cannot possibly be construed as anything other than sincere and unselfish. No one can suggest they have hidden agendas.

Federal programs promoting school health

Federal initiatives are aimed at only these two goals: (1) to guarantee that the 75 million students of all ages enrolled in schools, colleges, and regional vocational centers have equal access to the best possible education and (2) to improve, through constant and systematic development, evaluation, and dissemination of new teaching methods and materials, the quality of education for every student (*Introducing the U.S. Department of Education,* 1980). There is nothing that precludes the promotion of school health programs, and many federal initiatives are focused on both of these goals, particularly on the specifications of the second as it applies to health education in school.

Jimmy Carter, when he was running for president in 1976, promised that, if elected, he would propose to the Congress and vigorously support the creation of a cabinet level department of education. Many federal programs to aid education were administered at that time by the U.S. Office of Education, then a subdivision of the Department of Health, Education and Welfare (HEW). Other educational programs were placed within a variety of other federal agencies.

To improve management, eliminate duplication, and save money, it was proposed that most of these programs be consolidated in a new agency concerned solely with education. Thus, on October 17, 1979, President Carter signed into law an act passed by Congress establishing the U.S. Department of Education as the thirteenth cabinet level department. On May 4, 1980, all the organizational work had been completed, and the president, by executive order, announced the opening of the new department.

During the planning stages, several important decisions had to be made related to which programs would be placed within the new Department of Health and Human Services (the newly titled other part of the former HEW) and which programs would go to the Department of Education or to other federal agencies. Because health education includes the major words in the titles of both departments, this posed some interesting problems.

Office of Disease Prevention and Health Promotion One of the programs discussed was the Office of Disease Prevention and Health Promotion (ODPHP), Public Health Service (PHS), which had been located within the office of the assistant secretary for health. It had been established by Public Law 94-317, the National Consumer Health Information and Promotion Act of 1976, and functioned under the provisions of Title XVII of the amended Public Service Act.

The mission of the Office of Disease Prevention and Health Promotion was to help promote health and prevent disease among Americans by overseeing federal initiatives and programs concerned with disease prevention. Special attention is given to facilitating the prevention activities of the five public health service agencies (i.e., the Alcohol, Drug Abuse, and Mental Health Administration—ADAMHA; the Centers for Disease Control—CDC; the Food and Drug Administration—FDA; the Health Resources and Services Administration—HRSA; and the National Institutes of Health—NIH).

It was decided that the office should remain intact within the assistant secretary for health's office. It has since played a leadership role in several health education programs, including many related to school health. For example, this office had major responsibility for producing the document *Promoting Health/Preventing Disease: Objectives for the Nation* (1980). Their nutrition initiative works to strengthen the department's (DHHS) capabilities and national leadership in nutrition research, nutrition monitoring, nutrition services and training, nutrition education, food safety and quality, and international nutrition. Their preventive services initiative fosters the delivery of personal preventive services in clinical settings. Through the national worksite health promotion initiative, ODPHP has sponsored conferences, made case studies, conducted surveys, and assisted with evaluation of programs. Through their school health initiative, they have fostered the development of a special review of the use of computers for health education; are in the process of assessing the health attitudes, knowledge, and skills of fifth, eighth, and twelfth grade students in the United States; have assisted in the development of seven evaluation handbooks for health education programs; and joined the Centers for Disease Control in a major evaluation of certain curriculums developed for school health education (U.S. Department of Health and Human Services correspondence, July 1985).

Office of Comprehensive School Health The only program with a specific focus on school health education with the Office of Education at the time the U.S. Department of Education was created by law was the Office of Comprehensive School Health, which had been established just one month earlier. It was created at the urging of several legislators who were concerned that the Office of Education was not giving enough attention to the health and health education of children and youth. In its haste to fulfill the wishes of the legislators, the Office of Education did not wait until the lengthy process of establishing a new office by law had been completed. Therefore, it was implemented by initiative. An office can be created by initiative when an agency sees a need. It is not protected by any law, nor is it supported with dollars authorized and allocated by Congress. Only salaries for staff and expense monies are set aside for its operation within the agency.

The Office of Comprehensive School Health was charged with coordinating the efforts of the various health-related programs within the U.S. Department of Education and serving as the department's liaison with other governmental programs and community-based programs that had school health-related objectives. Additionally, its director oversaw the School Health Education Program (Public Law 95-561, Part I). Other activities included serving as a resource for information regarding school health instruction and services, opening lines of communication, establishing linkages at every level, and representing the Office of Education on advisory committees and with professional organizations (Cortese, 1981, p. 89).

Typically, a new administration wishes to create its own initiatives. (It is not possible to quickly eliminate programs that have been established by law. Initiatives can be eliminated by a stroke of a pen.) Thus, when President Carter was defeated for reelection, the new administration almost immediately canceled all initiatives. That was the end of the Office of Comprehensive School Health. As of this writing, the U.S. Department of Education is without a focal point for the health education and health promotion of the children and youth in the nation's schools.

The Elementary and Secondary Education Act of 1966 The major piece of legislation within education that has had a continuing impact on school health was the Elementary and Secondary Education Act of 1966. It was designed to strengthen and improve the educational quality and opportunity in the nation's schools. It was originally divided into five titles, and in 1967, a sixth title was added. Three of the six titles specifically concerned health education.

Title I recognized the close relationship between poverty and lack of educational development and poor academic performance. Money was appropriated through this section of the act to provide for improvement of elementary schools located in poverty areas. This program provided financial support for guidance, supplementary health and food services, school health, and psychological and psychiatric services. Using these funds, many schools were able either to begin or to improve their school health service programs.

Title III was designed to support supplementary educational centers and services of a model or exemplary nature. They were referred to as "Teacher Centers." Another program was called "Teacher Corps." In school districts where health education was a high priority, grant money was secured to develop innovative school health programs.

Title VI supported programs for handicapped children. Through its grant-giving mechanism, there were many opportunities for school districts to secure financial support to demonstrate effective health education aimed at the handicapped population.

Through the years, these titles of the Elementary and Secondary Education Act have been amended, but the major purposes remained the same. Expressing his concern that there was too much bureaucracy at the federal level in the area of education, President Reagan outlined a program in February 1981 for consolidating more than forty federal elementary and secondary education programs into a block grant to the states and local communities. On August 13, 1981, he signed into law the Omnibus Reconciliation Act of 1981, which included a modified consolidation of many of these programs but continued the Title I grant program for low-income school districts as a separate, categorical program. Other programs that remained categorical (i.e., they were not consolidated into a block) included bilingual education, education of the handicapped, rehabilitation services, and vocational and adult education.

The following programs were consolidated into a block grant: Emergency School Aid, School Libraries and Instructional Resources, Support and Innovation, Teacher Corps, Teacher Centers, Precollege Science Teacher Training, Gifted and Talented, Career Education, Consumer's Education, Metric Education, Cities in Schools, PUSH for Excellence, Ethnic Heritage, Community Education, Basic Skills, Law-Related Education, Biomedical Education, and Follow Through.

These programs were unfunded but were included in the block grant program (that is, they could be funded at the state and local levels if desired): Preschool Partnership, Youth Employment, Environmental Education, Health Education, Corrections Education, Dissemination of Information, Population Education, and Guidance and Counseling.

All of the above programs had to this point been operating as independent grant-giving entities (unless there were no dollars allocated for that purpose, as in the case of the last group listed). Thus, in the consolidation process, it became possible for school health programs to be funded only if these programs had enough support at the local or state level. Everything depended upon the strength of local coalition efforts. Each state receives a percentage share of appropriations based on the number of residents age 5 to 17 in its total population. Eighty percent of the funds must pass through to the local educational agency. Block grant funds can be used for the same purposes as were the previous individual programs, but not all programs must be continued (even if funded in the past). Those determinations are made by state and local agencies.

Bureau of Health Education The first major health education office established within the federal government was located in Atlanta, Georgia, as a part of the then Center for Disease Control. It began under the authorization of the Secretary of HEW as the Bureau of Health Education in September 1974. Its mission was to provide leadership and direction to a comprehensive national health education program for the prevention of disease, disability, premature death, and undesirable and unnecessary health problems (*Bureau of Health Education Facts,* 1975).

One of the bureau's first actions was to adopt a working definition of health education. After considering several proposals, the definition agreed upon by the 1972–1973 Joint Committee on Health Education Terminology was selected as follows: Health education is "a process with intellectual, psychological, and social dimensions relating to activities which increase the abilities of people to make informed decisions affecting their personal, family, and community well-being. This process, based on scientific principles, facilitates learning and behavior change in both health personnel and consumers, including children and youth" ("New Definitions," 1973).

When it was established, the bureau made it clear that it did not view health education as the exclusive province of professional health educators. It was pointed out that physicians, nurses, dentists, and other health care professionals; teachers; behavioral and social scientists; outreach workers; and consumers are all important in health education and should be included in deliberations involving the development of program potentials.

There were three major divisions of the bureau as originally organized. The first, the National Clearinghouse for Smoking and Health, administered a national program to reduce death and disability due to smoking. The second, the Community Program Development Division, initiated, monitored, and evaluated community health education projects. The third division, the Professional Services and Consultation Division, provided technical assistance and consultation to public and private agencies and groups.

In 1974, the new bureau established several action priorities that have been continued. Their primary major efforts were concerned with (1) helping to assure that health education is included in major developments on the national health scene (i.e., health resources planning and development and national health insurance); (2) developing and maintaining a useful data base on health education efforts in federal agencies; (3) stimulating cooperation among federal agency health education programs that are directed toward common target populations or share mutual educational goals; (4) encouraging the development of effective mechanisms for collaboration among voluntary professional, industrial, and other private sector groups with health education interests; (5) selecting specific projects for direct intervention and support that are designed for population groups in special need of health education (e.g., ethnic and linguistic minorities, youth, rural and inner-city communities, the aged, and the handicapped); and (6) providing technical assistance and consultation to public and private agencies and groups.

The Health Education Division of the Center for Health Promotion and Education The Bureau of Health Education was reorganized early in 1981 as the Health Education Division of the Center for Health Promotion and Education. At the same time, the overall title of the Atlanta group was changed to the *Centers* for Disease Control. What had been the bureau was combined with the Family Planning Evaluation Division and the Nutrition Program, and the Clearinghouse for Smoking and Health was moved to another jurisdiction.

Among its major school health initiatives carried out since its inception, the Health Education Division has continued to oversee the development of the primary and elementary grades health curriculum project entitled "Growing Healthy" and the "Teenage Health Teaching Modules" developed under contract for the secondary level. In addition, the division has cooperated with ODPHP in supervision of the School Health Education Evaluation Project ("Results of the Health . . . ," 1985). Again in collaboration with ODPHP, the division produces and distributes *Focal Points,* a newsletter discussing current health education programs and issues, as well as reporting activities of the two agencies. "Current Awareness in Health Education" includes citations and abstracts of current journal articles and nonpublished documents acquired and selected by the Center (CHPE). It also contains descriptions of programs in health education. Both publications are available only by subscription.

National Institutes of Health programs The National Heart, Lung, and Blood Institute has funded studies to evaluate school health education projects such as the Chicago Heart Health Curriculum Program and the Coronary Risk Factor Intervention in Childhood Study (Gilbert, et al., 1985). In collaboration with ODPHP, the institute sponsored a Working

Conference on School Health Education Research in the fall of 1983 (*Health Education,* 1984).

The National Cancer Institute supports several research and evaluation programs aimed at school-age children. The "Smoking Prevention and Youth: Motivational Strategies Project" assists in the development of school-based interventions to prevent smoking and tobacco use. They have also developed a program to be used in schools concerning adolescents who have cancer. It is entitled "Help Yourself—Tips for Teenagers with Cancer." "Project Choice" is a cancer risk reduction curriculum designed for students K–12. The institute's Office of Cancer Communication has prepared "Smoking Programs for Youth," which is a comprehensive review of available information (Gilbert, et al., 1985).

The Alcohol, Drug Abuse, and Mental Health Administration (ADAMHA) is comprised of the National Institute on Alcohol Abuse and Alcoholism (NIAAA), the National Institute on Drug Abuse (NIDA), and the National Institute on Mental Health (NIMH). Many of the programs of ADAMHA related to school-age children. For example, they have produced a guide, "Prevention Plus: Involving Schools, Parents, and the Community in Alcohol and Drug Education." They have also supported the development of "Being Friends," a mental health curriculum for children 9 to 12 years old (Gilbert, et al., 1985).

Other federally sponsored programs The Health Resources and Services Administration, primarily through its Division of Maternal and Child Health, has always shown an interest in the school-age child. They have developed elementary grade programs on human genetics and on accident and injury prevention. Several of their programs have evolved from their Indian Health Service Program.

The President's Council on Physical Fitness and Sports has as its major goal promoting physical fitness of all citizens, including children and youth. Children 10 to 17 years of age can earn the Presidential Physical Fitness Award, which is based upon the results of a fitness test developed to encourage increased physical activity.

The Office on Smoking and Health, originally in the Bureau of Health Education, is now housed as a staff unit of the Office of the Assistant Secretary for Health. It maintains an inventory of information that can be useful to those working in schools and, depending upon its physical capacity to do so, provides technical assistance on request (Gilbert, et al., 1985).

The National Highway Traffic Safety Administration within the U.S. Department of Transportation provides the schools with educational materials related to the use of alcohol, traffic safety, pedestrian and bicycle safety, and occupant protection. Their curriculum materials are developed for all age levels.

An important school-based program of the U.s. Department of Agriculture is the Nutrition Education and Training Program (NET). State agencies are supported in developing or purchasing nutrition education and training materials. These are designed to instruct children and to provide training for teachers, as well as those who work in school food service programs. Essentially, the program aims to develop good eating habits by reaching both children and adults. The department also assists with providing nutritious food to school lunch programs (Gilbert, et al., 1985).

If recent experience is an indicator, there will continue to be administrative modifications and changes in the titles of offices administering federal programs in school health and school health education. Whatever the changes in the names and the legislation supporting school health, it is predicted that the federal commitment to the provision of health care for children will continue to increase. Let us hope that it will be possible to maintain a balance between federally established guidelines and local autonomy. All must work together with confidence and flexibility if the unique needs of children in every community are to be met.

COMMUNITY GROUPS IN OPPOSITION

Unfortunately, every community group does not accept health education. Critics of the schools like to attack it, particularly with regard to teaching certain parts of the curriculum. The vast majority of parents are in favor of the school's provision of education about sexual behavior, abuse of illegal drugs and alcohol, decision making, problem solving, and other topics that have been criticized for one reason or another. But opposition groups do exist, and they also represent a community whose influence on health education is real.

Typically, such groups make up for their small numbers by being well organized and very vocal. Although most groups are opposed to instruction relative to certain topics in the curriculum, others oppose the health services program for religious reasons or other personal reasons (for example, in objecting to the immunizations required as a condition of their children's admission to school). Generally, program adjustments are made to meet the objections of these groups. In the event that parents prefer that their children not be present in mixed group discussions of sexuality, students are excused to spend the class period in the library. Parents can be excused from having their child immunized in some communities so long as this does not jeopardize the health of other children or the community.

There have been occasions when minority coalitions have been successful in destroying entire segments of the health instruction or services program. As a result, not just specific children but all children in the school are denied this education. This can happen only when the majority who approve simply fail to stand up and make their voices heard.

Chapter 6 has presented some very good analyses of the kinds of problems that occur and the reasons they do. A number of excellent suggestions for constructive ways of avoiding controversy or coping with it if necessary have been discussed. Be sure that you have internalized that information well enough that you could apply its principles in a real situation. If you can, it's far less likely that you will have to.

SUMMARY

1. A community can be defined in many ways. Generally, it is any group of people who share the same kinds of needs, concerns, values, and organizations.
2. Each of us is simultaneously a member of many communities, political jurisdictions, family groups, neighborhoods, age groups, ethnic, social, or cultural groups, professional groups, and more.
3. School health programs are carried on in a community, the school, for an age group of learners, by a community of professionals, and aided by the many community organizations interested in promoting health education as a means of promoting student and community health.
4. Community health-concerned groups can be categorized as they interrelate with schools as:
    a. parents and parent groups
    b. health care professionals
    c. private health agencies and organizations
    d. professional associations
    e. commercial associations
5. School-community liaison bodies facilitate communication and cooperation between schools and the community.
    a. Community health councils, although more broadly concerned with total community health needs and problems, include the schools among their primary interests. Membership in the council is typically representative of major community organizations and professional groups.
    b. School health coalitions may be local, state, or national in scope and seek to promote the health of school-age children and to further health education programs at all community levels, either by ex-

tension or directly. Membership may represent private industry or business, professionals, and individual citizens, the criterion being interest in promoting school health.
6. At the federal level of community, numerous offices, agencies, and health institutes are specifically working to promote school health in special ways.
    a. Following the report on health education published by the president's committee in 1973, new federal offices were established to reflect its recommendations—for example, the Bureau of Health Education (now the Health Education Division of the Center for Health Promotion and Education, CDC); the Office of Comprehensive School Health, Department of Education (since abolished); and the Office of Disease Prevention and Health Promotion in the Department of Health and Human Services.
    b. Specific federally funded and supported school health projects abound. Examples include development of the "Growing Healthy" curriculum (K–7); the teenage health teaching modules; the School Health Education Research Conference, sponsored by the National Heart, Lung, and Blood Institute; the Alcohol, Drug Abuse, and Mental Health Administration's curriculums for children such as "Being Friends" and "Prevention Plus"; and the several school health initiatives of the Office of Disease Prevention and Health Promotion.
7. Groups opposing school health education either in part or in total, although few in number, undeniably can and do influence the nature and emphasis of health education in schools unless care is taken to avoid criticism or misunderstandings about the program.

QUESTIONS AND EXERCISES

Questions

1. In what ways does a community of solution differ from most other community groupings?
2. Why is it important to involve the community, or a community's many communities, in planning and carrying out a school's health program?
3. How might an abundance of free curriculum materials offered by organizations outside the school be a hindrance rather than a help to health teachers? What is the best way to deal with that problem?

4. In what ways would a health program intended to promote the health of faculty and other school personnel help protect and promote the health of students?
5. What is the relationship between health education in schools and the promotion of community health?
6. How would you rank the different categories of community health-concerned organizations discussed in this chapter in terms of their potential impact on school health programs? Explain your rationale for that ranking.
7. How can parents be involved most effectively in the school health program? Could the program function in the absence of parental cooperation? Why or why not?
8. Given that schools are themselves an important part of the community, what should be the role or roles of community health educators in promoting school health programs?
9. In what kinds of situations would it be more efficient to contact single health agencies directly rather than submitting a need or problem to a council of such agencies?

Exercises
1. Assume that you have just been hired to serve as the health instructor and part-time health coordinator in a new high school in your district. The principal tells you that he will want you to familiarize yourself with the community and then prepare a proposed list of policies regarding a proposed curriculum in human sexuality. What community members might you ask to serve as an advisory committee as you began your work? How would you survey the areas served by the school to gather the data that you need in order to develop a curriculum appropriate to student needs and acceptable to parents? What kinds of policies would you recommend as essential as insurance against misunderstandings and controversy?
2. Find out whether there is an actively functioning community health council, or its equivalent, in your area. How many members are there, and whom do they represent? If you were asked to evaluate its representativeness and commend it as is or make suggestions to strengthen or improve its potential for assisting the school health program, what would be your response? Describe the present membership of your community health council. List other members who ought to be added. If there is no council, list a set of members that ought to be included.

3. Seek the names of the chairs of the Education Committees of the House of Representatives and the Senate. Then select a school health issue or problem that you believe needs to be addressed by the Department of Education directly and at once. For example, you might urge that the Office of Comprehensive Health be reinstated, that comprehensive health education be vigorously supported by every means possible, or that the free lunch program be upgraded. Write and mail a short, professional, knowledgeable, and persuasive letter on this topic. Share your answer with the class.

REFERENCES

Bureau of Health Education Facts, CDC, Atlanta, 1975.

Center, New York: National Center for Health Education, Number 2, 1984.

Center, New York: National Center for Health Education, Number 3, 1985.

Cortese, P., "School health funding sources in the public sector." *Health Education Quarterly,* spring 1981, pp. 88–89.

Gilbert, G., et al., "Current federal activities in school health education." *Public Health Reports,* Sept.-Oct. 1985, pp. 499–507.

Gorton, R., *School Administration: Challenge and Opportunity for Leadership.* Dubuque, IA: W.C. Brown, 1976.

"Healthy Me," *Center.* New York: National Center for Health Education, Number 3, 1985, p. 38.

Introducing the U.S. Department of Education. Washington, DC, 1980.

Kreuter, M., Christenson, G., and Davis, R., "The role of school health education research: future issues and challenges." *Health Education* 15:4, 1983, pp. 27–32.

Metropolitan Life Foundation, "Healthy Me Awards." *Journal of School Health,* March 1986, pp. 117–119.

NaSHEC *Newsletter,* New York: National Center for Health Education, Number 1:1, 1983.

NaSHEC *Newsline,* New York: National Center for Health Education, March 1986.

National Commission on Community Health Services, *Health is a Community Affair.* Cambridge, MA: Harvard University Press, 1966.

"New Definitions." *Health Education Monographs,* Number 33, 1973.

Promoting Health/Preventing Disease: Objectives for the Nation. Washington, DC: Department of Health and Human Services, 1980.

"Results of the Health Education Evaluation Project." *Journal of School Health,* Oct. 1985, entire issue.

Wellness at the Worksite. Washington, DC: Health Insurance Association of America, American Council of Life Insurance, 1985.

Appendix A

Selected Federal Health Information Clearinghouses and Information Centers

Aging
National Clearinghouse on Aging
330 Independence Avenue, SW
Washington, DC 20201
202/245-2158
Provides access to information and referral services that assist the older American in obtaining services. Distributes Administration on Aging publications.

Alcohol
National Clearinghouse for Alcohol Information (NCALI)
P.O. Box 2345
Rockville, MD 20852
301/468-2600
Gathers and disseminates current knowledge on alcohol-related subjects.

Arthritis
Arthritis Information Clearinghouse
P.O. Box 34427
Bethesda, MD 20034
301/881-9411
Identifies materials concerned with arthritis and related musculoskeletal diseases and serves as an information exhange for individuals and organizations involved in public, professional, and patient education. Refers personal requests from patients to the Arthritis Foundation.

Cancer
Cancer Information Clearinghouse
National Cancer Institute
Office of Cancer Communications
9000 Rockville Pike, Building 31, Room 10A18
Bethesda, MD 20205
301/496-4070
Collects and disseminates information on public, patient, and professional cancer education materials to organizations and health care professionals.

Office of Cancer Communications (OCC)
Public Inquiries Section
9000 Rockville Pike, Building 31, Room 10A18
Bethesda, MD 20205
301/496-5583

Answers requests for cancer information from patients and the general public.

Child Abuse
Clearinghouse on Child Abuse and Neglect Information
P.O. Box 1182
Washington, DC 20013
202/755-0590

Collects, processes, and disseminates information on child abuse and neglect.

Consumer Information
Consumer Information Center
Pueblo, CO 81009
303/566-1794

Distributes consumer publications on topics such as children, food and nutrition, health, exercise, and weight control. The *Consumer Information Catalog* is available free from the center and must be used to identify publications being requested.

Diabetes
National Diabetes Information Clearinghouse
805 15th Street, NW, Suite 500
Washington, DC 20005
202/842-7630

Collects and disseminates information on patient education materials and coordinates the development of materials and programs for diabetes education.

Digestive Diseases
National Digestive Diseases Education and Information Clearinghouse
1555 Wilson Boulevard, Suite 600
Rosslyn, VA 22209
703/522-0870

Provides information on digestive diseases to health professionals and consumers.

Domestic Violence
National Clearinghouse on Domestic Violence
P.O. Box 2309
Rockville, MD 20852
301/251-5172

Serves as a central resource for information on the problems and issues of domestic violence. Collects and disseminates information in the areas of sexual abuse in the family, psychological studies on domestic violence, counseling the abused and abuser, program management, prevention, acute medical services, and community networking.

Drug Abuse
National Clearinghouse for Drug Abuse Information
P.O. Box 416
Kensington, MD 20795
301/443-6500

Collects and disseminates information on drug abuse. Produces informational materials on drugs, drug abuse, and prevention.

Emergency Medical
National Clearinghouse for Emergency Medical Services
P.O. Box 911
Rockville, MD 20852
301/436-6267

Gathers and disseminates information on emergency medical services for accidents and other medical emergencies.

Family Planning
National Clearinghouse for Family Planning Information
P.O. Box 2225
Rockville, MD 20852
301/881-9400

Collects family planning materials, makes referrals to other information centers, and distributes and produces materials. Primary audience is federally funded family planning clinics.

Food Drug
Food and Drug Administration (FDA)
Office for Consumer Communications
5600 Fishers Lane, Room 15B-32 (HFE-88)
Rockville, MD 20857
301/443-3170

Answers consumer inquiries for the FDA and serves as a clearinghouse for their consumer publications.

Food Nutrition
Food and Nutrition Information Center (FNIC)
National Agricultural Library Building, Room 304
Beltsville, MD 20705
301/344-3719

Serves the information needs of persons interested in human nutrition, food service management, and food technology. Acquires and lends books, journal articles, and audiovisual materials dealing with these areas of concern.

Genetic Diseases
National Clearinghouse for Human Genetic Diseases
805 15th Street, Suite 500
Washington, DC 20005
202/842-7617

Provides information on human genetics and genetic diseases for both patients and health care workers and reviews existing curricular materials on genetic education.

Handicapped
Clearinghouse on the Handicapped
330 C Street, SW
Washington, DC 20202
202/245-0080

Responds to inquiries from handicapped individuals and serves as a resource to organizations that supply information to, and about, handicapped individuals.

Health Education
Division of Health Education
Center for Health Promotion and Education
1300 Clifton Road
Atlanta, GA 30333
404/329-3235

Provides leadership and program direction for the prevention of disease, disability, premature death, and undesirable and unnecessary health problems through health education. Inquiries on health education can be directed to the division.

Health Indexes
Clearinghouse on Health Indexes
National Center for Health Statistics
Division of Analysis
3700 East-West Highway
Hyattsville, MD 20782
301/436-7035
Provides informational assistance in the development of health measures to health researchers, administrators, and planners.

Health Information
National Health Information Clearinghouse (NHIC)
P.O. Box 1133
Washington, DC 20013
703/522-2590 in VA
800/336-4797
Helps the public locate health information through identification of health information resources and an inquiry and referral system. Health questions are referred to appropriate health resources that, in turn, respond directly to inquirers.

Health Planning
National Health Planning Information Center (NHPIC)
3700 East-West Highway, Room 6-50
Hyattsville, MD 20782
301/436-6736
Provides information for use in analysis of issues and problems related to health planning and resource development. Limits information services to the health systems agencies and the state health planning and development agencies.

Health Standards
National Health Standards and Quality Information Clearinghouse (NHSQIC)
11301 Rockville Pike
Kensington, MD 20795
301/881-9400
Collects materials concerning standards for health care and health facilities, qualifications of health professionals, and evaluation and certification of health care providers serving federal beneficiaries. Although free to federal agency personnel, searches are billed at cost to other requesters.

High Blood Pressure
High Blood Pressure Information Center
120/80 National Institutes of Health
Bethesda, MD 20205
301/652-7700

Provides information on the detection, diagnosis, and management of high blood pressure to consumers and health professionals.

Injuries
National Injury Information Clearinghouse
5401 Westbard Avenue, Room 625
Washington, DC 20207
301/492-6424

Collects and disseminates injury data and information relating to the causes and prevention of death, injury, and illness associated with consumer products. Requests of a general nature are referred to the Consumer Product Safety Commission's Communications Office.

Mental Health
National Clearinghouse for Mental Health Information
Public Inquiries Section
5600 Fishers Lane, Room 11A-21
Rockville, MD 20857
301/443-4513

Acquires and abstracts the world's mental health literature, answers inquiries from the public, and provides computer searches for the scientific and academic communities.

Occupational Safety
Clearinghouse for Occupational Safety and Health Information
4676 Columbia Parkway
Cincinnati, OH 45226
513/684-8326

Provides technical information support for National Institute for Occupational Safety and Health research programs and supplies information to others on request.

Physical Fitness
President's Council on Physical Fitness and Sports
Washington, DC 20201
202/755-7478

Conducts a public service advertising program and cooperates with governmental and private groups to promote the development of physical fitness leadership, facilities, and programs. Produces informational materials on exercise, school physical education programs, sports, and physical fitness for youth, adults, and the elderly.

Poison Control
Division of Poison Control, FDA
5600 Fishers Lane
Rockville, MD 20857
301/443-6260

Works with the national network of six hundred poison control centers to reduce the incidence and severity of acute poisoning. Directs toxic emergency calls to a local poison control center.

Product Safety
Consumer Product Safety Commission
Washington, DC 20207
800/638-8326
800/492-8363 in MD
800/638-8333 in AK, HI, VI, PR

Evaluates the safety of products sold to the public. Provides printed materials on different aspects of consumer product safety on request. Does not answer questions from consumers on drugs, prescriptions, warranties, advertising, repairs, or maintenance.

Project Share
Project Share
P.O. Box 2309
Rockville, MD 20852
301/428-3100

Provides reference and referral services designed to improve the management of human services by emphasizing the integration of those services at the delivery level.

Rape Information
National Rape Information Clearinghouse (NRIC)
5600 Fishers Lane, Room 11A-22
Rockville, MD 20857
301/443-1910

Maintains a listing of rape prevention and treatment resources to help people locate services available in their community and to facilitate networking among those working in the field of sexual assault. Has very little information for inquiries from the general public, and prefers to refer them to local resources.

Rehabilitation Information
National Rehabilitation Information Center (NARIC)
Catholic University of America
4407 Eighth Street, NE
Washington, DC 20017
202/635-5822

Supplies publications and audiovisual materials on rehabilitation, and assists in locating answers to questions such as dates, places, names, addresses, or statistics. The collections include materials relevant to the rehabilitation of all disability groups.

Smoking
Office on Smoking and Health
Technical Information Center
Park Building, Room 158
5600 Fishers Lane
Rockville, MD 20857
301/443-1690

Offers bibliographic and reference service to researchers and others, and publishes and distributes a number of titles in the field of smoking.

Sudden Infant Death Syndrome (SIDS)
Sudden Infant Death Syndrome Clearinghouse
1555 Wilson Boulevard, Suite 600
Rosslyn, VA 22209
703/522-0870

Provides information on SIDS to health professionals and consumers.

Surgical Opinion
National Second Surgical Opinion Program
330 Independence Avenue, SW
Washington, DC 20201
202/245-7897
800/638-6833
800/492-6603 in MD

Provides information for people who are faced with the possibility of non-emergency surgery. Sponsors the toll-free number to assist the public in locating a surgeon or other specialist.

This list was prepared by the National Health Information Clearinghouse. For additional copies or further information, contact the NHIC staff toll-free at 800/336-4797 (for Virginia only, call collect 703/522-2590) or write to:

National Health Information Clearinghouse
P.O. Box 1133
Washington, DC 20013

Appendix B

Criteria for Evaluating the School Health Services Program

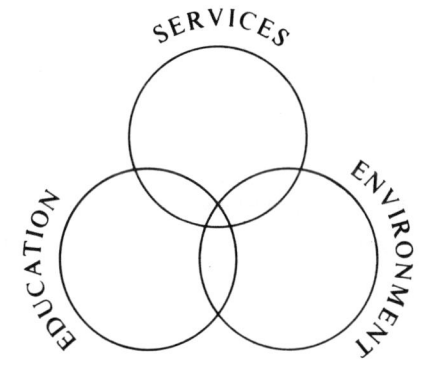

CALIFORNIA STATE DEPARTMENT OF EDUCATION
Wilson Riles, Superintendent of Public Instruction
Sacramento, 1982

Introduction

A school health services program strengthens the educational process by improving the health status and health knowledge of children and youths.

Criteria for Evaluating the School Health Services Program is designed to be used by school personnel in a self-evaluation process. The purpose of the evaluation is to identify strengths and weaknesses of the program. On the basis of the findings and recommendations, plans can be developed to improve and enhance health services for students and families.

This evaluation instrument may be used by any of the following:

- An individual
- An interdisciplinary school group
- A broadly representative district group
- A school or district/community group
- An outside team of experts

The criteria are expressed in terms of desirable practices. Provision is made for judging, on a five-point scale, the extent to which a program meets each criterion (completely; to some degree—75 percent, 50 percent, 25 percent; or not at all). Space is provided for listing changes that may be needed. At the top of each major section, space is provided for recording recommended steps to be taken in relation to the changes needed. Care should be taken to make recommendations that will not have an adverse effect on provisions or practices already meeting the criteria. Changes that are needed will undoubtedly have to be evaluated in terms of short- and long-range goals, and recommendations will need to be developed accordingly. Obviously, provision should be made for follow-up of the recommendations.

Some suggested procedures for using the evaluation criteria to improve a school health services program are the following:

1. Determine the membership of the group to conduct the evaluation.
2. Determine the need for consultant help.
3. Review the criteria for making the evaluation.
4. Conduct the evaluation.
5. Determine the degree to which the program meets each criterion.
6. Note the changes needed.
7. Develop recommended steps for making needed changes, and record these changes in the appropriate spaces on the form.
8. Set up a priority order for accomplishing the changes.
9. Submit a report, including recommendations, to the administration.

Evaluation Criteria

Criteria	Com-pletely	To some degree Percent 75 | 50 | 25	Not at all	Changes needed
I. Administration				
A. The policies of the district's governing board provide a school **health services program** designed to help all pupils achieve the degree of health their potentialities permit.				Recommended steps for making needed changes:
1. The policies provide for a comprehensive and well-planned program of health services that reflect current legal requirements.				
2. The policies provide for the maintenance of a healthful school environment.				
B. Written goals and objectives for the district's school health services program are available.				Recommended steps for making needed changes:
1. The goals and objectives determine the direction of the health services program.				
2. The goals and objectives determine the program for providing and maintaining a healthful school environment.				
C. The district has assigned qualified personnel to provide leadership for implementing and maintaining a comprehensive health services program and has provided the necessary resources.				Recommended steps for making needed changes:
1. A qualified person with professional preparation in health services and administration has been delegated responsibility at the district level for providing leadership to the district's health services program.				
2. Job descriptions define the duties of each person who has responsibility in the health services program.				

364 Planning and Implementing Health Education in Schools

Criteria	Com-pletely	To some degree — Percent 75 / 50 / 25	Not at all	Changes needed
3. All personnel responsible for providing direct health services receive a formal evaluation according to district policy.				
4. The district provides the resources (funding, personnel, and materials) necessary to operate the health services program.				
5. The district utilizes special funding resources for health services.				
D. The principal of each school is responsible for implementing the school health services program.	Recommended steps for making needed changes:			
1. A school health advisory committee provides input to the health services program.				
2. Each member of the staff is informed regarding the district's health services program.				
E. Qualified health services personnel are adequate in number to implement the school health services program.	Recommended steps for making needed changes:			
1. Credentialed school nurses are employed in accordance with a district-established nurse-pupil ratio.				
2. The nurse-pupil ratio is determined by student health needs, legal requirements, number of individuals with exceptional needs, availability of clerical assistance, mobility of population, and geographic area.				
3. Physicians, dentists, and other medical specialists are available for consultation.				
F. Adequate facilities, equipment, and supplies are provided for the health services program.	Recommended steps for making needed changes:			
1. Appropriate health office facilities that allow for implementation of the program are provided.				
2. Essential equipment is provided and properly maintained.				

Criteria for Evaluating the School Health Services Program 365

Criteria	Com-pletely	To some degree Percent 75 | 50 | 25	Not at all	Changes needed
3. Essential health supplies are available in the school.				
G. The staff development program for school personnel provides information on health issues and practices.	Recommended steps for making needed changes:			
1. Staff development training opportunities in health receive emphasis comparable to that given to staff development opportunities in other subject areas.				
2. School nurses are involved in the planning of staff development programs.				
H. A health services guide is provided by the school district or by the office of the county superintendent of schools.	Recommended steps for making needed changes:			
1. A health services guide provided by the school district or the office of the county superintendent of schools is available in the school.				
2. The guide contains the objectives, procedures, and sample forms used in providing health services.				
I. Student and family responses to school health and nursing services are assessed.	Recommended steps for making needed changes:			
1. The attitudes of students and parents and their degree of satisfaction toward school health services are evaluated.				
2. Students utilize school nursing and health services when appropriate and in constructive ways.				
3. Most parents respond positively to referrals made by school nurses.				

Criteria	Com-pletely	To some degree Percent 75 | 50 | 25	Not at all	Changes needed
II. Program—The Nurse's Role A. The health and developmental status of students is assessed and evaluated.		Recommended steps for making needed changes:		
1. A general health and developmental history is obtained on kindergarten students and new enrollees.				
2. First-grade students comply with the Child Health and Disability Prevention Program requirement (Health and Safety Code Section 308.5).				
3. Teacher-school nurse conferences are conducted at least annually.				
4. A vision screening program is conducted for students in kindergarten and grades three and six (Education Code Section 49455), grades nine or ten (Motor Vehicle Code Section 12805), and for new enrollees and referrals.				
5. Color vision screening is conducted on boys in kindergarten or first grade (Education Code Section 49455).				
6. A hearing screening program is conducted for students in kindergarten and grades one, two, five, eight, and ten or eleven (Education Code Section 49455 and California Administrative Code, Title 17, Public Health, Section 2951), and for new enrollees and referrals.				
7. Scoliosis screening is conducted for seventh-grade girls and eighth-grade boys (Education Code Section 49452.5).				
B. Health services personnel inform and advise parents and appropriate school personnel of the results of health assessments.		Recommended steps for making needed changes:		
1. Results of health assessments are reported to parents and pertinent school personnel.				
2. Students with suspected health problems are referred to an appropriate source of health care, and follow-up continues until the student receives care (Education Code Section 49456).				

Criteria for Evaluating the School Health Services Program 367

Criteria	Com-pletely	To some degree Percent 75 | 50 | 25	Not at all	Changes needed
C. The school nurse recommends necessary school adjustments for students with health problems.	Recommended steps for making needed changes:		
1. The regular school program is modified to accommodate the students' individual needs; i.e., preferential seating, shortened school day, and special bus passes.				
2. Students are referred by the school nurse for special education evaluation as needed.				
3. Arrangements are made for home/hospital instruction as indicated.				
D. The school nurse periodically reviews the health status and health maintenance plans of students with health problems.	Recommended steps for making needed changes:		
1. The school nurse reassesses the health status of students at least annually by:				
a. Consulting with the classroom teacher regarding the students' progress				
b. Conferring with the parents or guardians regarding the students' health				
c. Consulting with the students' source(s) of health care				
2. The school nurse updates the students' health maintenance plans as needed.				
E. The school nurse provides individual or group health counseling to students, parents, and teachers to effect behavioral change.	Recommended steps for making needed changes:		
1. The school nurse counsels students, school personnel, and families regarding health problems.				
2. Case conferences are held to assist pupils with special health problems to make the best possible personal and social adjustments.				

368 Planning and Implementing Health Education in Schools

Criteria	Com-pletely	To some degree — Percent 75 | 50 | 25	Not at all	Changes needed
F. The school nurse assists in the appropriate special education placement of individuals with exceptional needs and provides designated health-nursing services.	\multicolumn{4}{l|}{Recommended steps for making needed changes:}
1. "Informed Consents for Assessment" are obtained, and "Parent Rights" are explained.				
2. When students are being considered for special education placement, the school nurse conducts a special health assessment which includes a developmental and health history, home environment assessment, neurological assessment, and a review of all pertinent medical information.				
3. The school nurse prepares a report for the individualized education program (IEP) team.				
4. The school nurse serves on the IEP team.				
5. The school nurse participates in the review and update of the IEP at least annually.				
6. The school nurse is responsible for writing and implementing the IEP goals for "standardized procedures" (Business and Professions Code Section 2725(d)) for the administration of "specialized physical health care services" (Education Code Section 49423.5 and California Administrative Code, Title 5, Education, sections 3112(s), 3217, 3438, 3584, 3773, and 3797).				
G. The health services program includes prevention and control of communicable disease.	\multicolumn{4}{l|}{Recommended steps for making needed changes:}
1. All students comply with state legal requirements regarding immunizations (Health and Safety Code sections 3380—3385 and 3400—3407), plus the new code sections in California Administrative Code, Title 17, Public Health, Subchapter 8, 6000 series.				
2. The school nurse interprets and implements policies and procedures concerning communicable diseases.				

Criteria	Com-pletely	To some degree — Percent 75 | 50 | 25	Not at all	Changes needed
3. The school nurse administers immunizations (Education Code Section 49403(b)) in accordance with "standardized procedures" (Business and Professions Code Section 2725(d)).				
H. Health services personnel establish and maintain standards to minimize the effects of accidents and illness in school.	Recommended steps for making needed changes:			
1. Written policies and procedures for first aid and emergency care are provided to all school personnel.				
2. First aid is administered promptly to injured or ill pupils by the first person on the scene.				
3. The school nurse is available for consultation in cases of accident or illness.				
4. Phone numbers of parents and physicians are on file for each pupil to facilitate notification in cases of injury or illness.				
5. The school nurse provides periodic staff development on up-to-date first-aid procedures for all school personnel.				
6. Fully equipped first-aid kits are available in strategic locations on each campus and for field trips (Education Code Section 32040).				
7. First-aid equipment, such as stretchers and splints, is readily accessible.				
8. Accidents are analyzed to determine causes, and safety hazards are reported to the appropriate administrator for remedial action.				
I. The school nurse practitioner (SNP) provides primary health care to selected individuals.	Recommended steps for making needed changes:			
1. Criteria and priorities are developed for selection of individuals to be examined.				
2. The SNP identifies and manages specific conditions in accordance with "standardized procedures" (Business and Professions Code Section 2725(d)).				

370 Planning and Implementing Health Education in Schools

Criteria	Com-pletely	To some degree — Percent 75 / 50 / 25	Not at all	Changes needed
3. The SNP reports findings and develops a health care or case management plan.				
J. The school nurse assists in promoting the optimum health of the school staff.	Recommended steps for making needed changes:			
1. The school nurse provides leadership in the development, periodic revision, and enforcement of school district policies regarding staff health and safety.				
2. The school nurse orients school personnel regarding district staff health and safety policies.				
3. The school nurse counsels individual staff members regarding health problems and provides first aid as needed.				
4. The school nurse provides staff development programs and distributes current information concerning pertinent health issues.				
K. School health personnel assist in the provision of a safe and healthful school environment.	Recommended steps for making needed changes:			
1. School health personnel participate in the development and periodic revision of district policies regarding environmental health and safety.				
2. School health personnel assist administrators in achieving compliance with legal requirements.				
L. School nurses participate in the planning and implementation of a comprehensive health education program.	Recommended steps for making needed changes:			
1. The school nurse serves on curriculum development committees.				
2. The school nurse stimulates the incorporation of health instruction in the school curriculum and in each classroom.				

Criteria for Evaluating the School Health Services Program *371*

Criteria	Com-pletely	To some degree Percent 75 | 50 | 25	Not at all	Changes needed
3. The school nurse searches out, evaluates, and recommends new materials and community resources.				
4. The school nurse serves as a resource to teachers and presents individual lessons in the classroom.				
M. The school nurse serves as the school liaison to community agencies and medical and dental care providers.	Recommended steps for making needed changes:			
1. The school nurse maintains current information regarding community resources and referral procedures.				
2. The school nurse serves on community committees or boards and promotes cooperation, communication, and understanding among community resources and the schools.				
N. The school nurse participates as a team member in the development, implementation, and periodic evaluation of policies and procedures related to critical health issues, including substance abuse, adolescent pregnancy, venereal disease, child abuse, and the like.	Recommended steps for making needed changes:			
1. The school nurse assists in the identification and documentation of the scope of the problems.				
2. The school nurse participates in the development, review, evaluation, and revision of policies and procedures that apply to critical health issues.				
3. The school nurse serves as a team member to implement the policies and procedures.				
O. School health personnel provide assistance to families by referral for social services when needed.	Recommended steps for making needed changes:			
1. School health personnel facilitate family contact with local community resources.				
2. School health personnel assist families to obtain free or part-pay health services.				

372 Planning and Implementing Health Education in Schools

Criteria	Com-pletely	To some degree Percent 75 | 50 | 25	Not at all	Changes needed
P. The student health record is a mandatory component of the student's cumulative school record.	Recommended steps for making needed changes:			
1. A health record is initiated for each student upon enrollment (California Administrative Code, Title 5, Education, Section 432).				
2. Individual student health records are transferred, retained, or destroyed as required by law and regulations (California Administrative Code, Title 5, Education, sections 437 and 438).				
3. The "California School Immunization Record" is completed for each student and is a "mandatory permanent pupil record" (Health and Safety Code Section 3389(a) and California Administrative Code, Title 5, Education, sections 430—432).				
4. Required and pertinent health information is recorded on the individual student health record.				
5. Confidentiality of and rights of access to individual student health records are observed as required by law and regulations (Education Code sections 49060—49078 and California Administrative Code, Title 5, Education, Section 434).				
Q. The school health services program is evaluated at least annually in terms of established objectives.	Recommended steps for making needed changes:			
1. There is an established procedure for compiling and analyzing health services data.				
2. The health services program is evaluated to determine:				
a. Compliance with legal requirements				
b. Program effectiveness				
c. Program needs				
d. Staffing patterns				
3. A report on the school health program is submitted annually to the appropriate district administrators and the school governing board.				

Work Sheet

Summary of recommended steps to be taken:	Priorities, time lines, and resources:

Appendix C

Administration of the school health program

Successful school health programs involve understanding and leadership by school administrators in their roles as top-ranking coordinators and liaisons with the board of education, staff members, and the community. They must be able to present school health needs to their board and utilize all resources and facilities in the community for fostering the health of the schoolchildren. They are responsible for the enforcement of the state laws regarding school health, including immunizations. The school experiences of students in our school health programs will largely determine their knowledge and their attitudes about health. It is the responsibility of every school to offer a comprehensive and effective health education program taught by adequately prepared instructors. This effort should be supported by all groups in the community. Administrators set the keynote for effective working relationships with school personnel, students, and the community. Schools should be responsive to and involve the community in planning, developing, implementing, and evaluating programs in a variety of ways, including the establishment of and/or the participation in school-community health committees.

Standards and Recommended Practices	*What Are We Doing*
Program Organization and Administration	
A. A well organized school health program should be planned jointly by the schools, the health department, educational and health professional associations and other responsible community groups.	A. What methods are used to provide for joint planning of the school health program? 1. on a community-wide basis? 2. on an individual school basis?
B. Both the Board of Health and Board of Education may be charged with specific responsibilities. If this is so, the administration of the duties should be the result of joint planning, and roles and responsibilities of personnel clearly defined.	B. List the responsibilities of the: 1. School 2. Department of Health

Adapted from the Ohio Department of Education, *A Self-Appraisal Checklist for School Health Programs*. Used with permission.

376 Planning and Implementing Health Education in Schools

Standards and Recommended Practices	What Are We Doing

C. A school health program is best integrated when a well qualified school person is appointed to coordinate it.

C. 1. The person responsible for the coordination and administration of the school health program is:
   a. Superintendent _____
   b. Health Coordinator _____
   c. Principal _____
   d. School Medical Advisor _____
   e. School Dental Advisor _____
   f. School Nurse _____
   g. Other (list): _____

   2. The person responsible for the development of the health curriculum is:
   a. Superintendent _____
   b. Curriculum Director _____
   c. Health Coordinator _____
   d. Principal _____
   e. Nurse _____
   f. Supervisor, Health, Physical Education and Recreation _____
   g. Other (list): _____

   3. The person responsible for Health Services is:
   a. Superintendent _____
   b. Health Coordinator _____
   c. Nurse _____
   d. Supervisor, Health, Physical Education and Recreation _____

D. Administrative objectives are:

   1. To develop sound school health policies and to facilitate and make more effective the work of teachers, school health service personnel, and other related non-teaching staff

D. 1. Does the school have written policies that:
   a. Clearly define agency responsibility including legal. Yes ___ No ___
   b. Clearly define roles of personnel, e.g., nurses, administrators, teachers, etc.

Standards and Recommended Practices   *What Are We Doing*

Standards and Recommended Practices	What Are We Doing
(cafeteria workers, bus drivers, custodians).	Yes ___ No ___ c. When were the policies last reviewed?
2. To provide for special in-service education programs to be conducted for the personnel directly involved in the school health program.	2. Special in-service education programs are conducted for these personnel? Yes ___ No ___ How often? These in-service education programs are evaluated to determine their effectiveness? Yes ___ No ___
3. To provide for periodic evaluation and improvement to help keep the program in step with changing needs and trends.	3. Periodic evaluations and improvements are provided in the program? In what ways? How often?
4. To define and develop sound and effective working relationships among agencies directly concerned with the school health program, and to communicate school health concerns to the community-at-large.	4. There are sound and effective working relationships between those involved in the school health program and agencies? Yes ___ No ___ If not, what plans are being made to improve these relationships? Check ways the school health concerns are communicated to the community: P.T.A. or P.T.O. _____ School Health Committee _____ School Communications Official Agencies _____ Voluntary Health Agencies _____ The person responsible for helping to insure sound and effective working relationships is: a. Superintendent _____ b. Principal _____

Standards and Recommended Practices   *What Are We Doing*

	c. Health Coordinator _____ d. School Nurse _____ e. Supervisor, Health, Physical Education _____ f. Other (list): _____

E. Well prepared personnel, in all phases of the school health program are essential for its effective and successful implementation.	E. Qualifications of school health personnel.
	  1. Check the qualifications and experience of the school health coordinator:
	    a. Certificated _____
	    b. 3 to 5 years experience in health education or school health programs _____
	    c. Recent courses or workshops related to school health _____
	    d. Other (list):
	  2. What percent of the school nurses are:
	    a. Registered in the State of Ohio? _____
	    b. Certificated? _____
	    c. Have has post-baccalaureate courses in school health? _____
	  3. How many elementary teachers have background (a minimum of three semester hours) in health education and/or health science? _____
	  4. Are the secondary teachers assigned to teach health certificated in health education? Yes __ No __
	  5. The school provides an in-service education program for:
	    a. Teachers?
	      Yes__No__
	      Date:
	      One-half day or less _____

Standards and Recommended Practices   *What Are We Doing*

	One day or more _____
	College Credit _____
	b. Nurses? Yes __ No __
	Date:
	One-half day or less _____
	One day or more _____
	College Credit _____
	c. Administrative Personnel? Guidance counselors, social workers, etc.
	Yes __ No __
	Date:
	One-half day or less _____
	One day or more _____
	College Credit _____
	d. Non-teaching (non-certified) personnel?
	Yes __ No __
	Date: _____
	One-half day or less _____
	One day or more _____
	College Credit _____
F. The school administration promotes the integration of health and safety in all curricular and extra curricular activities of the school.	F. The school administration promotes the integration of health and safety in all curricular and extra curricular activities of the school by:
	Leaving to individual teachers _____
	Combined efforts of teachers/coordinators _____
	Suggestions in teachers guides _____
	Written policies and procedures _____
G. If available, schools utilize their community directory of health services.	G. The directory is readily available to all school personnel? Yes __ No __
H. Schools should know what health resources are available in the	H. The school utilizes the following community resources:

Standards and Recommended Practices   *What Are We Doing*

community and how they can be utilized effectively.

    Health Department   ———
    Other official agencies   ———
    Medical Society/Auxiliary   ———
    Dental Society/Auxiliary   ———
    Voluntary Agencies   ———
    Civic Groups   ———
    Other (list):

First Aid for Sudden Illness and Accidents:

A. State law (Sec. 3313.712) requires that an emergency medical treatment authorization form be annually filled out on each student by his parent or legal guardian before October of each year. This form is to be kept on file in the school.

A. Emergency medical treatment authorization forms for all students are filled out annually and are on file in each school?
Yes ___ No ___

B. First aid and sudden illness procedures agreed upon by administrator and staff are written and disseminated to all staff.

B. 1. Are policies agreed upon by administrators and staff?
Yes ___ No ___

2. Are written copies of first aid and sudden illness policies made available to all staff?
Yes ___ No ___

C. Persons (other than nurses) trained in first aid procedures should be available for administering first aid or providing direction in cases of sudden illness.

C. 1. How many persons with current first aid preparation are available? ———

2. Are all teachers working in high risk areas qualified in first aid, such as:
Science Labs   ———
Shops   ———
Home Economics   ———
Physical Education   ———

D. First aid procedures should be briefly written for quick reference and posted in special areas, such as science labs, shops, home eco-

D. Check areas posted:

Administration of the School Health Program   *381*

Standards and Recommended Practices   *What Are We Doing*

nomics rooms, school health clinic, and physical education areas.
Science Labs   _____
Shops   _____
Home Economics Room   _____
Health Clinic   _____
Physical Education   _____

E. First aid equipment/supplies should be kept in stock and readily accessible. All medicines, compounds, bandaging materials should be clearly labeled for use. A designated person should be responsible for ordering supplies.

E. 1. In what locations are first aid supplies stored?

2. All supplies are clearly labeled? Yes ___ No ___

3. Check the person responsible for ordering and restocking supplies?
Superintendent   _____
Principal   _____
Nurse   _____
Supervisor, Health Physical Education and Recreation   _____
Health Coordinator   _____

Accident Reporting System

A. Written policies and procedures (developed by administration and faculty, outlining a system for reporting school accidents) should be available to all school personnel.

A. Policies are written and made available to all staff? Yes ___ No ___

B. The Ohio Department of Health has an Accident Reporting Form, No. 4966.32. They may be utilized if the schools will report the statistical data to the Accident Prevention Program at the end of the year.

B. Does your school use the Ohio Department of Health Accident Reporting Form? Yes ___ No ___

Standards and Recommended Practices   *What Are We Doing*

C. The reporting system should:
   1. define a "reportable accident"
   2. indicate the time lapse in reporting the accident
   3. record information to include: who, what, where, when, why
   4. include follow-through on treatment or referral
   5. indicate who is responsible for recording and reporting accidents

C. Does the reporting system include:
   1. definition of a reportable accident _____
   2. time lapse in reporting accident _____
   3. who-what-where-when-why _____
   4. follow-up-
      a. number of days lost from school _____
      b. determining cause of accident _____
      c. possible action in future to avoid or eliminate future occurrences _____
   5. who is responsible for recording accidents?

D. School personnel should be familiar with school accident forms and should complete or use them uniformly.

D. School personnel are informed regarding the use of accident forms by:
   1. Staff conferences _____
   2. News bulletin _____
   3. Teacher handbooks _____
   4. Other (list):

E. At the end of each school year, all accident data should be reviewed, analyzed, and compared with last year's records to determine the needs for next year's program.

E. List recommendations as a result of reviewing this year's records.

F. A safety committee is recommended to provide leadership for planning a comprehensive safety education program. It should include such people as: administrator, safety specialist, teacher, driver education teacher, physician, school nurse, sanitarian, custodian, student, parent, etc.

F. 1. Do you have a safety committee?
     Yes ___ No ___
   2. Who is on the committee?
   3. List the name of the Specialist in Safety.

Appendix D

Criteria for comprehensive school health education

What do we mean by the term "comprehensive school health education"? Broadly speaking, it is health education in a school setting that is planned and carried out with the purpose of maintaining, reinforcing, or enhancing the health, health-related skills, and health attitudes and practices of children and youth that are conducive to their good health.

Comprehensive school health programs traditionally encompass three interdependent components: health education (instruction), health services, and healthful school environment. Each of these program components complements and is complemented by the procedures and the activities of the others. Although such a program is school based, it is recognized that not just school personnel and students, but their families and communities, must be involved in its planning, implementation, and evaluation.

In every state, school health services and healthful school environments are supported by an elaborately detailed framework of specific mandates and permissive legislation. However, the laws concerning health instruction are few, often ambiguous, and even mandates are largely left to local option for enforcement.

Comprehensive school health education exists nationwide far more in theory than in practice. One reason for this may be the lack of a definitive statement describing the distinctive concepts and processes of such instruction. It is believed that a statement of such significance must come from the school health education profession itself. With this in view, the following guidelines have been designed in an attempt to fulfill this need.

The term "criteria" as used in this document refers to a qualitative or quantitative standard of either performance or design by which a program of comprehensive school health education may be judged. Comprehensive school health programs include health instruction, services, and concern for the quality of the school's physical, social, and emotional environment. However, the statements that follow are concerned solely with aspects of curriculum, administration, and teaching methodology.

A comprehensive school health instructional program is defined by the following:

1. *instruction intended to motivate health maintenance and promote wellness and not merely the prevention of disease or disability*

Source: National Comprehensive School Health Education Guidelines Committee, "Comprehensive school health education." *Journal of School Health* 54:8, Sept. 1984, pp. 312–314.

Comprehensive school health education focuses on the entire continuum of health status and not merely disease identification and prevention. Such education has goals and objectives aimed at assisting students in making the kinds of decisions that can help them build or maintain the best health status possible as well as to eliminate or prevent disease.

2. *activities designed to develop decision-making competencies related to health and health behavior*
   Comprehensive school health instruction provides the cognitive information, behavioral skills, and affective experiences necessary for students to more effectively decide which health behavior(s) they will choose. The focus is on the processes the student encounters or participates in as well as the final behavioral outcomes. It does not merely prescribe a set of health behaviors that a student should adopt.

3. *a planned, sequential Pre-K to 12 curriculum based upon students' needs and current and emerging health concepts and societal issues*
   A comprehensive school health education program is designed to meet the specific health needs and interests of all students as they progress through the various (Pre-K to 12) grade levels. The learning experiences are based and built upon past learning experiences as a means of ensuring continuity. Health needs and interests vary within any grade level. A comprehensive program is flexible and responsive to changes in the learners and in the social settings in which they live.

4. *opportunities for all students to develop and demonstrate health-related knowledge, attitudes, and practices*
   Comprehensive school health education functions in all three domains of learning (cognitive, affective, and psychomotor). The providing of knowledge alone is usually insufficient in addressing all the complexities of human health status. Thus, comprehensive school health education programs include activities related to the development of feelings, attitudes and behaviors conducive to good health. It is important that a comprehensive program include a balanced approach in which all three domains are emphasized.

5. *integration of the physical, mental, emotional, and social dimensions of health as the basis for study of the following topic areas:*
   "Mental health" has always been considered an essential area of health education content. However, comprehensive school health education places greater emphasis on mental health by considering it as an inseparable dimension of health status. As such, comprehensive programs devote substantial curricular time to the mental aspect of *each* topic area.

It is generally accepted that human health consists of at least four dimensions (physical, mental, emotional, and social). A comprehensive school health education program addresses *each* topic area with attention given to each of the four dimensions.

The content of a comprehensive program also is balanced so as to provide adequate coverage to each area somewhere within the entire K–12 curriculum. Emphasis on only a few topic areas is avoided because such an approach fails to address the complex nature of human health and thus is not comprehensive.

The following topic areas are listed in alphabetical order. One does not have precedence over the others.

- community health
- consumer health
- environmental health
- family life
- growth and development
- nutritional health
- personal health
- prevention and control of disease and disorders
- safety and accident prevention
- substance use and abuse

6. *specific program goals and objectives*

    Comprehensive school health education program goals and objectives are clearly stated. They define the nature and character of the curriculum and instruction, and they provide the foundation upon which educational planning and evaluation are based. Objectives are addressed to the needs and interests of students and reflect what they can reasonably attain as a result of planned program activities. Objectives are written in measurable terms so that their attainment can be evaluated.

7. *formative and summative evaluation procedures*

    Evaluation is essential in providing information on program effectiveness. It furnishes useful information about the quality of instruction and the comparative needs, status, and progress of students. Evaluation should be continuous and concurrent with program activities because it provides both an inventory of present status and an assessment of progress.

8. *an effective management system*

    Comprehensive school health education programs are complex. Effective administration of the diverse affairs associated with such programs requires management policies and personnel responsible for the planning, implementation, coordination, and continuation of program activities that are at least equal to those received by other academic disciplines. Without such management, the effectiveness or existence of programs may be compromised.

9. *sufficient resources: budgeted instructional materials, time, management staff, and teachers*

The extent to which comprehensive school health education objectives can be attained is directly dependent upon the nature of the resources provided for such purposes by the school system. Resources include up-to-date instructional materials available for teaching health; the provision of class time equal to that afforded other basic disciplines; assignment of teachers who are qualified health education specialists by virtue of their professional preparation or as an outcome of extensive in-service or postgraduate study in school health education; and a management system capable of providing the necessary leadership, support, and coordination required to ensure a successful education program.

RECOMMENDED CONTENT AREAS TO BE INCLUDED IN COMPREHENSIVE SCHOOL HEALTH EDUCATION CURRICULA

Community health

Study of the ways in which individuals contribute in both positive and negative ways to the overall health status of the many communities of which each is a member, and how they can employ the support systems of these various communities to assist them in the protection, maintenance, and promotion of personal health status.

Consumer health

Examination of the many factors that influence the selection and use of health services, products, and information. The establishment of personal criteria for selection of health services and usage that are conducive to good health.

Environmental health

Investigation of the causes, effects, and methods of eradication of all external factors (e.g., pollution, overpopulation, radiation, hunger, waste disposal, etc.) that negatively affect human health. This study is approached on both a local and worldwide basis and employs a model that examines the totality of relationships between humans and their environment.

Family life
Investigation of the multiple roles and personal life-styles of individuals as members of larger family and societal units. Changes in the responsibilities and privileges each person encounters during the life cycle are studied, in addition to the multitude of factors that influence the expression of human sexuality. The biological, sociological, and psychological variables that affect the total development of the personality and interpersonal relationships are studied.

Growth and development
Study of the functions and structure of the human body systems, their interdependence, and how they function as a whole and contribute to health status from birth to death.

Nutritional health
Study of the principal nutrients necessary to maintain basic body needs and how nutrients can best be provided. Consideration of the essential components of a balanced diet, need for a wide variety of foods, influence of peers, family, culture, media, and so forth on what the individual does or does not consume.

Personal health
Exploration of the life-style activities individuals undertake that influence their health. The focus is on problem-solving techniques, achievement of positive self-concept, and acceptance of responsibility for those personal health actions over which the individual has some control (e.g., care of teeth and gums, eyes, ears, skin, hair, as well as balance between rest and physical activity).

Prevention and control of diseases and disorders
Investigation of the factors contributing to the incidence of the major chronic and communicable diseases and disorders that affect individuals and communities. Study focuses on measures for the prevention, early detection, and control of such health problems.

Safety and accident prevention
Exploration of the methods that can be employed to reduce or eliminate hazardous conditions in all aspects of daily life. Studies of techniques for first aid and emergency care are included.

Substance use and abuse

Examination of the appropriate and inappropriate uses of chemical substances that are commonly used. These include those substances that are legally available, such as alcohol, tobacco, or over-the-counter drugs, and those illegally available through a variety of sources.

Appendix E

Sample test specifications

SMOKING AND ITS EFFECTS

General description

Individuals are presented with statements about biomedical, economic, and social consequences of smoking behavior. Individuals indicate whether each statement is true or false.

Sample item

> This test consists of 20 statements about the effects of smoking. Some of the statements are true and some are false. If you think a statement is true, put a check in the column labeled TRUE. If you think a statement is false, put a check in the column labeled FALSE.

TRUE   FALSE

_____   _____   1. More people gain weight than lose weight after giving up smoking.

Stimulus attributes

1. A test item will consist of a single-sentence statement that the individual is to judge as true or false. This statement will contain information related to a potential biomedical, economic, or social consequence of smoking.
2. All test items will be derived from the specifications supplement *Smoking and its Effects*. This supplement presents statements about smoking that are based upon either empirical evidence or expert consensus. The statements are organized into sections, with each section containing information about one aspect of the consequences of smoking.
3. Each statement on the supplement consists of one main idea related to the effects of smoking. A statement (a) describes the nature or effects of a particular subject, (b) compares two subjects with respect

Source: Centers for Disease Control, *An Evaluation Handbook for Health Education Programs in Smoking*. Atlanta, GA, 1983, pp. 233–240.

to a particular attribute, or (c) presents a correlational or causal relationship between two subjects.
4. A test item will be based on a single statement selected from the supplement. If the supplement statement contains multiple parallel elements, only one of the elements will be used in the test item.

Example of a supplement statement with multiple parallel elements:

Cigarette smoking increases the risk of developing cancer of the lung, larynx, pharynx, mouth, esophagus, kidney, pancreas, and bladder.

5. A test item will present a supplement statement in either *accurate* or *inaccurate* form. An *accurate* test item can be created in one of the following two ways:
   a. *Direct restatement:* Reiterating a statement exactly as it appears on the supplement.
   b. *Paraphrase:* Rephrasing a supplement statement to communicate the same message in different words. This rephrasing may include substituting synonyms for words in the statement and/or reordering words within the statement. The quantitative portion of a supplement statement may not be paraphrased.

   Example of a test item created by paraphrase:

   Supplement statement: Millions of workdays are lost each year because of diseases related to cigarette smoking.

   Test Item: Every year, illnesses related to cigarette smoking cause the loss of millions of workdays.

6. An *inaccurate* test item will be based on a supplement statement or a paraphrase of that statement. An inaccurate item can be created in one of the following two ways:
   a. *Negation:* Rewording a supplement statement to have the opposite meaning. If the statement is worded positively, negation is accomplished by adding a negative word or phrase to the statement. If the statement is worded negatively, negation is accomplished by taking out a negative word or phrase.

   Example of a test item created by negation:

   Supplement statement: Nicotine causes the heart to beat faster.

   Test item: Nicotine does not cause the heart to beat faster.

   b. *Mutual exclusivity:* Transforming a supplement statement to communicate a message that is mutually exclusive with the original message. This transformation can be accomplished by (1) changing a single verb, adjective, or adverb in the original statement to a word or phrase with a contradictory meaning, (2) changing a comparative statement to either reverse the direction of the comparison made or make both terms being compared equal, or (3) changing a quantitative value to one that is different than the one given. A quantitative change must result in a new value that makes the original statement false, rather than a value that allows the statement to remain true because it represents a subset of the original statement. A quantitative change must be expressed in the same terms as the original value.

Examples of test items created by transformation to a mutually exclusive statement:

Supplement statement: Nicotine causes the heart to beat faster.

Test item: Nicotine causes the heart to beat slower.

Supplement statement: Smokers of filter cigarettes are at less risk of developing lung cancer than smokers of nonfilter cigarettes.

Test item: Smokers of filter cigarettes are at the same risk of developing lung cancer as smokers of nonfilter cigarettes.

Supplement statement: About 10 percent of all hospital and medical costs in the United States are related to tobacco.

Test item: About 25 percent of all hospital and medical costs in the United States are related to tobacco.

7. A test item will contain a maximum of twenty-five words. These words will be no higher than an eighth grade reading level on the *IOX Basic Skills Word List*. Technical terms not found on the word list may be used only if they are listed on the *Technical Terms Supplement*.

8. A test will contain an approximately equivalent number of accurate and inaccurate test items. These items will be selected according to the following procedures:
   a. One item will be randomly selected from each section of the supplement.
   b. The rest of the items will be randomly selected from the supplement as a whole.
   c. All of the items will be reviewed by content experts and modified as needed based upon this review.

9. All of the procedures for creating accurate and inaccurate test items will be used as equally as possible, with the exception of negation of a positively stated supplement statement. This type of change will be used only when no other transformation is possible because it results in a test item that requires the respondent to recognize that a negatively stated idea is not accurate, in effect creating a double negative.

Response attributes

1. Two response columns will be provided. One column will be labeled "TRUE," and the other will be labeled "FALSE."

2. The correct answer to a question will be "TRUE" if the statement is accurate or "FALSE" if the statement is inaccurate.

SPECIFICATIONS SUPPLEMENT: SMOKING AND ITS EFFECTS

General biomedical consequences of smoking

1. Tobacco smoke consists of dangerous particles and gases.
2. Tar, nicotine, hydrogen cyanide, and carbon monoxide are inhaled when you smoke.
3. Tar consists of numerous chemicals, some of which are believed to cause cancer.
4. Some scientists believe that nicotine is addictive.
5. Nicotine causes blood vessels to decrease in size, which reduces the amount of blood that can be transported.
6. Nicotine causes the heart to beat more rapidly.
7. Hydrogen cyanide damages the respiratory system.
8. Carbon monoxide decreases the amount of oxygen in the blood.

Smoking and disease

9. The risk of developing coronary heart disease is twice as great for cigarette smokers as for nonsmokers.
10. The risk of developing coronary heart disease increases with the number of cigarettes smoked.
11. Cigarette smoking is directly related to one in every three deaths from cancer.
12. Cigarette smoking increases the risk of developing cancer of the lung, larynx, pharynx, mouth, esophagus, kidney, pancreas, and bladder.
13. The risk of developing lung cancer is ten times greater for cigarette smokers than for nonsmokers.
14. The risk of developing lung cancer increases proportionately with the number of cigarettes smoked each day, the number of years of smoking, and the depth to which the cigarette smoke is inhaled.
15. Cigarette smoking increases the risk of developing lung cancer for both men and women.
16. Cigarette smoking increases the risk of developing chronic bronchitis and emphysema.

Interactive effects of smoking

17. Cigarette smoking increases the risk of being harmed by exposure to other dangerous materials such as asbestos or coal dust.
18. Cigarette smoking increases the dangers associated with taking birth control pills.
19. Smokers have an increased risk of developing a respiratory infection after an operation.
20. Cigarette smoking during the later months of pregnancy increases the risk of having a stillborn baby, a baby that dies shortly after birth, and a baby of lower than average birthweight.
21. If a woman smokes during pregnancy, the nicotine and carbon monoxide she inhales enter the blood of the fetus.
22. Cigarette smoking during pregnancy increases the risk of having a baby that will get "sudden infant death syndrome."

Effects of smoking filter cigarettes

23. Smokers of filter cigarettes are four times more likely than nonsmokers to develop lung cancer.
24. Smokers of filter cigarettes are at less risk of developing lung cancer than smokers of nonfilter cigarettes.
25. Smokers of filter cigarettes are at less risk of developing respiratory diseases than smokers of nonfilter cigarettes.
26. Smokers of most filter cigarettes inhale more carbon monoxide than smokers of nonfilter cigarettes.
27. Smokers of most filter cigarettes are probably at greater risk of developing coronary heart disease than smokers of nonfilter cigarettes.

Effects of smoking low-tar and low-nicotine cigarettes

28. Death rates are lower for smokers of low-tar and low-nicotine cigarettes than for smokers of high-tar and high-nicotine cigarettes.
29. Death rates are higher for smokers of low-tar and low-nicotine cigarettes than for nonsmokers.

Effects of smoking pipes and cigars

30. Pipe or cigar smokers are less likely than cigarette smokers to develop lung cancer.
31. Pipe or cigar smokers are more likely than nonsmokers to develop lung cancer.

32. Pipe or cigar smokers who inhale while they are smoking are at greater risk of developing lung cancer than pipe and cigar smokers who do not inhale.
33. Pipe or cigar smokers are at the same risk as cigarette smokers of developing cancer of the esophagus, pharynx, larynx, and mouth.
34. Pipe smoking increases the risk of developing lip cancer.

Effects of quitting smoking
35. The health risks associated with smoking decrease when a person stops smoking.
36. If a person does not smoke for ten to fifteen years, that person's chances of developing lung cancer are the same as a nonsmoker's chances.
37. The same number of people lose weight as gain weight after giving up smoking.
38. If a woman stops smoking by the fourth month of her pregnancy, the risks of health problems or death to her infant are probably reduced to the levels of those for nonsmoking women.

Effects of involuntary smoking
39. Smokers and nonsmokers can suffer eye irritation, headaches, and nose and throat discomfort from cigarette smoke.
40. Cigarette smoke may fill an enclosed area with higher levels of carbon monoxide and other pollutants than are usually present during an air pollution emergency.
41. Infants whose parents smoke have a greater chance of developing respiratory infections than infants whose parents do not smoke.

Economic and social consequences of smoking
42. Cigarette smoking creates health problems that increase the costs of health insurance and tax-supported health programs.
43. About 10 percent of all hospital and medical costs in the United States have some relation to tobacco use.
44. Millions of workdays are lost each year because of diseases related to cigarette smoking.
45. If a person smokes more than two packs of cigarettes a day, that person probably spends over $600 each year on cigarettes.
46. Cigarette smoking can leave noticeable stains on a person's teeth.
47. Cigarette smoking can leave a noticeable odor on a person's breath and clothing.

48. Parents who smoke are more likely to have children who smoke than are parents who do not smoke.
49. Teenagers are more likely to smoke if they have lower educational goals and achievement, do not accept the health risks of smoking, and have more smokers than nonsmokers among their friends.

Appendix F

Responsibilities of the Generic Health Educator

Responsibility I—assessing individual and community needs for health education

Competency A: obtain health-related data about social and cultural environments, growth and development factors, needs, and interests

Competency B: distinguish between behaviors that foster and those that hinder well-being

Competency C: infer needs for health education on the basis of obtained data

Responsibility II—planning effective health education programs

Competency A: recruit community organizations, resource people, and potential participants for support and assistance in program planning

Competency B: develop a logical scope and sequence plan for a health education program

Competency C: formulate appropriate and measurable program objectives

Competency D: design educational programs consistent with specified program objectives

Responsibility III—implementing health education programs

Competency A: exhibit competence in carrying out planned educational programs

Competency B: infer enabling objectives as needed to implement instructional program in specified settings

Competency C: select methods and media best suited to implement program plans for specific learners

Competency D: monitor educational programs, adjusting objectives and activities as necessary

Source: National Task Force on the Preparation & Practice of Health Educators, Inc., *A Framework for the Development of Competency-based Curricula for Entry Level Health Education*, 1985.

Responsibility IV—evaluating effectiveness of health education programs

Competency A: develop plans to assess achievement of program objectives

Competency B: carry out evaluation plans

Competency C: interpret results of program evaluation

Competency D: infer implications from findings for future program planning

Responsibility V—coordinating provision of health education services

Competency A: develop a plan for coordinating health education services

Competency B: facilitate cooperation between and among levels of program personnel

Competency C: formulate practical modes of collaboration among health agencies and organizations

Competency D: organize in-service training programs for teachers, volunteers, and other interested personnel

Responsibility VI—acting as a resource person in health education

Competency A: utilize computerized health information retrieval systems effectively

Competency B: establish effective consultative relationships with those requesting assistance in solving health-related problems

Competency C: interpret and respond to requests for health information

Competency D: select effective resource materials for dissemination

Responsibility VII—communicating health and health education needs, concerns, and resources

Competency A: interpret concepts, purposes, and theories of health education

Competency B: predict the impact of societal value systems on health education programs

Competency C: select a variety of communication methods and techniques in providing health information

Competency D: foster communication between health care providers and consumers

Index

Abortion, 196
Accountability, demands for, 229, 234–35
Achievement tests
 criterion-referenced, 277–79
 definition of, 277
 norm referenced, 277
 meaning of, 278
Acquired Immune Deficiency Syndrome (AIDS), 192, 194, 197, 200, 328
Action domain, 86, 242–45
 definition of, 242
Activity descriptor words, 90–91
Addictive behaviors, 199–202
 beliefs opposing education about, 201
 scope of, 200
Adler, M., 19
Administrative roles, 303–09
 health educator, 307
 principal, 303–04
 school health coordinators, 305–06
 school nurse, 307–09
 teachers and health specialists, 307
Affective
 behavioral terms, 90–91
 domain, 86, 241–42
 measures, scaling methods for, 284–87
  Likert scales, 285
  semantic differential, 285–87
  self-report, 241
  unobtrusive, 285

AIDS (Acquired Immune Deficiency Syndrome), 192, 194, 197, 200, 328
Aims of health education, (See Goals)
Alcohol, Drug Abuse, and Mental Health Administration (ADAMHA), 344
Alcott, W., 3
Alternate patterns of instruction
 correlated teaching, 314–16
 direct teaching, 310–12
 incidental teaching, 316
 integrated teaching, 312–14
 role of administrator in selection of, 310
Alternate response tests (See Tests, true-false)
American Association for Advancement of Science, 90
American Association of School Administrators, 57
American Cancer Society, 20
American Heart Association, 20
American Medical Association, 332
American Public Health Association, 4
American Social Health Association, 192
Appraisal, definition of, 231
Assessment, definition of, 231–32
Attitudes, definition, 241
Attitude scales
 Likert, 285
 semantic differential, 285

399

Baranowski, T., 6
Bartow, G., 37
Behavioral:
  change:
    as goal of community health education, 238
    as goal of patient education, 239
    as goal of school health education, 238–39
  objectives
    compared to behavioral changes, 243
    (See also Objectives, measurable)
  problems, 15–16
Beliefs, definition of, 284
Binary choice test item (See Tests, true-false)
Bloom Taxonomy Model of educational objectives, 94–95, 129
Bloom, B., 236, 286–87
Body of knowledge, 57–59
Boyer, E., 35
Bronfman Foundation, 33–34
Broudy, H., 144
Bureau of Health Education, 26–27, 342–43
  (See also Division of Health Education, Center for Health Promotion and Education)

Carlyon, W., 12, 62
Center for Health Promotion and Education (CHPE-CDC), 26–27, 343
Centers for Disease Control of the U.S. Public Health Service, 202, 343
Cereal Institute, 333
Chernobyl disaster, 328
Child sexual abuse, 197
Chlamydia, 198
Clarifying responses, 168
Clark, A., 176
Coalition of National Health Education Organizations, 31–33, 333–34

Cognitive
  behavioral terms, 90–91
  domain, 85, 240
  process, definition of, 58–59
  skills, 143, 152, 172
  terms, glossary of, 92–93
Combs, A., 37, 144
Commercial organizations and alliances supportive of school health education, 20, 333–34
Community
  concept of, 327–28
  definition of, 52
  as curriculum source, 52–55
    health needs and concerns, 55
    influence on curriculum planning, 55
    groups opposing school health education, 345–46
  health councils, 334
  involvement in school health programs,
    definition, 328
    of solution, 327–28
  resources, individual and groups, 329–36
Competencies, as measurable objectives, 88
Competency-based education, 235
  goals and objectives of, 86–89
Competency statements, formulation of, 87
Comprehensive School Health, Office of, 28–29, 340
Computer-Assisted Instruction (CAI), 176
Computer courseware, 176
Connecticut Study, *Teach Us What We Want to Know*, 17, 49–50
Controversial health topics, 191–203
  guiding principles for implementation, 215–18
  in school health teaching, 212
Controversy, prevention of, 213–15
Correlated teaching, 314–16

Criteria for selecting teaching techniques, 131, 135, 150
Criterion-referenced tests versus norm-referenced, 278–79
Culminating activity, 156
Curriculum Commission of the Health Education Division of American Association for Health, Physical Education, and Recreation, 64, 68, 69
Curriculum designs, 63–72
  body system design, 63–64
  competency-based, 71–72
  conceptual approach, 67–71
  health content area design, 66–67
  health problems design, 64–66
  health topic design, 67
Curriculum guides:
  essential elements, 117–27
  function of, 116
  as general framework, 115
  purposes of, 115
  sources of, 114
  ways to evaluate, 116
Curriculum implementation
  definition of, 113
  models of (See Health Curriculum)
  organizing elements of, 63
  planning, sources of,
    body of knowledge, 57–59
    community, 52–55
      local influences on, 55
      national health curriculum research, 53–54
      national health needs, 53
      state and local health needs, 55
    learners, 47–52
      developmental tasks, 52
      growth and development, 51–52
      needs and interests, 47–51
  scope, definition of, 63
  scope and sequence of, 63, 72
  sequence, definition of, 72
Curriculum patterns of instruction, 310–16

Curriculum patterns of instruction (continued)
  correlated teaching pattern, 314–16
  direct teaching pattern, 310–12
  incidental reaching pattern, 316
  integrated teaching pattern, 312–14

Dale, E., 125
Death and dying education, 202–03
  beliefs opposing education about, 202–03
  justification for, 203
Decision making
  bases of, 147
  definition of, 147
  and health behavior, 147
  as outcome of problem-solving method, 147
  skills, 20, 59
Denver Study, *The Health Interests of Children*, 49
Department of Health and Human Services, 339
Development, sexual, 193
Direct teaching, 310–12
Discussion, definition of, 154
Disease Prevention and Health Promotion, Office of, 29, 339
Division of Health Education, Center for Health Promotion and Education, 26–27, 343
Drucker, P., 84
Dubos, R., 5
Dunn, H., 167

Earl, A., 35
Education
  competency-based, 174
  for health, 58
Education Commission of the States, 58
Elementary and Secondary Act of 1966, 340–42
Enabling objectives, 104, 119–20, 133
Essay tests, 267–70

Evaluating health
  attitudes and values, 241–42
  behavior, 242–45
    (*See also* Action domain)
  concerned printed matter, criteria for, 247–49
  knowledge, 240–41
Evaluation
  activities, 279–84
    definition of, 280
  assumptions of procedures, 246
  audio-visual media, 249
  of classroom evaluation procedures, 253
  compared with measurement, 231
  of curriculum plans, 251
  definition of, 230–31
  effects on students, 287–89
  of environment of school, 254–55
  formative roles of, 236–37
  health course of study, 250
    effectiveness of, 252
    quality of, 251
  as major responsibility of health educators, 235–36
  purposes of in school, 237–38
  in school health, definition of, 231
  of school health services, 254
  of student health status, 245
  summative roles of, 236–37
  of teacher effectiveness, 249–50
  of teaching materials, 247
  terminology of, 230–34
  tools, tests as, 263
Evaluative research, 232–33
Experiential learning activities, 173–76
  definition of, 173
  versus experiential education, 173
Exxon Foundation, 33–34

Federal initiatives in school health, goals of, 338
Festinger, L., 148
Food and Drug Administration (FDA), 339

Forces affecting evaluation of health education:
  accountability demands on teachers, 234–35
  federal and private agency funding requirements, 235
  funding requirements for evaluation, 235
  minimum competency movement, 235
  Role Delineation Project, 235–36
Functional health objectives, 96–98

Gallup poll, 20
Games as social simulations, 162–63
General objectives, 119–22, 133
Glossary of cognitive terms, 92–93
Goals
  characteristics of statements of, 85
  as competencies, 86–87
  definition of, 84
  of federal initiative in school health, 338
  formulation of, 85–89
  of school health instruction, 12
Gonorrhea, 198
Goodlad, J., 54, 151
Grade placement, spiral and cycle plans, 73
Green, L., 21, 26
Growth and development, 51–52
Guilbert, J., 90

Handicapped, employment of, 318
Hands-on learning (*See* Experiential learning activities)
Havighurst, R., 52
Health
  attitudes, 284
  beliefs, 284
  definitions of, 58–59, 145
  facilities, 160–161
  as goal of education, 6
  habits, 7
  instruction, primary methods of, 144

Health (continued)
  intentions, definition of, 284
  interests, perceived needs or concerns, 17
  Interests of Children, the Denver Study, 49
  needs, 14–17
  practices, definition of, 7, 242
  problems:
    as curriculum-organizing elements, 63, 64–66
    definition of, 58–59, 145
    as needs, 14–17
  promotion, national objectives for, 24
  Promotion and Education, Center for, 26, 27, 343
  Resources and Services Administration (HRSA), 339
  services, 191, 300–302, 330
    administrative patterns of, 300–02
    of community health care professionals, 330
    definition of, 300
    lack of preventive, 191
    primary procedures of, 300
    purposes of, 300
  of teachers, 317
  teaching, 144
Health actions
  multiple factors influencing choice of, 243
  problems in evaluating, 243–44
Health behavior:
  as curriculum goals, 4
  definition of, 6–7
  as life-style, 7
Health care professionals, 330
Health curriculum, models of:
  health belief model, 60–61
  ideological, 62–63
  PRECEDE, 61–62
  Tyler rationale, 47, 59–61, 74, 100
Health education:
  behavior and attitude changes affected by, 202

Health education (continued)
  Bureau of, 26–27
  content commonalities across settings for, 2
  definition of, 8, 11, 342
  as discipline, 8
  National Center for, 27–28
  origins of, 4
  as outcome, 11
  as process, 11–12, 143
  as profession or occupation, 9–10
  President's Committee on, 22
  settings of,
    community, 1
    school, 1
    medical care, 1
    work site, 1
Health Education Division of Center for Health Promotion and Education, 27, 343
Health educator
  entry-level, 10
  generic, 10
  teacher, 307
Healthful school environment
  dimensions of, 303
  provisions for, 302–303
Healthy Me, 334
Healthy People, Surgeon General's Report, 23, 53, 65
Herpes, 198
High-level wellness (*See* Health)
Hochbaum, G., 36, 60, 244–45
Honig, B., 37
Horizontal curriculum sequence, 72–74
Humanism as threat, 203
Humanistic topics, 191
Hunt, M., 4
Hurlock, E., 52

Ideological curriculum models, 62–63
  medical—public health, 63
  school—developmental, 63
Impact evaluation, definition of, 237
Incest, 197

Incidental teaching, 316
Instructional media for health teaching, tools
  artifacts, 182
  authoring systems, 177
  computer assisted instruction, 176
  educational television, 178
  films, slides, filmstrips, 180
  health risk appraisal programs, 177
  human resources, 182–83
  printed teaching material, 181–82
  overhead projection transparencies, 179
Integrated curricula, 312–14
Integrating agencies supportive of school health education, 31
Intentions, definition of, 284

James, T., 176
Robert Wood Johnson Foundation, 33–34
Joint Committee on Health Problems in Schools of the NEA and the AMA, 8

Kaiser Family Fund, 33
R. K. Kellogg Foundation, 33–34
Kinsey, A., 192
Knowledge as process, 58–59
Kreuter, M., 244

Lalonde, M., 6
Learner participation
  direct, 150
  vicarious, 150
Learning
  experiential, 174–76
    definition of, 173
  opportunities, 120, 123–26
  outcome of instructional objective, 97
Legal aspects, local
  policies and regulations based on state law, 296–98
  sources of policy statements, 298–99
  superintendent's responsibility for, 297

Legal aspects, state:
  mandatory legislation, 14, 295
  permissive legislation, 14, 295
  tort laws, 296–99
Legislation (*See* Legal aspects)
Legislation in support of school health education, 14
Lesson plan
  anticipated problems, 132–33
  content and process defined, 128
  culminating activity, 131, 135, 256
  do's and don'ts, 136
  enabling objectives, 130
  initiation of, 131, 133
  resources and materials, 127
  sample, 133–34
Life-style and health behavior, 7, 15
Local coalitions supportive of school health, 335–38

McAlister, A., 6–7
Madaus, G., 288
Mager, R., 94, 95
Mann, H., 3
Mastery tests (*See* Achievement tests)
Matching item tests, 276–77
Means, R., 3, 144
Measurable objectives, 84, 88
  function of,
    in curriculum development, 84, 89–90
    in evaluation, 246
Measurement, definition of, 231
Method versus techniques of teaching, 144
Metropolitan Life Foundation, 33–34
Multiple choice tests, 274–76

Naisbitt, J., 52, 55
National Cancer Institute, 344
National Center for Health Education, 27–28
National Conference on School Health Education Research, 30
National Congress of Parents and Teachers (NCPT), 19, 21, 329

National Consumer Health Information and Promotion Act of 1976, 339
National Dairy Council, 333
National Education Association, 86
National Health Council, 27–28
National Health Education Organizations, Coalition of, 31–33, 333
National Health Information Clearing House (NHIC), 178
National health needs (*See* Healthy People)
National Heart, Lung, and Blood Institute, 30, 343
National Highway Traffic Safety Administration, 344
National Institute on Alcohol Abuse and Alcoholism (NIAAA), 344
National Institute on Drug Abuse (NIDA), 344
National Institute on Mental Health (NIMH), 344
National Institutes of Health, 29, 30, 343–44
National Livestock and Meat Board, 333
National organizations supportive of school health education, 26–35, 336–45
National School Health Education Coalition (NaSHEC), 336–38
National Task Force on the Preparation and Practice of Health Educators, Inc., 10, 72
Needs and interests, definition of, 47–49
Negligence, definition of, 299
Nutrition Education and Training Program (NET), 345

Oberteuffer, D., 35, 49
Objective-based testing (*See* Tests, criterion-referenced)
Objectives
  advantages of, for health teaching, 104
  in the affective domain, 90–91, 99–101

Objectives (continued)
  in the cognitive domain, 90–93
  definition of, 84–85
  measurable, 84, 88–89, 105
    characteristics of, 96–98
    feasibility of, 98
    function of in curriculum planning, 89–90, 96, 101–04, 119–20
    function of in evaluation, 105, 246
  models of, 94–96
    Bloom taxonomy model, 95
    operational model, 96
    programmed instruction model, 94–95
  national, health promotion, 24–25
Objectives for the Nation, U.S. Department of Health and Human Services, 53
O'Donnell, C., 83
Office of Comprehensive School Health, 28–29
Office of Disease Prevention and Health Promotion, 29, 339
Office on Smoking and Health, 344
Outcome evaluation, 237

Paedeia Proposal (*See* Health education as general education)
Patterns of instruction (*See* Curriculum patterns)
Parent and community support of school health education, 19–21, 334–35
Payne, A., 251–52
Personnel management, considerations of, 317–20
  collective bargaining, 319
  cost of school health programs vs. effectiveness, 319–20
  employment of handicapped, 318
  preemployment health evaluation, 317
  postemployment health evaluation, 318
  safety protection and occupational health, 319
  sick leave, provisions for, 319

Popham, W., 84, 89, 100, 101, 279
PRECEDE framework, 61–62
President's Committee on Health Education, Report of, 22
President's Council on Physical Fitness and Sports, 344
Pretesting, 245, 286
Preventive health services:
national objectives, 24
Private foundations supportive of school health education:
Bronfman Foundation, 33–34
Exxon Foundation, 33–34
Robert Wood Johnson, 33–34
Kaiser Family Fund, 33
R. K. Kellogg, 33–34
Metropolitan Life, 33–34
Rockefeller Foundation, 33
Zellerbach Family Fund, 33
Problem behaviors, 15–16
Problem-solving
definition of, 145
method, 146–47
(See also Scientific method)
skills, 58–59
steps in, 145
versus problem-solving method, 147
Process
definition of, 143
evaluation (See Evaluation, formative roles of)
Professional associations supportive of school health education, 30–31, 332–33
Proficiency tests (See Tests, criterion-referenced)
Prospects for a Healthier America: Achieving the Nation's Health Promotion Objectives, 24–25
Psychomotor:
domain, 85
skills, definition of, 242

Question asking, 155

Ranking and choosing activities, 168–69
Rape, 197
Raths, J., 151
Reliability of tests, 233–34
Report of the Sanitary Commission of Massachusetts, 3
Rockefeller Foundation, 33
Role Delineation Project, 10, 28, 235, 336
Rosenbaum, R., 58
Rugen, M., 4

School administrators, managerial functions of, 304–05
School board policy statements, 317–19
School health:
coalitions, 334
council/committee, functions of, 309
role in administration and management of health program, 309
Curriculum Project, 232–33
education:
definition of, 8
justification for, 13–26
Education Evaluation (SHEE) Project, 323–33
programs
administrator's responsibility for quality, 297
broad scope of, 295
community resources involved in, 329
components of, 295
cost of, 319–20
enabling legislation for, 296–97
local control of, 297
role of parents in, 329–30
role of state law in supporting, 296
sources of policy statements for, 298–99

School health (continued)
  team, 303–309
    health coordinator responsibilities, 305–307
    principal's roles, 303–05
    school nurse role, 307–08
    teachers and health teaching specialist roles, 307
Scientific method, 146–47
Scope of health curriculum
  alternate organizing elements of, 63
    (*See also* Curriculum designs)
  definition of, 63
Scriven, M., 236
Self-report
  devices for, 264
  survey, purpose of, 264
Sex education
  opposing beliefs about, 194
  opposing materials, 206–11
  outside schools, 218–19
  positive outcomes of, 195–97
  preventing controversy about, 213–15
  subtopics of, 193
Sex Information and Education Council of the United States (SIECUS), 206
Sexual development, 193
Sexual preference, 197
Sexually Transmitted Diseases (STDs), 192
  AIDS (Acquired Immunity Deficiency Syndrome), 192, 194, 197, 200, 328
  chlamydia, 198
  gonorrhea, 198
  herpes, 198
  syphilis, 199
Shane, H., 47
Shattuck, L., 3
Shattuck Report, 3
Skills
  cognitive, 152
  decision-making, 20, 59
  psychomotor, 240–42

Sliepcevich, E., 19, 62
Smoking and Health, Office on, 344
Solleder, M., 47
Solution, community of, 327–28
Spady, W., 72
Specific determiners in tests, 272
Sterilization, 196
Student health status, evaluation of, 245–46
Students Speak, the Washington State Study, 17, 50–51
Suicide, 202–03
Surgeon General's Report, *Healthy People*, 23, 53, 65
Syphilis, 199

Teach Us What We Want to Know, the Connecticut Study, 17
Teacher
  as facilitator, 146, 156, 172
  as information provider, 144
Teaching techniques
  criteria for selection of, 150–51
  data sources for planning of, 148–50
  group activities
    brainstorming, 155–56
    buzz sessions, 156–57
    case study and games, 162–63
    committee work, 158–59
    discussion, 153–55
    field trips, 160–62
    lecture-discussion, 157–58
    panel discussion, 157
    role playing, 159–60
    simulation and games, 162–63
    team projects, 158–59
  individual activities, 163–76
    curriculum modules, packaged, 171
    guest speakers, 165–66
    learning tasks, 171
    lecture, 164–65
    projects, 172–73
    textbook use, 169–71
    values activities, 166–69

Teaching method, definition of, 144
Teaching plan (*See* Lesson plan)
Teaching strategy (*See* Teaching method)
Test performance, variables affecting, 264
Tests, 264–287
   of achievement, 264
   as aptitude measures, 264
   of attitudes, beliefs, and intentions, 284–287
   competency-based (*See* Criterion-referenced tests)
   construction of, 267–79
   criterion-referenced, 235, 277–78
   definition of, 264
   effects on learners, 289
   essay, 267–70
   free response, 267–71
      definition of, 267
   Likert, 285
   matching item, 276–77
   multiple choice, 274–76
      distractors for, 275–75
   norm-referenced, meaning of, 235, 277–78
   norms, 265
   objective, 271
   semantic differential, 285
   short answer and completion, 270–71
   specific determiners in responses to, 272
   standardized
      definition of, 265
      versus teacher-made, 265–66
   structured response, 271–77
      definition of, 266, 271
   table of specifications for, 265
   teacher-made, 265–66
   true-false, 271–74
   unobtrusive, 287
   validity of, 265–66

Thomas, L., 35
Tools of evaluation, tests as, 263
Tort law, definition of, 299
Transferability, 150–51
   definition of, 151
Trucano, L., 17, 50
Tyler, R., 60, 242
Tyler rationale curriculum model, 47, 59, 60, 61, 74, 100

U.S. Department of Education, 340
Unruh, G., 172

Validity of tests, 233–34
Values:
   clarification of, 281
   definition of, 147
Values education
   basic teaching strategies of, 168–69
   clarifying response for, 168
   ranking and choosing, 168–69
Venereal diseases (*See* Sexually transmitted diseases)
Vertical curriculum sequence, 72–74

Washington State Study, *Students Speak*, 17, 50–51
Wilhelms, F., 46
Wilson, V., 36
Women's Christian Temperance Union (WCTU), 4
World Health Organization (WHO), 4

Yarber, W., 19
Youth Gives a Damn (YGAD), 174–75

Zellerbach Family Fund, 33